NATURE'S GARDEN

Samuel Thayer

A Guide to Identifying,
Harvesting, and Preparing
EDIBLE WILD PLANTS

Forager's Harvest

FORAGER'S HARVEST PRESS • BIRCHWOOD, WI

Cataloging-in-Publication Data
Thayer, Samuel.
Nature's garden : a guide to identifying, harvesting, and preparing edible wild plants / by Samuel Thayer.
p. cm.
Includes bibliographical references and index.
LCCN 2009931282
ISBN: 978-0-9766266-1-9

1. Wild plants, Edible—North America—Handbooks, manuals, etc.
2. Wild foods—North America—Handbooks, manuals, etc.   I. Title.

QK98.5.AIT43 2009   641.3'03   QBI09-600101

Book Design by Fiona Raven
Photographs and artwork by Samuel Thayer, except as otherwise credited.

First Printing January 2010, 16,130 copies
Second Printing July 2011, 19,135 copies
Third Printing January 2013, 20,000 copies
Printed in China

Published by
Forager's Harvest
N8757 Breakneck Road
Birchwood, WI 54817
www.foragersharvest.com

Forager's Harvest

To Rose Barlow,
 who left this life with grace

And Myrica Gale,
 who began it with promise

Claimer

Since we live in a society rife with frivolous lawsuits, most wild food books published today contain statements whereby the publishers disclaim liability for use of the information contained in their books. Older wild food books do not contain these disclaimers; they began to appear in the 1970s. By now disclaimers are standard, and virtually all wild food guides printed within the last eight years commence with them. Although it is doubtful that such disclaimers actually provide any significant legal protection, it is hard to blame publishers for including them. Most disclaimers, particularly the early ones, simply state the very reasonable fact that the author and publisher are not responsible for mistakes made by the readers. Indeed, this is true whether it is expressed in a disclaimer or not.

However, in recent years some of these disclaimers have become ridiculous. The Falcon Guide *North American Mushrooms* (Miller and Miller, 2006) contains the wordage, "Neither the authors nor the publishers in any way endorse the consumption or other uses of wild plants that are mentioned in this book." This raises the question of why, then, they would include the information to begin with? Lone Pine's *Edible and Medicinal Plants of the Rockies* (Kershaw, 2000) warns, "This guide is not meant to be a 'how-to' reference guide for consuming wild plants. We do not recommend experimentation by readers." Really? After reading the sections on "gathering tips" and preparation information, I never would have guessed that. This disclaimer seems two-faced and disingenuous. Why else would anyone buy this book? It is clearly conceived, designed, and marketed with the foraging crowd in mind.

It is one thing to disclaim responsibility for the actions of the inevitable idiot who reads the book and then does something stupid, but many publishers today are going way beyond this. In Van Wyk (2005) we read that "neither the author nor the publisher makes any expressed or implied representation as to the accuracy of the information contained in this book." I find this statement deeply disturbing. How can a reader trust a reference with such a caveat? Indeed, some books with these strong disclaimers contain egregious, even dangerous errors.

I would find these extreme disclaimers less offensive if litigation were the only thing at stake. The more important risk, in my opinion, is that such disclaimers will deter people from eating wild food, since they perpetuate the irrational fear that most people associate with foraging. (Indeed, similar disclaimers are not found in books dealing with far more dangerous activities, such as bicycling or hunting.) The wording of many of these disclaimers marginalizes and trivializes the use of wild food, as if those who forage are foolishly toying with death. I cannot conscionably begin my book with a disclaimer that essentially contradicts the core of the book's message and hope that readers will fail to notice my dishonesty, or forgive me for it as a "necessity of the times."

Instead of disclaiming the contents of this book, I claim them. Every photograph and piece of text herein was included through my own discretion. Any mistakes, unless cited to another source, are mine, and I take full responsibility for them. I approve this book's message, and encourage readers to use the plants as described and suggested herein. That's why I wrote it.

But of course, I am not responsible for your mistakes.

Acknowledgments

I have built two small houses and written two books. The houses were easy in comparison. One big difference between these two projects is that, with a book, you can't wait five years to finish the trim. What these endeavors have in common is that a lot of people get excited and lend their assistance, adding quality and value to the final product.

A few people gave continually of their advice, assistance, and encouragement: Josh Morey, Abe Lloyd, and my wife, Melissa. I owe them more than I am likely to repay. I thank all who have provided criticism, comments, and suggestions, particularly Mike Krebill, who spent many hours poring over the manuscript. Arthur Haines asked me difficult and thought-provoking questions, plus kept me from making a few embarrassing mistakes. I'm lucky to have friends like that. Bill Merilees provided several important photographs that enrich the book. I thank Steven Price for generously offering the use of his fine photos and providing constructive criticism, even while he was training to set a world record for pull-ups. Matt Nelson found acorns when I could not, and the readers benefit from his proficiency. Stephen Barstow helped me get alpine sweetvetch seeds and some obscure references on black nightshade. I am grateful to Sarah Mason, who provided me with her thorough and helpful treatise on acorn eating. Rose Barlow has been a teaching and foraging comrade; her combination of pragmatism and enthusiasm makes real things happen.

I am also deeply indebted to many other wild food authors and educators—not simply because they have provided me with an enormous amount of information and encouragement over the years, but more importantly, for their work advancing our common message. In this spirit I thank Nancy Turner, Steve Brill, John Kallas, Christopher Nyerges, Kelly Kindscher, Sunny Savage, Peter Gail, Vickie Shufer, Teresa Marrone, Tom Elpel, François Couplan, and all of our other allies.

I have been deeply moved by the encouraging feedback received from hundreds of readers since the release of my first book, *The Forager's Harvest*. It is for you that this work has been undertaken, and I hope it serves you equally well. Most delightful is the letter, displayed on my refrigerator, from ten-year-old Natasha; thanks for letting me know that I've done something right.

Contents

Nature's Garden

A few turns down the dirt road from my cabin there is a place I have come to call simply *The Garden*. To get there you cross a small river by way of a swinging foot bridge suspended between two black willow trees. In May, some of my neighbors come here to fish for trout. I come to pick vegetables.

The Garden is a virgin forest of black and green ash, balsam poplar, boxelder, and white cedar. Two decades ago it was dominated by magnificent American elms, all of which have now succumbed to Dutch elm disease. A few of their massive skeletons remain standing, but most lay strewn about the forest floor, where their hollows shelter porcupines and raccoons. The death of these giants left openings in the canopy through which sunlight poured down onto the shrubs and herbs below, and they responded prodigiously. Nannyberries and highbush cranberries grew into thick, laden clumps. Gooseberries grew robust, and chokecherries leaned out into the sunny openings and fruited profusely.

A Spring scene in Hopniss Valley. In this lush site there are more than thirty edible plants, growing more thickly than in any tended garden.

Healthy clumps of raspberries and red currants appeared. But more than anything, this garden grows vegetables.

The garden spreads for acre after acre, thick and lush with incredible quantities of food. The moment you hop off the bridge you are surrounded by a dense colony of ostrich fern covering several acres, the crisp fiddleheads in various stages of uncoiling. A short distance from the river the ferns give way to groves of cow parsnip, their lemony, aromatic stalks just beginning to reach toward the sun. The wood nettles grow exuberantly here, with unusually thick and juicy shoots. The luxuriant wild leeks grow half again as large as those in any maple forest. Mixed among their leaves are blooming spring beauties and white trout lilies, whose delicate blossoms hardly hint at the sweet, hearty food underneath them. In seemingly random places, a thick, pure carpet of spicy toothwort leaves spreads between the tree trunks. Delicate, snowy blossoms of sweet-rooted dwarf ginseng grow discretely in the shelter of rotten elm buttresses. In more sunlit places, the stinging nettles are already knee-high, and the dead stalks of last year's jerusalem-artichokes signal where to look for crisp tubers now. Enormous, succulent shoots of carrion flower rise above the tangled greenery. Along the trail, burdock, thistle, dandelion, and winter cress offer themselves to the hungry visitor. Here and there are mucky swales, where spring's meltwaters remain until July. Along the edges, thick, juicy stalks of swamp saxifrage are beginning to push up from their rosettes. Water parsnips and water plantain are greening up under several inches of icy runoff.

Food is everywhere, in all directions. Up the red clay side of the valley there are great thickets of raspberries, chokecherries, serviceberries, hawthorns, and wild plums; while upon the sandy slope opposite, one can spend days picking blackberries, thimbleberries, pin cherries, blueberries, and serviceberries. The top of this hill is a forest of red oak, dropping bread for an Arcadian people. The sugar trees, birch and maple, populate the hillside. In their light shade false Solomon's seal and bracken fern grow large and robust. Delicate salad greens bask here: twisted stalk, bluebells, and clintonia. Clumps of beaked hazelnut grow every few steps in the understory, and a plethora of savory mushrooms crop unpredictably from the duff. A few old pastures and meadows boast a riot of milkweed, chicory, dandelion, wild carrot, burdock, thistle, sheep sorrel, and asparagus. Feral apple trees produce bushels of orchard-quality fruit.

Just downstream from my floodplain garden, the river widens out into an estuary before flowing into Lake Superior. These wetlands boast an entirely different complement of food plants: cattail, bulrush, sweet gale, sweet flag, wapato, yellow pond lily, and bog cranberry. The sandy, conifer-covered ridges along the great lake teem with bunchberry, chokecherry, serviceberry, and pin cherry, while the beaches grow sandcherry, evening primrose, rose hips, and beach pea.

This is my special place. I'd give you directions, but luckily, you won't need them. Because Nature's Garden is everywhere. Your wild paradise is not in some far off land; it is in your own neighborhood. All you need is to discover it: see it, smell it, feel it, unveil its secrets; make it your own. Enter The Garden.

Archeologists tell us that gardening began 5,000 to 11,000 years ago in various parts of the world. This refers to our modern, civilized concept of gardening, which entails removing the native ecosystem and replacing it with a few exotic plants organized in a simple, geometric fashion. People have been tending Nature's Garden for much, much longer.

All around the world, hunter-gatherers carefully managed their environments to provide food, medicine, and craft materials. A well-documented example is the Kwakwaka'wakw of coastal British Columbia, who tended "root gardens"— natural coastal stands of silverweed *Potentilla anserina*, springbank clover *Trifolium wormskjoldii*, rice-root *Fritillaria camschatcensis*, and Nootka lupine *Lupinus nootkatensis* (Turner and Peacock, 2005). Rather than destroying the native plant community of these coastal wetlands, the Kwakwaka'wakw maintained healthy, exemplary versions of them. Likewise, the nearby Coast Salish carefully tended natural stands of camass (genus *Camassia*) by burning, weeding, tilling, and mulching (Suttles, 2005). When Europeans first encountered such

A dense bed of Pacific silverweed in coastal British Columbia. Native peoples managed, tended, and expanded prolific colonies such as this.

landscapes, they did not recognize them for what they were. They admired the immense natural beauty and productivity of the environment without realizing that these were largely artifacts of careful wild gardening. The idea of working *with* the inherent tendencies of a natural plant community to produce food was so foreign to the European way of thinking, it was assumed that these people remained hunter-gatherers only through ignorance of the techniques and concepts of plant cultivation.

Western anthropologists find these economies frustrating to classify. Civilized cultures, heirs to an ages-old prejudice against hunter-gatherers, are obsessed with the dichotomy between foraging and cultivating. There simply is no such dichotomy; it was invented to serve that prejudice. The Kwakwaka'wakw, Coast Salish, and hundreds of other hunter-gatherer peoples *did* cultivate plants; they cultivated them in wild gardens and then gathered them there. They didn't just cultivate plants, they cultivated ecosystems, working *with* the existing plant community. This isn't agriculture—it is *ecoculture.*

If modern authorities overlooked the wild gardening of dozens of peoples when they saw it in the present tense, certainly they cannot be expected to see it in the past through archeology. How long ago this practice began is unknown and probably unknowable. But we don't need to know; we need to *do*. Because foraging turns the ordinary woods into something sacred.

I am not saying that we should abandon our traditional gardens. I have one myself. Nor am I saying that we should manage or manipulate the plant community of every piece of wild ground; we need our share of true wilderness. But we also need to develop a deep connection with Nature by tending and using it in a responsible way. We need to understand how the plants, animals, fungi, soil, and weather interact—and how we interact with them. If we are to care for the wild, we must maintain a relationship with it. There is one fundamental way to do this: eating from Nature's Garden.

The Purpose of This Book

Nature's Garden has a different vision than other wild food guides. Rather than attempting to discuss several hundred edible plants with short, terse paragraphs, this book covers a smaller number of species in far more detailed accounts, replete with thorough instructions and multiple photos. The reason for this format is simple: people need more than one picture, a short description, and three sentences of instruction to make them feel comfortable consuming an unfamiliar plant. There are already a number of books that serve as long lists of edible plants; practicing foragers crave greater detail. This book is not a dictionary of edible wild plants; it is forty-one lessons about developing forty-one relationships with forty-one plants. Nature's Garden is not designed for armchair foragers; it is a guide to *actually foraging*. Although this book is a sequel to *The Forager's Harvest*, it is designed to stand equally well on its own.

This book is intended to provide something for every forager. The beginner will find enough instruction and advice to feel comfortable taking those daunting first steps of a new hobby. The casual forager with some experience will find this book opening the doorway to new adventures. The household cook will find new and exciting fruits, nuts, and vegetables to add to the family's meals, along with variety, fun, and a nutritional boost. Even chefs will find that these pages cover some of the most exotic, amazing, and gourmet ingredients available anywhere. Nature's Garden opens an economical new dimension for the homesteader, gardener, and health-conscious consumer. Those who live on raw foods will find many nutrient-dense live foods discussed in this volume. Campers, hikers, anglers, and backpackers can lighten their load and enliven their trail fare with fruits and vegetables from Nature's Garden. And the survivalist will learn how to recognize some of the most nourishing sustenance found in the wild.

However, this book is not a field guide. A field guide is carried with you; upon encountering a plant that strikes your fancy, you look through the guide and attempt to identify the plant. That won't work with this book, since it contains only a small fraction of the hundreds of plant species growing within walking distance of your home. Nature's Garden is best used in the opposite way: choose a plant in the book, carefully read its account, and then go looking for it. If you identify a plant with another field guide, refer to this book to confirm your identification and learn more about the plant's uses. For identifying the plants it contains, Nature's Garden is better than any field guide—yet it is more than a field guide, picking up where they leave off.

Likewise, this is not a cookbook. Cookbooks are useless unless you have food to cook. Nature's Garden is about getting the food. Some people feel that all wild food books must be cookbooks. This baffles me, since nobody feels that way about gardening books. When a cookbook says "two cups of wheat flour," it doesn't tell you what the wheat plant looks like, where it grows, when it ripens, how it is harvested, how long to dry it, what equipment to thresh it with, how to winnow it, or how to grind it. *Nature's Garden* covers everything *before* the recipe.

The bulk of this book is composed of forty-one chapters or plant accounts. These are arranged in standard taxonomic order rather than alphabetically, by season, or by the type of edible product the plant bears. Each account is organized into several sections for the reader's convenient reference. First, there is a story or essay introducing the plant, followed by a detailed description of the plant and its identifying features. The range and habitat are discussed together, since each is of limited value without the other. (Continent-wide range maps are not included because they have the tendency to mislead; due to habitat requirements, plants are typically absent from vast areas within their geographic range. Readers are advised to consult plant distribution resources that refer specifically to their state or region.) The harvest and preparation may be covered separately or together, depending on the length of the discussion. Some of the accounts contain additional sections with more specific information. Occasional warnings and important terms or ideas are highlighted to ensure their notice.

In this book I give you the tools to confidently identify these plants at any stage of growth, and to select the choicest specimens among them. I want to help you recognize their habitat and find them within it. I show you the right parts to eat, and how to distinguish when they are at the best stage to be eaten. I want you to know what to expect from their flavor and texture. I share with you the best ways that I have found for harvesting, processing, preparing, and storing these plants.

But there is more than the practical. I want you to *understand* these plants. I want you to get to *know* them: what they need, why they grow where they do, how they reproduce, how they interact with the plants and animals around them. I want to get you excited enough to spend a day outside, to inspire you to develop your own personal relationship with these plants. These relationships change the way we see the world, and in doing so, change the way we live.

I wrote this book to share my vision of Nature as a garden—*our* garden, *The Garden*—from which we are nurtured into life.

The Plants and Region Covered by This Book

The plants in *Nature's Garden* are not just edible; they are *foodworthy*. Typically, these are plants that I enjoy greatly and eat every year when they come into season. I crave and anticipate them, and store some of them so they can be used year-round. I have not included an account for any plant unless I have eaten it dozens of times or more. I do not claim that the plants in this book are *the best* wild foods, or even my favorites; they are some of the best, and some of my favorites.

Some people will inevitably complain that this book fails to include one favorite plant or another. However, there is simply no way that all of the edible plants in North America, or even in a limited region, could be covered this thoroughly in a volume of reasonable size. In fact, this book covers only a small fraction of our wild edibles. That's OK, because the only appropriate way to learn edible plants is one at a time—carefully, slowly, and thoroughly.

The plants in this book were chosen to represent a variety of produce types (nuts, greens, shoots, roots, tubers, teas, fruits, berries, seeds, and flowers) and a variety of landscapes (desert, city lawn, garden, mountain wilderness, swamp, farm woodlot). While the book is not intended to be a regional guide, it does have a regional bias because it is based on my personal experiences. Since I have spent most of my life in the Midwest, and I refuse to write about plants that I don't have extensive experience with, plants endemic to the Far North, West, or Deep South are underrepresented in this book.

The strongest criticism of my first book, *The Forager's Harvest*, was that it contained too few plants—in particular, too few Western plants. While I didn't change the fundamental vision of this second book, I have been careful to select more plants with a cosmopolitan distribution.

The chart on the following page has been included to show readers how pertinent this book is to their region. The listed figures represent the percentage of the plants covered by this book occurring in each state or province. Information on ranges comes primarily from the USDA online plant database, augmented by regional floras. The presence or absence of a plant was determined at the taxonomic level that heads each chapter. For example, I didn't determine the presence or absence of each individual species of blueberry in every state; I looked at the group as a whole and counted it present if one or more species was present.

Keep in mind that just because a plant is found in a particular state or province does not mean that it will be common, easy to find, or even legal to collect there. This chart is meant only to give the reader a general idea of where this book is most applicable.

United States

Alabama – 85%
Alaska – 43%
Arizona – 61%
Arkansas – 95%
California – 73%
Colorado – 71%
Connecticut – 98%
Delaware – 100%
Florida – 80%
Georgia – 93%
Hawaii – 39%
Idaho – 66%
Illinois – 100%
Indiana – 100%
Iowa – 100%
Kansas – 90%
Kentucky – 93%

Louisiana – 88%
Maine – 93%
Maryland – 100%
Massachusetts – 98%
Michigan – 98%
Minnesota – 98%
Mississippi – 85%
Missouri – 95%
Montana – 73%
Nebraska – 85%
Nevada – 49%
New Hampshire – 95%
New Jersey – 98%
New Mexico – 68%
New York – 95%
North Carolina – 98%
North Dakota – 80%

Ohio – 100%
Oklahoma – 85%
Oregon – 80%
Pennsylvania – 100%
Rhode Island – 98%
South Carolina – 88%
South Dakota – 83%
Tennessee – 95%
Texas – 80%
Utah – 68%
Vermont – 93%
Virginia – 100%
Washington – 76%
West Virginia – 100%
Wisconsin – 98%
Wyoming – 73%

Canada

Alberta – 56%
British Columbia – 68%
Manitoba – 76%
New Brunswick – 80%

Newfoundland – 59%
Northwest Ter. – 38%
Nova Scotia – 78%
Nunavut Ter. – 15%

Ontario – 98%
Prince Edward Is. – 68%
Quebec – 93%
Saskatchewan – 68%
Yukon Ter. – 29%

Figures represent the percentage of the plants covered by this book that are found in each state, province, or territory.

A Note on Plant Names

I begin each account with the most widely used common names for a plant. A well-known plant will often go by several common names, while other plants do not have any legitimate common name at all. Unlike the common names of birds, those of plants are not standardized, so no particular common name is "technically" or "officially" correct. I favor the names that I think are most useful and least confusing.

When a hyphen is used between two words of a common name, such as "Russian-olive," this indicates that the two words create a distinct noun. If the hyphen were absent, the first word would be interpreted as an adjective modifying the second word (noun). In other words, Russian-olive is *not* an olive, and jerusalem-artichoke is *not* an artichoke; they are distinct plants.

Latin or scientific names are intimidating to many readers, but they are integral to accurately communicating about plants. They are actually quite easy to remember once you decide that they are important to know. When you cross-reference sources, you should always refer to the scientific name, since one common name may be applied to several very different plants. The Latin name is a *binomial*, composed of two parts. The first part is the genus or *generic* name, and it is *always* capitalized. The genus is a group of organisms that are genetically very closely related. The second part of the binomial is the species or *specific* name, which is *never* capitalized. Two plants that share the same generic name, such as *Acer rubrum* and *Acer saccharum*, are closely related. Contrarily, sharing the same specific name does not indicate any relationship, as in *Ulmus americana* and *Prunus americana*.

Unfortunately, scientific names can also be confusing, since they may change as new discoveries regarding plant genetics and relationships are made. Often, authorities disagree on how to classify a plant. When this happens, two different scientific names may be used for the same plant. Although both names may be "correct," the tendency is for authors to automatically use the more recently proposed name, lest they seem outdated. This creates confusion when trying to cross-reference the names. The more helpful sources will list alternative scientific names or *synonyms*, as I have tried to do here.

Getting Started With Edible Wild Plants

Why Wild Food?

This is where I am supposed to tell you that: a. Foraging will make your life better, and b. Everybody's doing it. But actually, only a is true.

Some people think that it's silly to go for an invigorating walk on a beautiful May morning and come home with a lush heap of delicious gourmet vegetables when it would only take slightly longer to drive to the grocery store and spend hard-earned cash to get weeks-old inferior produce with half the nutritional value, doused with deadly chemicals. I see their point, but I'm sticking to the wild food just because it's a lot more fun.

Wild food is not for everyone. Many people don't like being outdoors, where mosquitoes live and it sometimes rains. Many people prefer eating frozen egg rolls, microwave pizza, and fast food. Some people hate cooking. Others hate vegetables. Three percent of the population is terrified of spiders. Some folks work a mandatory eighty-six hours per week and clean the garage on Sunday. And of course, most people would love to go outside, but can't miss their favorite TV show.

For the rest of us, there's foraging.

Where to Forage

Wild food can be found nearly everywhere. I have foraged in vacant urban lots, city parks, backyards, flower beds, pastures, farmland, gardens, swamps,

seashores, marshes, bogs, fens, ponds, lakes, rivers, prairies, meadows, roadsides, gravel pits, sidewalk cracks, construction sites, lawns, fence lines, hardwood forests, mountain slopes, pine barrens, deserts, canyons, conifer forests, and even on the roofs of old buildings. Every environment has its own unique set of plants. While some landscapes offer better foraging than others, everyone lives near a good supply of wild food.

At a rest stop in South Dakota, this highway department worker is spraying deadly chemicals on purslane. Watch what you eat.

Before foraging in any area, you need to determine if you are allowed to do so. If it is private land, you will need permission. If it is public land, you need to know what foraging restrictions may be in place.

You also need to ask yourself if the foraging site you have your eye on is likely to be seriously polluted or sprayed with pesticides, herbicides, or other toxic chemicals. Suspect areas include power line and railroad rights-of-way, roadsides, landscaping, lawns, golf courses, farms, orchards, and the immediate environs of large factories. Spraying may be evidenced by dead plants, wilting leaves, abnormal or twisted growth, fall colors in summer, or signs saying, "Caution: Pesticide Application!" Unfortunately, the signs of spraying may be subtle, so it is best to forage in areas that you know well.

Conservation

The responsible gathering of wild food requires a caretaker attitude and the exercise of reasonable moderation. All foragers should be deeply concerned about the plants they collect and the ecosystems the plants come from, remembering that they are gathering from a sacred garden that belongs to all. You should never harvest plants except where they are thriving, and never take more than the remaining population can easily replace. Always collect food in the way that is least disturbing to the plant and its environment. Carefully observe the area where you collect, noticing any effects you may have on the vegetation and alter your collecting practices accordingly.

One can practice this stewardship only by understanding the ecology and life history of the individual plants one harvests. This is why I explore these topics with each account later in the book. However, a few general guidelines can be given.

Annual weeds (lamb's quarters, amaranth, purslane, prickly sow-thistle, chickweed) can be collected with little restraint. In fact, people expend a great deal of energy trying to eradicate them. These plants reproduce prolifically by seed and are usually limited only by the availability of moist, exposed soil. The greens of many weedy perennials, such as dandelion and chicory, can also be harvested with little restraint.

Invasive plants (garlic mustard, kudzu, autumn-olive, Japanese knotweed) are typically biennials or perennials. These plants damage or alter ecosystems by displacing and outcompeting native species. Your local ecologists hope that you collect as many of them as possible.

Biennials (thistle, burdock, lettuce, carrot, evening primrose, salsify) are completely destroyed when their roots are collected, and their flowering is hampered by harvesting the flower stalks and greens. However, these plants are heavy seed producers and generally benefit from soil disturbance. The act of digging up a root creates an ideal germination and growing site for the next generation. Let half or more of the colony go to seed each year.

Perennial greens (nettle, honewort, dock, milkweed, wapato, basswood) can be collected with little harm to the plant, unless they are systematically picked multiple times in a season. Take less than a third of the available foliage.

Perennial shoots (milkweed, wood nettle, asparagus, carrion flower, cow parsnip, Solomon's seal) are more sensitive than greens, since at this stage the entire aboveground portion of the plant is picked. Take fewer than one third of the shoots in a colony each year.

Fruits, seeds, nuts, and berries are gifts from the plant, and taking them will harm it in no way. They are part of the reproductive strategy, but overharvest is usually, for all practical purposes, impossible unless the plant is already rare, in which case you should not be collecting from it anyway. Unless the plant is invasive, return its favor by spreading or planting its seeds where appropriate.

Multiple underground storage organs, such as tubers and sometimes rhizomes (jerusalem-artichoke, toothwort, hopniss, cattail, wapato, lotus), can be collected in moderation from healthy colonies. Leave at least half of the tubers to grow. Harvesting these parts often cultivates the soil and actually benefits the colony—but only if enough tubers are left behind.

Single underground storage organs such as taproots, bulbs, corms, and some rhizomes are the most easily overharvested plant parts. (Examples include wild leeks, onions, spring beauty, trout lily, dandelion, and chicory.) These plants, though small, often live for many years. Collect them judiciously, taking only a small portion of what is available. Thin the plants carefully to maintain the extent of the colony, rather than removing clumps or patches.

Does Foraging Harm the Environment?

Our culture embraces, in the words of the ethnoecologist Kat Anderson, a "schizophrenic" approach to Nature: we destroy it for profit, or we idealize its beauty and preserve it untouched. Although these attitudes appear opposite, they go hand-in-hand; both reflect alienation from our environment. When we limit our discussion to the two extremes of human intervention in Nature, one of which is impossible and the other unsustainable, we deprive ourselves of any opportunity for responsible stewardship. But there is a scarcely explored middle ground between exploitation and protection, and it is here that many answers to our environmental troubles reside.

In spite of the environmental movement, our relationship with Nature continues to weaken, our ecosystems continue to sicken, and our insane consumerism grows more unquenchable. Environmentalism has fallen short in the most fundamental way, failing to appreciably change (or even address) the human relationship to the landscape. The dominant conception of Western environmentalism is one of detached appreciation. We need a new paradigm—one of attachment and participation. We don't need more concerned intellectuals pondering the importance of Nature from third-floor offices; we need people who know the land because they live and work there, who love the woods because it nourishes them. All of our abstract theorizing, meticulous computations, and predictive models mean nothing until we have practical applications for them. Only participation in Nature can produce the intimate knowledge necessary to guide us in establishing a sustainable lifestyle.

Yet there are those who somehow believe that foraging, the oldest and most sustainable occupation on Earth, destroys the environment. They would have us treat the woods as a museum, to be admired but never touched. The most dangerous falsehoods often sneak in unseen, holding hands with a truth they resemble. Such folks may call themselves preservationists, but their irrational fear of human interaction with the landscape is one of the greatest challenges to establishing a healthy pattern of interaction with the natural world. Strictly proscribed limits on the outdoor experience simply keep people indoors, breeding yet greater indifference to the environment.

There are times and places where collecting wild plants should be forbidden, to protect extremely rare or precarious populations. But we are seeing much more than this—a total onslaught against harvesting wild plants in many areas, as authorities seek to forbid collection where there is simply no ecological basis for this prohibition. The influential and often outspoken anti-foraging faction presents no evidence that gathering food harms the environment. (The rare cases of overharvest are invariably perpetrated by commercial collectors.) Instead, it makes subtle appeals to covert elitism and taps into the long-standing prejudice against hunter-gatherers to support its agenda.

I am deeply offended that many parks bulldoze forests to build tennis courts, ball fields, and even golf courses—destroying habitat and permanently displacing or killing millions of plants and animals—but forbid the picking of dandelion, sorrel, and wild lettuce. A parking lot and hiking trail, standard at most Nature preserves, cause far more damage to the ecosystem than allowing plant gathering ever would. And as "Wildman" Steve Brill points out, so does lawnmowing.

This is perhaps an eerie vestige of the feudal system, where the wealthy claimed ownership of the forests and everything they produced as part of their subjugation of the peasantry. Social posturing has long been disguised with specious reasoning and make-believe morality. The real reason that golf is catered to and mushroom collecting forbidden is that one is pursued by the wealthy and one is associated with lower-class rural folks who do hard labor for a living.

The misbegotten belief that foraging harms the environment is based on

A scene for those who think edible plants are rare and elusive. The trees are sugar maple, the herb layer is wild leek.

A wapato marsh in Iowa. Wild food often grows as lushly and prolifically as the most carefully tended farmland.

two prevalent myths about Nature: its scarcity and its fragility. Jared Diamond (1997, p. 88) presents the ridiculous (and uncited) figure that in natural plant communities, 0.1 percent of the biomass belongs to species that produce food for humans. Obviously, he is not a forager, because he has missed something—or should I say, almost everything. Where I live, the average figure is closer to 60 percent, and in many places it approaches 100 percent. The biomass of edible plants is similar over much of the continent.

Every time I read this ridiculous underestimation, I think of places like Hopniss Valley, where virtually all the biomass belongs to an assortment of several dozen edible plants, and the namesake vines produce thousands of pounds of tubers per year. I think of the vast wetlands along the Mississippi River, where a "patch" of lotus or wapato covers hundreds of acres, and each acre produces more food than I could eat in a year. I see the miles and miles of California foothills that, despite human abuse, bring forth millions of bushels of acorns. I see fields of camass in Idaho, parsnip in Iowa. I envision the desert washes in Arizona, from which millions of pounds of amaranth sprout after summer downpours. I envision the endless nut groves of the South, persimmon fence lines, and the millions of acres of untapped sugar maples in the Northeast.

Nature provides lavishly.

We are told that Nature is fragile, and that anything we do to it is negative and constitutes "impact." This reflects the otherness with which we view Nature, for we would never make the same argument regarding human-to-human interactions—that any effect I have on your life, or you on mine, is

23

automatically detrimental. Nor do we claim that every effect of a squirrel, deer, fern, or mushroom upon its ecosystem is inherently negative. Why should the principle apply to us? We also can *do* without destroying.

The hands-off philosophy that these myths promote makes a proper relationship with our world impossible. It overlooks the experiences and innovations of hundreds of cultures that have achieved a sustainability that our Western civilization has never come close to. It precludes the only way forward.

Many of the beautiful "wild" landscapes that European explorers and settlers encountered as they populated the American continent, such as Yosemite Valley, were actually carefully managed landscapes in which the Native Americans had hunted and collected foods and other materials for thousands of years (Anderson and Barbour, 2003). There is no reason to believe that the many activities of numerous full-time foragers were "damaging" to these ecosystems. In fact, there is mounting evidence that many plants benefit from responsible patterns of human harvesting. Loewen et al. (2001) report that populations of the glacier lily *Erythronium grandiflorum*, once a staple food for some Native cultures, respond positively to the disturbance caused when humans (or grizzlies) dig up the bulbs. Yet foragers are commonly admonished not to do this.

Since the Nature-as-museum attitude is a practical impossibility, it must necessarily be applied in an inconsistent, illogical, and hypocritical way. Most public forest lands are managed to produce timber and are logged on a regular rotation. This management determines the composition and age of the trees, shrubs, and herbs. It removes massive amounts of biomass from the carbon and nutrient cycles, kills millions of animals, compacts soil, promotes erosion, and introduces exotic species. Yet we are somehow expected to believe that digging wild onions and gathering walnuts will have unbearable ecological consequences in this same forest.

The vast majority of the western United States, public and private, is grazed by livestock. This has caused ecological damage on a scale that few even comprehend, since ungrazed places that could serve as benchmarks of a healthy landscape are seldom seen. Somehow, the complete elimination of wild lilies from tens of millions of acres through grazing is acceptable; but for me to dig up enough of them for a meal is a crime.

I don't think they are really afraid that too many foragers would harm the environment. I think they know that "too many" of us will force them to protect it.

Plant Identification and Safe Consumption

The fear of eating the wrong plant and being poisoned runs deep for many (see "Poisonous Plant Fables," page 41), yet such cases are extremely rare and totally preventable. The consumption of an object is a deliberate act and can therefore be done with care and scrutiny. Anybody can avoid eating the wrong plant by following one simple rule: **never eat a plant unless you are 100 percent positive of its identity.**

Of course, the forager needs to be attentive and careful when collecting wild food, but the overblown horror with which many non-foragers view this activity is irrational. Dining out is *far* more dangerous. Most people get sick from restaurant food multiple times in their life, and many die from such food poisoning every year. Yet no comparable fear is attached to eating out. In fact, foraging is probably less dangerous than the average hobby—and the primary peril associated with wild food, that of eating the wrong plant, can be completely eliminated.

Identifying Edible Plants: A Step-by-Step Tutorial

Wild food harvesters need to be absolutely certain of the identity of any plant consumed. Every plant can be identified with this level of certainty if proper attention to detail is applied. The process of identifying a new plant can be difficult and intimidating for beginners, and for experienced foragers it is still an exacting and carefully administered task. But don't be discouraged; you can do it.

Once you have positively identified a plant, you need to carefully read that plant's account to determine which parts are used, when they are harvested, and how they should be prepared. The consequences of ignoring this information could be as serious as those of

The roots and young leaves of water hemlock, one of the world's deadliest plants. You need to be absolutely certain about the identity of any plant you consume.

misidentifying the plant. The same plant can produce one edible part and one toxic part. An example of this is the mayapple; its ripe fruit is delicious, but the root is deadly. Certain plant parts may be toxic if harvested at the wrong time or in the wrong stage of growth. Others are poisonous unless subjected to specific treatments that render them edible.

The Five Steps to Positively Identifying a Plant

1. Tentative Identification

Let's say that an attractive berry catches your eye, and you think, "Hey, that looks like autumn-olive!" So you grab this book, turn to the autumn-olive section, and see that your berry indeed resembles the photos of autumn-olive. This is your *tentative identification*; it is only the *beginning* of the identification process. You may reach the tentative identification in a variety of ways, such as using a botanical key or picture field guide, remembering a photo previously seen, or by simply following a clue or hunch.

The unfortunate truth is that many people stop at the tentative identification. This brash laziness accounts for most misidentified plants. You **must** go through the next four steps to be certain of your identification.

2. Reference Comparison

Sit down beside your tentatively identified plant and observe it carefully. Compare every available part of the plant to the descriptions and photographs in this book. Your plant should closely match both of them. Don't ignore the description just because you like pictures better. No matter how clear the photographs may be, written descriptions have a vital role in plant identification because they tell you which features to look at and which you should weigh most heavily. The most important identifying characteristics are not always the first ones noticed, and some will not be visible in the photographs.

As you compare the characteristics of a real plant to a book's description and image, it is vitally important that you ***do not mentally force your plant to fit the description***. If the leaf is supposed to have smooth margins, do not look at a leaf with very small or blunt teeth and say, "Well, it looks smooth enough." Do not call any cluster of flowers a raceme just because a raceme is a type of flower cluster. You may be very excited and want to prove your tentative identification correct, but don't be brash. Your plant should fit the description easily and reasonably, without any lenient comparisons or stretched definitions.

Certain identifying characteristics are more constant than others. Plant identification manuals usually focus on the form and arrangement of the flowering and fruiting parts because these are typically the most reliable. Features and patterns of the stems, leaves, and underground parts are also generally quite consistent. With all plant parts, form is more important than size or color. The least reliable characteristics are those of habitat association, phenology, size, and color. These traits should still be considered, but not as heavily as the more consistent ones listed above.

Many newcomers expect a plant to have one or two unmistakable characteristics that positively identify it. This is unrealistic. Wild plants don't come with labels; you must verify numerous characteristics to identify them. Since most features of a plant can vary from the norm in certain circumstances, you should ***never identify a plant by a single characteristic***.

During the process of identifying your plant you will encounter botanical terms such as *alternate*, *pinnately compound*, and *umbel*. If you don't know what such words mean, look them up in the glossary. You need to understand them to make a positive identification—and you will see these terms repeatedly as you learn about plants.

3. Cross-Referencing

If, after carefully, impartially, and reasonably comparing your plant to the description and image in your first book, you feel confident that you have identified it correctly, run through the same process with at least two more field guides to double and triple-check your identification. Read about look-alikes and use the descriptions of those plants to ascertain that your plant is not one of them.

4. Specimen Search

If careful cross-referencing verifies the conclusion you made with your first reference, and you are certain that you have positively identified your plant, go find *many* more specimens. This specimen search develops your *search image* of the plant. It is preferable to find and examine your plant in diverse stages of growth and growing conditions to get an idea of its range of variability. If it is a biennial, for example, you want to see it in flower and also in the rosette stage. Just as all people look different, there is a degree of variability between individual members of each plant species. Newcomers to botany are always surprised at how many sizes and forms a single plant can take. Learn to understand and appreciate this variability.

The specimen search teaches you to *recognize* your identified plant. Continue the search until you have found dozens of specimens of your identified plant and are ***never*** confused or even slightly doubtful about them. This may take half an hour, two weeks, or six years. Wait as long as it takes; you should be able to recognize a plant instantly and with unwavering certainty before eating it.

5. Contradictory Confidence

Before you eat a plant you need to be absolutely positive that you have identified it correctly; you need to be sure enough to bet your life on it.

Have you ever picked up a banana, peeled it, and then, just as you were about to take a bite, stopped suddenly, thinking, "Wait a second! What if this is ***not really a banana***?" I doubt it. Your ability to recognize bananas is probably well developed. If you brought a bunch of bananas to the grocery store checkout and were charged for grapes, you would (kindly, of course) point out the mistake—because you can positively recognize bananas. If the cashier called the produce manager, who then insisted that the bananas were grapes, you would probably laugh, and certainly contradict him. If he then pulled out a produce guide, with a clear color photo of bananas labeled "grapes," you would inform him that the produce guide must be misprinted. Because you *know* what a banana looks like, and nobody can convince you otherwise; you have *contradictory confidence.*

That's how absolutely and unwaveringly sure you need to be about the identity of a wild plant before you eat it.

You may reach this point on the first day you encounter a certain plant, or it may take many encounters over a period of months or even years. It depends on many factors: whether the plant is in an easy or difficult stage to recognize, the quality of your field guides, and most of all, your own level of experience with plant identification. Your first few plants will be the most difficult, and you should take great care not to rush the process.

Sometimes you may know a certain plant in one stage of growth but not in another. The slightest hesitation or doubt indicates a lack of contradictory confidence regarding the specimen in question. This means the field guides must come out again to verify the identification. If your guides do not adequately display the plant in a certain stage of growth, you may need to mark the plant and observe it through the seasons, waiting until next year to harvest it.

Learning From Others

One of the best ways to learn about edible wild plants is to accompany an experienced forager into the field (and hopefully the kitchen as well). Having somebody else identify a food plant for you is certainly far easier than going through the process on your own. However, if you do this you need to keep in mind that you are trusting your life to another person.

If you don't have total faith in the person identifying the plant, treat it as a tentative identification and go through the last four steps of the identifying process. And even if you completely trust another person's knowledge, you must complete steps four and five before collecting and eating the plant on your own.

Recognition and the Search Image

Identification and recognition are two completely different things. Identification, discussed above, comes first; it is a careful and deliberate process that one must go through to ascertain the name of a particular plant. However, people do not *recognize* things by carefully examining their specific distinguishing characteristics. You have probably never picked up an orange and given it a thorough inspection to identify it as such. Instead, we recognize a familiar thing through its search image, which is like a file folder in the brain where everything you have ever observed about that thing is stored. The search image contains more details and nuances of texture, shape, position, color, smell, and other such things than we could possibly remember or convey verbally. Every encounter with a plant enriches and refines the search image until recognition is instantaneous and effortless, just as it is when you see a banana or a strawberry.

Once you recognize a plant, you will not have to go through the tedious process of identification every time you harvest it. However, if there is *any* doubt, go back to the five-step identification process and reassure yourself.

Look-Alikes

The term "look-alike" can be misleading. Two different species of plant may look similar, but not identical. The more you observe them, the more different they will appear. If you are thoroughly familiar with a plant, any other plant will

Many people have trouble telling spiderwort (left) from salsify (right). To a forager who is familiar with and gathers both, however, they appear quite distinct.

look different from it. This is why the specimen search (step four above) is so important—it increases familiarity and strengthens the search image, decreasing the danger of confusing your plant with a look-alike.

Some edible plants appear similar to harmful plants, and such similarities can fool those who practice insufficient care in identification. A good example is wild carrot and poison hemlock. Although there are over a dozen easily observed differences between these two species, and a person familiar with them can differentiate them consistently and easily, many foragers have been fooled by their similarities. Before collecting an edible plant that has a dangerous look-alike, you should memorize several features that distinguish the edible species from the toxic one.

However, any edible plant can be consistently and reliably distinguished from similar-looking toxic plants by the trained eye. Your eye is trained by carefully going through the five-step process of identifying the plant and developing a search image for it.

First-Taste Procedures

The first time that you eat a new plant, exercise some restraint. Cook it by itself and taste a small portion carefully. **If it is bitter or otherwise distasteful, spit it out.** This is an extremely important secondary line of defense. The tongue was designed to tell us which foods are safe and which aren't, and it does a remarkably good job of this. Most toxic plants taste terrible.

If, on the other hand, you like the taste of your new plant, go ahead and consume a small serving. Even if it's really good, resist the temptation to pig out. Wait a day and see how the plant affects you. (Refrain from eating two or more new foods on the same day; otherwise, if there is a problem, you will not be certain which food caused it.) Perhaps this particular plant, though edible, disagrees with your metabolism and gives you gas or nausea. Most likely, however, you will feel great afterward. If all goes well, treat the plant as you would any other fruit or vegetable with similar qualities, incorporating it into your diet in a sensible fashion.

Food Allergies

There is a slight possibility that you could be allergic or intolerant to a plant that is normally edible. Thousands of people are affected by allergies to familiar foods such as peanuts, almonds, mangoes, and cashews. People are typically exposed to most common foods during early childhood, and experience new foods only rarely thereafter. But the forager is exposed to new foods on a regular basis, which increases the likelihood of experiencing an allergic/intolerant reaction.

Food allergies and intolerances are serious and can make a person extremely ill. Symptoms of the first reactions are usually similar to food poisoning or stomach flu: the body purges itself of the unwanted substance by vomiting and diarrhea, accompanied by nausea and general physical discomfort. Certain groups of plants, such as nuts and legumes, cause allergies more frequently than others. Unfortunately, these reactions do not typically occur upon the first exposure to a plant. If you ever get unexpectedly ill from a plant food that you know to be edible, suspect such a reaction. ***If you confirm that you are allergic or intolerant, treat the plant as if it is toxic***, since symptoms generally get more severe with each exposure, and can become deadly.

Food allergies are an inescapable and unpredictable fact of life. To use wild foods you must assume this risk. However, such reactions are rare.

Poisons in Plants

Most people believe that there is a clear dichotomy between edible and poisonous plants. This view is misleading; the two properties are not mutually exclusive. All of us eat poisonous substances on a regular basis. Rather than a dichotomy of edible and toxic, there is a continuum between two extremes. At one pole you have potent, deadly plants such as water hemlock, while at the opposite you have rather benign foods like the apple. However, toxicity is dosage dependent; every food and drink has the potential to harm you if you consume too much of it.

Every plant contains hundreds of chemicals. Some are useful macronutrients (sugars, starches, oils, proteins), some are beneficial vitamins, minerals, and antioxidants, while others are toxins and antinutrients. Since plants can't run and hide, they defend themselves by producing toxins. One reason we have kidneys and a liver is that *every* food we eat contains toxic substances. The proper question is not *if* a substance can harm you but *how much* it will take to harm you.

Despite the fact that our food contains toxins, we eat things in safe portions because our bodies tell us when to stop. Cravings and revulsions keep our diets in line. Through culture, we develop norms and habits regulating the use and consumption of familiar foods. We don't serve garlic or cilantro as a main course. However, we have not developed such norms for wild foods, increasing the likelihood that somebody will overindulge and suffer the results of poisoning. Which brings us to another safety guideline: **Don't force yourself to eat more of any food than you find appetizing.**

Certain plant species contain extremely potent or destructive toxins in dangerously high amounts. These should never be consumed. Such plants are unambiguously called *poisonous*, *toxic*, or *deadly*.

Plant Poisonings

Serious poisonings from wild plants are quite uncommon, and they are generally the result of neglect, or from a failure to follow the guidelines set forth in this section.

The majority of serious plant poisonings occur when children under five years old put unknown vegetation in their mouths (Turner and Szczawinski, 1991). Most other poisonings occur when adults put unknown vegetation in their mouths. This may be from failure to properly identify the plant, but more often—and surprisingly—it occurs when *no legitimate attempt* has been made to identify the plant. Another scenario with dangerous potential is when a toxic plant is growing beside an edible one and is haphazardly collected along with it. Some poisonings also occur due to misinformation, encountered either in person or in print. Finally, a plant that is generally safe can sometimes cause toxic effects due to overindulgence.

Some Thoughts on Wild Food

(A collection of important stories and essays to entertain, educate, stimulate, and enrich your campfire discussions)

Don't Make it Fit

After a presentation that I gave at a small-town library, an older gentleman approached me and said, "I've got something I'd like to ask you about," pulling out a clear plastic bag that contained a nannyberry twig, complete with several leaves and a cluster of unripe fruit.

"I see you've got some nannyberries," I smiled, welcoming his inquiry.

He gave me a sharp look and quickly replied, "Nannyberries? These aren't nannyberries. I wanted to ask you about pin cherries."

"OK. What about pin cherries?" I asked, sensing his defensiveness.

"Well, that's what these are," he proclaimed, adding, "I think," after an awkward pause during which he must have remembered that this conversation supposedly entailed a question. After an even longer pause, during which he presumably realized and then rejected the fact that I had already answered the question that he was about to ask, he held up the nannyberry twig and demanded, "Is this a pin cherry?"

I paused for a moment, considering the implications of not giving the answer he wanted, and calmly stated, "No, that's a nannyberry." He skeptically asked me how I could tell, and I showed him some of the more obvious differences: the opposite leaves instead of pin cherry's alternate arrangement, the larger and thicker leaf, the winged petiole, the larger fruits. I explained how pin cherries are borne on long individual stems attached directly to the twig, while nannyberries grow in complex, branching, terminal clusters of a dozen or more fruits. After this he sat down without a word, staring intently at his twig, and I entertained several other questions.

Several minutes later, just as I was about to leave, the man with the nannyberry twig approached me again, armed with a copy of *The Forager's Harvest* opened to the pin cherry chapter. He pointed to the photo of pin cherry bark and triumphantly proclaimed, "The tree that this twig came from had bark with large lenticels exactly like this one!"

I stood dumbounded, realizing that no amount of evidence was going to convince him of the truth. Forget the irony that he was trying to use *my own book* to prove me wrong—I was astounded that he could still even be considering that his branch might be a pin cherry. It was as if he had brought in a porcupine

If you can't tell nannyberry (left) from pin cherry (right), even while armed with accurate, thorough descriptions and clear photos, you're manufacturing delusions.

and asked me if it was an owl, and I had told him that it couldn't be because it had teeth and no feathers, and then he pointed to one of the porcupine's claws and said, "That sure looks like an owl talon to me!"

"Observe the fruit as it ripens," I said, "and see what it becomes."

This guy wasn't stupid. He was just doing perhaps the stupidest thing that a wild food gatherer can do: what I call *making it fit*. He wanted this tree to be a pin cherry so bad that everything that he saw was going to be interpreted to that end. It was, in fact, perfectly obvious that his plant was not a pin cherry. Both the text and the photos made this readily apparent. Any literate person should have come to that conclusion after only a few seconds. Yet here was an intelligent man engaged literally in magical thinking, trying to turn his nannyberry into pin cherry. Unfortunately, no book can prevent this kind of self-delusion.

I have no statistics for such things, but I suspect that this process of making it fit accounts for a large portion of plant misidentifications. I understand that the search for a plant can be exciting and even mesmerizing. But you can't let go of reality. As the reader and forager, it is your responsibility to consider the facts rationally and objectively observe what you see. Don't decide what a plant is before you actually know. The consequences could be serious.

There Are No Instant Experts

National Geographic Adventure magazine has run a feature called "Instant Expert," providing a tiny bit of information about an enormous topic and implying that this rudimentary introduction somehow qualifies the reader as an authority. It's no surprise. Our society reveres experts. We watch them on TV shows, listen to them on the radio, and place faith in their testimony in the courtroom. We read their articles and buy their books. Many of us want to be one.

It is fascinating to observe how, after only a year or two of avid interest in a topic, some people begin to feel like experts. Whether it is basketry, yoga, or tracking, some people feel the need to be teaching something almost as soon as they begin learning it.

I recently watched an "instructional" video about harvesting "wapato tubers." The makers of the video stated in the beginning, "I don't recommend anyone does this without the proper education and know-how." In the video they simply pull the plants from the mud and break off the bases of the stems, calling these "tubers." Later they pick the broken rhizome pieces from these stem bases, clean the rhizome chunks, and cook them. They talk about wapato "tubers" throughout this video, but never collect or show one—it seems almost certain that they have never even *seen* one. They obviously have no idea what they are talking about; the video is as absurd as one about making strawberry jam from the leaves.

The makers of this video seriously overestimated their expertise, and it is anybody's guess as to why they felt compelled to share their "information" with the world. Such egregious examples of the "expert" fantasy gone wrong are mostly funny, but they reflect something that is deeply dysfunctional about our culture: an impatience, lack of diligence, and almost pathological lust for instant reward. People do something once and feel like they are entitled to homage from those who have *not* done it. Magazines and advertisements cater to this "expert" fantasy because they know it sells. But in fact, there are things you might not learn until the 75th or 300th time you do something.

I have a book called *Why Wild Edibles?* by Russ Mohney (1975) in which the account of wild carrot is so fundamentally flawed that it is confusing to even explain the mistakes. It's so funny that it's worth it, but I'll have to give you a little background first: wild carrot (*Daucus carota*) is also known as Queen Anne's lace; poison hemlock (*Conium maculatum*) is likewise sometimes called Queen Anne's lace.

In his book, Mohney calls "wild carrot" *Daucus pusillus*, but that name actually refers to a small, related, annual species—not the one gathered and eaten, and not the one shown in his photos or drawings. He then says, "The edibility of Queen Anne's lace has long been in dispute." This actually isn't true: if you're calling *Conium maculatum* Queen Anne's lace, then Queen Anne's lace is definitely deadly, but if you're calling *Daucus carota* Queen Anne's lace, then it is unquestionably edible. But Mohney seems to have no idea which one he's talking about. He uses the name *Daucus carota* for Queen Anne's lace, which he labels "poisonous"—but this is actually the scientific name for the garden carrot, as well as the edible wild carrot that he shows mislabeled in his photos. But the photos and drawings he has labeled as "Queen Anne's lace (*Daucus carota*)" don't show any of the species mentioned above; they show tansy *Tanacetum vulgare*, an unrelated and remarkably different plant. He then describes how to tell tansy from wild carrot, the whole time calling the tansy "Queen Anne's lace" and using the wrong Latin name for wild carrot. To top it off, he then has a set of drawings which show features used to differentiate wild carrot from "Queen Anne's lace" (tansy). The drawing that is supposed to demonstrate that the leaves of "Queen Anne's lace" are pinnately compound shows *a single leaflet*—which is about as useful as drawing a dot and labeling it "the corner of a triangle." The drawing beside it, which is supposed to show us that wild carrot's leaves are "palmately compound" (which isn't true), actually shows the carrot leaves as *pinnately* compound—which Mohney tells us is *the distinguishing feature* of the plant we are trying to tell it apart from!

This gives special irony to the back cover's claim that the "excellent photographs and drawings make accurate identification a real joy."

This kind of irrational assessment of our own knowledge and skill level is a cognitive cousin to the delusional process of making it fit discussed already. Likewise, it can be exceedingly dangerous. But in this case it has the potential to not only harm ourselves, but others—like when the subject of a recent survival television show pukes up some *Nymphaea* water lily root, which he learned to eat from a book written by an "expert" who lacked "the proper education and know-how."

There is no shortcut to becoming an "expert" forager—that requires many years of diligent study and practice. And there is always much more to learn—never imagine that you know all the worthwhile wild edibles in your area, or everything important about a particular plant. Resist the temptations of experthood: overestimating your own knowledge, dismissing new information and differing opinions, and especially, answering questions to which you don't actually know the answer.

You don't need to be an expert. All you need is to thoroughly and positively know the plants you collect and use.

The Ethnographic Void

There is an enormous disparity in the depth and breadth of the information on edible wild plants in different parts of North America. The literature provides much more and better information about edible wild plants of the West than those of the East. This should come as no surprise.

Most of what we know about edible wild plants has been given to us by (or taken from) various indigenous cultures around the world. The careful description of these cultures is called *ethnography*, and it is upon ethnography that the study of *ethnobotany* (examining the role of plants in human cultures) is based. For our knowledge of North American edible wild plants, we are largely indebted to the pre-European cultures variously called American Indians, Native Americans, or First Nations. Most of what is written in the wild food literature comes directly or indirectly from ethnographies of these cultures.

As Europeans spread across North America, they conducted a staggering campaign of genocide against the Native Americans who preceded them. Europeans looked upon the Natives' diets with disgust and disdain and had little desire to record what was being eaten or how it was prepared. Their only interest was in those American plants, such as maize and tobacco, that fit well into the European economic model and could be used to make a profit. For over two hundred years, as Europeans colonized eastern North America, there were very few written accounts of Native American food uses—and those few were often written scornfully from the viewpoint of a prejudiced outsider who had no firsthand knowledge of the matter. It was not until the late nineteenth century that scholars began to seriously take an interest in ethnography. By this time, many Native American cultures in the East had been so disrupted that they had lost most of their traditional wild plant knowledge. Thus, the vast majority of our ethnobotanical knowledge comes from western North America, which was generally conquered later by Europeans.

Daniel Moerman's *Native American Ethnobotany* (1998) is an attempt to compile information from all the available primary ethnographic sources for North America that identified plants by their scientific names. Moerman lists 291 groups or cultures whose plant uses were recorded in North America. Of these, 215 lived west of the Great Plains, 22 in the Great Plains, 16 in the Arctic or sub-Arctic, 11 in the Deep South, and 13 in the Eastern Woodlands north of the agricultural region. The most productive agricultural region of the United States, an enormous area stretching from southern Minnesota to New York, south to Virginia, Tennessee, and Missouri, has only *13* ethnographic references. This area had probably the largest and densest population of any area of comparable size in pre-Columbian North America, yet we know very little about what wild plants the Natives here used for food. In fact, there are no ethnographies at all from Pennsylvania, Ohio, Indiana, Illinois, Kentucky, Missouri, and most of Iowa: in other words, the American heartland. (Note: I do not mean to be critical of Moerman's work in any way; *Native American Ethnobotany* is a remarkably useful resource, excellent in both concept and execution. The biases it reflects are simply those of the sources that were available to the author.)

Many food plants that are extensively discussed in the western ethnographies, such as cow parsnip, water parsnip, and red elder, are rarely mentioned in literature pertaining to the East, though they abound there as well. Very little is recorded about the use of certain eastern species that are suitable as dietary staples, such as American lotus, while a great deal is written about similar western staples, such as camass. The bark collecting and cooking methods of many western tribes have been recorded, yet we know essentially nothing about the food economy of the Adirondack people—a northeastern tribe whose name is reported to mean "tree eaters" because of their use of bark as a food. The primary ethnographic source detailing the harvest and use of wapato has been Meriwether Lewis's journal entries from western Oregon—yet this plant was and is found in far greater abundance around the Great Lakes and large eastern rivers.

Contributing to the informational bias against eastern wild plants is the fact that, while most Native Americans in the West lived by hunting and gathering, most eastern tribes subsisted on a mixed economy that involved both farming and foraging. Certain staple wild foods, such as acorns, were far more prevalent in the East but were used there less than in the West because they had been largely or partly replaced by agricultural products.

There are some excellent wild food books that draw upon the knowledge contained in the western ethnobotanies. Nancy Turner's *Food Plants of Interior First Peoples* and *Food Plants of Coastal First Peoples* come to mind. However, no ethnography-based compilations of comparable quality exist for eastern North America. In this book, I cite ethnographic sources where I find it appropriate, and these are usually references to the West. However, the lack of ethnographic information from the East does not mean that a plant wasn't eaten there. An enormous amount of knowledge has been lost, but we are wrong to lament it as lost forever. It is all still out there, waiting to be rediscovered.

This book is not ethnobotany; it is economic botany. Ethnobotanists record how *other people* use plants; I record how I use plants. In ethnographic terms, I am both investigator and informant. I am, of course, keenly interested in how other people use and have used plants, and I study this avidly. But ethnobotany is not the end, nor the means of my study; it is the beginning. The human relationship to wild plants is far from dead. My primary purpose in these accounts is to share my experiences, so that hopefully others will go have experiences of their own. Together, maybe someday we can fill in that ethnographic void.

What is a Meristem and Why Should I Care?

In general, edible plant parts fall into three categories: storage organs (roots, tubers, etc.), reproductive parts (flowers, fruits, seeds), and *meristems*. Most people quickly grasp what the first two categories are, but meristems aren't quite as obvious. The meristem is the part of the plant where growth occurs. A tree, for example, has only two meristems above ground: the tips of the branches, and under the bark. No other part of a tree grows. The basswood is one edible tree. Besides the reproductive organs, its only edible parts are the meristems: the new leaves and cambium. An asparagus spear is also one big meristem. So are nettle tops, Japanese knotweed shoots, young dock leaves, and even the submerged lateral shoots of cattail. The art of picking vegetables at the best stage of growth is the art of recognizing meristems.

There are several reasons that meristems are preferred for consumption. Perhaps most important is that they contain little cellulose or lignin, non-digestible components of woody tissue. A meristem must stretch as it grows; it *can't* contain long cellulose fibers because cellulose won't stretch—its very purpose is to provide rigidity by not stretching. The biological processes of cell division occurring within meristems require high concentrations of proteins and sugars. This means that meristems taste better and have more calories than older tissues. Meristems also typically contain fewer toxins and antinutrients than mature plant parts.

The recognition of meristems is a skill that every forager should have. Once you can do this, you don't need me, or anyone else, to keep explaining at which stage a green vegetable should be eaten, or what it looks like in this stage. The answer is always the same: you harvest it when it is a meristem. Following is a list of meristem characteristics to help you develop this skill.

How to recognize meristematic stems:

1. They bend, break, or snap more easily than mature stems.
2. They may droop or bend over at the top, due to lack of cellulose.
3. The leaves they bear are not fully formed.
4. They are thicker in proportion to their length.
5. They come to an abrupt end.
6. They may be lighter or different in color than mature stems.
7. Features such as hairs, ridges, thorns, or roots may be absent or not fully developed.

How to recognize meristematic leaves:

1. They are usually smaller than mature leaves.
2. They may be folded, curled, curved, or corrugated in ways that mature leaves are not.
3. Features such as hairs or lobes may be absent or not fully developed.
4. The surface may be glossier.
5. The color may be lighter or of a different hue.
6. Here's the fun one: meristematic leaves usually stretch a little. Gently grab at two points, pull apart, and watch the leaf stretch.

above left Meristem: Every part of this young amaranth plant.

above right Meristem: The uncurling leaf of wapato.

below left Meristem: The leaves, petioles, stems, and flower buds of this marsh marigold.

below right Meristem: The succulent shoot of this swamp saxifrage flower stalk.

Remember, only meristems grow. Asking if a plant part is meristematic is the same as asking if it is still growing. Many of the features listed above follow logically from that question. You can always simply observe if a plant part is still growing. Wrap two twist-ties around an asparagus spear, measure the distance between them, and then measure again a day later. If the distance increases, the portion of the stem between the ties *was* a meristem (it may not be any longer). You can deduce that a head of broccoli is a meristem if you know that it will spread out and flower if left in the garden, since it has to grow to do this. Once a plant part matures and ceases to grow, it will not revert to being a meristem.

Anyone with a garden has already learned to identify meristems. When we select the best lettuce leaves, rhubarb stalks, or asparagus shoots, that is exactly what we are doing. (However, many garden vegetables have been bred to retain their meristematic characteristics, such as mild flavor and tenderness, as long as possible.)

Another good way to find meristems is to "follow the calories." At any particular time of year, unless dormant, a plant will be investing its energy (calories) somewhere. An evening primrose puts energy into its root the first summer; the next year it invests it in young leaves, followed by its stalk, flowers, and finally seeds. Each of these parts of the evening primrose is edible, and they represent the three categories of produce: storage organs, meristems, and reproductive parts—in that order. Thinking about what the plant is *doing* will tell you where the calories are *going*, and that's where you'll find them.

This discussion of meristems isn't about passing a botany exam. It is about learning the all-important difference between ingesting roughage and eating food.

Poisonous Plant Fables

About ten years ago, a man approached me after a presentation that I had given on wild edibles. Obviously quite agitated, he stuttered a few syllables before launching a frantic diatribe, "You need to warn people that there's some edible plants that look **exactly** like deadly poisonous plants, and they grow side by side, and **nobody** can tell them apart. **Nobody!** Not even an **expert!**"

I paused, in a mild state of shock, before responding, "That's not really true. Some plants might . . . ."

"It **is** true," he interrupted. "Books tell people they can eat these plants, but they don't tell them that there's deadly poisonous plants that look *exactly the same*. It's like playing Russian roulette."

Of course, it **isn't** true, but the fear of wild plants runs *very* deep in Western civilization. While it certainly *is* true that people *can* poison themselves with wild vegetation, the fear that we attribute to plants is monstrously out of proportion with the actual danger they pose. Like many profound and unexamined fears, this one breeds irrationality, causing many people to suspend all logic and refuse to participate in rational discourse.

Such was the time when some friends and I stood at a beach, stuffing our faces with serviceberries, and two children, a brother and sister, took interest. As they were about to partake, their father intervened. From his lawn chair fifty feet away, he warned them that they'd poison themselves and die if they ate "those berries." His son piped in, "But Dad, I already ate some and they're really good!"

His father didn't budge. A little later, the children passed by again and surreptitiously asked, "Are they really poisonous?"

As I shoveled in another handful, I smiled and asked, "What do you think?" They giggled back, recognizing the absurdity of their father's logic: "These people are eating something they enjoy very much; it must be deadly poisonous."

Our culture is spellbound and beguiled by the story of someone mistaking a poisonous plant for an edible one and dying from the error. It is a magnetic motif with a suite of admonitions that we find economically and socially useful: don't stray too far from the beaten path; what civilization has given you is better than you realize; Nature cannot be trusted; be normal and live a predictable life of routine. These messages are compelling when a torturous death is presented as the cost of disregarding them.

Every culture builds its own propaganda to promote stability. An important aspect of this propaganda is *fables*—stories made up to teach particular lessons. Since we have trouble finding sufficient examples of wild plant poisonings, we fabricate the story again and again.

The Poison Plant Fable assumes many forms. When the world-famous forager Euell Gibbons died of a ruptured aortic aneurysm (which had absolutely nothing to do with wild plants or mushrooms), the public immediately began fabricating stories about his death, claiming that, in one way or another, he was killed by a "toxic diet." These falsehoods are more widely believed than the truth and are still commonly circulated today, even by the media. I am frequently confronted by people who, believing this Euell Gibbons fable, present it as "proof" that foraging is stupid and dangerous. Several foraging-death urban legends are commonly told, even among foragers. In her *Encyclopedia of Country Living* (1994), Carla Emery uses this same tactic in an attempt to terrify her readers away from foraging:

> Even Euell Gibbons, who wrote a whole series of books extolling the glories of wild food foraging, finally goofed and tried the wrong wild leaf in his lunch. That's how he died. (Emery, 1994, p. 401)

The Poisonous Plant Fable is accorded more power when perpetuated by highly respected individuals. In his Pulitzer Prize winning book *Guns, Germs, and Steel*, Jared Diamond tells of his reaction when some of his native New Guinean friends collect some mushrooms to eat:

> I patiently explained to my Foré companions that I had read about some mushrooms' being poisonous, that I had heard of even expert American mushroom collectors' dying because of the difficulty of distinguishing safe from dangerous mushrooms, and that although we were all hungry, it just wasn't worth the risk. (Diamond, 1997, p. 144)

To members of the Foré tribe, this probably sounded about as absurd as "let's not eat these bananas; perhaps they are deadly false bananas" would sound to us. Most Americans, having been indoctrinated with the Poison Plant Fable, would have given Diamond's warning serious consideration, but the Foré were properly offended and would have none of it. In Diamond's words, they "got angry and told me to shut up and listen while they explained some things to me." That is exactly how I often feel.

The people who repeat this garbage have become tools in the perpetuation of a fable they have internalized. Their ignorant fear-mongering dissuades many from a safe and rewarding hobby. It is a disservice to everybody.

Into The Wild: Another Poisonous Plant Fable?

At nearly every workshop or presentation that I have given over the last ten years, I have been asked my opinion about Jon Krakauer's book *Into The Wild*. "You should read it!" I was advised, dozens of times. Many people outlined the story for me, dwelling especially on the "cause" of Christopher McCandless' death. The ending sounded disturbingly like another rendition of the Poison Plant Fable to me, but many very intelligent people, convinced by Krakauer's skillful prose, would argue, "No, it's really true!" I eventually realized that reading this book and researching Chris's death were requirements of my job.

Into The Wild is about an emotionally embattled young man named Chris McCandless who left his affluent upbringings behind, renamed himself Alex, and wandered the West searching for purpose and identity. His decaying body was found by a moose hunter in Alaska on September 6, 1992.

Through an autopsy, medical examiners determined that McCandless had starved to death, and all evidence pointed clearly and unambiguously to that conclusion. But the Poison Plant Fable proved irresistible to Krakauer, who first wrote about the tragedy in "Death of an Innocent," (a January 1993 article in *Outside* magazine). He conjectured that Chris had died by poisoning when he mistook the wild sweet pea *Hedysarum mackenziei* for the "wild potato" *Hedysarum alpinum.* But since Chris had clearly starved to death, Krakauer had to reach further, positing that McCandless was "laid low" by the poisoning, and thus unable to feed himself. Since we have all internalized the Poison Plant Fable, this unlikely and scientifically unsupported explanation for Chris's death was immediately and widely accepted as fact.

But there is no evidence that Chris McCandless ever ate even a single seed of *H. mackenziei*. Krakauer doesn't even try to provide such evidence; he simply tells us that the two plants grow beside each other and are "very difficult to distinguish." Provided with these facts, most people immediately and unquestioningly conclude that McCandless mistook wild sweet pea for wild potato. Like Krakauer, they don't need any evidence because the Poison Plant Fable says that it happens this way. But how plausible is this?

An important component of the Poison Plant Fable is the insistence that "even experts" have trouble identifying edible plants. In *Into The Wild*, Krakauer writes, "Wild sweet pea looks so much like wild potato that even expert botanists sometimes have trouble telling the species apart" (p. 191).

Of course, if they are both *unfamiliar,* any two related plants may be confusing to an "expert botanist." This is a meaningless and irrelevant point. *Hedysarum alpinum* and *H. mackenziei*, like any other two plants, can be consistently, reliably, and easily told apart by any person who has become familiar with them. Despite Krakauer's misinformed insistence that the veins on the underside of the leaflets are the only reliable characteristic distinguishing them, there are actually numerous features of the two plants that are notably different. In fact, experienced foragers can readily distinguish these plants by their roots alone (Schofield, 1989).

Krakauer's hypothesis requires that, after more than a month of collecting *H. alpinum* safely, McCandless suddenly couldn't recognize the plant and accidentally ate a significant volume of *H. mackenziei* seeds. This explanation displays a gross misunderstanding of how pattern recognition works in the human brain. Once a person becomes thoroughly familiar with two plants, they appear distinct. Thus, every household cook can easily differentiate a head of green cabbage from one of iceberg lettuce, even though they look identical to the uninitiated. The same cook would not be able to point out a single readily visible diagnostic feature that she uses to distinguish these plants. After weeks of collecting wild potato and successfully distinguishing it from wild sweet pea, Chris would have developed an excellent search image for both plants. Misidentification at this point would be about as likely as a man making love to the wrong woman and not noticing. In a foraging culture, such an absurd proposition would be immediately ridiculed and discarded. The fact that our society swallowed this hypothesis and regurgitated it as fact demonstrates a systemic gullibility based on profound ignorance.

The second fatal flaw in Krakauer's poisoning hypothesis is the fact that *H. mackenziei*, the plant that supposedly poisoned Chris McCandless, is **not** poisonous. Although *Tanaina Plantlore*, the field guide that Chris was using, says that the plant is "reported to be poisonous," the author does not actually call it "poisonous." Although "reported to be poisonous" may sound alarming, it is actually rather insignificant. I can find printed references reporting about two-thirds of all wild edibles to be poisonous. The familiar garden parsnip, *Pastinaca sativa*, is listed as poisonous in dozens of wildflower books, some written by reputed botanists. I even have one book that calls it "exceedingly lethal." Indeed, some plants called poisonous or inedible in *Tanaina Plantlore* were regular food items for other Native American tribes.

Krakauer calls *H. mackenziei* "poisonous" in his *Outside* article. When he elaborates in *Into The Wild*, he admits that "accounts of individuals being poisoned from eating *H. mackenziei* are nonexistent in modern medical literature" (p.191). He goes on to counter that, "the aboriginal inhabitants of the North have apparently known for millennia that the wild sweet pea is toxic," but he does not tell us what makes this assumption "apparent." Krakauer finds one account of a poisoning "attributable" to wild sweet pea, but this report, from 1848, is highly questionable (a point also argued by Treadwell and Clausen, 2008).

In the wake of the Chris McCandless case, extensive laboratory analyses have been conducted, attempting to verify the toxicity of *H. mackenziei*. Roots, seeds, flowers, leaves, and stems were all analyzed. These tests have turned up no alkaloids or toxins of any kind (Treadwell and Clausen, 2008). The authors of this study also state that there is no credible chemical, historical, or ethnobotanical basis for the anecdotal belief that *H. mackenziei* is toxic. They believe that the wild sweet pea is nontoxic and has not been traditionally used simply because of the smaller size of its roots.

The hypothesis that Chris McCandless died from eating *H. mackenziei* seeds is supported by no evidence whatsoever, has absolutely no factual basis, and in fact relies on disproven assumptions. It should be discarded.

Krakauer's Second Hypothesis

Krakauer himself recognized the preposterousness of advancing misidentification as Chris' cause of death. When he elaborates on the story in the book *Into The Wild*, he writes, "For three weeks beginning on June 24, McCandless had dug and safely eaten dozens of wild potato roots without mistaking *H. mackenzii* (sic) for *H. alpinum*; why, on July 14, when he started gathering seeds instead of roots, would he suddenly have confused the two species?" (p. 192). After discarding his original explanation for McCandless' death, Krakauer proposes a new one: that Chris was poisoned by the seeds of *H. alpinum*—the plant that he thought he was eating. If the Poison Plant Fable didn't work, he would try the next best thing. Now, the story went, Chris hadn't eaten the wrong plant, he had eaten the wrong *part* of a plant, and this caused him to starve to death. Krakauer's eloquent and captivating rendition of the Poison Plant Fable has inculcated millions with its insidious message.

We know from McCandless' journals and photos that he actually had eaten *H. alpinum* seeds. However, evidence for toxicity of these seeds is entirely non-existent. Krakauer himself points out that "the seeds of *H. alpinum* have never been described as toxic in any published text: an extensive search of the medical and botanical literature yielded not a single indication that any part of *H. alpinum* is poisonous" (p. 191).

Yet Krakauer's second hypothesis doesn't just require wild potato seeds to be poisonous; it requires them to be poisonous in a very specific, rare, and unusual way: by promoting starvation through inhibiting digestion and metabolism. **Chris McCandless clearly starved to death, and Krakauer has never denied this**—he just argues that eating a wild plant *made him* starve to death. At face value, this is a very odd proposition. Last time I checked, starvation was caused by *not* eating things. Krakauer is breaking new ground; not just arguing that McCandless died this way, but indeed, introducing the very idea that people can die this way at all—something that the medical and toxicological community has never confirmed. Krakauer identified a chemical called swainsonine as

Hedysarum alpinum , a nonpoisonous legume that Jon Krakauer argued killed Chris McCandless. This is a common range plant in parts of the northern U.S. and Canada. Note the flowers tending toward one side of the raceme.

a hypothetical culprit—although he was apparently, like me, unable to find a single reported case of swainsonine poisoning in humans.

Krakauer doesn't test the implications of this exceedingly improbable hypothesis to determine if it is valid. Instead, he carefully crafts a series of specious arguments and illogical conclusions, by which the readers of *Into The Wild* are misled to believe that this hypothesis has somehow been verified. First, Krakauer tells us that the plant family *Leguminosae*, to which *H. alpinum* belongs, "is rife with species that contain alkaloids" (p. 193). (Krakauer is factually wrong here; Deshpande and Deshpande [1991, P. 247] state that "although widely distributed in the plant kingdom, alkaloids are not common in legumes.") As soon as this is incorrectly suggested, wild potato is treated as if it is *known* to contain alkaloids. As soon as it is implied that alkaloids *may be* toxic, they are treated as toxins. We are told that alkaloids *may be* localized in one part of the plant, and that the seeds are the *most likely* site for this localization. When we are then told that "preliminary testing" indicated that the seeds contain "traces of an alkaloid," we are beguiled into the totally unsupported conclusion that wild potato seeds contain toxic alkaloids despite their roots' edibility. (Thorough later testing contradicted these irreproducible preliminary results; but Krakauer didn't change his story until the media exposed this fact more than ten years after *Into The Wild* was published.)

Hedysarum mackenziei in flower. Another nonpoisonous plant that didn't kill Chris McCandless, despite what one might see on television. Photo by Bill Merilees.

We are then told that there is "a strong likelihood" that the (non-existent) alkaloid is swainsonine. Krakauer never explains why he thinks the likelihood is "strong"—since there are many thousands of known alkaloids, and swainsonine is not known from the species in question, any reasonable assessment would place the likelihood as "very small." In fact, the proposition that *Hedysarum alpinum* or *H. mackenziei* contains swainsonine is rather absurd. These are common, widespread range plants that are considered good forage for livestock (Larson and Johnson, 2007). If they contained swainsonine, this would almost certainly be well known, since virtually everything we know about this chemical is due to its toxic effect on grazing livestock, and a great deal of research has gone into identifying which legumes contain it. After all this, Krakauer tells us that wild potato seeds *may* contain swainsonine (they do not). Then he proceeds to treat them as if they *do* contain this alkaloid, and discusses the physiological effects of swainsonine poisoning in livestock.

The above is not an *explanation*; it is a meaningless string of unverified assumptions. It is not a *theory*; it is an untested progression toward a predetermined conclusion. It does not withstand even cursory examination under the scientific method. Yet it fulfills the Poison Plant Fable.

If Krakauer is correct in assuming that swainsonine poisoning in humans would be accompanied by symptoms comparable to those in animals, then it should be easy for him to conclude that Chris McCandless was *not* suffering from it. Chris only exhibited one swainsonine symptom, emaciation, and this was observed well before the alleged poisoning by *H. alpinum* seeds, and can clearly be attributed to the caloric deprivation that he was suffering. Krakauer ignores the fact that Chris was not exhibiting the widely known classic symptoms of swainsonine poisoning, which appear *before* weight loss: uncoordination, hypersensitivity, depression, blank-staring eyes, loss of awareness, and similar neurological symptoms (Harries et al., 1972). It is for these symptoms that *Astragalus* plants containing swainsonine are known as "locoweeds"—*loco* is Spanish for "crazy." When you read Chris's journal and see the photos he took of himself just before death, along with his final note, it seems obvious that he was not suffering swainsonine poisoning.

Dr. Thomas Clausen, a biochemist at the University of Alaska, extensively tested *H. alpinum* for toxins and concluded that no part of it is poisonous. No traces of swainsonine or any other alkaloid were found in any part of the plant. Dr. Clausen admits that he wanted Krakauer's tale to be true, since it made a nice story, but laments that this view has been found untenable. Indeed, he states of *H. alpinum* seeds, "I'd eat them myself" (Lamothe, 2007).

Just to lend a firsthand anecdote, I cooked and ate a small portion of *H. alpinum* seeds. Quite frankly, they were delicious—much like black locust seeds, but far better. No wonder Chris ate them for two weeks.

The Moldy Seed Hypothesis

In September 2007, Matthew Power wrote an exposé, "The Cult of Chris McCandless," in *Men's Journal*, in which he made the point that Krakauer's explanation of Chris' death in *Into The Wild* was effectively refuted, since chemists had tested these seeds for toxins and found none. Power's article received significant media attention, and at about this time, a new printing of *Into The Wild* hit the bookstore shelves across the country—in which Krakauer presents yet a third explanation for McCandless' death—which, of course, *still* blames it on eating a wild plant.

This third, the "moldy seed" hypothesis, is the most fanciful, forced, and inane of all. It states that, although the seeds of *H. alpinum* are not poisonous and do not contain swainsonine, they might become infected with a certain mold, *Rhizoctonia leguminicola*, which could produce swainsonine. If you ignore the fact that *Rhizoctonia leguminicola* is not known to infect *H. alpinum*, and the fact that Chris' symptoms appear incompatible with *Rhizoctonia* poisoning (a hyper-salivating condition known as "slobbers"), you are still left with the problem that there is no evidence that Chris actually ate any moldy seeds—much less the "enormous quantities" that Krakauer proposes (and which would be required to cause poisoning). The only evidence that Krakauer gives to support this hypo-hypothesis is that McCandless collected some seeds during a rainy period and put some of them in a Ziploc bag. That's it? Yup, that's *it*.

The moldy seed explanation is patently ridiculous. By this time, one begins to wonder if Krakauer will just continue to change his hypotheses *ad infinitum* as each one is logically and scientifically refuted. This capriciousness is the hallmark of "science" with a predetermined conclusion. Clearly, Krakauer's predetermined conclusion is that Chris McCandless died from a wild plant that he ate. Leaving the first and second hypotheses intact, though refuted, in his book, lends credibility to his latest story by making it seem like the author is searching earnestly for the truth, rather than grasping desperately for tenuous explanations to defend his fundamental belief in the Poison Plant Fable. It also adds to the feeling of peril associated with eating wild plants: "Behold all of these potential causes of death-by-plant that were *almost true*."

It doesn't upset me that Krakauer was *wrong*; it bothers me that he was *wrong-headed*. These explanations of Chris' death should have been recognized as deficient, if not the moment they were conceived, then certainly after minimal investigation. Yet Krakauer has labored and belabored for fifteen years to perpetuate them. Rather than make a genuine effort to gather facts and draw sensible conclusions, he drew extravagant conclusions first; then facts were conjured, contorted, or ignored to support them. Journalism should be an exercise in finding and communicating the truth, not in obfuscating the obvious explanations in favor of sexier ones that find no factual support. Krakauer's presentation of the matter seems stubbornly defiant at best. If his reasoning is not obstinately perverse, his arguments are disingenuous.

There is a reason that his entire book, save for this one part, is thoughtful and masterfully crafted: the deep, irrational, unexamined prejudice about foraging that prevails in our society. Edible wild plants remains one of the few topics about which such journalistic irresponsibility is still tolerated. Such conjectural nonsense about most topics would never pass the editors. But in reference to wild food, logic and scrutiny are totally suspended. The result is a best-selling book, and now a movie, together constituting the single largest message about wild food that the media has ever given our society, perpetuating the Poison Plant Fable.

Sean Penn's Deliberate Deception About McCandless's Death

In the movie version of *Into The Wild*, Sean Penn chose to portray McCandless poisoning himself according to Krakauer's first hypothesis—mistaking wild sweet pea for wild potato. Although this scenario is irreconcilable with the facts and had long ago been abandoned by Krakauer himself, it produced the strongest drama and the scariest anti-foraging message. This motif is integral to the film's plot and development. It is introduced almost immediately, as Chris writes to Wayne Westerberg about his "new book on the local flora and fauna." Soon after Chris arrives in the Arizona desert, there is a close-up of the cover of his copy of Outdoor Life's *Field Guide to North American Edible Wild Plants*. In another early scene, Jan Burres, who he met on the road, says to him, "That book of yours is really cool and all, but you can't depend entirely on leaves and berries."

Later, after Chris is starving and trapped by the high waters of the Teklanika River, the film shows him having an epiphany after reading the words "to call each thing by its right name" in *Doctor Zhivago*. After this, he takes the field guide *Tanaina Plantlore* and goes on a plant identification spree. Among the plants he identifies is *Hedysarum alpinum*. (In reality, Chris had already been collecting and eating this plant for several weeks by this time.) After eating this plant's seeds, McCandless becomes very ill. Upon a second look at his book he realizes that he has mistakenly eaten *H. mackenziei*, the wild sweet pea. Further reading reveals that he is bound to die a slow, agonizing death. He throws the book down in rage, screaming, "Fuck it all!"

To the viewer who may admire Chris or hold some of his ideals, it is a powerful scene: the wilderness sojourner and independent seeker of wisdom from Nature, brought to his knees and murdered for an innocent mistake by the treachery of a poisonous plant, now finally able to throw away all of his foolish ideas—but it is too late. Just before Chris expires, so that nobody forgets how he perished, the movie hauntingly repeats the words, "To call each thing by its right name. By its right name."

The message is clear: *Eating wild plants will kill you.*

But it's a lie.

Although it is understood that some details of a story will be changed to make it more friendly to the motion picture format, most viewers assume that a film "based on a true story" depicts things that at least remotely approximate the truth—especially when it comes to the most significant event in the entire story. The deception in this fictitious scene is careful, extensive, integral, exceptional, and inexcusable.

There is no reason to believe that Chris ever ate even one wild sweet pea seed, and these seeds are not poisonous anyways. But the film's most egregious deception occurs when Chris opens up *Tanaina Plantlore* (Kari, 1987). The book's actual cover is shown, but when Chris flips to page 128 to read about *H. mackenziei*, the movie shows a counterfeit page that the producers have forged and inserted. The excerpt from the book that McCandless reads in the film goes like this (Yes, it really does go like this; the apparent errors and omissions are original.):

> The lateral veins, nearly invisible on leaflets of wild sweet pea the plants poisonous seedlings. If ingested symptoms include partial motor paralysis, inhibition of digestion, and nausea. If untreated leads to starvation and death. Another way to distinguish is that the stem of the wild sweet pea is mostly unbranched.

That's strange, because when I open to page 128 in *my* copy, it only says *this* in the same place:

> The lateral veins of the leaflets of wild sweet pea are hidden, while those of the wild potato are conspicuous. Another way to distinguish between the two plants is that the stem of the wild sweet pea is mostly unbranched, while that of the wild potato is definitely branched.

In real life, the book has no mention whatsoever of "partial motor paralysis, inhibition of digestion, and nausea," nor of "starvation and death." The movie paused on a fragment of text representing each of the primary components of the Poison Plant Fable: "poisonous," "and death," and "the plants resemble each other." The focus on "lateral veins" corresponds to the "even experts" component of the fable, as does the subtly changed wording from "hidden" to "nearly invisible." The film also focuses on the words "starvation" and "digestion" so that we remember the imaginary effects of the plant that the filmmakers are pretending is poisonous.

This bogus text—displaying poor grammar, worse compositional skill, and profound ignorance of botany—is an insult to the actual author of the book.

The movie's fictitious death scene is an insult to the viewers. But more than anything, it is an insult to Christopher McCandless.

If this movie was made "in memory of Christopher Johnson McCandless," as it claims, then why was a fraudulent, insulting scene fabricated for his death? Chris's life story has been usurped by the very same propaganda machine that he so vehemently rejected, twisted into a fable for the purpose of casting fear and doubt into those who would seek what he sought. The greatest lessons that could be learned from his life are now buried under lies.

So how did Chris McCandless die?

There has never been debate about this: Chris starved to death. His autopsy, performed by the crime lab in Anchorage, confirmed this. When Chris's body was found, it weighed 67 pounds; it was estimated that his weight at death was 83 pounds, with a body mass index of 13.3 (Lamothe, 2007). Death from starvation usually occurs when body mass index falls to about 13 (Shils et al., 1994; Henry, 1990). The proportion of weight that Chris lost was comparable to that normally associated with victims of concentration camps, severe famine, anorexia nervosa, and death by starvation (Keys et al., 1950). Even Chris' own journal, nineteen days before his death, says, "Starving. Great Jeopardy."

Keys et al. (1950), in their famous and fascinating study of human starvation, point out that starving people become exceedingly preoccupied with food, writing and talking of little else. Krakauer and others were struck by this very feature of Chris's journal: Andrew Liske, who accompanied Krakauer to the bus after Chris's death, noted after reading the journal, "He wrote about hardly anything except food" (p. 183). Chris displayed this obsession for the entire stay, because he was starving through all of it. The journal entries clearly show that he was not getting nearly enough calories. He took pictures of himself that document his steadily decreasing body mass throughout his stay in Alaska. He appears dangerously malnourished weeks before ingesting the seeds that Krakauer claims killed him. The medical examiners who performed Chris' autopsy noted telltale signs of starvation: severe deterioration of his muscles and a lack of subcutaneous fat. **No other individual who has investigated the matter finds Krakauer's explanations necessary or even credible.**

The only reasonable conclusion is that Chris died of starvation—the regular kind of starvation, which results from not eating enough food over a prolonged period—not from some farfetched and imaginary sort of starvation.

Then why does Jon Krakauer insist that Chris McCandless died from eating a wild plant?

When the story of Chris McCandless' death hit the media, it produced a strong negative reaction among some people, particularly many Alaskans. McCandless was publicly ridiculed and lambasted. Krakauer saw through the shallowness, insensitivity, and irrationality of much of this criticism and wanted to provide a counterpoint.

I don't disagree with him. Although Chris made serious and egregious mistakes, this is not a sensible reason to become furious at him or about what he did. The impulsive disparagement levied toward Chris displays the insecurities of a kind of redneck found in every rural district—one who feels deeply threatened by those who do things that he would not dream of trying and can't understand. Only on the surface is this criticism about his fatal mistakes. Chris's death verifies his critics' self-image as rugged frontierspeople, and renders him a defenseless target.

Shortly after the story broke, the Alaskan hunters who found McCandless's body ridiculed him, saying that he had killed a caribou and mistaken it for a moose. In the words of Gordon Samel, "When I read in the paper that he'd thought he'd shot a moose, that told me right there he wasn't no Alaskan. There's a big difference between a moose and a caribou. A real big difference. You'd have to be pretty stupid not to be able to tell them apart," (p. 177). But there is no doubt that Chris did, in fact, kill a moose; his photos clearly show it. These Alaskans not only couldn't identify the animal's remains, but they derided Chris for getting it right.

This is a microcosm for much of the criticism Chris has received. When people say that Chris's adventure was pitiful and insignificant, and imply that "Alaskans do that kind of stuff all the time," they are kidding themselves. What they actually mean is that Alaskans go into the bush with snowmobiles or ATVs, lots of gear, and ample food supplies; why couldn't Chris just do the same? This is as irrelevant and hollow as mocking a marathon runner because you can get to the finish line faster in your car. There is nothing inherently moronic about what Chris tried to do; he just failed. No person who has the ability to successfully do what Chris attempted would detest him for trying.

I understand Krakauer's desire to defend McCandless from such crude and childish attacks. Having Chris die from a poisonous plant that could even fool "experts" makes him seem less foolish and overconfident than if he died by simple starvation. Krakauer's incongruous interpretation of the evidence seems to be based on this desire to preserve a more positive image of McCandless—both for the readers and for himself. But his beliefs rest on two demonstrably false assumptions: first, that starvation alone is inadequate to explain Chris's death; and second, that Chris's journal entry from July 30 somehow indicates that a plant eaten on that day is what killed him almost three weeks later.

Krakauer is in obstinate denial about Chris's state of health during his stay in the bush, and this is reflected in a strange dismissive attitude. Krakauer says that Chris "feasted regularly" from mid-May to late June, when in fact he was only eating sufficiently perhaps once or twice a week. He points out "a bounty of wild meat" in early June—the only stretch of his 113-day stay when Chris *might* have been consuming sufficient calories. Krakauer speaks of an "apparent munificence" and claims that "the country was a fecund riot of plant and animal life, and his food supply was adequate" (p. 188). Meanwhile, Chris's journal and photos clearly document his own starvation.

Krakauer also shares that "game seems to have been plentiful: In the last three weeks of July, he killed thirty-five squirrels, four spruce grouse, five jays and woodpeckers, and two frogs" (p. 188). Perhaps he never did the math, but this is a *striking shortage* of game. And this was a period of relative abundance in comparison with much of the trip. An examination of Chris's journal shows that he went without food on many days and almost always had an extreme caloric deficit. His starvation clearly began on April 28, not July 30 as Krakauer proposes.

When Chris tried to leave the wilderness in early July, he probably did so because he realized that starvation was a real threat. He took a picture of himself at that time, about which Krakauer says, "He looks healthy but alarmingly gaunt. Already his cheeks are sunken. The tendons in his neck stand out like taut cables" (p. 169). How does Krakauer deduce "healthy" from that description? This photo was taken almost seven weeks before McCandless died, and four weeks before he ate wild potato seeds and felt ill. Clearly, he was gravely malnourished and on a trajectory toward death long before the alleged "poisoning" even occurred. But Krakauer still maintains the fallacy that Chris was doing fine. Only one page after the above description, he states that Chris had "been fending for himself quite nicely in the country" (p. 171).

Krakauer is trying to squeeze blood from a turnip, so to speak, because he rejects the obvious. This denial helps explain his bizarre juxtaposition of incompatible statements: "His meager diet had pared his body down to a feral scrawn of gristle and bone, but he seemed to be in reasonably good health" (pp 189). Krakauer argues that starvation alone can't explain Chris's death because, before July 30, there was "nothing to suggest that McCandless was in dire circumstances." If a hundred days of drastic food shortage doesn't sound dire, what does? There is, in fact, overwhelming evidence that Chris had been starving before this date; the photos he took of himself show visual proof. Chris's own journal says "Starving" on July 30. Starvation doesn't happen suddenly.

Nothing about the journal entry "Extremly weak. Fault of pot seed. Much trouble just to stand up. Starving. Great Jeopardy" indicates that *H. alpinum* seeds killed Chris, or that Chris feeling ill that day caused his death nineteen days later. There is no plausible theory connecting these events. Most likely, this entry simply reflects that he overindulged on wild potato seeds and felt ill. Almost any fruit or vegetable will do this when eaten in immoderate quantity. Considering Chris's nutritional state, he seems a likely candidate for overindulgence.

The papery seedpods (*loments*) of *H. alpinum*. Each loment contains a tiny seed about 3% of its size, far too small to be of any practical value as food.

As a child, I once became extremely ill from eating way too many green peppers. Another time, as an adult, I seriously pigged out on bearberries and developed terrible stomach pains that doubled me over for an hour. In neither case did I die of starvation three weeks later.

Lamothe (2007) modeled Chris's food intake versus requirement, based on World Health Organization guidelines, and showed that his caloric deficit alone was sufficient to cause death. This supports the conclusion that Chris McCandless died of starvation—just like the medical examiner had said, and still contends. This also explains the "mystery" of why Chris didn't do more to save himself: the advanced stages of starvation are characterized by an extreme listlessness, weakness, and depression (Keys et al., 1950), all of which were probably aggravated by low-level lead toxicity from the game he was eating (ND Dept. of Health, 2008).

I can sympathize with Krakauer's desire to portray McCandless in a positive light, but there comes a time when you must let go of extravagant, unsupported guesses. There is simply no reason to believe that Chris McCandless was killed by a plant.

What lessons about wilderness survival and wild food can be drawn from the story of Chris McCandless?

Whatever you think of Chris as a person, it is hard to deny that he overestimated his skills and underestimated how much knowledge—and food—he would need. Despite some vocal anti-McCandless opinions, he was not ill-equipped or under-equipped; he was unskilled and unprepared. He didn't need a better map or a high-powered rifle. There are many knowledgeable and skillful people who have returned from similar adventures in good health, and who would have thrived with the same gear and in the same circumstances under which he starved to death.

In a short-term survival situation, food is of minor importance. However, in long-term survival or "living off the land," it is of paramount importance.

Chris grossly underestimated the amount of food that he needed. Before his trip to Alaska he had spent periods on a negative calorie budget and lost a great deal of weight. At one point his journal (oddly written in third person) said,

"Malnutrition and the road have taken their toll on his body. Over 25 pounds lost" (p. 37). Yet he was always able to access food after these excursions and restore his body mass. During such a replenishment period, after a time of living on wild plants, Jan Burres described him as "big-time hungry. Hungry, hungry, *hungry*" (p. 30). It is OK to lose twenty pounds over three weeks, but continuing that same negative calorie budget over several months is deadly.

We get food so easily and automatically that we hardly consider the quantities that we require, or its calorie content. Most Americans are profoundly out of touch with these things. What Chris did is common for wilderness survivalists today, who typically "survive" on negative calorie budgets, steadily losing weight. The only difference is that their excursions are normally of less than a month's duration, and they simply gain back the lost weight after returning to civilization. (An excellent description of this process of survivalist starvation followed by binge eating can be found in *The Last American Man* [Gilbert, 2002], pp. 52–63.) I believe that this is exactly what Chris intended to do, just as he had done before; but his attempt to leave was thwarted by a collusion of unforeseen conditions, weakness, and injury.

Maintaining one's weight and health over the long term is an entirely different proposition. It doesn't help that many survival books and instructors teach that only very small amounts of food are needed in the bush. McCandless's experience should serve as a lesson to any survivalist who entertains these caloric delusions. Making believe that Chris died by poisoning robs us of this important and potentially life-saving lesson, and instead imbues us with an unrealistic and unfounded fear that only makes us more likely to perish in the wilderness.

I like to measure my food in *calorie-days*—the number of days of my full caloric requirement that the food represents. I calculated Chris's calorie requirement as 3,300 per day based on his age, gender, a body weight of 145 pounds, and heavy physical activity, using guidelines from Grodner et al. (1996). This estimate is rough, and the true figure would depend on many unknowable variables. Still, my point is easily demonstrated: McCandless didn't have nearly enough food. He began his journey on April 28 with a ten pound bag of rice—which constituted less than five calorie-days. By May 9, he had only killed one grouse and had written "4th day famine" in his journal. The rice was already long gone.

When Krakauer insists that McCandless had sufficient food in the Alaska bush, it makes me suspect that he has never lived on red squirrels. I eat three in one *meal*, and that's *with* wild rice and vegetables.

The squirrels that McCandless was eating (*Tamiasciurus hudsonicus*) typically weigh five to nine ounces (Whitaker, 1996). Using seven ounces as an average, and realizing that after subtracting the skin, tail, head, bones, feet, and entrails, the edible flesh would constitute about 40 percent of that weight, or 2.8 ounces of meat per squirrel. This means that *he would have needed to eat about twenty-five squirrels per day to meet his caloric requirement.* If he carefully removed and ate the liver, kidneys, kidney fat, heart, lungs, and brain of each squirrel, he would have about doubled the calories that he received from each animal. Since he probably did this to some extent, I estimate that he needed roughly sixteen squirrels to equal a calorie-day.

I can find no estimate of the caloric value of *H. alpinum* roots. I use figures for parsnips in these calculations, since they seem like the most physically similar cultivated vegetable. (Note that, despite the common name "wild potato," *H. alpinum* is not closely related to potatoes, nor similar in form.) If parsnips have similar energy content, Chris would have needed about nine pounds of wild potato roots to equal one calorie-day.

Since we don't know exactly which berries Chris was eating and in which proportions, I calculated with the caloric value of blueberries (which is actually higher than that of some of the berries he was eating). It would have taken about thirteen pounds of blueberries to equal one of Chris's calorie-days.

A hypothetical day's food for Chris might consist of half squirrel meat, and a quarter each of berries and wild potato roots. In this case he would have needed eight squirrels, 2 ¼ pounds of roots, and 3 ¼ pounds of berries *each day*. I don't propose that he ever ate exactly this complement of food—that detail is insignificant. What matters is that his food journal clearly shows him getting only a small fraction of the calories he needed. (Note: the calorie content of various foods used in this section are derived from Grodner et al., 1996, except for dry rice, which is from Van Wyk, 2005.)

If this seems like a high volume of food, that's because it is. We have sought, developed, cultivated, and become accustomed to calorie-dense foods for so long that most of us have never been without them. We've never had to eat food in volumes like this. When you realize that a stick of butter has as many calories as two and a half quarts of blueberries or seven pounds of broccoli, you can see why the innate human desire for calorie-rich, low-fiber food developed.

You can't just eat whatever is edible; you must eat food in appropriate proportions.

This is a big shocker to modern folks, who get to pick and choose their dietary proportions from an almost endless variety of easily acquired food. Most of us have never really faced this challenge. The survivalist often imagines that she can find an edible plant and just eat it until she is full, but this is simply not so.

Chris had access to a lot of lingonberries. If he didn't get any meat, couldn't he just eat more lingonberries and get all his calories that way? Absolutely not. He would have needed to eat almost *three gallons* of lingonberries *per day*. He'd probably be vomiting before finishing the second quart. No matter how many lingonberries were available to him, his body would have only accepted them for a small portion of his caloric requirement. This doesn't make lingonberries "poisonous"; the same is true of virtually *every* food, although the appropriate proportions vary. Toxicologists do not consider an illness from overindulgence to be a poisoning (Kingsbury, 1965). When Chris wrote, "Extremly weak. Fault pot seed," it was not because *H. alpinum* seeds are poisonous, but simply because he had eaten too much, and his body rejected them.

The concept that foods can be eaten only in appropriate quantities is taken so much for granted that, to my knowledge, it has never been given a name in the medical literature. I call it the *maximum caloric proportion* (MCP). Some foods have a very high MCP, such as milk, meat, and potatoes. They are easily digested and contain few antinutrients or toxins, thus they are suitable as dietary staples. Others, such as cabbage, rhubarb, and raspberries, cannot serve as staple foods and are only suitable to supply small portions of the diet. As one travels north, there tends to be fewer plants with a high MCP; this is why hunter-gatherers from northern latitudes ate meat for the great majority of their calories.

Don't underestimate the skills and knowledge that living off the land requires.

Chris was neither a good hunter nor a good gatherer. He either didn't realize these facts, or didn't think they mattered. Identification represents perhaps one percent of a seasoned gatherer's knowledge about a particular plant. The rest is learned from experience, not books. Each plant is a complex skill, which often takes much time to master, but many neophyte foragers don't appreciate this fact. An experienced harvester might locate a plant in half the time of a novice and select better specimens, harvest them six times as fast, then process and prepare them in only a quarter of the time. Even with a skill as deceptively simple as berry picking, skilled collectors typically acquire two to four times as much as inexperienced pickers beside them. Such disparities add up *enormously* and can be the difference between life and death in a survival situation.

McCandless was also a complete novice when it came to hunting. Skilled hunters kill many times more game than the inexperienced. Porcupines, red squirrels, and spruce grouse are notoriously easy to kill. Of course, he should have eaten easy prey, but mention of the more elusive game is mostly lacking. Snowshoe hares, for example, are found in the same area and provide about six times the meat of a squirrel, but they also require more skill to hunt. It takes years to become a proficient hunter, and Chris sorely lacked such experience. This callowness is all the more egregious when you consider that Chris was attempting to survive in a landscape where high-calorie plant foods do not exist, and hunter-gatherers subsisted largely on meat.

In a very real sense, Chris was killed by the ignorance he displayed when he killed the moose. It took him two days to finish removing the internal organs, which should have been done within an hour or two. He didn't even commence with smoking the meat until *four days* after the kill. In *June*! Beyond this, it is honestly quite hard for me to imagine the naivety that would be required to not know that meat should be preserved by cutting it into thin strips and drying. Sure, plenty of people don't know this—but they aren't going into the wilderness alone without provisions. Chris was attempting to live off the land. If he had all this time to read Tolstoy, why didn't he have time to read about what he was *doing*? There is an abundance of literature on this topic, and he could have easily done a *little* research and discovered that this was the standard way to store meat before freezers, almost everywhere in the world. Even a small moose would have provided at least sixty calorie-days, virtually ensuring his survival if he had only known a few basic facts.

Everything he needed was amply supplied, except for knowledge and resourcefulness. He just failed to take advantage of it.

If you are going to live off the land, food needs to be a priority, not an afterthought.

In a long-term subsistence situation, food is the priority. In former times, the native people of the Far North planned each move according to *food availability*. McCandless largely ignored this consideration, planning his entire wilderness experience based on aesthetic and philosophical considerations.

Moreover, the entire trip was ill-conceived from this standpoint. If Chris was really planning on feeding himself from the wild, he should have gone to a place with a lot of wild food. Instead, he chose what is arguably one of the most difficult places in the country to feed oneself. This is a mistake that I often encounter. People want to go to a remote, wild area to live off the land. Ironically, these areas are remote and wild precisely because of their limited biological production (i.e., hardly any food).

Chris did not seem to think food mattered very much. One wonders how much this had to do with the influence of Tolstoy and Thoreau. Shortly after his terrible experience wasting the moose, he highlighted this passage from *Walden*:

> I believe that every man who has ever been earnest to preserve his higher
> or poetic faculties in the best condition has been particularly inclined
> to abstain from animal food, and from much food of any kind.

This was not a vacation to Chris; it was a vision quest. I believe that, in the early part of his stay, he saw his caloric deprivation as some kind spiritual necessity and moral statement. By the time he changed his mind, it was too late, and his inexperience caught up with him.

Survival or "Earth living" entails more work than many people claim.
There is a prevalent myth that living by hunting and gathering requires only "two hours of work per day." Many authors and teachers of wilderness survival preach this, but it is groundless. The idea is based on the work of a few anthropologists (Richard Lee, Irvin DeVore, James Woodburn, and McCarthy and McArthur), popularized by Marshall Sahlins (1972). If you take the findings of these anthropologists out of context, they may seem to support this claim, but careful reading of the original studies brings to light a few things worth pointing out. First, two hours per day was the lowest estimate made in any of these studies. Second, the subjects were life-long professional hunter-gatherers who had been familiar with their respective areas all their lives. Third, most of these estimates did not include the time required for food preparation and other tasks such as building shelters or crafting tools. Further, the estimates are for groups of people, and so represent the many advantages that collaboration and division of labor provide. And finally, the observations come from tropical cultures which invested little to no labor in shelter, clothing, long-term food storage, or containers. Two hours of work per day might feed you—if all of these conditions apply to your "survival" situation.

Many survivalists have been confused and rattled by this myth, thinking that things are so hard for them either because they are inept, or because they just can't find the hamburger tree. Today we are fed with such ease that, when thrust into a subsistence or survival situation, most people find it remarkably difficult to muster the diligence and effort necessary to acquire sufficient calories. When this frustration is compounded by inexperience, some people are shocked into near paralysis. I suspect that, at least to some degree, this happened to Chris McCandless.

In this essay, I do not wish to pass any judgment on Chris McCandless. He made incredible mistakes, overestimated himself, and underestimated "The Wild," but that does not make me scornful of him. In fact, I admire his courage despite his fatal hubris. I also admire his search for truth and meaning in a world that is often disgusting in its shallowness and materialism. The fact that he died in this search in no way diminishes the lasting truth of the answers he found. To that end, I hope he would appreciate what I have written here.

One Month Eating Wild

In the spring of 2008 my wife and I decided that it would be fun to eat all wild food for a month. We had gone on "wild diets" together for a short time before, and I had done so for longer before we met, but a month seemed like a reasonable goal for the two of us—exciting but not daunting.

Why go on a wild diet, one might ask? Certainly not to prove that it can be done, since for most of human history, everybody was on a life-long wild diet. Not to prove, even, that we could do it, since I had already done it and we had no doubt that we could do it together. Really, we didn't want to *prove* anything—we just wanted to focus on eating really good, healthy food and to feel the satisfaction of being self-sufficient. We also knew that an exclusively wild diet would force us to learn new recipes and preparation techniques, and get us to experiment further with plants that we often overlook. But more than anything, eating wild makes each meal an adventure; we did it for the excitement.

Anytime I talk about eating a wild diet, people want to know the "rules" of the diet. The parameters that we set up were pretty simple: all of our calories were to come from food that was not farmed or raised for food. We allowed ourselves to use salt and spices that were not wild, since these don't contribute any measurable calories. We also allowed ourselves to use some venison that we had previously canned with a taco seasoning mix that had a small number of calories.

It amazes me how some people wish to complicate things, like a wild food diet. Many have asked, "Are you allowed to use a refrigerator?" Excuse me, but where within the term "wild food" do you hear reference to refrigerators? I was even asked if we were allowed to use toothpaste. Yes, we used toothpaste—and toilet paper too.

These questions are laden with challenges and assumptions. People decide what they think I am trying to prove with this diet, and then try to prove that I am not proving it. They ask about the refrigerator so they can say, "But our Paleolithic ancestors didn't get to use refrigerators," as if that somehow makes the food in the refrigerator not wild. I am not Paleolithic, by the way. Unlike many Paleolithic children, I grew up watching MacGyver and playing Atari. Why would I need to prove that people can live with Stone-Age technology? That was proven in the Stone Age.

In a way, it is hard to blame people for taking a defensive and doubtful position against an "extreme" diet. After all, most groups who define themselves by diet take extremely irrational or self-righteous positions toward those who eat otherwise. Every meat eater has experienced a guilt-trip laid on by a vegetarian, while many vegans scoff at the deficient morality of vegetarians. Raw food purists have trouble arguing that cooking food is *immoral*, so instead many of them act as if cooked food is extremely harmful and avoid it like poison. Although irrational, this absolutism does prove useful. Food is addictive, and treating dietary change like an attempt to quit smoking makes the change mentally easier.

But relax. I am not implying that cultivated food is immoral or physically harmful. My message is simply that wild food is extremely healthy, tasty, and fun.

What Did We Eat?

Of course, we were supposed to be monumentally excited about this endeavor and keep meticulous records of every snack and meal. We should have recorded our reactions and feelings in a diary, analyzed our gastrointestinal reaction to the change, and documented our weight. We should have had our blood pressure, blood sugar, triglycerides, and electrolyte levels monitored. But we are not an experiment. This was not a study; it was our life, and it's already complicated enough.

I started out keeping a careful dietary journal, which went like this:

May 1
Breakfast: Wild rice hot cereal with hickory nuts and maple syrup
Lunch: Deer meat, nettle greens, plum-apple sauce
Supper: Deer meat, dandelion crowns, parsnips, canned black raspberries
Snacks: Dried chokecherry

May 2
Breakfast: Wild rice cereal with maple syrup and butternuts, black raspberries
Lunch: Deer meat, dandelion greens, parsnips, wild leeks
Supper: Deer meat; hot dish with wild rice, leeks, ostrich fern, wood nettle, grated parsnip; canned huckleberries
Snacks: Dried chokecherries

May 3
Breakfast: Wild rice with hickory nuts and syrup, dandelion coffee
Lunch: Out hiking, didn't eat
Supper: Deer steaks, parsnips, canned serviceberries
Snacks: Dried chokecherries, black walnuts, dandelion coffee

May 4
Breakfast: Rice with hickory nuts and syrup, dandelion coffee
Lunch: Deer steaks, leftover hot dish from May 2, stinging nettle greens, nettle tea sweetened with maple syrup, acorn pudding.
Supper: ? I never recorded this.

The journal is interrupted here by the statement "It gets so old writing down what you eat all the time! We eat a lot of nettles, parsnips, dandelion greens, venison, maple syrup, canned berries, wild rice, nuts, and dried chokecherry." I was busy transplanting and watering trees, erecting fences, washing sap buckets, and doing plant presentations. After that, the entries became sporadic and incomplete—I only recorded some of the meals that felt more exciting and interesting. These four days are fairly representative of how we ate, except that the meals were fairly small; as the diet progressed, we ate more food, and of a greater variety.

When looking at this food diary, people are inclined to see our dining as monotonous, but compared to conventional diets, it's not. We are largely blind to the monotony of our everyday fare. Many people actually think that spaghetti and cheeseburgers are different foods. That confused look on your face tells me that you do too. They are both composed primarily of wheat, beef, and milk—only two species of organism. The only difference is in the proportion and type of complimentary vegetables, which comprise just a small percentage of the calories in these meals. When analyzed objectively, most people's diets are revealed to be shockingly simple.

In general, our wild meals were excellent. I'm sure this is largely because we made our days revolve around food, and everything was real, whole, and home-cooked. We took the time to prepare some foods which, although highly preferred, are also labor-intensive. The meals were generally larger than my meals on a conventional diet, but there were fewer snacks in between.

Normally, I eat a lot of fresh fruit and often drink fruit juice. No fruits were in season during our wild diet, so we had to rely on those that were canned, dried, or frozen. They were precious desserts, but I craved fruit much less than I normally do—probably because I was getting an ample supply of the same nutrients from fresh vegetables. The things I did crave were, not surprisingly, sugar and fat. There was no more discarded gristle from the edge of my steak—I swallowed every scrap. We traded some friends a gallon of maple syrup for some bear fat, then fried smelt in it and rejoiced in the incredible fatness of it all. We didn't drain the fried fish on a paper towel because we didn't want to waste the oil. I licked the droplets from my plate. My sugar craving could only be met by maple syrup; it was my junk food. I tried to reduce the shots I took, but often found it irresistible. But overall, my appetite achieved more of a steady state on wild food than it does on a conventional diet: I rarely felt famished, and I rarely felt full.

During the course of our diet, we consumed a surprisingly large array of plants and animals: 104 different species. (Actually, there almost certainly were more than we remembered to record.)

American elder
American hazel
American plum
Anise root
Apple
Asparagus
Basswood
Bear
Beechnut
Birch (2 kinds)
Blackberry
Black huckleberry
Black raspberry
Black walnut
Blueberry
Blue elder
Burdock (2)
Butternut
Camass
Canada goose
Cattail
Chicory
Chokecherry
Clam (species?)
Coho salmon
Cottontail rabbit
Cow parsnip
Crab (species?)

Dandelion
Dock (3)
Eurasian rabbit
Fennel
Fiddleheads (5)
Field garlic
Garlic mustard
Halibut
Honewort
Hopniss
Lake trout
Largemouth bass
Lettuce (3)
Lomatium nudicaule
Maple (2 kinds)
Milkweed
Morel
Oyster
Parsnip
Prenanthes
Red oak
Red raspberry
Rough cinquefoil
Ruffed grouse
Salmonberry
Salsify (3 kinds)
Sea urchin
Serviceberry

Shagbark hickory
Silverweed
Slippery elm
Smelt
Snowshoe hare
Sockeye salmon
Solomon's plume
Solomon's seal (2)
Spring beauty
Stinging nettle
Strawberry (2)
Swamp saxifrage
Sweet cicely
Thistle (2)
Toothwort (2)
Virginia waterleaf
Walleye
Wapato
White-tailed deer
Wild carrot
Wild leek
Wild onion (2)
Wild rice
Wild turkey
Winter cress
Wood nettle
Wood sorrel (3)
Yellow trout lily

The most memorable meal of the whole experience was my birthday dinner. My wife's grandmother wanted us to come over for the meal. She typically laughs at my wild food interest and wonders aloud why anyone would go to all that trouble. Normally, she would refuse any wild food except for well-known berries and maple syrup. But she really wanted us over for dinner, and said she'd supply some wild Alaskan salmon as the entrée if we could bring some vegetables and maybe even dessert. At this time, we hadn't eaten any wild food except what we'd collected ourselves, but we couldn't refuse the invitation if the salmon was really wild—and we didn't want to. We went all-out and made a meal to remember.

Melissa collected and cleaned the largest pile of spring beauty roots and trout lily bulbs that I've ever seen—knowing that I consider these together to be the world's finest vegetable dish. She also made my favorite pie—huckleberry. I had painstakingly made some cattail rhizome flour that, along with bear fat, made a fantastic crust. The filling was sweetened with our lightest amber maple syrup poured over the top, and thickened with cattail rhizome flour. To all of this was added a pot of steamed ostrich fern fiddleheads. Not only was this meal intensely satisfying—it also made a convert of her grandmother, who liked every part of it.

How Did We Feel?

The civilized American diet is based on wheat and milk, neither of which I digest very well. For both of us, the first and most dramatic physiological effect of eating wild was that flatulence stopped. What I had grown up believing was a normal aspect of life became abnormal—perhaps one small fart every two or three days. Along with this, my intestines shrunk in volume. The first few days I lost several pounds—far more than could have possibly resulted from a deficiency of calories. I attributed this weight loss to my gastrointestinal tract simply decreasing in volume because the foods I was eating were easier for my body to digest.

Besides my shrinking gut, I simply felt better. I had notably more energy, slept better at night, and woke up earlier. Small annoying problems, such as a frequent tickle in my throat and an itch on the back of my neck in the evening, ceased. I don't want to romanticize foraging too much, but it is truly amazing how healthy wild food is, and how great it feels to eat healthy food.

Did We Lose Weight?

This is an interesting question. Whether or not losing weight is considered a good thing or a bad thing speaks volumes about our culture. For most people on Earth, the challenge is still getting enough calories. That's why we crave low-fiber, high-energy foods like cheese and potato chips. Humans have invested thousands of years of labor and innovation into refining, selecting, cultivating, and processing energy-rich foods, all to ensure access to sufficient calories. We have been so successful in this endeavor that millions of us now try desperately to get fewer calories.

In the first week or so, I lost about five pounds, which I attributed to my shrinking gastrointestinal tract. After that, my weight largely stabilized, fluctuating by about three or four pounds.

When experiencing a drastic dietary shift, people have a strong tendency to eat significantly less until their bodies become used to the new food. This is not conscious—the body tells them to stop eating. The students in my foraging workshops consistently eat servings of wild food that are only about a third of what I eat. Immediately afterward they report feeling full, but two hours later they are stopping at their cars for snacks. Many will (usually discretely) head to town for a meal after the class. For this reason alone, anyone switching to a wild diet will probably lose weight for a week or more. This "skimpy meal syndrome" affected Melissa far more than it affected me, since I had eaten most of these foods in larger volumes before, and she lost more weight than I did. But the test of long-term success on a wild diet is whether you can maintain a normal, healthy body weight.

On the other hand, for the millions who *want* to lose weight, a wild diet is nearly ideal. Low-calorie, satisfying foods high in vitamins and minerals are easy to come by, and junk food is almost impossible to make.

How Much Time Did It Take?

To get an accurate picture of the labor required to feed oneself with wild food, it would have to be done for a whole year. During our wild diet, the majority of our calories came from a few stored foods—wild rice, hickory nuts, maple syrup, and deer—that had been harvested during other seasons. Many days, we spent no time gathering food, and no more time cooking than we would have spent preparing food from the grocery store. Most days, we spent between thirty minutes and an hour harvesting. A few times, we spent all day foraging. From August through October, however, I suspect we would have spent ten or twelve hours per day gathering and processing food. A reasonable average for the whole year might be three or four hours per day. That might not seem like much, but the average American works only about thirty-five minutes per day for his food. This means that, to the forager, food is about six times as valuable. That is certainly how it felt.

What Was Difficult?

The hardest part, in a sense, was never being able to let down our guard; there was no plan B. Every meal, snack, and drink had to be made from scratch, and if we were lazy, forgot, or miscalculated, we went hungry. We had no village to fall back on during the hard days.

If you eat a strictly raw, vegan, vegetarian, or kosher diet, you can still stop at many restaurants and grab a bite to eat. If you are adamant about organic, you can walk into almost any grocery store in the country and grab some grub. But how much wild food can you find? Seafood, maple syrup, and that's usually about it. Interestingly, you'll find hundreds of items labeled "wild" that have absolutely nothing even remotely wild about them—from bubble gum and soda to pork chops and wild rice.

I know, the point of eating a wild diet is not to *purchase* wild food. But on any other diet, you'd be cut some slack. Eating wild, you can't visit anybody and expect to eat over, and you can't travel and eat on the go. I went to a family function at my sister's house and had to pass up her fantastic cooking. Another time, I drove to Minneapolis for a presentation, which finished late, and decided to spend the night rather than fall asleep and "harvest" a roadside tree. However, I hadn't brought enough food for the extra day. I decided to climb a bluff and look for rattlesnakes and interesting flowers on the way home, and by the time I got back to the car, I was famished. The asparagus, salsify, and garlic mustard stalks I'd been eating on the hike were good, but not filling. All I had was a quart of maple syrup that I had failed to sell, and I drank half of it on the way home.

These frustrations weren't reserved for me. Melissa worked twelve-hour shifts as a nurse, and sometimes had to do three in a row. I tried to prepare as much of the food as possible when she worked, but sometimes I wasn't around. It could be hard keeping up with long shifts, a long commute, food preparation, and other inevitable duties. I guess that's why fast food and frozen pizza were invented.

It might be tempting to point out that our hunting and gathering ancestors didn't have these obligations and just had to feed themselves. But this isn't true; their lives were also probably full of social obligations and non-food ambitions. There may have been athletic competitions to train for, wedding gifts to craft, ceremonies to attend, gossip to spread, cave bears to fend off. However, they didn't have to do it alone; trading and sharing was an everyday part of life. Since money is a way of trading labor for labor, we decided that it was only fair to be able to spend as much on wild food as we earned by selling it. Of course, there's very little wild food to trade for, and we never came close to this amount; but there were a few times where it made life much more convenient to be able to buy a smoked trout while traveling.

The hardest part of the diet, however, was *temptation*—something that the Paleolithic ancestors we keep measuring ourselves against never had to contend with. There was no Dairy Queen taunting them on the way to the library, no grilling brats at a friend's picnic. It's hard to resist food when you're hungry—especially the food you crave because you grew up eating it.

Normally, all of this wasn't a problem, but on a few occasions the temptations became all-consuming. By June 5, when I had a planned trip to visit a friend and colleague in Washington State, I had already exceeded my original goal of a month, but I was entertaining less practical notions of maintaining the diet for longer. This friend, Abe, was flying in thirteen hours later from an ethnobotany conference. I was supposed to take a bus to his brother's house, where his vehicle was being temporarily kept, get the key from his brother, kill some time, and then pick Abe up at the airport in his own vehicle.

There were complications. His brother wasn't home. None of his housemates knew where the key was. Abe's plane was delayed twelve hours. But I didn't know that, since neither of us had a cell phone. Nor did his brother, who was in Costa

Rica. All the while, I was stranded in a strange city, committed to a strange diet, and hungry. I put on a lot of miles foraging the alleys, parks, and vacant lots of Seattle, and somehow made it through until it all got straightened out.

After two hungry days in the city, we miraculously heard about a Native American seafood festival that was *free*, and I gorged like I hadn't done in months, maybe years. There were clams, oysters, salmon, crab, even raw sea urchin gonads! After that, foraging went well. We dug camass bulbs and roasted them in a pit, steamed silverweed roots, and peeled an enormous heap of burdock stems. We visited Nancy Turner, North America's foremost wild food expert, and in her fantastic hospitality she donated to my cause: dried seaweeds, frozen elderberries, halibut jerky, and other delicacies. The highlight of our foraging was when we caught a rabbit and made a huge pot of delicious stew, adding field garlic, sow-thistle stems, fennel stalks, carrot stalks, wild rice, salsify flower buds, burdock stalks, and *Lomatium nudicaule* leaves as a seasoning. It was one of the best meals I'd eaten all summer, and a fabulous culmination to my foraging adventure.

All of this was fun, and I was eating well, but at some point I realized that my special diet had become the overbearing focus of the trip. We still had some other activities planned, and I felt satisfied with forty days of eating wild, so on the evening of June 9, we ordered pizza. And man, was it a strange thing to eat. Meanwhile, back at home, Melissa had started eating civilized food four days earlier, as she had to work four consecutive twelve-hour shifts and I wasn't around to help with meal preparation.

Secrets to Success on a Wild Diet

In a true survival situation, when the alternative is starvation, success is measured by sustenance. You need to identify which foods are calorie rich, invest lots of time in acquiring them, be successful, and then figure out efficient ways to process and prepare them. You must let the food set your agenda. This applies to both plant and animal foods. You will almost certainly be unsuccessful at this unless you *practice it beforehand*. Bringing a book will probably not cut it.

However, we were not in a "survival" situation. Our wild diet was voluntary, so the threat to success was temptation. The way to fight temptation is through satisfaction. In this case, you need to identify calorie rich foods *that you really enjoy*, successfully harvest a lot of them, and become efficient at preparing them. As long as we had planned well and had rich, full, satisfying meals with several courses, we never dreamed of straying. There is *nothing* I'd rather eat for breakfast than wapato mush with wild strawberries, hickory nuts, and maple syrup (except maybe lotus mush). In my mind, no dinner can top venison steaks, salsify stalks, and morels, with huckleberries for dessert, washed down with leadplant tea. Don't eat wild and deprive yourself; *indulge* yourself, and you'll have no problem sticking to it. And traveling, as we all know, is not very compatible with cooking.

For a successful wild food diet, unless you live in the tropics, you should have a lot of food stored: buckets of seeds, jugs of syrup, gunnysacks of nuts, gallon jars of dried fruits, a cellar full of roots and canned goods.

To eat wild, you need knowledge and experience. The best way to get this knowledge and experience is to eat wild—even if you start with one day, one meal, or one mouthful.

Timing the Wild Harvest

Over the years I have kept careful note of the ripening times of the wild foods I collect. Many fruits and vegetables have long seasons of availability, while others can be gathered for only a week or two. The calendar on the following pages will help you organize your foraging activities throughout the year. However, the dates listed (unless otherwise indicated) pertain to my climate: 45 degrees N and 1,000 feet (300 m) elevation in the Midwest.

There are a few very general guidelines for adjusting these dates. In spring, subtract one week for each 100 miles (160 km) south or 1,000-foot (300 m) decrease in elevation, and add one week for each 100 miles north or 1,000-foot increase in elevation. Of course, proximity to the coasts and many other factors also play a huge role in climate. It is best to observe familiar plants in your area and adjust the dates on this calendar to reflect your local seasons. (The blooming of dandelions is one of the most useful and visible phenologic indicators.)

These times are averages; they may be as much as four weeks early or late in any particular year. The further south you go, the slower the seasons progress. In the North, spring plants grow unbelievably fast, and harvest availability of shoots may be remarkably short. In arid climates, seasonality may depend more on moisture than on temperature, and is less predictable. Also remember that, as you go north, spring plants ripen *later*; but in the autumn, many plants ripen *earlier* in the North.

One of the most important details for wild food gatherers is *exposure*. South slopes are warmer and drier than north slopes; the difference in vegetation may be equivalent to traveling several hundred miles. The same plants will ripen much later where the exposure is north versus a south exposure.

Different produce types predominate during different times of year, as listed below.

Early Spring: Underground storage organs, perennial greens, sap
Mid Spring: Underground storage organs, perennial greens, biennial greens, perennial shoots
Late Spring, Early Summer: Perennial and biennial shoots, perennial and annual greens, underground parts of spring ephemerals, cambium, flowers
Mid Summer: Small fruits, annual greens, flowering parts, underground parts of spring ephemerals
Late Summer: Small and large fruits, seeds, nuts
Early Fall: Nuts, small and large fruits, seeds, underground storage organs
Late Fall: Underground storage organs, nuts, seeds, fruits
Winter: Underground storage organs, leftover nuts and seeds, bark

Dates correspond to an average growing season at 45°N latitude and 1000 ft (300 m) elevation	Early Spring (Mar 25 – Apr 25)	Mid Spring (Apr 25 – May 10)	Late Spring (May 10 – June 5)	Early Summer (June 5 – July 1)	Mid Summer (July 1 – Aug 10)	Late Summer (Aug 10 – Sep 10)	Early Fall (Sep 10 – Oct 10)	Late Fall (Oct 10 – Nov 15)
Trout lily bulb	██	░	█░	█				
Trout lily leaf	░	██	░					
Solomon seal shoot			█░	░				
Solomon seal rhizome	██	█	█░	░				█
False solomon seal shoot			█░	░				
False solomon seal rhizome	█░				░	█░		█
False solomon seal berries							█░	█
Lotus tuber					░	█░	█	░
Lotus nut (soft)							█░	
Lotus nut (dry)							░█	░
Lotus leaf				░█	█	█░		
Mayapple						█░		
Hackberry	░						█░	█
Walnut							░█	█
Acorn (red)	░						░█	█
Acorn (white)							█░	
Beaked hazel						█░	░	
American hazel							█░	
Prickly pear fruit							░█	█
Prickly pear fruit (Southwest)						░█	█	░
Prickly pear flower				░█	░			
Prickly pear flower (Southwest)	░	█░	██					
Prickly pear pad			░█	█░	░	░	░	░
Prickly pear pad (Southwest)	██	█░	█░	░				
Amaranth greens			░	█░	░			
Amaranth seeds						░█	█░	█
Dock greens	░	█░	█░	░	░	░	░	░

█ = Peak of Season   ░ = Coming into/out of Season

Dates correspond to an average growing season at 45°N latitude and 1000 ft (300 m) elevation	Early Spring Mar 25 – Apr 25	Mid Spring Apr 25 – May 10	Late Spring May 10 – June 5	Early Summer June 5 – July 1	Mid Summer July 1 – Aug 10	Late Summer Aug 10 – Sep 10	Early Fall Sep 10 – Oct 10	Late Fall Oct 10 – Nov 15
Dock petiole	▓	▓	▓					
Dock stalk		▓	▓					
Dock seeds					▓	▓		
Maypop (Arkansas)							▓	▓
Toothwort tuber	▓		▓					
Toothwort greens	▓	▓	▓					
Garlic mustard greens	▓	▓						
Garlic mustard shoots		▓						
Blueberry					▓	▓		
Cranberry							▓	▓
Black huckleberry					▓			
New Jersey tea				▓				
Wild strawberry				▓				
Black cherry						▓		
Sand cherry						▓		
Wild plum							▓	
Aronia berry							▓	▓
Autumn berry							▓	
Bunchberry						▓		
Wood sorrel (annual)			▓	▓	▓	▓		
Wood sorrel (perennial)		▓	▓	▓	▓			
Honewort greens		▓	▓	▓			▓	
Honewort root	▓							▓
Honewort shoot			▓					
Wild carrot root	▓						▓	▓
Wild carrot shoot			▓					
Cow parsnip flowerstalk			▓					

This calendar may be photocopied and altered for private use.

Dates correspond to an average growing season at 45°N latitude and 1000 ft (300 m) elevation	Early Spring (Mar 25 – Apr 25)	Mid Spring (Apr 25 – May 10)	Late Spring (May 10 – June 5)	Early Summer (June 5 – July 1)	Mid Summer (July 1 – Aug 10)	Late Summer (Aug 10 – Sep 10)	Early Fall (Sep 10 – Oct 10)	Late Fall (Oct 10 – Nov 15)
Cow parsnip petiole		░	■	░				
Cow parsnip greens		░	■	■	░			
Cow parsnip bud			░	■				
Black nightshade greens			░	■	■	░		
Black nightshade berry					░	■	■	░
Bugleweed tubers	■	░						
Red elderberry					░	■		
Black/Blue elder flower				░	■	░		
Black/Blue elderberry						░	■	
Jerusalem-artichoke	■	■						
Ox-eye daisy greens	░	■	■	░				
Wild lettuce greens		░	■	░				
Wild lettuce shoot			░	■				
Sow-thistle greens (perennial)		░	■	░				
Sow-thistle greens (annual)			░	■				
Sow-thistle shoot (annual)			░	■				
Prenanthes greens		░	■	░				
Dandelion greens	░	■	■	░		░	░	
Dandelion crown	░	■	░					
Dandelion flower		░	■					
Dandelion root	■						░	■
Chicory crown	░	■						
Chicory greens		░	■	░				
Chicory root	■	░					░	■
Salsify root	■						░	■
Salsify shoot/greens		░	■					
Salsify bud/peduncle			░	■				

■ = Peak of Season   ░ = Coming into/out of Season

Trout Lily, Fawn Lily, Glacier Lily

Erythronium spp.

Liliaceae – Lily Family

Trout lilies are the essence of spring; they come and go with the vernal weather. Just to hear the name brings me back to the excitement of those first warm days of April, when the brooks flow strongly with melting snow and the moist ground is soft underfoot; when the robins sing mightily before dawn and geese honk overhead in the cool darkness. Every time I see a photo of a trout lily, I fondly remember my *first* trout lily, beside the leaf-strewn headwaters of Otter Creek in a marvelous place called Baxter's Hollow. I can still see the skunk cabbage leaves unrolling beside it, the marsh marigolds in bloom. I can smell the rich dirt and wet oak leaves. I can hear the lone peeper wailing from the flooded black ash, singing to me again and again about trout lily and a hundred other springtime miracles.

A colony of trout lily *Erythronium americanum* in bloom. When the sun shines, the petals curl back like this, exposing the anthers; in cloudy weather the flowers are bell-like and drooping.

Description

The variety of common names given to these plants indicates that they have intrigued a great many people. One name, "dog-tooth violet," is a reference to the tooth-like shape of the bulb, but this plant is no more closely related to violets than lions are to termites. It is, however, closely related to the tulips (genus *Tulipa*). This beautiful monocot is called "trout lily" because the mottled leaves of some species remind people of brook trout, and "fawn lily" due to these same spots (and perhaps because it blooms when the does give birth). A western species, the glacier lily, is so called because it inhabits alpine meadows, often beside glaciers. Whatever you call these striking wildflowers, they are thoroughly amazing. Through this account, I'll call the whole group "trout lily," despite the fact that some of them do not generally go by this name, and use more specific names where appropriate.

North America is home to 23 species of *Erythronium* lily, all of which are similar in form and life history. The one that I am most familiar with is the common trout lily *E. americanum*. This is a small plant with one or two basal leaves that are typically 3–7 inches (8–18 cm) long and 1–2.5 inches (2.5–6 cm) wide. Each leaf has a conspicuous crease running down its center. The leaves are lanceolate or elliptic in shape, tapering at both ends. Soft and pliable to the touch, they have a smooth surface and entire margin. They are very dull green, and upon first emerging they are strongly mottled with curvy, grayish-purple spots and streaks. This mottling fades through the growing season but is usually at least faintly visible. Typically, non-flowering plants have one leaf and flowering individuals have two.

Glacier lily *E. grandiflorum* is the most common and widespread species in the West. It grows significantly larger than our eastern species and may have multiple flowers per plant. Note the lack of mottling on the leaves. Photo by Bill Merilees.

The white trout or fawn lily *E. Albidum*.

Trout lily is a spring ephemeral that persists through the dormant season as a small bulb, growing for several years before flowering. When it finally blooms, a single flower is produced on a 4–8 inch (6–20 cm) scape directly from the base of the plant. About 1 inch (2.5 cm) wide, the flowers have six strongly recurved yellow petals and conspicuously protruding stamens. The scape takes a sharp turn at its top so that the flower faces sideways or hangs slightly downward.

The bulb is teardrop-shaped and averages about the size of a candy corn. It is brownish on the outside with a thin skin that peels off to reveal white or cream colored flesh. All of the roots are clustered at the base.

The glacier lily or yellow avalanche lily *E. grandiflorum* is similar in appearance but is larger and has larger yellow flowers. Its leaves lack the conspicuous mottling of the trout lily. Avalanche lily *E. montanum* also has unmottled leaves, but its flowers are white with yellow centers. The names white fawn lily and white trout lily refer to *E. oregonum* in the West and *E. albidum* in the East. Both of these species have white flowers and mottled leaves, but the western species grows larger. The coastal fawn lily *E. revolutum* is a large western species, sometimes exceeding 1 foot (30 cm) in height. This plant has mottled leaves and pink flowers. Other western species with mottled leaves include *Erythronium hendersonii*, *californicum*, *multiscapoideum*, *purpurascens*, and *citrinum*. The dimpled trout lily *E. umbilicatum* and beaked trout lily *E. rostratum* are yellow-flowered eastern species with mottled leaves. The prairie trout lily *E. mesochoreum*, with white flowers and unmottled leaves, grows in the moister parts of the southern Great Plains.

Consult a good regional field guide to identify the *Erythronium* species in your area, and be sure to find out if they are rare or protected. It is not certain that all of the *Erythronium* lilies are edible, although none are known to be toxic. Ethnographic records exist for the use of *E. albidum*, *mesochoreum*, *grandiflorum*, *oregonum*, and *revolutum* as food. Of course, the lack of records doesn't make a plant inedible; I can find no ethnographic records for the edibility of the one that I eat regularly, *E. americanum*.

Range and Habitat

The glacier, trout, and fawn lilies are found throughout most of the United States and southern Canada, in areas with moist, rich soil. These plants are absent from the deserts, dry plains, and far northern forests, but are abundant in the Eastern Woodlands, Rocky Mountains, Pacific states, and wetter parts of the Great Plains. Most of the trout lily species reach great abundance in the best habitat, forming dense, almost pure beds over large areas in early spring. The eastern trout lilies are typical of rich hardwood forests and the floodplains

Many species of *Erythronium* form solid, dense carpets over the forest floor, sometimes covering acres.

of small rivers and streams. Western species are found in hardwood forests at lower elevations, along streams, and in alpine meadows, talus slopes, and open woodlands at higher elevations.

The various lilies of this genus are ephemerals. Their very short growing seasons commence in early spring and terminate by early summer. Woodland species take advantage of the sunlight available on the forest floor before the trees leaf out, while some western and prairie species take advantage of the moisture available in spring and die back before the ground becomes too dry during the hot summer.

Harvest and Preparation

Trout lily has two or three edible parts: the leaves, bulbs, and sometimes the flowers. However, the bulbs are functionally two separate vegetables, depending on the time of year they are collected.

The **leaves** are the part mentioned most often in the edible wild plant literature, but I am not fond of them. These greens are best in early spring before they have fully unfurled. When raw, they have a pleasant sweetness and a nice texture, but I find their aftertaste to be bitter and somewhat acrid. While I know several people who like them, my palate rejects all but the smallest servings, and I use them only occasionally as a trailside nibble. As is true with many lily family plants, the leaves actually seem to taste worse after cooking, as if boiling releases the acrid chemical.

Herrick (1977) reports that the Iroquois used the above-ground portions of *Erythronium americanum* to prevent conception. I personally know one person who suspects that eating these raw greens caused her to have a miscarriage during early pregnancy. While the use of *Erythronium*

In spring, the bulbs are sweetest when dug very early—when the leaves are tightly curled like this or not yet emerged at all.

bulbs as food is well-documented, there is little to no ethnographic record of the leaves being eaten, and perhaps they should be viewed with caution.

The **flowers** taste similar to the leaves, but sometimes leave an unpleasant burning sensation in one's mouth and throat. I do not eat them, but those of some species may be better than what I have tried.

On the other hand, trout lily **bulbs** are an unsung delicacy. I first tried them one dreary day in early spring when I was digging up some highbush cranberries along a stream to transplant. With each bush that I dug I would unintentionally excavate some trout lily bulbs. Having read that these were edible, I put some in my pocket. After a while I went down to the water to rinse a few and see what they were all about. They tasted like sweet corn or snow peas and were very crisp, with no objectionable flavor of any sort. Sometime later, I realized that I had shifted to digging out highbush cranberries just to get trout lily bulbs. That afternoon, when I fed some raw to a friend who was helping me transplant the trees, he very calmly stated, "That might be the best vegetable I've ever tasted."

These were early spring bulbs: crunchy, sweet, and tender. They are at their best as soon as the ground thaws, before they have grown at all, for growth sucks the sugar out of their bulbs and sends it up into the leaves. This timing poses a conundrum, however, because it is nearly impossible to see where the bulbs

are before the leaves have appeared. One way around this problem is to mark a patch when the leaves are visible so you can find it year-round. Another solution is to learn to recognize the tiniest emerging leaves, which are rolled up so tightly they almost look like dull green needles. These have grown so little that their bulbs will still be excellent eating, and if you spot the earliest of them, there will still be many more bulbs beside them which have not yet produced any growth at all.

These are nice-sized bulbs of *E. americanum* collected in late spring. They are beginning to get starchy. The bulb to the right is in the "elongation phase," in which it moves itself over or plants itself deeper.

As the trout lily's leaves die back in late spring, the plant sends its energy back into the bulb. This is another good time to harvest the bulbs, but they are like another vegetable altogether: harder and, as I mentioned, starchy rather than crisp and sweet. You can get them all summer and fall if you know where they are. Over the course of the winter, cold temperatures stimulate the plant to convert its starches to sugars in preparation for the coming growing season, and the bulb becomes sweet again by spring.

Unfortunately, due to their small size, trout lily bulbs are difficult to gather in quantity even where they cover the ground in a solid carpet. A typical bulb is about 0.8 inch (2 cm) long and 0.3 inch (8 mm) thick. I prefer to collect mine with a shovel or a large digging stick. The bulbs are normally 2–5 inches (5–13 cm) under the surface, which is too deep for convenient use of a small digging stick. I can collect a little more than a cup of bulbs per hour in average conditions, but sometimes the harvest goes faster.

Above are dormant trout lily bulbs from midsummer; below are corms of jack-in-the-pulpit *Arisaema triphyllum*. They grow side by side, and *Arisaema* corms are often incidentally dug up during trout lily harvest. They contain calcium oxalate crystals and will cause excruciating burning in the mouth and throat. Note the rough, wrinkled texture of the *Arisaema* corms, especially on the bottom, as opposed to the smooth surface of trout lily bulbs. When not dormant, trout lily bulbs have all their roots concentrated in one knob at the base (see other photos) rather than scattered around the surface like *Arisaema* corms.

Trout lily bulbs are rather distinct, but I caution you to become thoroughly familiar with them while the plants are bearing leaves and flowers before collecting the dormant bulbs without these features, since there are other small bulbs, corms, or tubers which you might potentially confuse with them. I know of several instances where very young jack-in-the-pulpit *Arisaema triphyllum* corms have been mistakenly gathered with trout lily bulbs, in one case turning a foraged meal into a most unpleasant experience. See the photo for details on the differences.

After harvesting the trout lily bulbs, I wash them, break off the roots, and sometimes peel the thin skin off the outside. Then they are ready to be nibbled raw or cooked in a variety of dishes. Some Native American groups ate them raw (Gilmore, 1919, referring to *E. mesochoreum* and *E. albidum*, and Boas, 1921, referring probably to *E. revolutum*) while other individuals reported that they were unfit to eat raw (Turner, 1978, referring to *E. grandiflorum*). Personally, I relish the early spring bulbs of *E. americanum* and *E. albidum* raw, but I have never eaten them in greater quantity than a quarter cup simply because they are labor-intensive to collect. I suggest using moderation when eating raw bulbs.

Trout lily bulbs are small enough that I do not cut or chop them before cooking. A simple, gourmet wild vegetable dish is a cup of steamed trout lily bulbs, a cup of steamed spring beauty roots, and one-third cup of finely diced wild leeks or onions (bulbs and tops), mixed and sautéed in butter. These ingredients can all be harvested in early spring and are often found growing together. Cooked trout lily bulbs are excellent mixed with other vegetables or served alone. They are one of my favorite vegetables, and the labor invested in acquiring them is always well-spent.

The glacier or avalanche lily *E. grandiflorum* of the mountainous sections of western North America was formerly a staple and highly esteemed food source

A nice glacier lily bulb, several times larger than any eastern species. Photo by Nancy Turner.

for many groups of Native Americans (Teit, 1928; Turner et al., 1990). Bulbs of this species can be much larger than those of their eastern relatives, yet they also tend to grow in large, dense colonies. These factors combine to make the glacier lily a more practical vegetable than the smaller species. The bulbs were dug in spring just after emerging, sometimes several hundred pounds per family. For immediate use they were steamed, roasted, or boiled, and large quantities were dried and stored for later use. The dried bulbs were rehydrated by soaking before being cooked (Turner, 1978). Tom Elpel (2002) calls these bulbs "crisp and sweet" and has timed his harvest at one to two cups per hour, but states that the glacier lilies in his area are smaller than average.

The trout lilies are remarkably abundant in some areas, but because they are long-lived perennials, they should always be harvested with great care. Dig up small clumps from around the patch rather than removing all from one area. Thin out the colony by taking only the larger bulbs, leaving good growing conditions for the small ones left behind. In localities where they are not abundant, leave them alone. Trout lilies are being decimated in some areas by high deer populations, as they are a preferred spring food. Keep this in mind and don't harvest where the plants are abnormally small due to grazing.

Under *responsible* harvest practices, trout lily colonies will thrive. There is some evidence that digging the bulbs of glacier lily actually helps give them a competitive edge over other plants (Loewen et al., 2001).

To the forager, trout lily is not just a woodland decoration; it is also a delicacy. It is something to be not only observed and marveled at, but also experienced. I find it comforting to know that if I were ever forced by circumstances to live deep in the woods and away from modern groceries, I would have to live on things as delicious as trout lily bulbs.

Solomon's Seal

Polygonatum commutatum, P. biflorum, P. pubescens

Liliaceae – Lily Family

When I was a child, we had a set of railroad tracks running through our backyard. Along these tracks there was a strip of surprisingly lush and diverse vegetation. Before the railroad company began to spray it with herbicides, I used to eat a lot of this vegetation. Solomon's seal was not particularly abundant here, nor was this where I first identified the plant. But it was along these railroad tracks that my zeal for Solomon's seal gifted me with an awesome realization: that a plant can be recognized by no more than the dead, withered remains of its stalk.

One early winter in junior high, I was holed up in my bedroom after school, reading some plant books, when I came across the claim that Solomon's seal rhizomes were an edible potato-like vegetable. I knew there were some growing along the tracks down the block, and there was no way I was going to wait for next year to try a new wild food. I *had* to find a Solomon's seal plant before

Great Solomon's seal, about four feet tall.

the ground froze solid. I was outside within minutes, slowly walking along the tracks, my eyes searing every piece of dead vegetation.

I had never tried this in earnest before, and I was shocked to learn that I could identify the withered stalks of many familiar plants. Sometimes I had to puzzle over it for a few moments, but it was surprisingly easy: catnip, motherwort, goldenrod, milkweed, chicory. When I finally came to the Solomon's seal, I recognized its distinct form with ease. As I pulled its white rhizome from the dark, rocky ground, I smiled at my sweet success.

Identification

There are three species of Solomon's seal in North America, and these come in the usual sizes: small, medium, and large. All are perennial herbs with smooth, round, strongly arching, unbranched stalks. The leaves are alternate, elliptic, entire, and clasping or sessile. As with other members of the lily family, the venation is parallel. The leaves are a light silvery green beneath. Each leaf axil contains one thin stem, which bears a drooping flower or a tight cluster of up to nine of them. The drooping, bell-like flowers are whitish green and tubular, ending with six short lobes that curve slightly outward. The fruits, which develop in late summer, are spherical and dark blue with a white bloom on their surface. Growing to 0.2–0.4 inch (5–13 mm) in diameter, each of these inedible fruits contains several seeds. Overall, Solomon's seals are very distinct and are generally confused only with one another or their close relatives.

Small or hairy Solomon's seal *Polygonatum pubescens* is by far the most diminutive species, rarely exceeding 20 inches (0.5 meter) in height. It typically produces one fruit per leaf axil, sometimes two. The common or two-flowered Solomon's seal *P. biflorum* is typically 12–36 inches (30–90 cm) tall and most often has its fruit dangling in pairs. The large or great Solomon's seal *Polygonatum commutatum* has a robust stem that can grow into arches

Solomon's seal flowers.

Ripe fruit (non-edible) of great Solomon's seal, with several berries per axillary cluster.

8 feet (2.5 m) long and 5 feet (1.5 m) high, although somewhat smaller is more typical. On the great Solomon's seal, the fruit is most commonly found in clusters of three to nine. Some authorities claim that the two larger species are not truly distinct from each other. Without entering the fray on plant genetics, we'll consider them two species here.

Solomon's seal rhizomes are white or off-white. They range from 1.5 inches (3.5 cm) long and 0.2 inches (5 mm) wide on the smallest specimens to over 1 inch (2.5 cm) thick and more than a foot (30 cm) in length on great Solomon's seal. Regardless of their size, the rhizomes are irregularly constricted and have a surface heavily corrugated by ridges or rings around them. On the top of the rhizome one finds a few round depressions—the scars where stems were attached in previous growing seasons. These scars, imagined by some to resemble the "seal of Solomon," account for the plant's name.

Range and Habitat

The three species of Solomon's seal are found in the hardwood forest areas of eastern North America. As a group they range from North Dakota to New England and south to Texas and Florida.

The small Solomon's seal *P. pubescens* is the most shade tolerant, inhabiting mature, closed-canopy mesic forests as well as younger, drier, and more open woods. It is distributed across the northern half of the eastern United States and adjacent Canada.

Two-flowered Solomon's seal *P. biflorum* is slightly less shade tolerant; it does inhabit mature forests, but these are usually oak-hickory stands that allow more light to reach the understory. It does especially well in young woods and at forest edges.

The great Solomon's seal *P. commutatum* is found throughout the eastern United States but is especially common in the prairie-forest border region of the Midwest. It thrives at the edge of woods, in old fields, and along roadsides, power lines, railroads, and fencerows. Occasional specimens are also found in dry, sunny woodlands. This plant often forms dense colonies that spread by rhizome. For some reason, the great Solomon's seal does remarkably well on the large cleared shoulders and banks along interstate highways, and enormous clones can sometimes be seen in such localities.

Harvest and Preparation

Solomon's seals have two edible parts: the rhizome and the shoot. For both of these parts, the great Solomon's seal is the best food source, and the small Solomon's seal is the worst. This is not just a matter of size; the flavor of the larger plant is also superior.

Solomon's seals are widely distributed in the northern hemisphere and have been used for food by many cultures. *Polygonatum sibiricum* and *P. odoratum* are cultivated in northern and eastern China, both for their medicinal properties, and for their edible rhizomes which are used to make pastries, drinks, and candies. Several other species are locally harvested from the wild in China, including *P. inflatum, P. involucratum,* and *P. macropodum* (Hu, 2005). Sturtevant reports that the rhizomes of various species were used as food in Japan and Europe (Hedrick, 1919). Couplan (1994) reports that the young shoots of *P. odoratum* (also called *P. officinale*) can be used like asparagus, but that the rhizomes should be avoided, since they contain high levels of irritating calcium oxalate crystals. Hamel and Chiltoskey (1975) report that the Cherokee used the rhizomes and greens of *P. biflorum* for food.

Rhizome: This was the first Solomon's seal vegetable that I was introduced to. I grubbed one out of the crushed coal and gravel that formed the steep bank along the railroad tracks by my house. I was excited by its size, which dwarfed the wild carrots I often collected in the same area. I brought the rhizome home, cleaned it, boiled it, and decided that it tasted "like coal." Some time later, I

The rhizome of small Solomon's seal *P. pubescens* is not only small, but it also has a slightly acrid flavor.

hopefully tried a rhizome dug from nice, clean sandy soil, only to find the same unpleasant flavor that I had previously attributed to the crushed coal.

In the years since, I have tried Solomon's seal rhizomes many times in many ways and have liked them only raw, in early spring, when they are quite sweet. They don't ruin a stew, but neither do they add anything that I appreciate. Cooked by themselves, I can't bring myself to eat more than a few bites. However, some people report liking them cooked, so don't count them out simply because of my opinion. If you like Solomon's seal rhizomes, they are a convenient package of edible carbohydrates. The rhizomes of the small Solomon's seal *P. pubescens* have an irritating quality that the others lack or exhibit only slightly, presumably caused by the presence of a small amount of calcium oxalate.

I like to dig Solomon's seal rhizomes with a shovel, although I use my hands to loosen them carefully from the soil before pulling them out. They are typically 1–3 inches (2.5–8 cm) below the surface. Solomon's seal rhizomes can be collected at any time of the year, but they contain the most energy during the dormant season. Their flavor is sweeter in spring than in fall, presumably due

A rhizome of great Solomon's seal collected in fall. The leading end (toward the shoot at right) is always thicker and less fibrous. The distance between the scars represents one year's growth.

to inulin being converted to simple sugars over the winter. During the summer, the tender growing tip of the rhizome has the best flavor.

After harvest, pull off the roots and clean the rhizome well with a vegetable brush to get all the sand out of the grooves. Cut out any crevices that hold dirt. For cooking it is preferable to slice the rhizome perpendicular to its direction of growth, which will ameliorate the somewhat fibrous texture. These vegetables store very well in a root cellar or refrigerator, as long as they are not allowed to dry out.

If you do collect Solomon's seal rhizomes, be sure to do so conscientiously. Dig them only where the plants are abundant, and never take more than about 10% of the rhizomes in the patch. Since they reproduce slowly, they are very susceptible to overharvest, and in many localities they should be left alone except in case of emergency. Also, take care not to break up the rhizomes you leave behind.

Shoots: Unlike the rhizomes, the shoots of Solomon's seal are a first-rate vegetable. They look and taste remarkably like asparagus when steamed or boiled, and they are fairly good raw. You can use Solomon's seal shoots in place of asparagus in any recipe and will most likely find it delicious. However, when you consume Solomon's seal shoots, always remove the leaves; they taste bad when raw, and even worse cooked.

Harvest the shoots as long as the leaves are curled into a spear-like tip that points upward. The largest ones will be about a 0.5 inch (13 mm) thick and over 2 feet (60 cm) tall.

A Solomon's seal shoot at the right size to pick.

The shoot should break easily when bent just above the base. If you are a few days late, the top will begin hanging off to the side and the leaves will unfurl. At this time, you can use the upper portion of the shoot, but only if it remains tender and breaks off easily. Once the leaves are fully opened, it is too late.

Because Solomon's seal is a perennial, and the shoots are so good and so easy to collect, it practically begs to be overharvested. Don't do it! Every time you pick a shoot you will use up some of the rhizome's energy, and the shoot that grows back to replace it will be smaller. Never collect more than one-third of the shoots in a colony at one time, and never collect from the same colony more than once per year. If that means you get to eat only two shoots, so be it. Keep your eye on the colony to see how your harvesting affects it over the years and adjust accordingly.

Well known for its striking, elegant form, the Solomon's seal's culinary attributes make it doubly worth encouraging in the backyard or planting in the wildflower garden. Next time you pass its graceful dusty arches leaning over the edge of a gravel backroad, smile and be thankful for the provender of the countryside.

False Solomon's Seal, Solomon's Plume

Maianthemum racemosum (also *Smilacina racemosa*), *M. stellatum*

Liliaceae – Lily Family

There is nothing false about the false Solomon's seal. It isn't imitating anything else, attempting to fool us into mistaking it for a more reputable relative. The false Solomon's seal is a beautiful native wildflower, just as deserving of respect as the "true" variety. And although many people equate the word "false" with "poisonous," this plant has three edible parts.

Mature, flowering plants of western false Solomon's seal. Photo by Bill Merilees.

Description

Recognizing the injustice of this herb's name, many sympathetic wildflower enthusiasts and landscapers use the name "Solomon's plume." That sounds better, I suppose, but there is nothing about this plant's plume to associate it with King Solomon. It also goes by the name of "false spikenard." Unfortunately, all of this plant's common names are confusing and ridiculous.

In general description, the false Solomon's seal sounds a heck of a lot like Solomon's seal: It is a perennial woodland herb with a slender, arching, unbranched stem and alternate, entire, clasping, elliptic leaves with parallel veins. It grows singly or in small colonies from an irregularly constricted, occasionally branching rhizome. The most conspicuous distinction between Solomon's seal and false Solomon's seal is the arrangement of the flowers of the latter species into a large terminal panicle (rather than small ones in the leaf axils), which may contain from a dozen to many hundreds of tiny flowers. Each of these is about 0.2 inch (5 mm) across with six very narrow, spreading white petals. The tiny spherical fruits are gold at first, turning to bright red in the fall. Each fruit contains a single, hard, spherical, white seed, usually with a small gray circle where the stem was attached, and a darker gray dot in the center of this circle. This makes the seed look surprisingly like a little eyeball.

A colony of starry Solomon's seal *Maianthemum stellatum* in flower.

False Solomon's seal tends to grow in loose colonies. At maturity, the arching stems are typically 2–4.5 feet (60–140 cm) long and reach from knee to waist high. The leaves are elliptic, deeply grooved, slightly rough, and sessile, typically measuring 3–6 inches (8–15 cm) long and about half as wide. The rhizomes are proportionately thinner than those of Solomon's seal and are cream or pale yellow in color, but otherwise are similar in appearance.

A mature false Solomon's seal from the east; note the more arching form.

Western false Solomon's seal (generally considered a subspecies rather than a separate species) has a slightly different look than its counterpart east of the Great Plains, tending to be a little stouter and stand more erect. Also, its leaves are almost clasping and have more rounded bases.

This account deals primarily with *Maianthemum racemosum*, the largest and best-known member of the false Solomon's seal genus. Starry Solomon's seal *M. stellatum* (also called starry false Solomon's seal and starry Solomon's plume) is a closely related plant that, while edible, is much less practical to use. Starry Solomon's seal is more upright in posture than its larger relative, and the leaves are narrower, borne more densely, and not as much in plane with the stem. It often forms dense, extensive colonies in moist, open, sandy areas, moist coniferous woodland, and sandy prairies. This plant rarely exceeds 2 feet (60 cm) in height. The three-leaved false Solomon's seal *M. trifolium*, a small plant found in bogs, is not covered in this account.

False Solomon's seal inflorescence.

Range and Habitat

The false Solomon's seal ranges from the West Coast to the East, inhabiting hardwood and mixed hardwood-conifer forests. In the East it is found from northern Georgia and Alabama to Arkansas, and north well into Canada. It reaches its greatest size and abundance in oak and oak-pine forests of the Northeast, but it is found in nearly all forest types. In the West it grows in moist, open forests and in woodland openings. It grows commonly at low and medium elevations in the Pacific Northwest and in the mountain forests of the rest of the West, from British Columbia south to Arizona. The largest specimens grow at the edge of the woods, along roads and trails, or in places where a thin canopy allows a good amount of sunlight to reach them.

Harvest and Preparation

The **rhizomes** of false Solomon's seal are edible, and were eaten by several tribes of the Pacific Northwest (Turner, 1975, 1978). The rhizomes are not very hard to collect in quantity if the plants are large. The spaghetti-like roots are tough and stringy and somewhat difficult to remove from the rhizome, but once this is done they can be cleaned quite easily. By looking at the round seals on top of the rhizomes, which show you where the stems were previously attached, you can see that they grow only 1–3 inches (2.5–8 cm) per year; this indicates that they are very susceptible to overharvest. I have a simple formula for determining the amount that can be sustainably harvested. Count the number of large stems in the colony you are collecting from, then multiply this number by two.

False solomon's seal rhizomes.

This is the number of lineal inches of rhizome you can sustainably harvest per year in that particular colony. For example, if there are six stems, take no more than 12 lineal inches (30 cm) of rhizome.

The terminal—or new—end of the rhizome will be its thickest part; it is lighter in color and less fibrous than the older sections, especially in summer as it is actively growing. This thick terminal section has a passably good flavor when raw, although it is somewhat tough. After cooking, there is a pleasant, sweet flavor mixed with a mild unpleasant aftertaste. The older, thinner sections of rhizome have a similar flavor when cooked, but are very fibrous. The rhizomes have a mucilaginous texture.

Huron Smith (1932) reports that the Flambeau Ojibwa, very close to my home, soaked the "roots" in lye water and then parboiled them to get rid of the lye before cooking them "like potatoes." This account, and others, provide little detail, and we are left to wonder when and how the rhizomes were harvested, how they were cooked, how strong the lye solution was, how long the rhizomes were soaked, how highly preferred this food was, and a myriad of other questions. I have found only one author (Mohney, 1975) who claims to have performed this lye-soaking process, using one half cup of ash lye to a gallon of water. When I tried it, soaking in a stronger solution made from commercial lye and then boiling several times to get rid of it, the acrid aftertaste was eliminated and the flavor improved, but the rhizomes remained fibrous. More experimentation is in order here, but false Solomon's seal rhizomes would at least be a good source of calories for someone lost in the woods.

The **shoots** of false Solomon's seal make a good vegetable. They are similar to Solomon's seal shoots, with a soft texture and rich asparagus-like flavor, but they do have a faint aftertaste that I find unpleasant. I like them almost as much as I like Solomon's seal shoots, and use them similarly. They are excellent simmered until tender and served with butter, and they make a superb soup ingredient. Starry Solomon's seal has very small shoots of poorer flavor, and I seldom collect them.

The shoots of false Solomon's seal look similar to many other spring shoots, most of which are related and edible. Among these are Solomon's seals and the bellworts (genus *Uvularia*). However, it is important not to mistakenly collect shoots of false hellebore *Veratrum viride*, which is a dangerously poisonous plant whose range partially overlaps that of *Maianthemum racemosum* (see photos on pages 96–97).

False Solomon's seal shoots should ideally be collected when all the leaves are still closed up and the top cluster still points skyward. They should break easily at the base when bent. If only a few leaves have opened, you can still use the part of the stem that passes the break-easy test. But in all cases it is very important to remove the leaves, whether they are open or not. They are very bitter, and cooking only accentuates this bad flavor. The false Solomon's seal shoots that grow near me have an unpleasant aftertaste when eaten raw. However, the few that I have tried in the Pacific Northwest had a much sweeter, milder flavor when raw, with no unpleasant aftertaste. There are thousands of miles in between these localities; try the shoots in your area and decide for yourself.

Be careful not to overharvest this plant. It is already under great stress in some areas with high deer populations. I have seen hundreds upon hundreds of

below left Do not confuse false hellebore *Veratrum viride* shoots with those of false Solomon's seal! Photo by Bill Merilees.

below right Shoots of *Uvularia grandiflorum* resemble those of false Solomon's seal; however, they are smoother with a faint bloom. Fortunately, they are also edible. Note the drooping yellow flower in the background.

opposite page Shoots of false Solomon's seal (eastern on left, western on right) at the ideal stage for eating.

the young shoots nipped off within a few days—which makes my harvest seem insignificant. Collect shoots only where the plant is common and appears to be thriving. Even then, never remove more than a third of the shoots in a colony each year, and try not to pick a shoot from the same rhizome two consecutive years. Don't systematically pick all the largest shoots; let some of them grow and go to seed. And if you want to do the entire lily family a big favor, eat more venison.

In autumn the **berries** of false Solomon's seal turn bright red. Their beauty is striking, and when you find a quarter-pound cluster, it is natural to fantasize that they might taste like raspberries or strawberries. They don't. The flavor of false Solomon's seal fruit is quite unexpected: molasses-sweet at first, fading to an overbearing dose of that bitter/acrid flavor that permeates every part of the plant in varying concentrations. This acrid taste is too strong for me to enjoy more than a few berries, but the sweetness coaxes me to reach for another nibble later. As

with the shoots, I have found that the berries I have tried in the West are much better tasting than those I've had in the East. Their bitter aftertaste is reduced to the point that I enjoy eating them. Growing in large clusters, the berries can be harvested easily and in great quantity, and their sweetness indicates that they are high in calories. Look for false Solomon's seal berries in September or October, often after the leaves and stems have died and turned straw brown.

False Solomon's seal berries, from both *S. stellatum* and *S. racemosa*, were eaten raw by several tribes in British Columbia, but disdained by some others (Turner, 1975, 1978). *S. stellatum* has a much smaller cluster of five to ten berries, borne in a raceme rather than a large panicle, but the fruit is similar in appearance and flavor.

False Solomon's seal berries ripen in autumn and can often be collected after the stems and leaves have withered away.

American Lotus

Nelumbo lutea

Nelumbonaceae – Lotus Family

J ust south of Savannah, Illinois, there is a place called Spring Lake in the Upper
Mississippi River National Wildlife and Fish Refuge. Spring Lake isn't really
a lake so much as it is a giant field of lotus, stretching three miles from north to
south and more than a mile wide. Monocultures are rare in Nature, but this vast
expanse of lotus is broken only occasionally by islands, sections of open water,
and patches of wapato. It isn't a monoculture in the agricultural sense: carp
swim under the giant pads, minnows feed on the abundant insects, bullfrogs
and cricket frogs call from the shallow sections and sometimes sit picturesquely
upon the floating lotus leaves, while blue herons and great egrets stalk all of these

Thousands of acres of food.

smaller creatures. When the lotus blooming is at its peak in late July, Spring Lake is a wondrous sight to behold, the miles of mild, yellowish flowers melding one into the other to form a creamy sheet across the water.

If any plant can be called charismatic, it certainly must be the lotus.

The American lotus is spoken of with superlatives. Bearing the largest flower of any plant on our continent, it demands attention when in bloom. This plant is so unique that, although it hardly needs description, it is a joy to describe. There are only two species of *Nelumbo* in the world, the American and the Asian, and both have had mystical powers ascribed to them on their respective continents. Literature, mythology, and art from southern Asia often presents the magnificent lotus flower rising triumphantly from the muck below. While the symbolism of this is powerful, there are also equally valid practical reasons why this amazing plant might be held sacred.

Although Native Americans cultivated this food in the Tennessee and Cumberland Rivers (Bailey, 1916), the American lotus seems virtually unknown today; it is the most overlooked and underappreciated wild staple in North America. Our wild lotus is never seen for sale in fancy shops or markets as are hickory nuts, pinyons, or wild rice, even though it is considered a gourmet food in the Orient and was used extensively as a staple by Native Americans within its broad range. It is hardly discussed in the wild food literature. Its culinary value was systematically ignored by European settlers and would astonish those who live beside it today.

My hope is to let you in on the secret of the lotus, so that when you look across the ponds and sloughs from which its giant blooms arise, you will think of more than the alligators, frogs, catfish, and rails that hide there. You will know that under that murky water, buried in that rich muddy sand, there is provender in both quantity and quality that few would imagine.

Description

The striking appearance and obtrusive nature of the American lotus have given it a colorful variety of common names: alligator buttons, swamp rattles, water chinkapin, yonkapin, watering can, monocanut, yockernut, rattlenut, and duck acorn, to mention a few. Lotus looks similar to our common yellow (*Nuphar*) and white (*Nymphaea*) water lilies, but is much larger than either. This similarity has been the source of a great deal of confusion, and the lotus has often been carelessly referred to as a "water lily." However, the more familiar one becomes with these plants, the less similar they appear.

In deep water, lotus leaves typically float on the surface like those of *Nuphar* and *Nymphaea*; however, lotus pads always lack the slit-like sinus or cutout that

Unlike water lilies, lotus leaves will stand up to six feet above the water or mudflat. They also lack the cut-out of water lilies. Note the lotus' edible neighbor, wapato.

characterizes the various pond lilies and water lilies. Lotus leaves have a prominent vein that runs straight from the center of the leaf to one edge; all the other veins are curved. (Water lilies also have this prominent straight vein; it runs in the direction opposite of the cutout.) In the center of the lotus leaf there is a pattern of two half circles side by side, with the straight edges near each other—it reminds me of a stylized drawing of a human brain from above. Lotus leaves can be easily separated from *Nuphar* lilies by their round shape. (*Nuphar* leaves are oblong.) From a distance, when the presence or absence of the sinus may not be visible, lotus leaves can be distinguished from those of water lily by their darker green color—especially when the two are side-by-side. Another unique characteristic is that, due to microscopic hydrophobic hairs, water on the top of lotus leaves will bead up and roll off like drops of quicksilver.

Lotus leaves attain much greater size than water lily pads, sometimes reaching 3 feet (90 cm) in diameter in the southern part of its range. Lotus leaves do not always float, however; they also grow as emergents in shallow water and on mudflats, rising from a few inches to as much as 6 feet (2 m) above the surface. Each leaf is supported by a stiff, rough, unbranched stalk as much as 1 inch (2.5 cm) thick that is attached to its underside. The stalk has dark projections, almost like tiny pin feathers, scattered around its surface. If you cut this stalk you will notice that it exudes a latex and is characterized by eight hollow vessels or air chambers running its length, creating an appealing symmetrical design.

Lotus leaves may emerge or rest on the water's surface like this one. Notice how the water beads up into little silver droplets.

Emergent lotus leaves tend to be broadly funnel-shaped, a design which helps them support their mass.

If you break the leaf or flower stalks of lotus, you will see another amazing quality of the plant. As you pull the broken pieces apart, super-fine strands of coiled, silk-like xylem fiber will stretch between them—sometimes more than 6 feet (2 m) if you move slowly enough.

Lotus flowers open in the morning, close at night, and last only two days. Like the leaves, they are borne individually on long, unbranched stalks that have air-filled tubes running their length. These blossoms may appear from water level to 6 feet (2 m) above it—typically just slightly higher than the nearby leaves. The American lotus blooms from July to early September, the peak being in the middle or late part of July. Individual flowers range from 4–10 inches (10–25 cm) across, with 6–8 inches (15–20 cm) being typical. The numerous petals are a light creamy-yellow, surrounded by a few green sepals. Although not particularly fragrant, the mild scent of lotus blooms is sweet and pleasant.

To ensure cross-pollination, lotus flowers reveal their female parts first and their male parts later. In the center of the lotus blossom is a receptacle shaped like an inverted cone, holding several pistils. After pollination the petals and sepals fall away and this green receptacle widens to a broad funnel shape. Embedded in the receptacle are fifteen to twenty-five nuts the size and shape of small acorns, about 0.5 inch (13 mm) long. The fully formed receptacle or seedhead may be as much as 5–6 inches (13–15 cm) wide. After ripening, the seedheads and nuts dry out and turn brown, both shrinking considerably. Amazingly, not only do the nut *kernels* shrink, but the *shells* shrink, too. These dark brown dried nuts become as hard as stones. As the receptacle dries, some of the nuts usually fall out, but others remain loosely inside their individual chambers, where they rattle around when the seedhead is touched or shaken. Lotus seedheads are familiar to many people because of their frequent use as decoration, especially in dried flower arrangements.

American lotus is a perennial that spreads quickly by rhizomes, which inundate the mud or sand underneath a colony. Lotus rhizomes are typically about 0.8 inch (2 cm) thick and usually run for several feet before branching. They are creamy in color, rather hard, and have a smooth surface with only occasional roots attached. They differ dramatically from *Nuphar* and *Nymphaea* rhizomes, which may be 2–6 inches (5–15 cm) thick, are green, yellow, or brown in color, spongy on the inside, and have a scaly-looking surface with numerous roots attached.

Lotus is North America's largest native flower. Note the prominent midvein on the leaf to the right.

The sacred or Chinese lotus, *Nelumbo nucifera*, is not native to North America, but it has been widely introduced and has gone feral in many areas, particularly in the Southeast. This species is nearly identical to the American lotus except that it has light red flowers and slightly more elongated nuts. The two species can be used as food in exactly the same ways.

The name "lotus" engenders a great deal of confusion and has been applied to many different plants over the ages. The word comes from the Greek *lotos*, a word that referred to a few different plants. Some scholars believe that the original *lotos* was a hackberry, while others believe it was *Zizyphus lotus*, a fruit-bearing tree related to the buckthorns. In *The Odyssey*, Homer writes of the *Lotophagi* (Lotus Eaters), a group of people in North Africa who live off of the lotus fruit in dreamy contentment and indifference. Later, the name became attached to *Nymphaea lotus*, a water lily that was sacred to the Egyptians. Later still, the name was applied to *Nelumbo nucifera*, the sacred pink lotus of China. The Latin name *Lotus* is used by botanists to refer to a genus of leguminous plants that includes the common hay and forage crop bird's-foot trefoil. In this account, the name "lotus" is reserved for the genus *Nelumbo*.

Range and Habitat

American lotus is native to eastern North America, from Florida and the Deep South north to southern Minnesota, southernmost Ontario, and southern New England. It ranges as far west as Texas, Oklahoma, and western Iowa. In some parts of its range, such as Michigan, New England, and Ontario, American lotus colonies are quite rare, while in other areas, particularly in the Mississippi River Valley, it is considered a noxious wetland weed. In many sections of the South, lotus is a ubiquitous water plant found in nearly every pond, slow river,

Nymphaea water lilies. Unlike lotus, these leaves have a sinus or slit.

lake, or slough—as long as there is sufficient sunlight. It is quite prolific along major river systems, where it is known to cover enormous areas in pure or nearly pure stands—tens, hundreds, or even thousands of acres in a single patch. The vigorous rhizomes can grow up to 45 feet (13 m) in a single growing season; healthy colonies may have 45 miles (73 km) of rhizome and 75,000 leaves per acre (Hall and Penfound, 1944).

American lotus seems to prefer shallow lakes, sloughs, bayous, and rivers where the water is warm and the bottom has some organic matter but remains somewhat firm. In murky water, lotus has a distinct advantage over other aquatic vegetation because it can colonize shallow areas and out-compete floating plants by standing above them. It can then expand into deeper zones where the turbidity prevents other plants from being established by seed. Lotus grows at a greater range of depth than other emergent or floating plants that share its habitat, from mudflats to water as deep as ten feet. This versatility combined with its ability to expand remarkably fast by rhizomes makes it a fierce competitor.

The Asian lotus *N. nucifera* is found in many wetlands in the southeastern United States, where it has been planted outright or has escaped from cultivation. Like most exotic plants, it shows up erratically, and we do not yet fully understand its habitat requirements, nor how it will compete with native wetland plants, including the American lotus.

Ecology

The American lotus has a major impact on riverine ecosystems and is truly hated by many of the boaters, fishermen, and other people who must deal with it on a daily basis. It's hard to blame them. A fishing lure snagged on a lotus stem is often a lure lost. In some places where boating or water skiing were popular not long ago, the lotus has rendered it nearly impossible to navigate. However, this fascinating plant has been part of the eastern rivers for much longer than humans have. Lotus produces enormous amounts of biomass per year, and the pads provide habitat for insects, fish, mollusks, amphibians, birds, reptiles, and aquatic mammals. The rhizomes and tubers feed muskrats, nutria, and beavers, while the high-energy nuts are relished by waterfowl.

Lotus nuts remain viable longer than any other known seeds—nuts as old as 1300 years have been successfully germinated (Shen Miller et al., 1995). Under normal circumstances, the seeds don't germinate for decades and perhaps centuries. This might seem odd at first, but actually it makes perfect sense in light of the plant's ecology. A plant that reproduces vegetatively with such vigor has nothing to gain by planting itself where it already grows. So the nuts sink to the bottom and are covered with silt that accumulates year by year. Once a lotus bed is established, it slows the current, causing an increase in the rate of sediment deposition. Over many years this fills in sections of the river channel and changes flow patterns. Eventually the lotus bed becomes a sandbar, and then an island covered with silver maple, and finally the island connects to shore. The giant leaves and bold blossoms are not even a memory in this place. A few generations later a great flood tears out the maples and cuts a new channel—and guess who has been waiting there, deep in the sand, for a few hundred years, as the territory changed from nation to nation, in preparation for just such a moment? Now the nuts germinate, float to the surface, and wash into the shallows, where they take root. Like a conjurer's trick the great pads appear one summer and begin anew their takeover of the muddy waters. Indeed, lotus plants have been known to appear in lakes and rivers where they had seemed extirpated for decades.

Of course, a plant so unique can't just germinate in any regular old fashion. Each lotus nut encloses a little air pocket—which contains just enough oxygen for it to germinate in the oxygen-poor muck. No functional primary root develops from the germinating seed—an exceptional quality among plants. Instead, the new plant grows four little leaves and a small tuber. A few weeks later, the leaves wilt and the lotus appears to die—but in fact it is only in metamorphosis. The plant later recommences growth as if "germinating" from its little tuber, growing adventitious roots and a new leaf, assuming the familiar form of a lotus plant (Hall and Penfound, 1944).

Lotus Nuts – Harvest and Preparation

Lotus nuts ripen in late summer and early autumn. The time of ripening can vary greatly from one patch to another, depending on water depth and other conditions. As with most nuts, the crop can be exceedingly good in one year or one location and poor in others. They are highly sought by muskrats, who make large piles of the empty seedheads. Because the nuts are clustered into large receptacles, they are rather easy to gather despite their small size. If seedheads are growing at the edge of a waterway, you can break or snip them off while you stand on dry ground. In shallow water they can be obtained by wading.

However, the serious way to collect lotus nuts is by canoe, preferably with two people. One person paddles or poles the canoe through the lotus bed while the other grabs the seedheads and throws them into the boat. The poler/paddler grabs the occasional head that the first person misses. A light rod with a hook on the end can be a great help; use it to reach out and pull in those stems that are out of arm's reach. The seedheads break off easily enough, especially when dry, that no knife or shears are needed for collecting them. With this method, you can literally fill a canoe with seedheads in a few hours.

These are the yockernuts, yonkeynuts, rattlenuts, duck acorns, alligator buttons—whatever you want to call them. Some people say they look "alien." I say cool. This one stood about five feet above the mud. The nuts in here actually look aborted and unviable—not to be collected. See how they have darkened but do not fill their cavity even halfway; compare to seedheads with good nuts below.

Upon first ripening, the receptacles are green and soft and can be manipulated with the fingers to get the nuts out. The nut shells will also be soft and pliable, making them easy to cut, crack, or bite open to get at the nutmeat inside. At this stage the nutmeats are rather soft and chewy, reminiscent of chestnuts in flavor and texture (hence the name "water chinkapin"). They are delicious roasted; you can just put the entire seedheads on the coals of a campfire for a few minutes, then pull them out and pick out the roasted nuts. However, there is a small, green leafy embryo between the two halves of the nut; this embryo is bitter, and the flavor of the nut is better when it is removed.

After ripening, the receptacles and the nuts begin to dry and shrink, turning brown in the process. The nuts get extremely hard when dry and store practically forever in this state. Nuts or seedheads picked green can be allowed to dry, or

These are ideal, ripe, dry seedheads. Most of the nuts are large and plump, almost filling their cavities.

Lotus nuts go from green to brown and then shrink substantially. The full-sized nuts with soft shells, such as you see on the left, are excellent roasted and eaten.

Cracked lotus nuts, showing thin shells, meats, and bitter green embryos.

The kernels on top are good; those below are spoiled. Note the off color, which is not dramatically different.

you can pick them after they have dried on the stalk. You can tear the dry receptacles apart by hand to free the nuts. On a large scale, the efficient way is to put the dry, ripe seedheads in a gunnysack on a hard floor and thoroughly smash or stomp them; then dump the contents into a box or bin. Most of the nuts will fall out on their own, and the few that remain can be picked out by hand. Often, just bending the receptacle is enough to get the nuts to fall out. Discard any nuts that are exceptionally narrow or shriveled, as these will not contain sound kernels.

After the lotus nuts ripen and dry, the seedhead falls into the water. This is the culmination of a fascinating process that begins with flowering. After the petals fall away, the receptacle or *torus* nods downward to the east. As the seeds ripen, the "neck" turns again, so that the "head" faces into the sky once more. It looks skyward until it dries and turns brown and the nuts shrink and harden, finally nodding downward in a final bow, after which it falls into the river and floats away. All this nodding apparently loosens the tissue in an abscission ring on the stem just below the torus, allowing it to detach. Receptacles that remain attached into the late fall and winter usually lack any viable seeds.

In places where the plant abounds, the slough bottom may be littered with "lotus gravel"—an accumulation of nuts deposited over the years. These sunken seeds can be collected at any time of the year, but a higher percentage of them will be spoiled, so take only those with the normal plump shape.

Lotus nuts are a delicious starchy staple, easy to harvest, and eminently storable. The nuts of *N. nucifera* are a traditional food in India, China, and other parts of Asia, where they are eaten raw, boiled, roasted, or added to soups and stews. They are also sometimes ground into flour or candied. The nuts are 15 percent protein and 60 percent starch (Van Wyk, 2005), comparing favorably with wheat and other high-protein grains. Native tribes within the American lotus' range, including the Dakota, Meskwaki, Ojibwa, Omaha, Pawnee, Ponca, Potawatomi, and Winnebago, made use of the seeds as a starchy food, especially in soups (Moerman, 1998).

Dried lotus nuts are too hard to crack with most nutcrackers, but a hammer or wooden pestle works fine. I crack mine with the Davebilt nutcracker (see page 183), which is much faster. After cracking I separate the kernels and shells by hand, using a small nut pick, discarding the green embryo leaves as I come across them. The kernels should have a light creamy yellow color; any that are darker, or, more often, powdery and white, are probably spoiled—and spoiled lotus nuts are *nasty*. If in doubt, taste a few until you learn to spot the bad ones. After you separate the kernels they can be stored for as long as you wish, so long as they stay dry and safe from pests.

I like to grind lotus nuts into a coarse meal which is then boiled to make one of the finest hot cereals ever tasted. The meal even turns a light pink as it cooks. More finely ground, lotus flour has many uses. It is stickier than most other flours, and it is the only wild flour that I have used without the addition of wheat to make a product clearly recognizable as a loaf of bread rather than a chunk of stuff. I have also used it to make delicious tortillas and pancakes.

below left Lotus nut mush, a fantastic hot cereal.

below right Lotus bread, with no other flour added.

Harvesting Lotus Tubers

The time to harvest lotus tubers is late summer and early fall, generally in August, September, or early October. Earlier than this all the tubers will not have formed; later than this they get tough and woody. Unlike most other root vegetables, lotus tubers are not at their prime during their long dormant season, but only for a rather short window just before going dormant. Immature tubers are the best.

Lotus tubers mature somewhat erratically. One patch will have mature tubers forming in mid-August, and another nearby not until early October. It seems that those growing in mucky bottoms and deeper water ripen later than those in shallow water with a hard bottom.

Lotus usually grows in areas with a moderately solid bottom: clay-mud, mud, muddy sand, or sand. However, depending on the type of waterway and which plants it is competing with, it can be found in a great variety of soil conditions, which will substantially affect the ease of gathering the tubers. The tubers are generally deposited 6–12 inches (15–30 cm) under the mud or sand. You can sometimes dig lotus in shallow areas and only get your arms wet, but more common harvesting conditions are thigh-deep water with a softer bottom. Fortunately, the water is usually rather warm during the first part of lotus tuber season. Nothing will make you more effective at gathering lotus than the willingness to get wet and muddy. I was inspired by several students at a recent class who dove into the shallows of the Mississippi with me, getting completely submerged and coming up 30 seconds later with a "mud banana" (or "mubanana," as it comes out sounding) and giving whoops of victory with each one.

Lotus rhizome, terminating in a tuber. You can't take a picture of this in the mud, so I pulled it out carefully and cleaned it off. See how shortly before the tuber, the rhizome turns downward and begins to thicken.

(However, in the southern part of its range, lotus patches are home to water moccasins and alligators.)

To find a "mubanana," follow a leaf or flower stem down into the mud with your hands. From a few to several inches into the mud, the stem will meet a smooth rhizome that runs horizontally. You want to follow this rhizome until it ends, where a tuber will be. This means you have to choose which way to go: one direction leads backward to last year's growth, and the other direction leads forward to a tuber that will fuel next year's growth. The reward at the end of the rhizome is big, but it can be a lot of work to get there, and if you go the wrong way you might give up before ever finding a tuber. So here are a few ways to know that you are heading in the direction of growth rather than away from it.

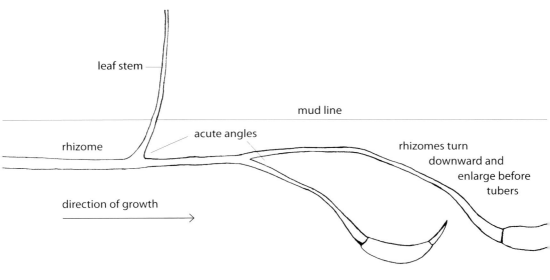

1. If the rhizome seems notably thicker on one side of the stem, go toward the small end.
2. Where the erect stem attaches to the rhizome, it tends to lean slightly in the direction of growth.
3. If the rhizome branches there will be an acute angle in the direction of growth, just as with a tree branch.

Once you have determined the direction of growth, keep going that way. If the rhizome branches, follow the smaller one, for you are probably closer to its end. (Return to the larger branch later.) If the rhizome suddenly changes angle and plunges deeper into the mud, don't give up—you're almost there. Lotus likes to lay its tubers a little deeper than most of its rhizomes grow, so the sudden down-turn indicates that a mubanana is just around the corner. Soon you'll feel the rhizome expand into a banana-shaped tuber 3–14 inches (8–35 cm) long. Loosen the mud around the tuber a little before trying to pull it out, and pull gently backwards, not up. The tubers are often connected end-to-end—I have found as many as three in a chain—and if you are not careful the distal tubers may break off and be difficult to find once the rhizome is detached.

There is another reason that you want to be very gentle with lotus tubers as you harvest them: they contain hollow air channels that run their entire length, and if you break either end of the tuber during collection, mud or muddy water will get into these channels. Sometimes the mud can be rinsed out, but this is an annoying and laborious extra step. Other times the mud ruins the tubers. Breaking the tuber also reduces its shelf life in storage.

Occasionally you will get to the end of a rhizome and find no tuber, just a slightly enlarged bud. This may be a place where the plant is still intending to put up a leaf during the current season or, more likely, it is a place where a tuber was going to form but had not yet done so. Sorry. Start over.

If you are collecting at the right time, you will occasionally find dead ends like this. Once most of the tubers are past their prime, you will find few to none. And if you find mostly dead-ends, you are collecting too early.

Sometimes, especially where the tubers grow in sand, it is easy to just dig in the middle of a thick lotus patch, fanning the sand away with your hands or feet. Eventually, you will find some tubers down there, or some rhizomes that you need to follow only a short distance to a tuber.

Tubers: Preparation

Lotus tubers have a light cream-yellow color, often with reddish-brown patches on the skin. They are generally about the length of a banana but slightly narrower. A length of 6–10 inches (15–25 cm) is common and the largest exceed a foot (30 cm). Younger tubers are lighter in color, often nearly white. After harvesting I rinse the tuber, cut off the ends, and check to see if the insides are clean. If not, I spray water through the hollow channels. Then I peel the tough outer skin with a vegetable peeler. After this I slice the tubers crosswise into sections. Due to the air channels, these slices have a distinct symmetrical look reminiscent of pasta wheels, which most people find very attractive.

Young tubers have almost translucent flesh, a crisp texture, and a mild sweet flavor that is delicious raw as a snack or in salads. Sliced tubers are sometimes candied or pickled in Asia and are frequently sold canned for use as a garnish. They are also fried as chips. Other traditional uses include boiling, roasting, baking, or stir-frying with meat and vegetables.

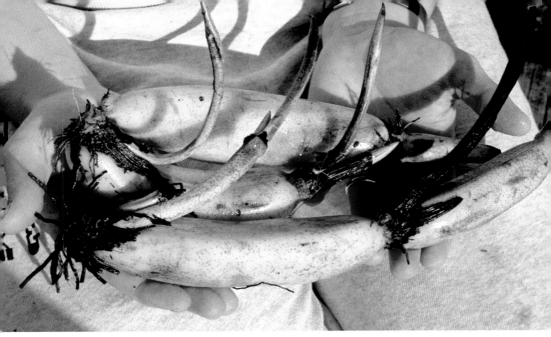

"Mubananas" often grow as doubles like these, or even triples. This is one of our largest wild tubers.

As the tubers age their flesh becomes less sweet, more opaque, and grows fine, tough fibers. These older tubers remain edible but are totally unpleasant when raw and require longer cooking—and even after prolonged boiling they will be rather firm. Their flavor becomes plain and starchy but not unpleasant. If you collect lotus tubers in late fall, winter, or early spring, you will get these fully mature tubers.

Starch can be extracted from fully mature tubers for use in noodles, pastries, and other goods. To extract starch in the home kitchen, first peel several mature tubers and cut them into a few large slices, making sure they are clean inside. Put them in a blender and cover with water, then puree. Pour the puree into a jelly bag suspended in a gallon jar, then pour water through the jelly bag until the jar is full, stirring as you go. Let the jar sit for a day or so; the starch will settle to the bottom and form a hard sediment, and the water can be carefully poured off.

Three unpeeled and one peeled lotus tuber. The rightmost of the unpeeled tubers is immature; young tubers typically lack the yellow tone.

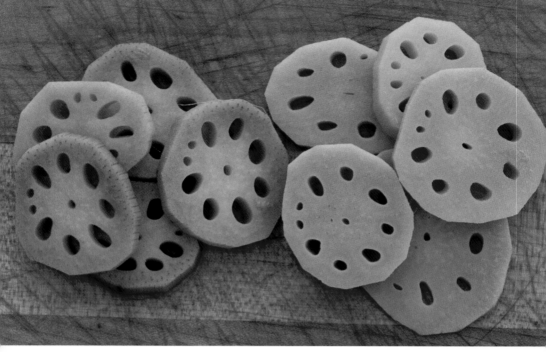

Sliced and cooked lotus tubers. The immature ones turn blue when boiled, the mature ones turn pinkish. Note the incongruous pair of small air channels; this is typical.

Lotus tubers can be pressure canned or parboiled and frozen. Traditionally, the Meskwaki, Potawatomi, and Ojibwa cut the tubers into sections crosswise and hung them on strings to dry for winter use (H. Smith, 1928, 1932, 1933). I like to cut mine into slices, boil them for twenty minutes, and then dry the slices in my electric food dehydrator. These can be tossed into soups or easily rehydrated for any recipe. As long as they are kept from drying out, intact lotus tubers will keep for at least three to six weeks in a refrigerator or root cellar. Damaged tubers should be used within a week or two.

Greens

The young, tender leaves of lotus and the new stems are also edible. These can be collected from late spring through midsummer. New leaves emerge from the water with both sides rolled up, looking like a lopsided scroll. As long as these leaves are still rolled up they are very tender. They can be broken off by hand, and when you do this you will feel that the tops of the stems are also tender. You can also pick the small, light green, newly-unrolled pads.

Lotus greens have some of that same mucky bitter flavor that is character-istic of every part of pond and water lilies, and which is also found in the leafy embryo inside of the lotus seed. They are rather disgusting to eat raw. Cooked in one or two water changes, they can be made palatable but are not exceptional. However, the cooked greens do have a nice texture and have been used traditionally to wrap cooked rice, meat, fish, and vegetables.

Young, curled lotus leaf—the kind to use for cooking.

Hopefully you have come to appreciate the lotus as more than just a perch for bullfrogs and shade for bass; more than a beautiful flower—more even than a sacred one. The lotus is all of these things, but it is also one of the most useful food plants that humankind has been blessed with.

Mayapple

Podophyllum peltatum

Berberidaceae – Barberry Family

Perhaps it is a maladaptive trait, but people would rather hunt than work. When given the choice between amassing a substantial quantity of food through diligent repetitive labor or finding a few scattered morsels of some elusive delicacy, people almost always choose the less economical but more exciting option. Available for but a fleeting moment in the cycle of seasons, the mayapple has long been popular as just such a quarry. Like the morel and the pawpaw, this unique fruit has been glorified in the folklore and conversation of

Ripe mayapple on plant.

rural people—because it demands our time in the thrill of pursuit rather than the drudgery of preparation.

I, too, have felt my heart pounding as I knelt down and peered among the half-yellowed leaves in search of a *second* mayapple. I have bolted among the white oak trunks to pounce on one dangling, shaded yellow treasure after another. I have run to exhaustion up limestone ridges in the waning dusk light, scratching my thighs on blackberry thorns and covering my socks with stick-tights in the hope of adding two or three pulpy mayapples to my precious dozen.

I have never examined the input/output ratio of calories for this pursuit, nor have I calculated my labor efficiency. But please don't do it for me. Let us mayapple hunters have our fun. Who cares how many hours are consumed; we are driven by our memory of *that one time*, when there was a fruit on every forked stem, some as big as kiwi fruits—and we got *hundreds*. You don't understand. You weren't there. Maybe someday we'll find that again. And if not, sixteen will keep the memory alive.

Description

The mayapple is one of our most distinct woodland herbs, both its uniqueness and its beauty helping to commit it to memory. The stalk is single, smooth, erect, and straight. It either is unbranched, supporting a single leaf, or forks once and supports two leaves. As a rule, the forked stems with two leaves produce a single flower, while the stems with a single leaf do not flower. When the shoots emerge in spring, each leaf unfolds like a tiny umbrella. Like many perennial herbs, the mayapple persists from year to year and spreads by its creeping rootstock.

Mayapple leaves are light green, shiny, large, and umbrella-like. The stem is attached to the

The umbrella-like shoot of mayapple. **Not edible!**

Fertile mayapple plants produce a single flower each spring.

middle (known as "peltate") on single-leafed plants, but the leaves on forked stems are slightly smaller and are attached slightly to one side. The leaves are typically 9–16 inches (23–40 cm) wide and divided into four to nine large lobes, each of which is coarsely and irregularly toothed and sometimes divided into smaller lobes. The ends of each lobe droop, adding to the umbrella-like appearance. The plant is typically 14–24 inches (35–60 cm) tall. Mayapples tend to grow in large colonies, sometimes forming enormous patches of knee-high leaves that hide the ground from view.

Flowering stems produce just a single blossom, which nods on a stem 1–1.5 inches (2.5–4 cm) long attached at the fork in the main stem. Mayapple flowers are striking and rank among our most popular woodland wildflowers, despite their strange scent. About 2 inches (5 cm) across, their six to nine waxy petals are white, contrasting with the pale yellow pistils and stamens in the center. The flowers are hidden by the leaves. Mayapples bloom in mid to late spring, just before the forest canopy closes above them.

If luck prevails and the flower is successfully pollinated, it will mature by late summer into a lemon or egg-shaped fruit 1–3 inches (3–8cm) long. Typical size is a little smaller than a medium chicken egg, but large specimens are comparable to kiwi fruit in size. The ripe fruit turns to a light, dull yellow or brownish yellow. It has a delicious tropical scent, often described as "ethereal," that makes my mouth water. The skin is smooth but tough and leathery; inside there is a nearly translucent, light yellow liquidy pulp mixed with many seeds about the size of apple seeds.

It is a mystery to me why this plant is called "mayapple." The fruit does not ripen in May, even at the southern extreme of its range; it typically blossoms in April or May. Other common names, all of which have more evident origins, include raccoon berry, yellowberry, wild lemon, custard-apple, American mandrake, and hog-apple.

Range and Habitat

The mayapple inhabits the hardwood forests of eastern North America, from eastern Texas to northern Florida, north to southern Minnesota, southern Ontario and Quebec, and central New England.

Mayapples prefer hardwood forests with rich soil, doing best in dry-mesic stands with a mixture of trees. Maple-beech forests are often too shady, but oak, ash, and hickory cast a lighter shade more favorable to the mayapple's growth.

A typical colony of mayapple plants in spring.

The densest, most vigorous colonies—which produce the most fruit—are usually in small openings, woodlands without a closed canopy, or at the edge of the forest. I have seen places where this plant completely takes over narrow power line corridors through the woods or lightly used pastures with scattered trees. It is also often abundant along small country roads through wooded areas. Mayapples are sometimes found in open country near woods, especially along road banks and in pastures.

Harvest

The edible part of this plant is the ripe fruit. **Roots, leaves, and stems are considered very toxic and have caused death when misused.** The unripe fruit are also considered toxic (Turner and Szczawinski, 1991). The fruit ripens in late summer across the northern states and southern Canada, but in midsummer in the southern United States. In Wisconsin the first mayapples ripen about August 15 or 20, and the last ones can be collected around September 10 or 15, with the peak of harvest about September 1. By the time the fruit is ready to pick, the plants may have toppled over and the leaves are likely to have begun turning yellow or brown. Often, the ripe fruit simply falls from the plant.

There is no special trick to collecting mayapples; just grab them as fast as you can. But make sure they are ripe. Unripe fruits are hard and green, often with very light, almost white, areas on the skin. Ripe mayapples soften considerably, become yellow or straw-colored, and develop a wonderful aroma. Their rind gets progressively thinner as they ripen—and the riper they are, the better they taste. Totally unripe mayapples taste horrible, especially the skins. Fruit that is almost ripe might trick you into eating it and give you a false impression about the mayapple's flavor. Nearly-ripe mayapples will ripen fully if you let them sit for a few days at room temperature, but as usual their flavor will remain inferior to that of fruit ripened on the plant. Severely underripe mayapples are hopeless.

The hardest thing about mayapples is *finding them*. Sure, the plants are common enough, even abundant—but the flowers are fickle about setting fruit. In some years, virtually every stem will be barren, and one can search for hours to no avail. Drought is the mayapple collector's enemy, for in such years the plants drop their fruit and die back prematurely to wait for a better growing season. In most years, however, you'll find an occasional mayapple hanging there beneath the leaves—enough to entice you onward in your diligent search, anticipating the next find as your collecting bag slowly gets heavier. And then there are the occasional growing seasons when the weather cooperates in every way with the mayapple's wishes, and a luscious fruit dangles from nearly every forked stem, filling pails and pockets with ease. Just take what you get and be happy with it.

Certain mayapple patches fail to set fruit year after year. There are two primary

An assortment of ripe mayapples (the greenish one is probably not ripe).

If the raccoons don't get them, mayapples will wrinkle as the leaves turn brown and shrivel. Still excellent eating.

reasons for this. Commonly, the plants are under stress from competition and shade. The mayapple plants may be decades old; perhaps when they became established, the canopy was more open. As the years passed and the overhead foliage grew denser, the mayapples slowly declined, and today they are barely hanging on, with no extra energy to invest in flowers or fruit. If this is the case in your mayapple patch, search elsewhere; or, if the property is yours and you need firewood, thin the canopy.

In many areas the mayapples, like a host of other native wildflowers, are stressed by an overpopulation of deer. I have watched deer pull up one mayapple plant after another, eating the stem and dropping the leaf. This robs the rootstocks of energy, causing the mayapple to grow back much smaller the following year with insufficient energy to bloom. The solution to this problem is to eat venison.

Preparation

My favorite thing to do with mayapples is to tear a hole in the skin, suck out the pulp, and enjoy its flavor as I spit out the seeds. It is said that raw mayapples can cause an upset stomach when eaten in a large enough quantity, but I have never had such an experience. (Better safe than sorry. If you think you may have collected too many, my address is on the title page.) Mayapples will store for a week or two at room temperature and a little longer in the refrigerator, as long as they are kept intact and not piled too deep (which promotes molding).

Most people who like fruit like mayapples. Taste a good one and you'll understand why it is almost legendary in the foraging world. They are sometimes compared to strawberries—which seems ridiculous to me—or more realistically to guava or passion fruit. Of course, their flavor is distinct and unique. Unlike embarrassment, it is much better experienced than described.

If you're lucky enough to get more mayapples than you want to eat raw, good things can be made from them. In the wild food literature you'll find instructions for processing them by cutting in half, boiling, and then straining out the seeds and skins. I think that's a very bad idea. The seeds and skins are very bitter and during cooking they impart this flavor to the pulp, utterly ruining it in some cases. The riper the fruit is, the thinner and less bitter the skins are, and you can get away with boiling with the skins on *if all the fruit is extremely ripe*—but it is rare to find super-ripe mayapples, except in the very best years, because other animals eat them too quickly. I think the flavor of mayapple products is distinctly superior when the pulp is scraped or squeezed from the skins when raw, and the seeds are removed with a strainer or colander before cooking.

The resulting puree makes a sensational jam, bursting with the deep, rich flavor for which mayapples are famous. It can also be used to make pies, tarts, and other baked desserts. Add a small amount of water to the mayapple pulp, boil it, and strain it through a jelly bag to get a wonderful juice to drink alone like precious wine, or to mix with other drinks or juices worthy of its company. This juice can also be used to make a superb jelly.

The raccoon berry is fit not just for raccoons: it is a gourmet fruit with few peers. In fact, I'd trade the raccoons sweet corn for mayapples any day.

Hackberry, Sugarberry

Celtis Spp.

Ulmaceae — Elm Family

On our city streets, the hardwood trees that we plant are almost always river floodplain species: silver maple, green ash, pin oak, cottonwood, pecan, and American elm. Several generations ago, a few Midwestern cities chose a more obscure floodplain tree, the hackberry, to complement the ubiquitous elms lining their thoroughfares. On the streets of La Crosse, Wisconsin, hundreds of these old hackberries can be seen today, towering gracefully above the homes and churches, some approaching 3 feet (1 meter) in diameter and exceeding 100 feet (30 m) in height. Now that decades have passed since Dutch elm disease swept through, the trees serve as a reminder of the urban arboreal splendor that we lost, and as a monument to our tunnel vision.

Fruit of the unknown tree. This one is net-leaf hackberry *Celtis reticulata*. How many stinkbugs can you count?

My earliest vivid memory of hackberry is almost too embarrassing to put in print. Before I knew they could be eaten, I used to put a hackberry in one nostril, push the other shut, turn my head in awkward positions, and "sneeze-shoot" the fruit at schoolmates. One time, with a hackberry in my nose, I hiccoughed, and the fruit disappeared into the nasal abyss. Too embarrassed to report the incident, I waited a few weeks for my irritated sinus to abate. A few months after this trauma, I sneezed into my hand—and what came out but a snot-coated hackberry stone. My first hackberry was ingested through the wrong hole.

You may not have heard much about the hackberry. It hides in plain view. Not only is it largely overlooked as a wild food—it seems to be largely overlooked that this tree exists at all. One of its French Canadian names is *bois inconnu*, or "unknown wood," quite appropriate for this common tree whose name often elicits blank stares even from people who have lived their entire lives in its shade.

I find this mystery mysterious, for the hackberry is quite distinct and not unattractive. Once people become acquainted with it, they usually find it among our easiest trees to recognize. Indeed, the bark is among the most distinctive of any North American tree, and once you look at it closely you will find it almost impossible to forget. But our cultural lens has blotted out this sylvan neighbor, and the horrendous and forgettable name of *hackberry*, which conjures up images of some worthless thorny bush rather than a stately tree, has unfortunately befallen it.

The wild animals, far more objective than people in their assessment of plants, pay much attention to the hackberry. Its fruit is eaten by an enormous number of creatures, from raccoons and bears to robins and woodpeckers. The hackberry mast ranks in importance beside the oak, hickory, walnut, and beech, and it is truly one of the most important wildlife foods in North America. White-footed mice, a keystone of the woodland food chain, thrive on them. Squirrels of all sorts relish hackberries and often depend on them during years when the larger nuts have produced poorly. Because the high-calorie fruits often remain attached to the tree all winter, they are available to wild turkeys even when deep or crusted snows have made it impossible to scratch for acorns and ground beans. Perhaps it is not coincidence that the original range of this magnificent game bird in the northern states closely mirrors that of the hackberry.

In the wild food literature, the hackberry, if given any space at all, is generally mentioned cursorily, as if it is a second-rate fruit worthy of no more than an occasional taste for the sake of curiosity. We seem to think that the hackberry wanted to be something plump and juicy like a cherry and failed miserably. But a hackberry is like no other fruit, providing the closest thing you can get to a complete meal from one plant. In sheer survival value it is unsurpassed, for it packs a remarkably high number of calories comprising all three sources: fat, carbohydrate, and protein. Furthermore, these calories are easily digestible without any cooking or preparation. All this in a food so delicious that you might start to crave it like I do.

Sound good? Read along and discover this unknown tree for yourself.

Description, Range, and Habitat

North America is home to six species of hackberry, all of which produce similar edible fruit. I will first describe the most widespread species, the common hackberry *Celtis occidentalis*, which serves as a reasonable representative, and amend the description with distinctive characteristics of the other species.

The common or northern hackberry is a medium to large tree that grows fairly straight with a moderately wide crown. Specimens regularly attain 50–70 feet (15–21 m) in height and occasionally exceed 100 (30 m). Perhaps the most distinct feature of this tree is its bark, which is rather thin with many high, narrow, corky ridges or wart-like growths. A closer look reveals that these ridges are composed of thin layers suggesting sedimentary rock, earning it the imaginative name of "Grand Canyon bark." The color of the bark is dull gray. On younger growth, and sometimes between the ridges on older trunks, the bark is smooth, almost like that of beech.

Hackberry produces slender reddish brown or greenish brown twigs. Another distinct feature of this tree is that the branches often produce "witch's brooms"—places where several twigs grow from the same point on a branch. This is caused

A close-up of the bark of *Celtis occidentalis*, the common hackberry.

by a mite and a fungus that infect the tree. However, these witch's brooms are common enough to be a good identifying feature of the leafless hackberry. Even in the absence of this pathogenic influence, the twigs are borne quite close together on the outer limbs, giving the tree a distinctive branching pattern that can be recognized from a distance.

Hackberry leaves somewhat resemble those of elms in size and shape but are broader at the base. They are 3–6 inches (8–15 cm) long, simple, alternate, and rough to the touch. The leaf margins are shallowly toothed, except near the base, where they are untoothed. Hackberry leaves tend to be asymmetrical, particularly at the base. Their color is somewhat lighter green than those of most trees, a fact that can aid in spotting hackberries from a distance. Hackberry leaves are typically infected by an insect (*Pachypsylla celtidis-mamma*) that causes wart-like growths to form on their lower surface—these are called "hackberry nipple galls." The foliage turns to dull yellow in autumn.

This disease, hackberry nipple gall, is so common that it is a good identifying feature of the tree, especially in the East.

Hackberry flowers appear just as the leaves emerge in spring. They are tiny, cream-colored, and inconspicuous, with four sepals. The flowers, and later the fruit, hang individually on long stems from the leaf axils. The fruits, which ripen to an orange, reddish-brown, or dark purple-brown in September, are about the size of a pea, 0.25 inch (6 mm) in diameter. (Several manuals state that the fruit of this hackberry reaches 2 cm in diameter, but I believe this is a typographical error that has been copied from one text to another. That is 0.8 inch, or about the size of a cultivated cherry, which would be almost forty times as massive as the largest hackberries I've ever seen. If you know of any that large, please contact me, because such a tree should be propagated!) Each fruit consists of a single large, spherical seed surrounded by a thin layer of dry, sugary pulp and a smooth skin. These drupes are almost perfectly round.

The common hackberry is found from the river valleys of the eastern Great Plains to the East Coast. The northern edge of its range is from South Dakota and Minnesota to southern Ontario, southern Quebec, and Vermont; it ranges south to Virginia, Arkansas, and Oklahoma. This is a common tree of river floodplains and valleys with rich soil, but it is also found upland in mixed hardwood forests, especially on limestone ridges. Moderately fast-growing, moderately long-lived,

In the East, hackberries can be large trees. This is *C. occidentalis*.

and not very tolerant of shade, *Celtis occidentalis* is most often associated with oak, elm, green ash, cottonwood, boxelder, hickory, and walnut.

The net-leaf hackberry *C. reticulata* is a small tree of the southwestern and western United States. This species occurs in rocky ravines, limestone hills, canyons, and along rivers, usually in semi-arid climates. Net-leaf hackberry reaches 30 feet (9 m) in height and has an open, crooked, branchy form. As its name suggests, the leaves have conspicuous net-like veins on their lower surface. This species ranges from Texas and Kansas west to California and northwest to Idaho and eastern Washington. Associates include cottonwood, sycamore, boxelder, walnut, and blue elderberry.

The sugarberry or southern hackberry *Celtis laevigata* does not grow quite as large as the common hackberry, rarely exceeding 60 feet (18 m) in height. It can be distinguished by its smaller leaves with untoothed margins. The bark also typically bears smaller and fewer warty ridges, sometimes with large areas of smooth bark between them, and the fruits are slightly smaller and lighter in color. This tree is common in floodplain hardwood forests and other moist sites across the southern half of the eastern United States, where it largely replaces the northern hackberry on similar sites. Sugarberry grows from Texas, Oklahoma, and southwest Kansas to southern Florida and north to Virginia, southern Illinois, and central Missouri. In many areas it is one of the most predominant trees.

Dwarf hackberry *C. tenuifolia* is a large shrub or small tree typically reaching 9–25 feet (3–8 m) in height. The leaves are only about 2.5 inches (6 cm) long and have only a few teeth toward the tip. Like all hackberries, the bark becomes warty, but smaller specimens may lack this feature. The fruit is slightly smaller and usually darker than that of the common hackberry. Dwarf hackberry is spottily distributed in dry, open hardwood forests, especially those that are sandy or very well drained, occasionally becoming abundant in the right habitat. It ranges from southeastern Kansas and eastern Texas to Georgia, and north to Pennsylvania, southern Ontario, and southern Michigan.

One species, *C. lindheimeri*, is confined to ravines and brushland of the Edwards Plateau in south-central Texas. This is a scrubby tree sometimes reaching 40 feet (12 m) in height, but due to its rarity it should probably be left alone.

Our most unique species is the desert hackberry *C. pallida*, which is confined to southern Arizona, southern New Mexico, and southwest Texas. This is a shrub rarely exceeding 10 feet (3 m) in height with short thorns and small, thick, coarsely-toothed evergreen leaves about 1 inch (2.5 cm) long. The drupe is smaller, brighter orange, and more fruity-tasting than that of the larger species.

Some History and Lore

Despite its near invisibility today, only a handful of food plants have equaled the hackberry in importance to hunter-gatherers. Remains of the fruit are found time and again in archeological sites throughout the surprisingly broad range of this tree. Hackberries were uncovered from every level of the famous site of Çatal Höyük in Turkey, inhabited roughly 9000 to 7000 years ago (Helbaek, 1964). These nut-berries were "by far the most common plant remains" recovered at the ancient Meadowcroft Rock Shelter in Pennsylvania (Adovasio et al., 1978). They have been found in archeological food remains from locations as widely

dispersed as Peru (Rossen et al., 1996), Honduras (Lentz, 1991), Mexico (Taylor, 1972), Arizona (Fish et al., 1986), Indonesia (Glover, 1977), Sudan (Haaland, 1995), and South Africa (Plug, 1981). In fact, an enormous number of hackberry seeds were found at the "Peking Man" site at Zhoukoudian, China, which is estimated to be 500,000 years of age, giving hackberry

The net-leaf hackberry *Celtis reticulata*, the common western species, is usually a small tree.

the distinction of being perhaps the oldest known human plant food (Brothwell and Brothwell, 1969).

Apparently the hackberry has been appreciated by certain more recent cultures, too. This fruit was a well-known food to the ancient Romans and Greeks. It was widely eaten by Native Americans, including the Acoma, Apache, Comanche, Dakota, Hualapai, Keres, Kiowa, Laguna, Meskwaki, Navajo, Omaha, Papago, Pawnee, Pueblo, Tewa, and Yuvapai (Moerman, 1998). In typical Western prejudice against this tree, Peattie (1953) states that it is still eaten by "some of the more sedentary and ill-nourished desert Indian tribes." I suspect, however, that they ate it not because they were ill-nourished, but because it was good.

What a shame that this tree has been assigned such a ridiculous and unpleasant name. And it is a misnomer, derived from the Scottish *hagberry* for a species of small and unappreciated wild cherry. The scientific name *Celtis* is derived directly from the Latin name for *C. australis*, a Mediterranean species of hackberry apparently once less obscure. This plant is believed to be the "lotus tree" of Greek legend (Lindley and Moore, 1876); eating its fruit was supposed to induce a state of contented forgetfulness and indifference. To me, the legend of the lotus sounds like a reflection of the common prejudices that agrarian people hold against their hunting and gathering neighbors and ancestors—that they are lazy and stupid. Is it coincidence that this legend was applied to a former staple of foragers in the region?

(Note: the name "lotus" has been applied to various species of trefoil, *Nymphaea* water lilies, and the genus *Nelumbo*, creating a confusing mess when trying to interpret any literary reference to anything called "lotus.")

The bark of sugarberry is typically smooth with only scattered corky knobs.

Harvest and Preparation

The edible part of the hackberry is its pea-sized fruit. These ripen in early September but may remain until midwinter or even the following spring, when they will be finally gobbled up by migrating birds. In years when the yield is poor the hackberries may be gone in early autumn soon after they ripen. Not only is the hackberry crop quite variable, its availability is affected by the yield of other local food sources such as acorns, hickory nuts, and wild grapes. When these neighbors crop poorly, the wildlife will focus heavily on hackberries.

I typically collect hackberries after the leaves fall, when they are easier to see. Late October and November is the peak of the harvest, but I have gotten excellent yields through April. The fruit does not spoil, since it lacks any appreciable amount of moisture—the pulp is mostly sugar like that of a date.

The most difficult part about collecting hackberries is reaching them; much of the time this is simply impossible. Open-grown trees sometimes have some lower branches within easy grasp, and I have many times stood on a snowbank, boulder, or picnic table to extend my reach, or used a berry hook to pull down slightly higher limbs. Oftentimes, and particularly after a fierce windstorm, one finds the ground under a productive hackberry tree heavily littered with fallen fruit. Because of their smooth skin and dry texture, they generally remain clean and undamaged after the fall. I have spent some pleasant winter hours chatting with

Unlike other hackberries, sugarberry leaves have entire margins.

The desert hackberry is a large, spiny shrub with small evergreen leaves and tiny berries.

friends under a hackberry tree, filling containers with the fallen fruit. Another fun and effective but more dangerous way to acquire hackberries is to climb the tree and shake or beat the limbs to dislodge the fruits—although sometimes they are reluctant to fall. Stuff any easily reached ones into your pocket as you climb, then descend the tree and pick up the rest from the ground. Hackberries can also be dislodged with a throwing stick. This may be a relief to the less arboreal, but is certainly not without its own dangers. A sheet or tarp spread on the ground to catch the fruit will speed up the harvest. You can also use a blueberry rake to strip them onto a tarp or cloth, which is very effective.

Whichever method you employ to collect hackberries, you will find it rather slow going—at least when measured by volume. I have never been able to harvest a gallon in an hour, and if you get half that volume you're doing well. However, remember that the fruit is dry already and high in oil. A gallon of hackberries is worth three to five gallons of raspberries or blueberries when measured by calories, so actually it compares quite favorably with other small fruits in terms of harvest efficiency.

Hackberries have no juice and their flavor lacks the tartness or sourness required for jam or jelly. Although I have occasionally seen recipes for such things, I think hackberry jam is about as appropriate as snapping turtle wine. Hackberries contain an enormous seed from which the pulp is nearly impossible to separate in any efficient way, rendering them useless for pies or most other baking. In fact, so long as you think of hackberries as *berries* they will seem quite worthless.

Instead, think of the hackberry as a small, thin-shelled nut, high in oil and protein, surrounded by a sweet pulp that is somewhere between a date and cooked squash in flavor. It seems that many wild food authors have noted the sweet pulp, but few have noticed the interior nut, which turns this bastard berry into something totally different. The easiest thing to do with hackberries is to chew them up, crushing the seedshells between your teeth, and eat them whole. The mixture of the nutty kernel with the sweet pulp is delicious, rich, and filling— totally unlike other "berries." I suspect that hackberries alone could sustain a person for months if necessary. The sweetness and thickness of the pulp varies from one tree to another, as does the thickness of the seedshells. My favorite trees produce seeds that crunch almost as easily as M&M's, but some others are hard enough to crack that you may be in danger of breaking a tooth if you try.

People who object to chewing up the seedshells still have many options. You can smash the whole fruit (which I do with a mortar and pestle), obliterating the pits into tiny pieces. This produces a substance with a texture like very stiff cookie dough. I call this "hackberry candy" and like to eat it with no further preparation, except maybe squeezing it into animal shapes, whose heads I then bite off. Of course, this mashed hackberry will still contain the pieces of seedshell, but you won't have to crunch them between your teeth. The shell bits are small enough to swallow, and if you chew gently while letting the candy melt in your mouth, your teeth won't have to bear down on the shell fragments at all.

Sometimes I mix this mashed hackberry with other kinds of dried berries. At my house we call this mixture something unmentionable, in reference to its resemblance to ursine spoor. Hackberry candy will keep for months, even years, at room temperature, but its taste is best when freshly pounded. The famous forager Euell Gibbons wrote of his first wild food recipe, when at age five he pounded together hackberries and shelled hickory nuts to make a wild "candy bar" (Gibbons,

The leaves and fruit of the common hackberry.

1973). Try it—it's seriously good, and with a touch of maple syrup it's exceptional. Although Euell later grew to dislike the texture of shell fragments in his mashed hackberries, I think it is quite tolerable. But if you can't get accustomed to it, there are still more options for partaking of the hackberry.

Take about two cups of mashed hackberry and break it up into small chunks. Place these in a saucepan with about six cups of water and boil for thirty minutes, stirring occasionally at first to be sure the clumps dissolve. Then pour the pan's contents through a fine-screen strainer and scrape the strainer's sides with a spoon until the liquid has percolated through. The seedshell pieces and skins will remain in the strainer, while most of the good stuff should go through with the liquid. This process produces a thick orange-brown liquid that I call "hackberry milk." It has a rich, hearty flavor that is hard to describe but easy to like—especially with a dash of maple syrup. Hackberry milk is very filling, and I prefer to drink it warm. You don't have to drink hackberry milk as is; you can use it as a base for soup (use a squash soup recipe) or you can cook your favorite hot cereal in it to impart a distinct flavor. You can substitute it for the liquid in pancake, muffin, or quick bread batter. You can also boil hackberry milk down to make a syrup that is sweet and oily.

Hackberries are easy to store for later use, since their high sugar and low moisture content conspire to prevent spoilage. Spread them shallowly (one

A bowl of sugarberries.

to five layers deep) in a tray or pan where they can sit for a few weeks to fully dehydrate, stirring occasionally. Once dried they will store indefinitely in a plastic bag or jar.

Sugarberries *Celtis laevigata* are smaller and have harder seedshells than the common hackberry. The flavor of their pulp has a slight hint of apple. They seem more sour, but not actually any sweeter than other hackberries. I have also collected dwarf hackberry *C. tenuifolia* and net-leaf hackberry *C. reticulata*, and these can be used in the ways described above. The net-leaf hackberry has a smaller fruit than the common hackberry, but it has a delicious flavor and is usually easier to reach. I have collected only small samples of the desert hackberry. While this species is extremely abundant in parts of its range, the diminutive fruit seems less practical to gather.

As you can see, this unknown fruit can be enjoyed in a variety of ways. Considering its storability, high calorie content, and excellent flavor, it is no surprise that hunter-gatherers around the world once sought hackberries with enthusiasm. Maybe now you will, too.

Walnut, Black Walnut

Juglans nigra, major, microcarpa, californica, hindsii

Juglandaceae – Walnut Family

The black walnut was one of the first wild foods that I learned. My grandparents had a few of them growing around their farmhouse, and I was shown the nuts at an early age. I loved to fill small pails, bring them to my grandfather, and watch him crack the nuts. My ornery old neighbor Ms. Swanson also had a huge walnut tree in her yard—but I dared not set foot on her lawn. Ms. Swanson seemed to have nothing better to do than calling the police and reporting on the activities of six-year-old boys. So I just got the lucky strays that rolled onto the sidewalk in front of her house. I loved to pick them up while they were still green and hard, sniffing their unique aroma. And I often carried one with me, for no projectile ever fit more snugly into a young boy's hand. As if I needed to give Ms. Swanson a *reason* to call the police.

A cluster of black walnut *Juglans nigra* on the tree. Astute walnut pickers can tell that these are not quite ripe by their constricted, nipple-like tips.

Description

The black walnut is a large deciduous tree that tends to have a straight and very dominant trunk. The bark is rather light grayish brown, thick and rough, separated into nearly parallel ridges by narrow fissures. The twigs are smooth, brown, and very thick. The buds are naked and the bud scars have a "monkey face" similar to that found on the closely related butternut.

Black walnut's leaves are pinnately compound, consisting of thirteen to twenty-one leaflets. Each leaflet is soft and lanceolate, from 2–4 inches (5–10 cm) long with entire or faintly toothed margins. The leaf is typically 18–32 inches (45–80 cm) long. Black walnut's foliage is similar to that of sumac, ailanthus, and butternut. Compared to butternut, with which it is often confused, black walnut's leaflets are narrower, smaller, slightly darker, and more uniform in size; also, the terminal leaflet is usually small or absent on black walnut, while it is well developed on butternut. Walnuts leaf out rather late in spring and lose their foliage early in autumn as the leaves turn dull yellow.

In late spring or early summer, as the branches begin the season's explosive growth spurt, inconspicuous catkins of drab green flowers appear. If pollinated successfully, small bumpy green balls will form in their place, hanging typically in pairs or threes. These will grow until they reach their full size of 1.5–3 inches (4–8 cm) in diameter nine to twelve weeks later. The nuts ripen in early fall, whereupon they begin dropping, although occasional trees hold the nuts well into autumn. They can be easily told from other large nuts by their round shape and the fact that their husks do not peel in sections; they cling to the shell like the flesh of a fruit.

Typically, the black walnut fruit is a little larger than a chicken egg (although not the same shape), but on exceptional trees they may be the size of peaches. Technically, the nut is not a "true" nut; rather, just as it appears, it is the pit of a fleshy fruit. But the flesh of the black walnut is nasty and inedible. This flesh is hard and green at first, but as the

Trunk of a large black walnut; such trees are uncommon, as this log is probably worth more than a thousand dollars.

nuts ripen and fall it softens, developing a yellowish hue and finally turning black and mushy. The nut itself is faintly heart-shaped with a brain-like pattern of low, rounded ridges—quite unlike the sharp ridges of the butternut.

While the eastern black walnut is by far the most common and widespread walnut species, there are four smaller western walnuts that can be used similarly. (The butternut or white walnut *Juglans cinerea* was discussed separately in *The Forager's Harvest*.)

The Arizona black walnut or nogal *Juglans major* is a smaller, spreading tree whose 8–14 inch (20–35 cm) compound leaves have nine to fifteen leaflets. The nut resembles an eastern black walnut in miniature. The Texas walnut or little walnut *J. microcarpa* is a smaller, almost shrubby species, seldom exceeding 15 feet (4.5 m) in height or a foot (30 cm) in diameter. The leaflets are narrower, almost willow-like, and more numerous, with fifteen to twenty-three per leaf. Everything is supposed to be bigger in Texas, but this species has the smallest nuts of any of our walnuts, usually less than 0.5 inch (13 mm) in diameter. The California walnut *J. californica* is a small, spreading tree typically growing

below left All walnuts have pinnately compound leaves; on black walnut they may exceed two feet in length.

below right Walnut flowers have few admirers.

The Arizona walnut or nogal *Juglans major* is a common tree of floodplains and stream valleys in the Southwest. When I took this photo in February the ground under the tree still had gallons of good nuts.

20–40 feet (6–12 m) tall. The compound leaves are typically 6–10 inches (15–25 cm) in length, composed of eleven to fifteen small ovate to elliptic leaflets 1–2 inches (2.5–5 cm) long. The shape of the leaflets is rather distinctive; they are broader than other walnuts and lack the acuminate tips. The nuts are small, and smoother than the species mentioned above. The northern California walnut or Hinds walnut *J. hindsii* is a large tree, sometimes growing straight and tall like the eastern black walnut. However, its leaves are smaller, like the other western species; only about a foot (30 cm) long, they are composed of thirteen to nineteen small, narrow, glossy leaflets. The nearly smooth, faintly grooved nuts are the largest among our western walnuts (although still much smaller than the eastern black walnut), sometimes 1 inch (2.5 cm) long.

Range and Habitat

Black walnut is typical of our eastern hardwood forests and the floodplain forests of the eastern Great Plains. The southern edge of its range extends from northern Florida to central Texas. It ranges north through Oklahoma, eastern Kansas and Nebraska to southeastern South Dakota. In the North it is found from southern Minnesota through southern Michigan, Ontario and Vermont. However, because of its edible nuts, attractive appearance, and valuable wood, the black walnut has been planted extensively outside of its native range, in some areas appearing naturalized.

In the wild, eastern black walnut is most common in rich-soiled mesic forests and in river valleys just above the floodplain. It does well colonizing old fields and is often prevalent along forest borders and fencerows. Black walnut is a pioneer tree, dependent on disturbance, and grows extremely fast. I have seen seedlings exceed 6 feet (2 m) in their first season. Unlike many pioneer trees, it has a long life span and can remain dominant in a stand for hundreds of years.

The Arizona walnut *J. major* is found in southwestern New Mexico, southern and central Arizona, and extreme western Texas. It grows along streams, rivers, washes, and canyons at low to middle elevations, where it is associated with cottonwood, boxelder, hackberry, and sycamore. The Texas or little walnut *J. microcarpa* is found along the floodplains of rivers and streams in central New Mexico, western and Central Texas, western Oklahoma, and south-central Kansas. Native stands of California walnut *J. californica* are restricted to sheltered hillsides and canyons at low elevations in coastal southern California, but the tree has been planted widely throughout southern California. The Hinds walnut *J. hindsii* is native to rich floodplains and valleys at low elevations in a very limited area of northern California—only a few natural stands are known. However, this species has been extensively planted outside of its natural range and has become naturalized widely in California.

Typical form of an open-grown California walnut. This one, on a cliff above the Pacific, had enough nuts to feed a village.

Harvest and Preparation

Black walnut is one of the easier wild foods in North America to collect. It is a more consistent producer than oaks, hickories, beech, pinyon, or butternut, and the crop tends to be heavy. Upon ripening, the nuts fall to the ground, where they can be easily picked up. Under good conditions, one can gather a few bushels per hour. If the nuts are ripe but remain on the tree, shaking the branches or throwing a stick will dislodge them. Even though the western species have smaller nuts, they are often produced copiously and can be harvested in great quantity with little effort.

Wild walnuts typically ripen in September or October. However, those that have been planted as street and yard trees often come from faraway seed sources and may ripen at odd and variable times. If they fall way too early or stick on the tree way too late, the nuts are likely to be bad. If you collect them too early, the husk will be extremely hard and totally green; the husks of ripe walnuts turn yellow-green and develop black spots, and their flesh softens.

The next step after harvest is to remove the husk. If the walnuts are left for several weeks, these husks will turn black, soften, and rot. If you let them dry after going through this process, you can easily crumble away the remains of

the husk, but this poses two serious problems. First, you must find an appropriate place to allow the rotting and drying to occur, where the ink that oozes from the blackening nuts will not stain a floor, but where the nuts are still safe from squirrels. Second, the ink from the rotting hulls may soak through the shells and taint the flavor of the kernels. For these reasons, it is preferable to remove the hulls soon after harvest, before they turn to ink or mush.

I told you it was loaded!

During those years when the crop is heavy, especially if the weather is wet, the hulls will rot away as the nuts sit on the ground under the tree. In this case all you'll have to do is pry the nut from this inky mess. Under such natural conditions, when the nuts are not piled deeply and the black juice from the hulls

After the green flesh is removed from these California walnuts, the nut is disappointingly small.

can percolate into the soil, the nutmeats generally do not become disflavored by their ink. Both species of California walnut have thinner husks, which are much easier to dry or remove immediately. You can put the whole nuts into a gunnysack once the hulls have softened, stomp on them, then dump them out and just pick the nuts out of the mashed hulls.

There are many ways to loosen black walnut hulls while they are still green. A popular one is to dump the nuts in a driveway and drive over them repeatedly, which crushes and often separates the hulls and leaves the nuts intact. Many people seem to think this method is so fantastic that any other option is ridiculous, but I think it reflects the American obsession with motor vehicles. You still need to collect the nuts, move them, dump them, drive over them, get out and check which nuts you've missed, move those back into the tire path, drive back and forth again, check again, repeat until you've gotten most of them, then separate and pick up the nuts by hand, and then, depending on where you've been doing this, clean up the hulls. I don't think it's generally a time saver. And, if done on pavement, this process will put hairline cracks in the nuts, causing them to go bad in storage. But when else do we get to run over things on purpose?

I used to just stomp on the walnuts where they lay on the ground. It worked, and I think I could solidly outperform an automobile operator this way, but it made my leg sore if I did a large quantity of nuts. This led me to devise an efficient method requiring no machinery that I'm currently very satisfied with. Instead of using my foot, I crush the walnuts with a wooden stomper, which does a better job and is much faster and easier. I just zigzag around under the tree, smashing the nuts right where they lay, and almost effortlessly exceed the rate of one nut per second. The only catch is that the nuts have to be at the proper stage of ripeness, where they are beginning to soften but are not yet inky. Sometimes in very soft forest soil the nuts don't get crushed by the stomper—they just get pushed into the ground. If the soil is not firm enough for on-the-spot stomping to work, you can collect them and dump them in another area to work on them.

After stomping, I pick the nuts from the crushed hulls by hand and toss

141

them into a gunnysack. This way, the nuts are only moved once, and the hard part is done right away in the field—and there are no gunnysacks of forgotten or neglected walnuts leaking ink on the back porch.

Handling walnuts brings up a significant problem: the juice of the flesh will stain your skin dark brown. Once it dries, it absolutely *will not* wash out. You will be stuck with "walnut hands" for ten to twenty days. I wear this as a badge of honor every autumn, but in some professions it may be unacceptable. To avoid getting walnut hands, wear rubber gloves whenever you come into contact with the flesh or juice—especially during the process of removing the hulls. I don't do this because I find that the gloves slow me down, but your priorities may differ. If you inadvertently get some juice on your hands, wash them vigorously *right away* and you can prevent most of the discoloration.

Besides staining your skin, heavy exposure to the juice of walnut hulls can also cause soreness, especially under the fingernails. If you get squirted by walnut juice (as might happen if you hit one with a hammer or stick) it is a good idea to wipe or rinse it immediately, as it can cause a burn-like sore, especially where the skin is thin. And of course, you want to avoid getting this juice in your eyes, as it burns intensely and may cause damage.

After removing the hulls, the walnuts will occupy only 20 to 35 percent of their original volume. At this point I give them a float test in a five-gallon bucket,

Hinds walnuts cracked, showing kernels and thick shells.

in batches of about two gallons of nuts at a time. Most of those that float will be bad nuts, but crack a few to be sure, as sometimes the meats are good but have just shrunk a little.

The next step is to dry or "cure" them. I do this in a cardboard box, layering them one or two nuts deep and drying for three to six weeks, shaking the box occasionally to mix the nuts and facilitate even drying. The cardboard will generally absorb the small amount of ink that may run from hull residue that is still attached, but to be safe I like to put them in a place where a small leak would not be a big deal. A thin hull residue will turn the nuts black as it dries, but don't worry about removing it; as long as the nuts dry reasonably fast, the liquid will not seep through and disflavor the meat.

It is possible to eat black walnuts fresh, without curing them. However, most people agree that the flavor is greatly improved by drying. The shrinking and hardening of the nutmeat also makes it easier to extract.

Simply because of their size, black walnuts are more labor efficient to crack and shell than most other wild nuts. A regular nutcracker will not work; these nuts are too large and their shells are too thick. Special heavy-duty nutcrackers are made specifically for black walnuts. I use a hammer, wearing a thin glove on the hand that holds the nut, and a nutpick for removing the pieces of meat. Hit the nut on its flat or narrow side, as hitting the end tends to crack the shell along its suture, which makes the nutmeat hard to get at.

I have been told over and over again that I need to get this or that special black walnut cracker—indeed, I've been mocked for not using one. Having tried several over the years, and having purchased an embarrassingly expensive one that came highly recommended, I have found none that come even close to the efficiency of a skilled hand with a hammer. However, I have seen one (and only one, but I don't know the manufacturer) that, while slower than a hammer, did an excellent job, and seemed to make the meats easier to extract than hammer cracking does. Still, I suggest a hammer, since it is simple and cheap. If you are not skilled or comfortable wielding a hammer, get a special black walnut cracker.

Black walnuts have a unique flavor that is very strong. It is very different from the cultivated English or Persian walnuts that most of us are familiar with. Some people love black walnuts and others hate them. I've been both of these kinds of people. As a child, I liked black walnuts and ate them often. But then, on a "survival" camping trip when I was fourteen, I made a stew of black walnut, wood nettle, and wood sorrel. Not exactly gourmet, but I was hungry enough to like it. However, I came down with mononucleosis that weekend, beginning to feel ill shortly after my second serving of that stew. After that experience, I couldn't stand black walnuts, and it took me ten years to start liking them again.

Whether or not you like black walnuts, their flavor is not easily described and not easily forgotten. I remember giving some to a friend once, at a time when I still didn't like them but had collected them hopefully (and perhaps because I am addicted to foraging). I told him, "They taste terrible, like paint. At least, they taste how paint smells."

After cracking and eating a half dozen, he looked at me and said, "You're right. They do taste like paint. . . . *Really good paint.*"

Of course, the flavor of black walnuts varies somewhat from one tree to another, but it is always strong. And while some people object to the flavor of the nuts by themselves, they have a way of turning baked goodies into outstanding culinary achievements. My liking for black walnuts finally returned some years ago at the Wild Foods Weekend held at North Bend State Park in West Virginia, where I had the opportunity to try brownies, cookies, cake, maple sugar candy, and ice cream containing them. The strong flavor of the black walnuts did not detract from these treats; in fact, it is exactly what made them exceptional. Since then, I have been eating wild walnuts with increasing frequency and appreciation.

Black walnuts, cracked: The eastern black walnut has much larger nuts than any of our native western walnuts.

Arizona walnuts are like black walnuts in miniature.

For many people black walnut is an acquired taste, achieved in the context of familiar sweets where the walnuts act partly as a seasoning while also adding texture, calories, and essential nutrients. My wife disagrees with this; she doesn't like walnuts in baked goods, but finds them acceptable by themselves. Of course, some people hate all nuts, and these folks just might hate black walnuts most of all. But to some epicures, this is the epitome of baking nuts.

I have decided that liking black walnuts is a good thing. I like a wild food with some real subsistence value, and this is where these nuts excel. They are incredibly abundant in many parts of the country, and they are quite easy to gather and at least relatively easy to shell. Once dried, they store well in the shell.

Our four species of western walnut can be used similarly to the eastern black walnut. I have spent many leisure hours along the Gila River in New Mexico gathering Arizona walnuts and cracking them on nearby rocks with a hammerstone. Their flavor is equal to that of the eastern black walnut, and oftentimes the ground under the trees is covered thickly with nuts—even several months after they have fallen. Their only drawback is their small size, making cracking and shelling a time-consuming proposition. The Texas or little walnut is reported to have excellent flavor, but is exceedingly small. I have never tried it. The California walnut is also small, which certainly detracts from its popularity, but it has good flavor. Peattie (1953) says that the kernels of Hinds walnut are "hardly worth eating, compared with those of the eastern Black Walnut," but I strongly disagree. I think the Hinds walnut tastes better, and its thinner shell makes cracking easier, although the smaller size might make up for this advantage. Any wild food cook in California should look for these nuts.

The gourmet black walnut commands high prices in fine stores—when you can find it. Yet every year, millions of pounds of them fall to the ground unwanted, many to be raked from yards and thrown out as trash. Under some trees, the walnuts cover the ground in such abundance that it is hard to walk, and rural roads with overhanging trees often have bushels of them accumulated in neat piles on the shoulder. Even after the insects and rodents have been fed, tons of black walnuts are left to rot. If you want any, there are plenty to go around.

Acorn

Quercus spp. and *Lithocarpus* spp.

Fagaceae – Beech Family

There is no food that means more to me than the acorn, for the acorn fulfills both a promise and a fantasy: that the forest will provide for me. When I gaze across an Ozark valley from a limestone precipice, I see more than scenery. I see thousands of acres of bounty, millions of pounds of delicious food dropped from the crowns of countless trees, waiting to be gathered up by eager hands. I see more food than I could ever eat—more than I can even fathom. A wilderness and an orchard in one.

The world looks different when you eat acorns.

For thousands of years our ancestors subsisted on acorns, living as part of the ecosystems they called home. From the hills of the Fertile Crescent to the great forests of Western Europe, from the coasts of Japan and Korea across the Pacific

Northern red oak, *Quercus rubra*.

to California, from the Eastern Woodlands of North America to the mountains and valleys of Mexico, the acorn was once a cherished food as basic as bread. The oak provided not only the staff of life, but also wood to build homes and tools, fuel for heating and cooking, tannin for making leather, shade, and shelter from the wind. It also fed much of the game that people hunted.

It is no surprise that the oak was widely held sacred. Even our very language hints at the acorn's former importance; no other fruit is given a name different from that of the plant which produces it. We still speak of oaks with a tone of reverence granted to no other tree, occasionally leaving one standing where it proves inconvenient.

Despite their long history as a food source for people over much of the world, acorns are widely believed to be poisonous or inedible. Even more widely, they are despised as being beneath the dignity of human beings to consume. We have no other plant food on Earth subject to a prejudice of such proportion and irony. As agrarian societies conquered the lands of acorn eaters, this prejudice served to dehumanize their enemies—until the world's last acorn-based societies were vanquished by the European-Americans who invaded California in the 19th century.

The acorn is among the most misunderstood and misrepresented of our wild foods. Ancient finds have often been misinterpreted by archeologists with strong preconceived ideas about acorns (Mason, 1992, 1995). Strangely, ethnography, archeology, and the surviving acorn traditions seem scarcely to have affected the accounts in the popular wild food literature, which often contain vague claims, unsupported conjecture, and inaccurate generalizations. Acorns deserve better than this. The following account is based on almost twenty years of experience collecting and eating many hundreds of pounds of acorns from over two dozen species across the United States, as well as extensive literary research. I hope that it can do the topic justice.

Description

An acorn consists of a rather large seed encapsulated by a smooth shell with no surrounding fleshy tissue. The shells are thin compared to those of most other nuts and also differ in being pliable until they are dry. All acorns terminate in a nipple-like point, and all of them are borne in tight-fitting scaly or bristly cups. These cups (also called caps) may cover only the base of the nut or they may enclose it entirely. No other North American fruits or nuts are borne in cups like these.

Acorns are produced by oaks of the genera *Quercus* and *Lithocarpus*, the latter of which only includes one North American species, the tanoak. (While

Acorns come in a surprising variety of shapes, sizes, and colors. Many species in the southern U.S. have very small acorns which are impractical to use. Note the pumpkin-orange flesh of these willow oak *Quercus phellos*.

tanoak may not be a "true" oak, it will be discussed in this account along with the other oaks, since its acorns have been traditionally used just like acorns from *Quercus*.) Eighty to ninety species of oak are found north of Mexico, and there are hundreds of species worldwide. Our oaks are all woody trees or shrubs; many are long-lived forest dominants. Their growth tends to be rugged in appearance, often with large, spreading limbs. Many open-grown oaks are wider than they are tall.

Oak leaves are alternate and rather tough; they vary dramatically in other characteristics. Some species have large, deeply lobed, deciduous leaves, while others have small, entire, evergreen leaves. One characteristic shared by all oaks, however, is the presence of multiple lateral buds clustered around the terminal bud.

Few people notice oak flowers. Appearing in late spring just as the leaves flush, the tiny male flowers grow along short, hanging strands (catkins) from the previous year's growth. The female flowers, comparably minuscule, grow singly or in small clusters from leaf axils of the new year's growth a few inches away. Though they may be green, yellow, or red, oak flowers remain inconspicuous due to their small size and lack of petals.

Members of the genus *Quercus* in North America are often divided into two groups or subgenera: *Lepidobalanus* or section *Quercus* (the white oaks) and *Erythrobalanus* or section *Lobatae* (the red and black oaks). A few oaks are intermediate between these in characteristics, and these are sometimes given their own section, *Protobalanus*. The red and black (hereafter referred to as red) oak group is endemic to the Americas, while the white oak group is found in Eurasia and Africa as well as the New World. Generally, the leaves of the red oaks have pointed lobes ending in a bristle, while those of white oaks have rounded lobes lacking bristle tips. However, some exceptions occur, and this criterion obviously does not work for the many oak species that do not have lobed leaves at all. Members of the white oak group also tend to have lighter-colored, softer, looser bark. The acorns of the two groups are also quite different; this will be discussed in detail later.

Sizes of Selected Acorns

Species	Location of sample and comments	Weight per acorn
Q. alba White oak	Northern Arkansas, average acorns	0.24 oz. 6.8 gm
Q. alba White oak	Northern Arkansas, large acorns	0.32 oz. 9.1 gm
*Q. chrysolepsis Interior live oak	Northern California, large acorns	0.34 oz. 9.6 gm
Q. douglasii Blue oak	Central California, average acorns	0.25 oz. 7.1 gm
Q. falcata Southern red oak	Northern Arkansas	0.03 oz. 0.9 gm
*Q. kelloggii California black oak	Northern California	0.28 oz. 7.9 gm
*Q. kelloggii California black oak	Northern California, large acorns	0.50 oz. 14.2 gm
Q. lobata Valley oak	Central California, from four average trees	0.34 oz. 9.6 gm
*Q. lobata Valley oak	Northern California, large acorns	0.45 oz. 12.8 gm
Q. macrocarpa Bur oak (southern)	Southern Illinois, from two typical trees	0.50 oz. 14.2 gm
Q. macrocarpa Bur oak (southern)	Southern Illinois, small sample of largest nuts	1.40 oz. 39.7 gm
Q. michauxii Swamp chestnut oak	Northern Missouri, from two average trees	0.40 oz. 11.3 gm
Q. muhlenbergii Chinkapin oak	Northern Arkansas	0.07 oz. 2.0 gm
Q. rubra Northern red oak	Northern Arkansas, tree with large acorns	0.41 oz. 11.6 gm
Q. shumardii Shumard oak	Northern Arkansas, tree with large acorns	0.21 oz. 6.0 gm
Q. stellata Post oak	Northern Arkansas	0.05 oz. 1.4 gm
*Lithocarpus densiflorus Tanoak	Northern California, acorns slightly dry	0.23 oz. 6.5 gm

The weights in this chart were determined by weighing acorns in batches with a postal scale and calculating averages. The acorns were collected from 2006 to 2008. I tried to use only sound, viable acorns that had lost minimal weight to drying. These acorns were collected by my wife and me, except for the samples marked with an asterisk, which were collected by Matt Nelson.

The variability in weight can be extreme within a single species. Also, note that the largest acorns in this chart are 44 times larger than the smallest.

The spreading arms of open-grown oaks, such as this bur oak, are a welcome sight around the world.

Descriptions of Individual Species

There are too many oaks in North America for me to describe each one, and that would start to get boring anyway. Instead, I'll just mention those whose acorns I think are most likely to be collected—generally because they are large, abundant, or widespread. This does not mean you should not use other kinds of acorns; all of them are edible.

White Oak Group – Section *Quercus (Lepidobalanus)*

White oak *Quercus alba*: White oak inhabits almost all of the woodlands of the eastern United States, from eastern Texas to Minnesota and eastward, as well as the southern reaches of Quebec and Ontario. Often a dominant tree, the white oak commonly reaches 70–100 feet (20–30 m) in height. The attractive leaves are deeply and elegantly lobed. White oak is not very shade tolerant and prefers well-drained soil, where it commonly grows alongside other oaks, hickories, white ash, white pine, tuliptree, beech, sweetgum, black gum, and black cherry. This is the most abundant oak in North America.

The acorns drop from late August to mid-October, with the peak from mid-September to early October. White oak acorns are remarkably variable in size and shape; the larger ones are good for collecting. The caps are relatively small, and

White oak, with its scaly, light gray bark, is the most prevalent hardwood tree in the eastern U.S.

the shells are a dark purple-brown and somewhat glossy, making white oak a particularly attractive acorn. Due to its abundance, this oak is among the most commonly used.

Valley oak, California white oak *Quercus lobata*: This is the largest of our western species, known to exceed 100 feet (30 m) in height and 5 feet (1.5 m) in diameter. Open-grown individuals develop a massive, spreading crown. Valley oak is very much the western counterpart of the previous species, only its range is much more limited. It is confined to the valleys and foothills of the inner and middle coastal ranges of California, where it grows in deep, rich, fertile soils. Vast stands have been cleared to make way for farmland, but this remains among the best-known trees of California.

Valley oak's bark is light gray and develops broad, flattened ridges on older trees. The leaves are rather small and broad with large, rounded lobes and moderately deep sinuses. The distinctive long, narrow, tapering acorns, with small cups covering only the base, are among the largest in North America, and this oak produces the heaviest crops I have ever seen. They can be gathered with remarkable ease and are popular with foragers, but they dry very slowly, making them prone to spoilage.

below left Valley oak, fruiting branch.
below right Valley oak's distinctly shaped acorns are one of our largest.

Swamp white oak leaves.

Swamp white oak _Quercus bicolor_: This is a rather large oak of river floodplains in the east-central and northeastern United States, reaching its greatest abundance in the rich agricultural sections of the lower Midwest. The bark of swamp white oak has long, peeling plates like white oak, while the two-toned leaves, with shallow lobes or large teeth, are more like a cross between those of bur oak and chestnut oak. This oak differs from potentially confusing species such as swamp chestnut oak in that its acorns are borne on peduncles many times their length.

The acorns of this species average somewhat larger than those of the white oak. If you can find a productive grove and avoid the poison ivy that almost always abounds under this tree, swamp white oak is an excellent acorn to gather. It typically ripens a little later than white and bur oaks in the same area.

Bur oak _Quercus macrocarpa_: This majestic tree grows in the central and eastern United States and adjacent Canada. Its range also extends south through the eastern half of the Great Plains into central Texas, and north several hundred miles into Manitoba—farther north than any other oak on our continent. Bur oak grows in bottomland forests but also tolerates harsh, dry prairie conditions where few other large trees survive. Its bark is thick and corky, imparting fire resistance, and the twigs of open-grown saplings are often encapsulated with a thick layer of cork to protect them from prairie fires. Bur oak's leaves are dark green on top and silvery beneath, often making it appear to change color when

Bur oak acorns get larger as one travels south. Those shown here were collected about 400 miles apart and do not represent either extreme in size.

the wind blows. The broad leaves are shallowly lobed toward the end but have a few deep sinuses near the base.

In the northernmost part of its range, bur oak acorns are quite small, but in the southern part of its range this tree produces the largest acorns in North America, occasionally larger than golf balls. The problem with bur oak, however, is that the cup, fringed with harmless "burs," often encloses most of the acorn. When this is the case, it is laborious to remove the nut. This sometimes outweighs the benefit of the larger size. These oval-shaped acorns typically fall before other species in the same area, from late August through September. Their color is drab gray-brown and they often become rippled soon after falling. The nutmeats dry out very slowly compared to those of most other acorns, and large ones should be shelled immediately.

Overcup oak *Quercus lyrata*: This oak is found in bottomlands, swamps, and floodplains in the southeastern United States, from Texas to Florida, north to New Jersey and Illinois. It can grow to 90 feet (27 m) in height and tends to form a broad, spreading crown. The distinct leaves may grow 6–10 inches (15–25 cm) long and have a small number of well-spaced, medium-length lobes. The acorns are equally distinct. Nearly spherical, they are completely or almost completely enclosed in their cups. While rather large, these acorns are annoying to use because of the cup that envelops them.

The leaves and acorns of overcup oak are very distinctive.

Blue oak *Quercus douglasii*: This is one of the most common oaks in California, ranging through most of the state. Blue oak inhabits hot, dry foothills in the interior, often forming savannas and woodlands where it is the primary component. It commonly attains 60 feet (18 m) in height and 2 feet (60 cm) in diameter, with a short trunk and broad, spreading crown. The leaves are deciduous, small, and dark bluish-green on top, typically from 1.5–3.5 inches (4–9 cm) in length. They may be entire with wavy margins, they may have a few large, rounded teeth, or they may be shallowly lobed.

Blue oak's dark brown, smooth, attractive, egg-shaped acorns generally ripen in October. While not as large as those of valley oak, they are still good-sized and abundant.

below left Blue oak acorns and leaves. **below right** Rugged form of blue oak, the most common species in California, with typical oak landscape in the background.

Chestnut oak, rock oak *Quercus montana*: This is a medium-sized oak of the eastern United States from Alabama and Georgia north to New England; its range is centered around the Appalachians. Chestnut oak grows on well-drained sites in dry-mesic stands. It is very abundant on rocky slopes and ridges, earning it the alternate name of *rock oak*. The trunks, tall and narrow on forest trees, are covered by dark brown bark that is distinctly ridged—it is one member of the white-oak group with bark that looks typical of the red oak group. The leaves of chestnut oak lack lobes but have large, rounded teeth along their margins. This shape, reminiscent of a chestnut leaf, accounts for the tree's name. Ironically, this oak grows in the same habitat once dominated by the American chestnut, and has now largely replaced it throughout much of its former range.

Chestnut oak leaves.

The acorns of chestnut oak are rather large and somewhat elongated, borne in a cup that covers almost half the nut. In years of heavy crop they can be quite easily gathered. (Note: this tree, along with the next species and one other, is sometimes called *Q. prinus*, a confusing name that has never been consistently applied. The name *Q. prinus* is better avoided and is now largely abandoned.)

Swamp chestnut oak, cow oak, basket oak *Quercus michauxii*: This is a tree of bottomlands and other moist, rich areas of the southeastern United States, from eastern

above Chestnut oak is unusual among the white oak group in that its bark has dark, hard ridges.

below Leaves and large acorns of swamp chestnut oak.

above left Gambel's oak looks much like the eastern white oak.

above right Oregon white oak leaves in early summer.

Texas to northern Florida, north to southern Illinois and New Jersey—a range that almost mirrors that of the overcup oak. It is found in the company of other impressive nut trees, such as bur oak, pecan, and shellbark hickory. The scaly, light gray bark resembles that of white oak, while the broad leaves with large teeth are somewhat reminiscent of chestnut oak leaves, although they are broader toward the tips. This is a large species with tall form, exceeding 100 feet (30 m) in height and 4 feet (120 cm) in diameter.

The oval or elliptic acorns of swamp chestnut oak are among the largest in North America and are often produced abundantly. They can be gathered with ease, and their large size will save time in shelling. Although somewhat smaller than southern bur oak acorns, the nuts of swamp chestnut oak readily fall out of their small cups, making them much easier to process. This acorn should be sought by those who live within its range. They should be shelled immediately because they dry slowly.

Gambel's oak, Rocky Mountain white oak *Quercus gambelii*: This is the most common oak in the Rockies in Utah, Colorado, Arizona, and New Mexico, and in many areas it is the only oak. The Gambel's oak grows in foothills, canyons, valleys, and on middle to lower slopes, sometimes forming dense thickets. It is typically a small to medium-sized tree, occasionally reaching 60 feet (18 m). The medium-sized, deeply lobed leaves resemble those of the eastern white oak, as does the bark.

Although the acorns of Gambel's oak are small to medium in size, they are often highly appreciated where they are found, since they may be the only acorns available.

Oregon white oak, Garry oak *Quercus garryana*: This species is native to the Pacific Northwest from the environs of Vancouver, BC, south to central California, mostly within 200 miles of the coast. Growing on lower mountain slopes, in valleys, and on rocky or coarse-soiled areas near the coast, Oregon white oak inhabits dry sites where larger, moisture-loving trees are challenged. This tree is rather small and gnarled in appearance, and its deeply lobed leaves resemble those of valley oak, but are larger.

Oregon white oak, like Gambel's oak, is the only oak species over much of its range. Even if this were not so, the somewhat elongated nuts are rather large and would still be an excellent choice for collecting.

Arizona oak, Arizona white oak *Quercus arizonica*: This is perhaps the largest oak of the Southwest, forming a broad, rounded crown. Arizona oak is found in central and southeastern Arizona, southern New Mexico, and far western Texas. In this region there are a number of gnarly oaks with small, unlobed, leathery leaves and small acorns, and Arizona oak fits this

Arizona oak acorns are small, but other species in the Southwest are even smaller. The nutmeats occasionally have purple flesh, especially when under-ripe.

Most Southwestern oaks are small and scrubby, but Arizona oak can become a large tree. They may be hard to see, but there are five javelinas eating acorns under this one.

description. The leaves may be entire or have sharply toothed margins; they are almost evergreen, not falling until spring a few months before the new leaves appear. The acorns of this common oak are not very large but are among the largest in this region. They typically ripen in October.

Live oak, southern live oak *Quercus virginiana*: Live oak is among the most cherished trees of the Deep South. It grows along the Coastal Plain from

southern Virginia to southern Florida, and west to central Texas, inhabiting moist sandy or rich soils. Live oak is well known for its spreading form and tendency to support garlands of Spanish moss.

Live oak is an evergreen with small to medium-sized, blunt-tipped, obovate to oblanceolate, usually entire leaves 1.5–4 inches (4–10 cm) long. The acorns are dark brown and egg-shaped or somewhat elongated, often with a narrow base and very small disk. Although small to medium in size, live oak acorns are often produced in great abundance.

Southern live oak, acorns and leaves.

Red Oak Group – Section *Lobatae (Erythrobalanus)*

Northern red oak, red oak *Quercus rubra*: This is an abundant and widespread tree, rivaling white oak in economic and ecological importance. Found in all of

the United States east of the Great Plains, except for the Deep South, red oak ranges north to northern Minnesota, central Ontario, Nova Scotia, and New Brunswick—farther north than any but the bur oak. Its form is tall and graceful for an oak. Northern red oak grows best on well-drained soils with high fertility and adequate moisture. It is associated with white oak, white ash, bitternut hickory, beech, tuliptree, sweetgum, sugar maple, black cherry, white pine, bigtooth aspen, and birch. It is the most shade-tolerant among our oaks. The dark gray bark starts out smooth with long, shallow fissures, but as the tree ages it gets thicker and rougher. The leaves are large with prominent, broad, pointed lobes.

Northern red oak trunk. Most members of the red oak group have hard and blocky rather than peeling bark.

Northern red oak produces medium to large acorns that fall primarily in late September and October. It has heavy crops of nuts compared to most other oaks. Because of their abundance and size they are an excellent species to collect.

Shumard oak *Quercus shumardii*: This is a large, beautiful oak of the southern half of the eastern United States, where it most often grows on well-drained sites along rivers and valleys. The leaves resemble those of the northern red oak but are broader with longer lobes. This species replaces the northern red oak in the Deep South; the two share territory over much of the South and the lower Midwest.

Shumard oak branch ready to drop food.

The acorns of Shumard oak average slightly smaller than those of northern red oak, but they are still worth collecting, especially since most of the southern oaks of the red oak group have tiny acorns. Shumard oak is also a very prolific nut producer.

California black oak *Quercus kelloggii*: This oak is confined to California and southwestern Oregon. It grows at low to middle elevations on mountain slopes, often in association with ponderosa pine, sugar pine, Oregon white oak, tanoak, redwood, sequoia, and madrone. California black oak grows as much as 4 feet (120 mm) thick and 80 feet (24 m) tall and tends to develop a broad, spreading form. The bark is dark brown or gray and smooth at first but develops thick, irregular plates as the tree ages. The leaves are larger than those of other California oaks and have long, broad, bristle-tipped lobes. They look very much like the leaves of red, Shumard, or eastern black oak, but are distinct among California oaks; no other western oak has deep sinuses and point-tipped lobes.

California black oak acorns are among the largest in North America. The cups enclose about half the nut. They often produce heavily, and when this is the case they can be

California black oak leaves cannot be mistaken for those of any other western oak.

Immature acorns on black oak
Q. velutina.

The small but attractive acorns of pin oak.

Acorns and leaves of coast live oak.

collected remarkably fast. Black oak acorns fall in September and October. They were once the staple food for several Native American peoples, and this culinary tradition is carried on by some today. This is a highly preferred acorn. It has soft flesh, dries readily, and seems less susceptible to spoilage than other large acorns.

Black oak *Quercus velutina* This is a common, widespread oak of dry soils in most of the eastern United States; its resemblance to California black oak is striking. Often confused with northern red oak, the leaves of black oak tend to be shorter and wider with one fewer set of lobes. The bark is also blockier and the shape less graceful than northern red oak. Black oak's acorns are much smaller than those of its west coast counterpart, but they are sometimes abundant. They dry readily and can be practical to shell with the water separation method explained later.

Pin oak *Quercus palustris*: A widely planted street tree, even outside of its broad native range in the eastern states, pin oak has a distinct, almost conifer-like form. Its natural habitat is river floodplains. The leaves have very deep sinuses and long, narrow lobes. The attractively striped acorns are small but often very abundant. Like black oak, they dry extremely well due to their size but are only practical to shell if water-separation is employed.

Interior live oak *Quercus wislizenii*: This is a short, stout, tree of foothills and dry mountain slopes of California. It has a densely branched, broad-spreading crown. Interior live oak often grows with gray pine and blue oak. The tiny evergreen leaves are ovate or lanceolate and may be entire or coarsely toothed. The medium to large acorns are very elongated and taper to a point. They are about half enclosed in their cups.

Coast live oak *Quercus agrifolia*: These medium-sized trees resemble the interior live oak but grow slightly taller and have larger leaves, up to 4 inches long. The evergreen leaves are tough

160

and holly-like, with margins that may be entire but are typically spiny. Coast live oak inhabits the slopes and valleys of California's coastal mountains, where it often forms pure stands. Coast live oak produces medium to large acorns that are elongated and taper gradually to a point. Unlike most other members of the red oak group, the acorns mature in a single season. They are a good species to gather when they produce well.

Emory oak *Quercus emoryi.* This is a small to medium-sized scrubby evergreen oak of Arizona, New Mexico, and the Trans-Pecos region of Texas. It grows in canyons, foothills, and lower mountain slopes, often accompanied by Arizona oak, silverleaf oak, alligator juniper, and pinyon pines. It can be identified by its small, stiff, shiny, evergreen leaves, which are broadest at the base, pointed at the tip, and usually have a small number of very prominent teeth. The acorns are about 0.5–0.7 inch (13–18 mm) long and cone-shaped with pointed tips. Although these acorns are small, they are produced abundantly and are reputed to be the best tasting in the region. They usually fall earlier than those of the nearby Arizona oak, and sometimes dry out while sitting on the ground beneath the tree. This species is unusual among the red oak group in that its acorns ripen in one year; for this reason it had been formerly placed among the white oaks by some authors.

Emory oak leaves.

Intermediate Oaks – section *Protobalanus*

Canyon live oak, Canyon oak *Quercus chrysolepis*: This is an extremely variable species, ranging from shrubby in form to a tall, slender tree. It grows best in canyons and deep, cool valleys but is also found on exposed ridges and cliffs. Canyon oak can become an enormous, spreading tree under the right conditions, reaching 10 feet (3 m) in diameter. This tree's range is primarily in California and southern Arizona, but it also extends a little into southwestern New Mexico, southern Nevada, and southwestern Oregon. The evergreen leaves are 1–3 inches (2.5–8 cm) long and can have smooth, toothed, or spiny margins. They are noted for their attractive yellow-green color.

The acorns of this species ripen over two years. They are oblong and variable in size, sometimes growing quite large. Their cups are very distinct; thick

Canyon oak acorns in their distinctive golden cups.

161

and shallow, they are covered with fine golden hairs when the acorns are still growing—the whole thing looks almost like an acorn propped up in a fuzzy, golden donut.

Tanoaks – *Genus Lithocarpus*

Tanoak *Lithocarpus densiflorus*: Tanoak is a moderately large tree of fertile seaward slopes in southwestern Oregon and much of coastal California. It commonly grows with redwoods. Large specimens will exceed 100 feet (30 m) in height, although the crowns tend to be narrow. The medium-sized evergreen

leaves are ovate or elliptic with sharply toothed margins. The twigs are notably hairy.

Tanoak is a prolific producer of medium to large acorns, which have been widely used by California native peoples. The acorns rest in a cup, as do those of the true oaks, but these cups are bristly, reminiscent of the husks of chestnut. These nuts dry readily. The acorn meat is very bitter before leaching. It is also exceptionally soft, which makes it easier to pound or grind. These acorns leach extremely well.

Dead leaf and acorn of tanoak, on redwood duff. Note the bristly cups. This acorn is rotten.

Red, White, and Tan

Acorns come in three basic types, those of the red oak group, those of the white oak group, and tanoak. (Throughout the rest of this chapter, I will say "white acorns" or "red acorns" in reference to their respective groups. When referring specifically to the individual species, I will use the whole species name, such as "northern red oak acorn" and "bur oak acorn.") The white and red groups differ far more than many would expect; in every step of harvesting and processing they need to be treated a little differently. For the purposes of our discussion, canyon live oak (considered intermediate between white and red oaks) will be lumped in with the red group, for its acorns are most similar to that group.

White acorns mature in one year; that is, they flower in spring, and the fertilized flowers develop into acorns that mature in the summer or fall. Red oaks likewise flower in the spring, but on most of them, the fertilized flowers develop into tiny embryonic acorns or *acornets* that remain on the twig unchanged for a year. In the following spring, the acornet begins to grow, maturing into a ripe

below left Red oak twig with flowers. The male flowers droop in long strands. The female flowers can be seen in the axils of the newly forming leaves above. Acornets fertilized last spring are below on last year's growth; they will reach maturity the coming fall.

below right With white oaks the male and female flowers are also borne separately, but the acorns will mature in one season.

acorn by late summer or autumn. This two-year ripening is highly unusual among temperate plants.

The fact that red acorns take two years to mature has been twisted into a very common misconception that the tree only produces acorns every other year. This is simply untrue; ripe acorns and acornets will be found on the tree at the same time, and some acorns will ripen every year. The acornets will always be found on the most recent season's growth, while the mature acorns will be behind them on growth from the season before. Contrarily, white acorns are borne on the present season's growth.

With a few exceptions, white acorns sprout within a few weeks of ripening. Red acorns, however, don't sprout until the spring following their ripening. This difference in germination strategies corresponds to significant differences in the physical properties of the two kinds of acorn, as expressed in the following chart. Some of the listed differences are largely incidental; the most important distinctions for the *balanophage* (a fancy term for acorn eater) are microscopic. Red and white acorns differ in composition and structure, thus they differ in hardness, texture, flavor, drying time, and permeability.

left Winter twig of red oak. With red oaks you can assess the number of acornets during the winter and predict the crop next autumn.

below This red oak acorn is germinating in May. This delayed germination probably accounts for most of the differences between the two types of acorn.

Which Acorns Are Best?

In the wild food literature it is frequently claimed that white acorns are better for eating than red acorns, or even that Native Americans preferred the white acorns. Ignore these statements. They are not based on ethnographic study, or on the experience of people subsisting on acorns. This idea is derived from the false assumption that the flavor of a raw acorn is the only important criteria in determining which kind to use. It is actually almost irrelevant.

Many Native American cultures subsisted on red acorns as their primary food source. The ethnographic evidence *does not* show a preference for white acorns; if anything, it indicates the opposite. For example, the most highly preferred acorns in California were the California black oak and tanoak (Heizer and Elsasser, 1980). An examination of the ethnographic evidence indicates that the most important factors in determining which acorns were used for subsistence were *size* and *availability*.

My own experience corroborates these observations. After thorough leaching, both red and white acorns are palatable and wholesome. I have not found it significantly more easy to thoroughly leach white acorns—despite frequent presumptions that this is the case. In fact, the red acorns seem to leach more easily—probably because of their softer tissues. There are many other factors, such as size, ease of harvest, ease of cracking, storability, and availability that are far more important considerations than the initial tannin content. I do not recommend red or white acorns; each group has advantages and disadvantages relative to the other. Seek the largest or most abundant acorns available and develop your own preferences and techniques from experience.

Tanoak *Lithocarpus densiflorus* deserves special mention. The acorns of this species have very different qualities from red or white acorns. In my opinion, tanoak acorns are the best for eating. They leach much more easily and thoroughly than any other acorn I have tried, and the final product has a better flavor. I would preferentially use them if they grew in my area.

About Tannin

If you pick up an acorn and eat it, you will most likely find it bitter, astringent, and inedible. Although these nuts have served as a staple food for thousands of years, they were and are generally eaten only after leaching to remove their bitterness. Tannin is what makes acorns and many other plant foods bitter. It is found in some quantity in nearly all plant material: it makes apples tart, chokecherries puckery, and coffee and tea bitter. Tannin is an everyday part of the human diet, and consumption of small amounts is not only safe, but probably beneficial due to tannin's action as an antioxidant (Meyers et al., 2006). Tannin is also considered a mild toxin because in large amounts it can

Tannin Content of Various Acorn Samples

Species	Tannin %	Source
Red oaks		
Q. agrifolia	20.3	Koenig and Heck, 1988
Q. agrifolia	19.6	Koenig and Benedict, 2002
Q. chrysolepsis*	9.1	Koenig and Heck, 1988
Q. coccinea	6.7	Korstian, 1927
Q. ilicifolia	11.3	Waino and Forbes, 1941
Q. kelloggii	2.9	Wagnon, 1946
Q. rubra	7.4	Korstian, 1927
Q. rubra	9.8	Waino and Forbes, 1941
Q. wislizenii	6.6	Wagnon, 1946
White oaks		
Q. alba	4.4	Henry, 1950
Q. alba	4.4	Korstian, 1927
Q. alba	3.3	Servello & Kirkpatrick, 1989
Q. alba	5.6	Waino and Forbes, 1941
Q. douglasii	6.1	Wagnon, 1946
Q. douglasii	31.2	Koenig and Benedict, 2002
Q. dumosa	9.4	Wagnon, 1946
Q. lobata	7.2	Chestnut, 1974
Q. lobata	10.9	Koenig and Heck, 1988
Q. lobata	4.1	Wagnon, 1946
Q. lobata	5.7	Koenig and Benedict, 2002
Q. prinoides	4.4	Waino and Forbes, 1941
Q. montana†	7.8	Korstian, 1927
Q. montana†	8.9	Korstian, 1927
Q. montana†	8.1	Servello & Kirkpatrick, 1989
Q. montana†	8.8	Trimble, 1986
Q. montana†	10.4	Waino and Forbes, 1941
Q. ilex‡	0.4–0.5	Mazueles Vela et al., 1967

Unfortunately, relatively few analyses have been done to determine the tannin content of acorns. I have included only those believed to be from acorn cotyledons (shells removed). There are several methods used to determine tannin levels in acorns, and these do not necessarily produce comparable results.

* This species is not a member of either group, but is more similar to the red oaks.

† This species was reported as Q. prinus, an invalid name, in the original source.

‡ For comparison, I have included *Q. ilex*, a Mediterranean species with low tannin content.

damage the mucus membranes of the digestive system. It is also classed as an *antinutrient* because it interferes with the body's absorption and utilization of minerals and protein. For these reasons, consumption of tannin must be limited.

Tannin is not a specific chemical; it is a group of many similar chemicals. Tannins are large-moleculed organic acids which bind to dissolved proteins. There are hydrolizable (water-soluble) and non-hydrolizable tannins. When you eat or drink something with dissolved tannin, the tannin binds with the proteins on the surfaces of your mucus membranes, which causes the cells to contract and the tissues to tighten. This process and feeling is called *astringency*, a characteristic of all tannins. Tannins also chelate free mineral ions such as calcium, phosphorus, potassium, and magnesium. Once they are chelated by the tannin, these minerals are unavailable to the body and pass from the system unused.

The Myth of the Sweet Acorn

I have been told over and over again about this or that species of oak with "sweet" acorns that can be eaten directly from the tree without being leached. Indeed, you can enjoy a few acorns from some trees. But after that, your mouth begins to pucker and the nuts seem more and more bitter. Grind and boil these same "sweet" acorns into porridge, and you probably wouldn't get past a few bites. Use them for flour, and you can bake bread that nobody likes. But a nut or two is pretty good, especially on a long hike. Acorns have a magical way of raising our hopes like this. The "sweet acorn," the acorn that doesn't need to be leached, is the Holy Grail of wild foods. Such acorns may be native to Israel or Portugal, but not here. Dream of these tannin-free acorns if you wish, hope if you like, but don't waste your time looking for them. No acorn myth has bred more disillusionment.

I fell into this trap for many years. I collected bur oak acorns and no others because one of my books said they were the only acorn that didn't require leaching. (Since then I have heard this exclusive claim also made for valley, chestnut, swamp chestnut, southern live, white, Emory, and swamp white oak. I have eaten every one of these acorns, and they all taste about the same to me, and all of them need to be leached.) I made bread, muffins, pancakes, and cookies with unleached bur oak flour and tried really hard to like them, but I couldn't. Neither did my family or friends. I eventually decided that acorns just weren't very good to eat, and stopped harvesting them.

A few years later, on a camping trip, I leached some red oak acorns—which I had read were far too bitter to use—just for the heck of it, expecting total disappointment. I made biscuits, and everybody liked them. Since then I have leached every kind of acorn, and people have generally liked the products made

167

above On the bottom right are the two cotyledons of a valley oak (white group); on the bottom left are the cotyledons of a California black oak (red group). Across the top, from left to right, are cotyledons of northern red oak (red group), tanoak (neither group), and swamp chestnut oak (white group). Note that the cotyledons of white acorns are roughly symmetrical, while those of red acorns are distinctly asymmetrical.

below Here we have the same kinds of acorns: valley and swamp chestnut on top, tanoak to the left, California black on the lower right, and northern red (small one in the center). The testa adheres to the red acorns, but not the white, and you can see that the red acorns have a deep groove in one or both cotyledons.

Characteristics of the Red and White Acorn Groups

Red	White
Mature in two years; ripe acorns borne on last year's growth; acornets on current year's growth	Mature in one year, ripe acorns borne on this year's growth; no acornets
Cups scaly	Cups bristly
Germinate the spring after falling	Usually germinate immediately after falling in autumn
Shell interior with fuzzy lining	Shell interior lacks fuzzy lining
Cotyledons (acorn halves) rarely equal, often fused, typically meeting with curved or angled surfaces	Cotyledons typically equal, not fused, meeting with smooth, flat surfaces
Cotyledon surfaces typically have one or more deep grooves	Cotyledon surfaces without deep grooves
Testa adherent, fuzzy	Testa usually flakes off easily
Flesh more permeable to moisture; dries and moistens much more rapidly	Flesh less permeable to moisture; dries and moistens much more slowly
Softer when dried	Harder when dried
Fresh kernels contain less water, shrink less in drying	Fresh kernels contain more water, shrink more in drying
3–20% tannin	3–30% tannin
15–30% oil	2–11% oil
3–8% protein	6–9% protein
Fresh kernels cream, yellow, to bright orange	Fresh kernels cream, sometimes purple

from them. Yet I still regularly meet people who excitedly claim to have made something delicious from some kind of "sweet acorn" that doesn't require leaching. When I have tried these foods, I have invariably found them disgusting, unless the acorns were used in a small proportion mixed with other flours, or masked with lots of sugar. If you are going to use nominal amounts of acorn in baked goods, it is possible not to leach them—although the tannin will still detract from the quality. But this chapter is about subsistence, which means using acorns as a food, not a coloring. This requires leaching.

Which Acorns Have Less Tannin?

It is commonly stated that white acorns are low in tannin and red acorns are high. This statement is much simpler than the truth and is not supported by chemical analyses. A much more reasonable statement is that both groups have tannin levels ranging from low to high, with tannin content of red acorns averaging somewhat higher. Looking at the tannin chart, you can see that there is great variability within both groups and within species. The highest tannin content I find reported for any acorn is from *Q. douglasii*, a member of the white oak group.

It you taste acorns of various species and compare their flavor to their composition, you can easily see that tannin content does not strongly correspond to the bitterness or astringency of the acorns. All white acorns taste about the same, regardless of tannin content. Likewise, all red acorns taste roughly the same, regardless of tannin content. Yet the flavor of the two groups is completely different, with red acorns consistently tasting less sweet and more astringent. A blue or chestnut oak, with high tannin levels, will usually taste less astringent than a California black oak, with rather low levels of tannin. While the astringency is caused by tannin, something more is going on here.

I hypothesize that white acorns taste less bitter because, due to the structure of their tissue on a microscopic level, the tannin is not released or dissolved in saliva as readily as the tannin from red acorns. This explanation finds strong empirical support. The slow drying and rehydrating of white acorns compared to red indicates that the white acorns are indeed less permeable to moisture, and therefore their tannin would dissolve in saliva less readily. Perhaps the tannins are stored in *hydrophobic vacuoles*—small pockets that repel water. Tannin stored in such structures would not dissolve unless the vacuoles were damaged or destroyed, such as through grinding or boiling. My observations fit this hypothesis as well, for white acorns that taste almost palatable from the tree seem to become much more bitter when ground into flour or boiled into mush.

In any case, the substantial differences in hardness, texture, and drying time make it certain that *something* about the tissue structure of the two types of acorns is significantly different.

Harvest

Depending on the species and location, acorns ripen from late summer through fall. The mature acorn is eventually dropped by the tree, but it may be held for several weeks after ripening. Acorns remaining on the tree can be identified as ripe if they will detach easily from their caps. You can pluck acorns directly from the twigs, but this method is time consuming. It is much more effective to use a heavy stick thrown forcefully into the limbs to loosen the acorns. You can also get the acorns down by climbing the tree and shaking the branches.

If the crop is heavy, it is most efficient to collect acorns after they have fallen of their own accord. Even at a leisurely pace I can fill a five-gallon bucket with medium-sized acorns under a typical tree in about an hour. Under ideal conditions I have gathered five gallons in ten minutes. When collecting, you'll greatly increase your speed if you toss the acorns into a shallow, open container like a small wash basin rather than directly into a tall bucket or gunnysack. (Depending on species, five gallons of fresh acorns produces twelve to eighteen pounds of dried, shelled nutmeat, or about eight calorie-days for an average person.) Because acorns store very well and the crop is extremely variable from one year to the next, it makes sense to gather a lot of them in good years.

"Mast Years" and Predators: Understanding the Acorn Crop

Anybody with an oak tree in the yard, or who pays any attention in the woods, knows that the acorn crop varies dramatically from year to year. One October the acorns will pop beneath the tires, form little piles in the street gutters, and make it treacherous to walk barefoot; the next two autumns there are few or none to be seen. Why? This is an essential part of the oak's survival strategy.

If the acorn crop were the same every year, the populations of the animals that eat them would stabilize at levels such that nearly every acorn produced would get eaten every fall. However, if there are almost no acorns for two years, the populations of squirrels, jays, mice, chipmunks, and especially acorn weevils

Acorns are just beginning to fall from this valley oak, which has produced an enormous crop. However, most of the acorns are infected with insect larvae.

will plummet. When a heavy crop comes the following year, there simply will not be enough consumers to eat all the acorns, guaranteeing that many of them will germinate. The poor seasons "train" the animals to prepare for scarcity, so that when a bumper crop comes, they hoard and cache more than they can possibly eat. Some of these acorns will always be forgotten, or their proprietors will pass away before dining on them, leaving them to germinate. This is how the oaks get their payment for feeding all those creatures.

The primary factor controlling the fluctuating productivity of acorns is the weather at the time of flowering. Although it seems counterintuitive at first, oaks are programmed to flower at a time when their flowers are likely to be destroyed by frost or go unpollinated due to wet weather. This is the easiest way to genetically produce the random crop fluctuation that the trees need. Oaks do not have heavy crops or "mast years" in any predictable pattern; a tree or stand may produce poorly or prolifically in consecutive years. However, there are rarely two true bumper crops in a row, perhaps because the trees cannot afford to invest this much energy into acorn production every year. Furthermore, the surge in populations of acorn-eating animals will make the nuts harder to obtain in each productive year that follows.

Acorn Weevils and Grubs

If you gather a bucket full of acorns and let it sit for a few days, you will find that many of the nuts develop holes in their shells. On the bottom of the pail there will be a surprising number of short, light-colored, legless grubs. These are the larvae of acorn weevils, and they are the bane of balanophages everywhere. In the eyes of many, these "worms" or "grubs" are the most frustrating part of using acorns. In some years these insects destroy the majority of the crop.

There are two genera of acorn weevils: *Curculio* (formerly called *Balaninus*) and *Conotrachelus*. Within each genus there are multiple species, and their relative importance varies by region and species of oak under concern. Some of these weevils feed exclusively on acorns, while others also attack hazel, chestnut, and other nut species. Since the life cycles of these various acorn weevils are substantially similar, we will lump them together for this discussion.

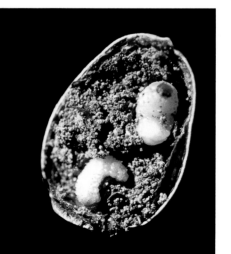

The adult weevil uses its long snout to make a hole in the acorn, into which the egg is deposited. These holes are tiny and inconspicuous; you are not likely to notice them.

Weevil larvae and the acorn they have ruined. Photo by Mike Krebill.

The egg hatches a few days later, and the larvae waste no time consuming the meat of the acorn. When it reaches full size, about 0.4 inch (1 cm), the "grub" chews an exit hole in the shell. (These are the small, round holes commonly seen in acorns, which many people mistakenly believe are *entry* holes.) Because acorn weevil larvae are soft and legless, they are able to work their way out through holes with a much smaller diameter than their bodies. After leaving the acorn, the grubs burrow under leaf litter and into the soil, where they pupate and spend the next ten months underground. They emerge as adult weevils in late summer or early autumn to seek acorns to infect, beginning the cycle again.

Some weevils lay their eggs in acorns as they are still growing upon the tree, while others lay their eggs in fallen acorns. Some do both. As an acorn harvester, you obviously want to avoid collecting weevil-infested or "wormy" acorns. In the novice collector's pail, it is likely that 20 to 70 percent of the acorns will be wormy. But armed with the proper knowledge you can almost completely eliminate the grub problem.

Acorn Inspection:
Separating the Good From the Bad During Collection

Weevils eat every kind of acorn; if you feel like you have observed otherwise, it is only coincidence. If you read about traditional Miwok acorn collection in *It Will Live Forever* (Ortiz, 1991) you will notice no mention of "floating" acorns to identify the bad ones, or of roasting them to kill the grubs. Instead, Julia Parker simply picks up the good ones and leaves the bad ones. Yes, it is that simple, and it *is* possible to tell. Infected acorns exhibit visible clues or defects indicating that they contain weevil larvae. Once you learn to read these clues you will be able to spot bad acorns instantly. After some practice, acorn inspection will be an automatic part of collecting, and your gathering container will fill up almost exclusively with sound nuts.

The defects to look for are listed below, with the most important ones first. Most of these defects are caused by weevil larvae, but some may indicate other reasons for rejection as well. Many are observed in the "disk"—the light-colored area where the acorn was attached to its cap while growing. The disk will often show signs of infection long before other parts of the nut.

Defects:

1. **Attached cup:** This is an easily observed and reliable indicator of worthlessness. Ripe acorns loosen from their cups unless they are infected. When an oak senses that an acorn is infected, it ceases to invest energy in ripening it and aborts it. The acorn and attached cup are dropped before abscission (the process of separating two bonded parts) takes place. If you pry one of

the acorns out of its cup and look at the disk, it will almost certainly exhibit one or more of the disk defects listed below.

Note that this defect is listed as "attached cup." An acorn isn't bad simply because it is *resting in* or *enclosed by* its cup. If the two parts fall away from each other with little or no force—a gentle touch of the fingertip or less—the acorn may still be sound. However, if they must be pried or pulled apart, they are *attached*. On species such as bur and overcup oak, which have cups that largely or fully enclose the acorn, this can be hard to tell—although often you can still get the nut to move easily within its enclosing cup, indicating that it is not attached.

When the attached cup is pried off, the acorn always displays other defects: the one to the right shows discoloration, shell separation, bulging disk, and rippled bottom. The other acorn in the photo is a good one for comparison.

Acorns with attached cups may be crafty, but they're not food.

2. **Exit hole:** A no-brainer, although a grub hole on a dark acorn can easily escape the attention of a speedy collector. Exit holes are about the size of a pencil lead.

This hole is not where a grub entered the acorn, it is an exit hole. Note the dying sprout on the white oak acorn on top, another indication that it is bad.

3. **Old acorn:** Acorns from the previous autumn are dull brown or gray and have lost any attractive color they may have had. When in doubt, crack them; they will not have any good meat inside, just some dark crud.

4. **Dark zone:** Sometimes the shell of a bad acorn exhibits a dark area. These seem to be caused by a bacterial infection of the nutmeat where a weevil has probed a hole, or where a grub has eaten part of the inside. Dark zones may be rather small or they may encompass as much as a third of the shell. They may be nearly black or they may be only a little darker than the rest of the acorn. They can appear on any part of the nut. If you crack the nut open you will usually see the dark zone corresponding to obvious spoilage inside the acorn.

    Sometimes acorns fall from the tree green, before they have fully changed to their ripe color. Those nuts in the process of changing color may have one area darker than another without being infected. At first it might be hard to tell such acorns from those with a dark-zone defect; however, their darker area should be the same color as that of the ripe acorns around them. (Note, however, that falling early in itself is a sign that acorns are more likely to be infected.)

below left The acorns to the left have the dull color of old acorns from last year. Usually the difference is even more pronounced.

below right This acorn has a dark zone down its side and several corresponding dark bundles on its disk, plus a small hole in the shell.

above left The acorn to the right shows an obvious disk separation.
above right Shell separation.

5. **Shell or disk separation:** Normally the shell of the acorn is bonded neatly to the disk. Shell separation is when the shell has peeled away from the disk at one or more points, resulting in a free edge. A disk separation occurs when the pressure inside the acorn pushes the disk away from the shell, or when the acorn was pulled out of a cup to which it was attached. In either case, the normal bond between disk and shell is interrupted.

6. **Rippled bottom:** The bottom part of the acorn's shell, just outside of the disk, is often slightly rippled, but an extreme or exaggerated ripple typically indicates a bad acorn.

7. **Dark spot:** Tiny dark spots, corresponding to weevil holes, can appear anywhere on the shell, but they are common and easiest to see on the disk. Weevils like to probe through the severed ends of the vascular bundles (these

below left The two acorns on top have abnormally rippled bottoms. This is one of the more subtle defects; compare to good acorns from the same trees below. The rippled acorns also have an off color. The cracked disk on the lower left is nothing to worry about.

below right The disk on the upper left has an enlarged, dark bundle in the 12:00 position. The disk on the upper right shows a dark spot (just out from the bundles) in the same position. The lower acorn has a dark spot in the 6:00 position, well off the disk. All of these probably indicate weevil infection.

appear as faint spots or tiny holes at regular intervals along the periphery of the disk) because they are softer than other parts of the shell. When this happens, one or more vascular bundles may become noticeably darkened. Dark spots can be a hard detail for some to see, as they are very small.

8. **Bulging or sunken disk:** The disk of an acorn may naturally be flat, slightly concave, or slightly convex. If the disk is sunken abnormally deep or bulging abnormally (compare to normal acorns from the same tree) this indicates a bad acorn. Sunken or bulging disks are often off-color.

9. **Dying sprout:** This is seen primarily on white oaks. The presence of a healthy sprout indicates that the acorn is alive, having suffered minimal to no damage from insects. However, if the grubs eat enough of the acorn as it is sprouting, the sprout tip will turn black and die. Leave these acorns behind.

Cracked disks and seams—not defects: It is common to find the disk at the bottom of the acorn cracked. I think this is from the nutmeat growing too large or absorbing moisture, exerting pressure on the shell and cracking it. A cracked disk is not an indicator of a bad acorn. Sometimes every nut from a very productive tree shows this crack. Prominent scars or seams are sometimes seen running the length of the acorn. I have no idea why they form, but they are nothing to worry about.

As you gather, you can use the **bite test** from time to time to verify what your visual inspection tells you. Put a clean acorn between your front teeth and bite, but not too hard. You are not trying to crack the acorn; you just want to feel how full and firm it is. It should be hard and not give easily; if it gives way like a ping-pong ball, the shell is empty and the nut is bad. Occasionally, if good nuts have been sitting in a sunny spot, the kernels may dry and shrink somewhat and will not be as firm, but otherwise the bite test is quite accurate. When in doubt, break a few acorns open and check. Also, the bite test will not detect *impostors* (see below).

Seams like this do not indicate a bad acorn.

These are all fine, healthy disks. (Look through acorn photos earlier in this chapter to see more healthy disks.)

Please don't imagine that you must give each acorn a thorough nine-point inspection; that would take ridiculously long. At first, looking for these defects will slow you down—but trust me, it will make up for it in time saved later. Sit down under an oak tree with this list and carefully separate the acorns you find into a good pile and a bad pile. Crack acorns and check your accuracy until you are satisfied with your skill. (Note: you are unlikely to find all these defects under one tree. Under some trees you will find virtually no defects, and under other trees you will find no good nuts. Often, all the bad nuts will exhibit the same one or two defects.)

Eventually, "inspection" will require no more than a momentary glance as you pick up the acorn and toss it into a container. You will develop a search image for good acorns, and the bad ones will be obvious. You are bound to miss a few, but your quantity of bad acorns should be reduced to 2 to 5 percent.

Impostors

After a weevil lays its egg, it takes a few days for the larva to hatch and begin seriously damaging the acorn, so most defects will not immediately show up. Visual inspection will miss most of the infected acorns in this brief time window. I call these acorns, which are presently sound and look good but actually have an egg or very small grub in them, *impostors*.

There are ways to avoid impostors or reduce the number you collect. The first thing to know is that acorns dropping earlier than usual are almost always infected. It is common for red oaks in my area to have one "drop" in late August and early September, and another drop in October and early November. Often, every acorn in the first drop is infected—that's why the tree is getting rid of them. Those that look good are impostors. Collect from the second drop. With white acorns, the early drop (infected acorns) often blends seamlessly into the later drop (good acorns) because the ripening is crammed into a shorter time period. Avoid collecting too early.

Acorns often fall in great quantity during windstorms. If you collect them immediately afterward, some kinds of weevils will not have had much time to lay eggs, and you will end up with fewer impostors. Of course, you can create your own windstorm, so to speak, by knocking down the acorns with a nut stick or by shaking the limbs and gathering them immediately. Acorns that fall during a period of freezing weather will also have fewer impostors if you collect them before it warms up, since the weevils will be inactive at this time.

For red acorns, you can reduce the number of impostors by waiting several months to collect them. With the colder weather in late fall or winter, the weevils will become inactive, so there will be no newly infected acorns. All the grubs will have had time to hatch and do their work, making it evident which acorns are bad. I prefer to gather mine at this time, when there are fewest impostors. Where I live, that means collecting just before Thanksgiving, or just before the snow covers the ground. In much of the United States, there are chances to collect red acorns all winter long. In productive years, the ground will still be covered with good acorns in early spring, and by then the good and bad ones can really be easily told apart. However, don't wait for these conditions unless you know there is a true bumper crop—otherwise you won't get any acorns at all.

This late-season collecting doesn't work for white acorns because they fall earlier and germinate soon after falling. For this reason, when collecting white acorns, one sometimes has no choice but to collect many impostors.

If you suspect that you have a high number of impostors, you should shell the acorns immediately and dry them before the grub does its work.

Three of these valley oak acorns are bad, three are good. You decide.

The Float Test

Good, fresh acorns are heavier than water, but as weevil grubs eat the acorn meat, they create a cavity that lightens the acorn. When this cavity gets large enough, the acorn will float. These facts are the basis for the "float test," which goes like this: Pour your acorns into a container of water and discard any that float. Those that remain suspended in the water but don't rise to the top are probably also bad. Stir the nuts a few times to make sure that any bad ones have the chance to rise.

The float test works, but its usefulness is limited and often misunderstood. It segregates those nuts which have been substantially eaten by grubs, and that's it. Like visual inspection, floating *will not* catch the impostors. Floating is less thorough and effective than visual inspection, but it will always find a few bad acorns that your visual inspection missed. Since it is a good idea to wash the nuts anyway, you might as well put them through the float test at the same time. As your acorn-inspecting eye gets better, you'll find fewer and fewer bad acorns with floating.

Floating works only on fresh acorns. If you have stored them for a while without drying, they may be molding inside the shell, and floating will not detect this. If they have begun to dry (and this occasionally happens even before you collect them), all of them will float, even the good ones.

Drying and Storing, Dead and Alive

Fresh acorns are more perishable than walnuts or hickory nuts. Many people collect acorns and leave them in a pail for a few weeks before cracking, only to find that they have become moldy or rotten in the meantime. Save yourself this disappointment—dry or use your acorns as soon as possible.

An acorn is a living organism. It doesn't spoil as long as you can keep it alive—but this is hard to do. An acorn can succumb to mold, rot, a very deep freeze, or excessive heat, so if you want to keep it alive for an extended period, you must store it in a refrigerator or other moisture- and temperature-controlled environment. Placing acorns in the shade or a cool basement will also slow down their death. **Once an acorn dies, it quickly spoils unless it dries**. It is vital to remember this. Some people freeze or roast acorns to kill grubs, but when you do this, you are also killing the acorns, which will then go bad within a short time. If you carry out such a treatment, you must quickly shell and dry the acorns.

Long-term live storage of acorns is possible in a refrigerator. However, it is not very practical; you should dry them instead. After dehydration, they can be stored for years without spoiling or losing much quality. In fact, some of the California tribes that subsisted on acorns stored a supply sufficient for multiple years as a buffer against crop failures (Bean, 1972).

I got some used baking trays and built this rack to hold them. On 15 trays I can dry about 22 gallons of acorns.

I dry my acorns by spreading them one nut deep on baking trays arranged on a rack by my woodstove. You can also use window screens, or spread them on a tarp or cloth laid in an attic or another warm place where they are protected from rodents. You can also sundry them, but you'll have to keep the animals away.

Acorns dry in one to eighteen weeks, depending on the species, size, and temperature. Some species dry more readily than others, and some are more prone to spoilage. Tanoak and California black oak seem to have the best drying qualities of all large acorns. Among white acorns, white oak *Q. alba* dries fairly well. White acorns take much longer to dry than red acorns of the same size; large ones are nearly impossible to dry in the shell before they spoil. (Some valley oak acorns that I picked this fall took almost four months to dry on a rack near my woodstove; on the same rack, similar sized acorns of California black oak dried in about twelve days.) When your acorns are fully dry, the nutmeat should be shrunken and hard. You can then place them in a mouse- and insect-proof container and process them further at your convenience.

Cracking

You will crack your acorns either fresh or dried. Cracking and shelling dried acorns is much easier, but you may need to crack some right away.

When cracking **fresh, undried acorns**, you will find that the nutmeats come out of the shell much more easily if you heat them first. You don't want to cook them—just warm up the shell and outer nutmeat. You can do this by "flash roasting" the acorns for a couple of minutes or, as I prefer, by putting small batches of them into a colander and dipping them into vigorously boiling water for about twenty seconds. Crack and shell them immediately after this treatment, while they are still warm.

Some people crack acorns with a nutcracker, between their teeth, or by hitting them with a hammer or rock. These methods work, but they are slow. After years of frustration with slow cracking methods, I came up with **the towel method**.

Lay a towel out flat on a hard floor. Place pairs of acorns of about the same size side by side on the towel, making several rows of such pairs spaced about three inches apart. Then you will need a stomper—a heavy, flat-bottomed piece of wood about five or six feet long. While standing and working from right to left (if you are right-handed), stomp your way rhythmically down the first row, cracking two acorns at a time. Hit them hard enough to really crack them, but don't obliterate them. If you go too fast, have poor aim, or place the acorns too close together or in odd pairs, some acorns will "squirt" away on impact, messing up the whole operation.

When you get to the end of the row, *go back to the right again and work the second row from right to left.* **Always work from right to left if you are right-handed**, or vice versa if you are left-handed. If you go the wrong way your view of the acorns will be blocked by the stomper, and this will cause poor aim. After you crack the middle row, go to the opposite side of the towel so you don't have to lean over it. When you've cracked a towel-full, pick them up, lay out new rows of acorns, and go at it again.

This method might sound slow because it took so long to explain, or ridiculous because I called it "the towel method," which sounds totally corny. But in fact it's totally acorny. The towel method has been repeatedly put to the test

The towel method.

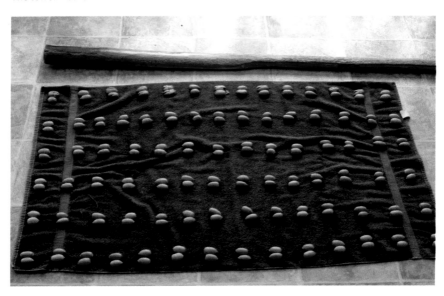

against nutcrackers, hammers, and rocks, and it is two to five times faster. *And* it's a lot more fun.

"Why the towel?" you ask. Try it without the towel and watch the acorns squirt all around the room.

A variation on the towel method uses a sturdy gunnysack. Place about two quarts of acorns into the sack, then fold it in thirds and lay it on the floor with the open end tucked underneath. Spread the acorns so they are about one layer deep and evenly fill the rectangle formed by the folded sack; adjust the folding if necessary. Now you can crack them with the stomper.

This **gunnysack method** is faster yet than the towel method. The disadvantage, however, is that you can't see the acorns as you crack them, so some always go uncracked while others get smashed to smithereens.

The best way that I have found to crack acorns is with a **Davebilt nutcracker** designed for small-scale commercial hazelnut cracking. It costs about $140 but is a good tool for a serious forager to have, working for acorns, hazelnuts, pecans, and lotus nuts. (It does not work with hickory or black walnut.) The Davebilt nutcracker works best with dried acorns. This hand-operated machine can be expected to crack about fifteen to twenty gallons of acorns (sixty to eighty pounds, dry weight) per hour. I figure that mine paid for itself on the first day, when my wife and I cracked thirty-two gallons in less than two hours. Furthermore, acorns cracked with this machine come out in larger pieces than those cracked by other methods, and this again saves hours with shelling later on.

The Davebilt nutcracker is the best acorn cracking device I've ever used. It also cracks hazel, pecan, and lotus nuts.

Shelling

Shelling is the process of separating the desirable kernels or nutmeats from the unwanted shells. The simplest way to do this is by hand, pulling out the nutmeat and discarding the shell. Since acorns have regularly shaped shells and meats they can be shelled more easily than most nuts, and this method is generally sufficient. When shelling acorns by hand you will quickly realize that: 1) Larger acorns go much faster than small ones, 2) Dry acorns are easier to shell than fresh ones because the nutmeats shrink, and 3) Fingernails are very useful.

If you are shelling a larger quantity of red acorns, especially a small or medium-sized type, you may want to try **water separation**. This works only with dry acorns of the red oak group. For this method of shelling, first crack your acorns with the gunnysack method detailed above. There is a difficult happy medium to achieve here: you want them broken up more than for hand separation, but not shattered into tiny pieces. Vigorously shake the gunnysack after cracking to make the kernels fall out of their shells. When you have about two gallons of cracked acorns, dump them into a pail with about three gallons of water and stir with your hand.

You will clearly feel the acorns separate into two layers—mostly nutmeats on the bottom and mostly shells on the top. (This happens because the shells have a fuzzy lining that makes them float. White acorn shells don't have this fuzzy lining, which is why this method doesn't work for them.) Remove the top layer and discard it. Scoop out the bottom layer with your hands and put it into a colander to drain. After draining, spread it out to dry again.

This bottom layer will not be pure nutmeat; any shell bit that has lost its fuzzy lining will sink along with the kernels. You will still have to go through it by hand; however, the water will have done 60 to 70 percent of the separation in just a few seconds. With large amounts of acorn, this can save hours of hand-shelling.

After the bottom layer has been removed and dried, it is helpful to winnow it. This will quickly separate an enormous quantity of shell bits, tiny kernel pieces too small too deal with, and pieces of the thin papery skin (testa) that adheres to the kernels. After winnowing, finish separating the kernels by hand.

The downside to water separation is that by using this process you will lose about 25 percent of your good nutmeats. When acorns are abundant and collecting is easy, this is not a big deal; the time saved in shelling more than makes up for the time required to get 25 percent more acorns. The discarded material is not waste—dump it back into the woods for wildlife, put it on your birdfeeder, or feed it to chickens. *You cannot be efficient with water separation unless you accept that you will lose a lot of acorn meat*—if you spend hours picking for all the tiny bits of kernel, or sorting through the discard layer for nutmeats, you will negate any potential time savings. One advantage to water separation is that this process loosens the testas from the acorns, so it does not have to be done later.

Water separation is useful for small or medium-sized red acorns. If you have larger acorns, pure hand separation is probably faster and definitely less wasteful.

As mentioned above, water separation doesn't work with white acorns. That's alright, because **winnowing** does. After drying white acorns and putting them through my Davebilt nutcracker, I winnow them by pouring from one container into another on a breezy day. White acorn shells are generally lighter than those of red acorn, and they seem to catch the wind better. The kernels are harder and seem to be heavier, too. A few minutes of winnowing white acorns can eliminate 50 to 80 percent of the shells, saving hours of hand-shelling time.

Removing the Skin (Testa)

The cotyledons of acorns are covered with a testa, much like that which covers peanuts. On white acorns it is thinner and tends to stick to the shell instead of the cotyledon, or it comes off the smooth cotyledons easily when the kernels dry. However, the cotyledons of red acorns usually have folds and valleys on their surface, to which the testa often holds on tenaciously.

Some people feel that it is very important to remove the testa. At least with some oak species, it is especially high in tannin. It is quite easy to get rid of it, so I generally do. If it loosens on its own, as with tanoak, just rub the shelled acorns between your hands and it will fall off. If it is not loose, immerse the dried, shelled acorn meats in water for five to ten seconds and stir vigorously, then drain. You can also wet the acorns with a spray bottle, and this will cause less discoloration than immersion. When the acorns are dry again, most of the testa will be loose or will rub off easily. (You may want to use a knife to split the cotyledon along its deepest groove to remove the testa.) The loosened skins can be easily winnowed away from the heavy nutmeats.

Grinding

You will need to grind acorns before cold leaching, and you may want to grind them into flour after hot leaching. You can try this in any type of flourmill or cornmeal grinder. Since flourmills are generally designed for small grains, many will not function well with larger pieces such as chunks of acorn. Hopefully you can try your mill out on acorns *before* you purchase it. If you use a flourmill, get iron burrs—the oily meal will clog stone burrs. I run my raw (unleached) acorns through a corn cracker before grinding, which gives me smaller pieces that pass more readily through my grain mill. Other grinding options include a coffee grinder or blender for small amounts. If you want to cold leach fresh, undried acorns you can puree them in a blender with a small amount of water.

Traditionally, most Native Americans who cold leached acorns pulverized them with a hand-held stone, pounding (not grinding) the acorns in a stone mortar (Fagan, 2003). For a detailed first-hand discussion of this method, read *It Will Live Forever* (Ortiz, 1991), a fascinating account of traditional Miwok acorn preparation. Choose whichever grinding or pulverizing method you like, so long as the final result is powdered acorn.

When grinding dried acorns there is a significant difference between the red and white types. Red acorns are semi-hard, like wheat, while white acorns are much harder, like corn. Red acorns are also much more oily. Grinding methods will work differently for the two types.

The finer the flour is, the more readily it will leach. However, it is difficult to get acorn flour *uniformly* fine, which is the key to cold leaching quickly and thoroughly. I sift my flour through a fine-screen strainer or a jelly bag suspended in a jar, regrinding the coarser meal. The Miwok method was very different. Acorn meal was placed into a tightly woven basket and the basket was shaken until the finer flour stuck to the weave by surface tension. The basket was then slowly turned on its side, being tapped or shaken all the while, as the coarser particles hopped their way down the slope and off the edge into another container; these were later pounded further. The finest particles that stuck to the fibers of the basket were then brushed off into another container and considered ready to leach (Ortiz, 1991).

Leaching

Leaching is the process of removing the tannins from acorns so that the kernels are safe and pleasant to eat. All North American acorns should be leached before being consumed in significant amounts. There are a variety of ways to do this, all of which take advantage of the fact that most acorn tannins are water-soluble. There is no single correct way to leach acorns, just some basic principles to follow. In this section I'll discuss various acorn-leaching traditions and share my own experiences as well. You can try whichever techniques appeal to you and develop your own preferences and innovations through experience.

There are two basic ways to leach acorns: with hot or cold water. Both methods were used around the world by various cultures, and both work well. However, they produce totally different food products.

Whichever method of leaching you choose, it is important to do it thoroughly. In my opinion, the most common mistake of acorn preparation is inadequate leaching. Adequate versus inadequate leaching is the difference between palatable and unpalatable. The more thoroughly you leach acorns, the more you will enjoy them, and the more you will eat them.

Hot Leach

Hot leaching was done in North America primarily by tribes of the Eastern Woodlands, often with the addition of wood-ash lye to neutralize tannins (Mason,

1992). This method uses boiling water to extract the tannin from the acorns. Hot leaching is for large pieces of acorn, typically halves or quarters. (If you boil acorn meal or flour, it will dissolve and turn into a gelatinous mass.) Place the acorn pieces in a pot and cover them with four or more cups of water for every cup of acorns. Cover the pot and place it over a heat source. Let it boil vigorously for 30–360 minutes, then pour off the water through a colander, refill the pot, and repeat the process three to fifteen times until the acorns are not bitter. By the time they are done, these acorns will become dark chocolate brown.

Hot leaching is not an exact science. The number of necessary water changes will depend on the amount of water used, how vigorously and how long it boils, the size of the acorn pieces, the original tannin content and type of the acorn, and the desired final flavor. Sample the acorns with each water change to determine when they are done. (Despite what you may read, the water may still turn brown when the tannin is gone.) I hot leach my acorns in a five-gallon pot on my woodstove, changing the water at my convenience, and find it very practical.

The main advantages of hot-leaching are that it is relatively quick and the acorns do not have to be ground first. A drawback is that it is energy-intensive and therefore not always practical unless you have a woodstove. Hot-leached acorns also lose more of their volume and nutrients than cold-leached acorns do, and they lose their ability to stick together when cooked.

Hot leach acorn flour.

Cold Leach

Cold leaching follows the same principles as hot leaching: the acorns are soaked, the water absorbs tannins, then the water is poured or percolated off and new water added. This is repeated until there is little to no tannin left in the acorns. However, since tannin does not dissolve as readily in cold water, and water does not pass as easily through raw acorn flesh, effective cold leaching generally requires the acorns to be ground into a flour or meal. Cold leaching of larger acorn pieces is theoretically possible. There are a number of ethnographic records of this, but they all entail leaching for extremely long periods of time. Since I have not found this practical, I won't discuss it at length here, but feel free to experiment.

Cold leaching was the primary technique used by those Native American peoples in California for whom acorn was the dietary staple (Mason, 1992). It has also been employed by cultures in many other parts of the world. Cold leaching is used in large-scale acorn processing plants today in Korea, producing an extremely fine acorn flour used in a traditional food called "dotorimuk" or "acorn jelly," which is something like a very soft acorn tofu.

One of the primary advantages of cold leaching is that it does not require heat. It also produces a more complete food than hot leaching, since it retains many of the soluble starches and other components that are lost through boiling. Cold-leached acorn flour will stick together to form cakes or flatbreads, while hot-leached acorn flour will not.

Cold leaching methods can be divided into quick leaching and slow leaching. Slow leaching involves letting the acorn meal soak for a period of days or weeks, changing the water occasionally. Quick leaching occurs in a day or less;

left Gallon jar strainer.
below Strainer for cold-leaching acorns.

it involves pouring acorn flour mixed with water onto a cloth and letting the water percolate out, usually adding water and letting it percolate one or more additional times.

I usually do my **slow leaching** in a five-gallon pail or a one-gallon jar. In either case I fill the container about one sixth with acorn meal or flour and the rest with water. I stir it and then leave it alone for anywhere from four hours to more than a day. Then I gently decant the water, being careful not to lose any acorn flour, add new water, and stir again. After six to twenty water changes, the acorn will be ready to use. I go by taste to judge when it has leached sufficiently. Patience is a virtue here; it is always tempting to stop the leaching early, which results in an inferior product.

When the acorn is deemed ready I pour the water off one last time and pour the wet acorn flour into a cloth strainer so that additional water can percolate. When the strainer stops dripping I pick up the cloth and thoroughly wring out the acorn meal until it is hard to squeeze a single drop from it. When I remove the cloth after this, the acorn will stick together and look like a ball of clay. It is now ready to use for cooking. It can be stored frozen or refrigerated, or it can be crumbled between the hands and dried for use later.

Both red and white acorns can be cold leached. However, I find that white acorns are more prone to spoilage; they have to be leached quickly or kept cool to prevent them from going bad.

Traditional methods of cold acorn leaching varied. If you live near a waterfall on a clean stream, you can suspend a mesh bag of coarse chunks in it for a month, as was done in one Japanese village (Matsuyama, 1981). However, most California tribes who used acorn as a staple did some form of **quick leaching**. The Miwok method demonstrated by Julia Parker (Ortiz, 1991) starts with creating a circular, flat structure from loose sand, with a sand lip built up all around the perimeter to hold water. A cloth was placed over this leaching basin and a mixture of acorn meal and water was carefully poured in to cover the bottom. The water was allowed to percolate, leaving about an eighth- or quarter-inch of wet acorn meal evenly spread over the cloth. More water was then poured in, through a conifer-branch "waterbreak" which spread out the impact of the water as it was poured, and allowed to percolate. This was done repeatedly until the acorn was thoroughly leached.

I have built a shallow basin with a screen bottom that is lined with a cloth; I suspend this over a tub that catches the water that percolates through. This setup allows me to do quick leaching in my house, which has no sandbar. An excellent "cloth" for leaching fine acorn flour is a nylon pre-filter used for filtering maple syrup. These pre-filters are designed to let liquid pass through readily while retaining small particles. They are inexpensive and available from any maple supply dealer in 36-inch square sheets.

The keys to quick leaching successfully are finely ground flour and lots of water. Quick leaching produces a slightly different—and I think better—flavor than prolonged leaching. Quick leaching also produces a flour with lighter color. However, quick methods tempt the novice to stop while the acorn is still too bitter for most palates. Nothing will disappoint you, dishonor the acorn, misrepresent tradition, and breed skeptics more than serving bitter acorn products to the uninitiated.

Lye, Lime, and Clay

Alkali processing (using lye or lime) can be incorporated into either hot or cold leaching. These alkaline chemicals combine with tannin and neutralize it—including the small portion of non-soluble tannins that can't be leached out with water alone. Any excess lye or lime can be easily leached out, since their relatively small molecules move through acorn tissue and dissolve in water more readily than tannin does.

Using lye (NaOH and KOH) and lime [Ca(OH)2] may sound unnatural, but these are simple compounds that have been used in traditional food processing for thousands of years by cultures all around the world. Lye has long been used to neutralize the tannin in olives, exactly as it is used with acorns. It was employed by many eastern tribes in North America in the leaching of acorns (Mason, 1992). It is also used to turn corn into hominy and grits, and cod into lutefisk. Lime, extracted from limestone, is used in the processing of cocoa as well as corn flour for tortillas. While these chemicals are caustic and can be dangerous, with reasonable caution you can use them safely.

Lye can be purchased in many grocery and hardware stores as a drain cleaner (only use pure lye for food processing), or it can be made by mixing white wood ash with water and straining out the solids. Lime can be purchased in enormous bags for just a few dollars at many feed mills and farm supply stores. Be sure to get *quick lime* or *hydrated lime*, rather than barn lime. Strong lye solutions, such as those needed for soap making, are never used for processing acorns. Still, one should be extra cautious with these chemicals and store them out of the reach of children.

As lye and lime combine with tannin they produce a byproduct with an unappetizing flavor that is reminiscent of green olives. I am fond of olives, but not of olive-flavored acorns. To minimize this flavor, I use both forms of alkali only in the later stages of leaching, when most of the tannin has already been removed. Do not use lye or lime with finely ground acorn flour, or it will turn into a gelatinous mass that cannot be rinsed or used. Instead, I use alkali with coarsely ground acorn meal to make a product that I call "**acorn grits**." After the acorn meal is mostly cold leached, I soak it in an alkali solution for twenty-four hours (during which time the water may become very dark), then leach out the alkali with several water changes over a few days. I do this in a gallon jar with a piece of cheesecloth attached to the mouth with a rubber band, which makes a convenient strainer. At the end, I boil the grits in a few water changes to rid it of any trace of alkali (just as is done with hominy or corn grits made from scratch) before calling it ready to eat.

I don't have an exact recommendation on the strength of the alkali solution to use, because every strength I have tried has worked. Stronger solutions soften the acorn more and turn it a lighter color, but even weak solutions seem to neutralize every last bit of tannin.

Acorn grits make a good hot cereal, served much like hominy grits, although they never get as soft. They can also be seasoned and used as a starchy accompaniment to meats and vegetables, much as couscous is eaten, but I don't find their texture as pleasant. Acorn grits can also be used in baked goods, especially cookies, where their texture is more appreciated.

Some people are fearful of lye used in food processing, believing that trace residual amounts in the food are very toxic. This is a misunderstanding. Lye is caustic and can burn tissues that it comes in contact with, but it does not become a systemic poison when ingested. Instead, it reacts with your tissues and is neutralized in the process. Certainly you want to remove all the lye, but a trace amount in your food will react with your stomach acid to become salt and water—two relatively safe substances. A trace of lye can cause indigestion by neutralizing your gastric acid, but it won't poison you.

Clay was mixed with acorn flour by some California peoples (Heizer and Elsasser, 1981). This was presumably done because the clay contains mineral ions that bind to tannin, preventing the tannin from chelating minerals consumed in other foods. I have not found much detail about this practice, nor have I tried it, but it warrants further investigation. **Gelatin** has also been recommended as an additive, since it binds with tannins (Fernald and Kinsey, 1958).

Acorn grits. Some pieces are brown, some yellowish, and some nearly white.

Nutrition in Acorns

Acorns provide calories: starch, oil, and a little bit of protein. The overfed majority tries so hard to reduce calories that we often forget that we will die without enough of them. The most significant component of acorns is starch, which comprises 50 to 90 percent of their weight. Starch levels are higher in white acorns. The oil content of acorns varies from 5 to 30 percent, being substantially higher in red acorns. Acorns are relatively low in protein at about 5 to 8 percent (figures from Mason, 1992).

The USDA's National Nutrient Database for Standard Reference, Release 21 (2008), contains analysis of a few samples of acorn cotyledon, but they oddly do not list the kind of acorn. However, since they report 31.4 percent fat, we can presume that the figures are for a member of the red oak group, since no white acorns are known to come even close to this figure. The USDA's analysis shows the acorn as a fairly good source of most mineral nutrients and B vitamins, as well as being an excellent source of niacin and exceptionally rich in potassium. The analysis also shows that acorns contain all essential amino acids—although they are low in tryptophan.

This compositional profile makes acorns among the most appropriate staple foods on Earth. The leaching process removes the water-soluble salts and vitamins, but the fat-soluble vitamins and mineral nutrients remain.

Cooking With Acorn

The dishes that can be made with acorn are as diverse as those prepared with wheat, corn, or rice. Your imagination, tools, and culinary creativity are the only limits to acorn cookery. My experiences hardly scratch the surface of the many possibilities.

Hot-leached acorn is very soft and mild in flavor. I like to mash these with a potato masher and use them in chili instead of beans. I also mix them with ground meat and refried beans to make filling for burritos, enchiladas, and chimichangas. Hot-leached acorn can be used in soup or casserole. A friend of mine makes fried meatless patties with wild rice, mashed acorn, and egg. I use hot-leached acorn mashed and topped with spaghetti sauce, served with mushrooms, zucchini, and parmesan cheese.

I also do much baking with hot-leached acorn flour. After the acorns are leached, I run them through my meat grinder to produce a finer texture, then dry them. Once dry they go quite readily through my flourmill. The dark brown flour stores extremely well and is used at our convenience in breads, pancakes, cookies, and muffins. It does not stick together on its own and therefore must be used with another sticky flour (generally wheat). I typically use a ratio of one part acorn to one and a quarter parts wheat. The acorn adds a nice color and hearty flavor to all of these baked goods

Cold-leached acorn flour is more versatile and is my favorite way to use acorns. Unlike hot-leached flour, it is able to stick together on its own and therefore does not require the addition of wheat flour. However, it does not rise or get fluffy like wheat, and if you expect it to act like wheat, you will definitely be disappointed. California Natives commonly made three different products from cold-leached acorn flour: a thin soup (called *akiva* in Miwok) from the finest flour, a porridge or mush (*nuppa*), and "biscuits" or congealed balls of dough (*uhlley*). The Koreans make a food called dotorimuk from super fine acorn flour mixed with water and congealed into a jelly-like consistency; this is then commonly fried with vegetables and seasonings. Acorn flour can also be used as a thickener in soup, although I don't think it makes good gravy.

I often use cold-leached acorn to make a sort of flatbread. We call this an "**acorn crust**," and often make pizza and pie crusts with it. Rewind to the cold-leaching section, where I had just unwrapped a clay-like ball of cold-leached acorn flour. This is what is used for the crust. The flour should be moist but not wet; its texture is hard to compare to anything made with wheat, and when cooking with acorn all of our grain-based culinary experience is useless. Let's make a pizza crust.

For an eleven-inch pizza I'll use about two cups of moist, cold-leached acorn flour. I'll add a little salt and about a quarter cup of tomato juice. The desired texture is probably much drier-looking than you think it should be. Little to no liquid should run from the acorn dough even when it is pressed hard. Mold the dough into the bottom of a non-stick frying pan, curving the edges slightly up the sides to hold the sauce. Even out the thickness and make it look nice. Put a cover on the pan and put it atop a burner on low heat for twenty to thirty minutes until the crust is cooked—you'll see and feel the texture change as the acorn starts sticking together.

above right Clay-like dough ball.

below right Acorn crust in pan.

Finished acorn crust.

Don't turn the heat too high, or bubbles may form that will break the crust. Once the texture changes, indicating that the acorn has cooked, take the cover off and let the crust cook a few more minutes until the surface is dry. Now you have a pizza crust. Remove from the pan, put on a pizza tray, apply your sauce, cheese, and toppings, and bake.

For a pie crust, use maple syrup instead of tomato juice to moisten your meal. Mold the acorn into the pie plate, bake, remove from the oven, add your pie filling, and bake again.

If you are starting with cold-leached flour that is dry, you can moisten it with egg to improve its cooking qualities, and then add the liquid of your choice for the remainder. Just be sure to let it sit for about an hour so the meal can totally assimilate the moisture before you cook it.

For a unique meal, moisten your meal with regular mustard, shape and cook like a pizza crust, and top with avocado slices. Or bake a crust from unseasoned acorn meal and eat it with gravy and a slice of roast venison on top. Or have it with coconut oil spread over it. You can also salt and season the meal, spread it very thin, and bake acorn chips.

Cold-leached acorn flour is slightly "dry" feeling due to its faint astringency; culinary use of acorn requires one to counterbalance this dryness. This counterbalancing can be accomplished with pie filling, pizza sauce, avocado, a slice of meat soaked in *au jus*, or in many other ways. It can also be accomplished simply with water: if you mix enough liquid with finely ground, thoroughly cold-leached acorn flour to make a soft, pudding-like consistency, and then bake it, you will get a nice product with a texture like cheese, tofu, or jello—depending on the amount of liquid used. You can season and salt the mixture, dice it up,

This moist "dough" of cold-leached tanoak flour will cook into a "bread" with a texture like soft cheese.

and serve it hot at dinner; or you can sweeten it, add a little cinnamon, and eat it as a snack.

Another product is "**acorn milk**." Remember when I was wringing out the acorn flour in a cloth? I save all the liquid that I squeeze out, which has the finest particles of acorn starch suspended in it. After bringing this liquid to a boil and mixing in a touch of maple syrup, it becomes a rich, delicious drink.

These are just a few things I like to make from cold-leached acorn—the possibilities are endless. It is hard to give very precise instructions when I know we are not working with uniform and standardized ingredients—everybody will grind and leach his or her acorns a little differently. But rest assured that with a little experimentation, you can develop some excellent and unique cuisine based on cold-leached acorn.

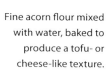

Fine acorn flour mixed with water, baked to produce a tofu- or cheese-like texture.

As you can see, the acorn is a versatile staple food. No wonder this nut has been the staff of life for a multitude of cultures around the world.

As the Greek poet Hesiod said almost three thousand years ago:

> Neither famine nor inward disaster comes the way
> of those people
> who are straight and just; they do their work
> as if work were a holiday;
> the earth gives them great livelihood,
> on their mountains the oaks
> bear acorns for them in their crowns
> and bees in their middles.

—*The Works and Days* (translated by Lattimore, 1991)

We can still do our work as if work were a holiday. The oaks still bear us acorns in their crowns. What will happen to us, and our world, if we eat them?

Hazelnut

Corylus cornuta, C. americana

Betulaceae – Birch Family

I still vividly remember the first wild hazel nut that I tasted, when I was thirteen years old. Early one wet September morning I walked from my campsite to a nearby lake, and on the way I spotted a shrub with clusters of deformed leaves. Stopping to investigate, I noticed that the odd leaf clusters seemed too symmetrical to be deformities. I plucked one from the bush and pried apart the "leaves" to reveal a small, smooth-shelled, light-brown nut. Having searched for these before to no avail, I instantly recognized my discovery as a hazelnut bush.

The nut was reluctant to pop out of its hiding place, but once I managed to remove it from the sticky depths of its sheath, I admired its form. Then came the second challenge: how to crack it. After positioning and repositioning it in my mouth several times, and hoping not to break a tooth, I managed to crack the shell between my jaws. And then, the taste test. . . . To this day there are few things I find as delicious as a hazelnut fresh from the bush.

American hazelnuts on the bush. The husks are green, but the nuts are ripe.

Description

North America is home to two types of hazelnut: the American hazel *Corylus americana*, and the beaked hazel *C. cornuta*. These two species are quite similar in appearance. I will describe them together here and detail the differences later.

The hazels are medium to large shrubs that form thickets, which can be dense and nearly impenetrable in sunny locations. Each stem or trunk is typically 0.75–2 inches (2–5 cm) in diameter. They are clumped at the base, typically with six to forty stems per clump. Hazels reproduce by suckers and some new shoots are almost always present in the clump. Individual stems are erect and branch little below their midpoint. Their growth tends to be crooked and slightly leaning. They are most commonly confused with alders and witch-hazel, but the nuts are unmistakable. The wood is quite strong and the twigs are thin and zigzagged. Hazel bark is gray, medium-smooth, and nearly uniform in texture, lacking plates, scales, or peeling sections. Sexually mature hazel bushes usually bear catkins on the winter twigs.

Beaked hazelnuts typically grow singly or in small clusters. Aborted nuts, descending in size, are almost always attached.

Beaked hazel leaves. Both species have irregularly toothed margins like this.

Hazels bear alternate, simple, deciduous, ovate leaves 2–5 inches (5–13 cm) long and about two thirds as wide. The tips are acuminate. Hazel leaves are rather thin and are hairy, especially on the lower surface. The petioles are proportionately short and rarely exceed 0.5 inch (13 mm) in length. The leaf margins are sharply and doubly or irregularly toothed. Winter buds are about 0.15 inch (4 mm) long , blunt-tipped, and rounded or oval in shape.

The flowers are unisexual.

Beaked hazel twig in winter, showing catkins.

Male flowers are borne in catkins 1.5–2.5 inches (4–6 cm) in length, and the tiny female flowers remain obscured by their bud scales and are extremely hard to notice. Flowers of both sexes emerge in early spring before the foliage.

Hazelnuts ripen in late summer and are borne in tight clusters of up to 15 nuts near the tips of the branches. About 0.5 inch (13 mm) in diameter, the nuts are hard-shelled, smooth, and an attractive light brown when ripe. Each nut is wrapped in an *involucre*, a pair of modified leaves that hides and protects it. All the nuts and involucres are packed in tightly together with no stems connecting them, forming a big, leafy ball. Large ones may weigh several ounces and are fun to toss around.

Our two species of hazel can be easily told apart by their fruit. The American hazelnut is enclosed in an involucre that consists of two ruffled halves narrowest near the nut, while the beaked hazelnut's involucre is wrapped tightly around it, extending to form a tapering tube or "beak" 1–2 inches (2.5–5 cm) in length. American hazel's sheath is covered with sticky, gland-tipped hairs, while that of the beaked hazel is armed with tiny spines. American hazels are borne in clusters of up to fifteen, with four to nine being typical; beaked hazelnuts may come eleven per cluster, but this is rare—more typical is three nuts or fewer. The nuts themselves are also shaped differently: the American hazel is somewhat flattened when viewed from the top, and the beaked hazel is round. However, the involucres are so different that you will never be wondering by the time you get the nuts out.

If there are no nuts on the bushes, there are still easy ways to differentiate them. The twigs of American hazel, like the involucres, are covered with sticky, gland-tipped hairs, which beaked hazel lacks. Also, the winter catkins of American hazel dangle from the twigs on short stalks, while beaked hazel's catkins are sessile or nearly sessile and often held erect or horizontally.

Range and Habitat

The beaked hazel ranges from Newfoundland to southern British Columbia and across the northern United States, extending southward in the mountains to central California and northern Georgia. Over much of its range, the beaked hazel is the only edible nut, making it highly valuable to wildlife and human foragers. Beaked hazel is primarily an understory shrub of younger, more open forests, especially those of birch, aspen, oak, and pine. It also grows along fencerows, at forest edges, and in abandoned fields, often forming small thickets. Over much of its range, beaked hazel is the most common upland shrub.

The American hazel is widespread from southeastern Saskatchewan to Maine, and south to Arkansas and South Carolina. It is most common in the prairie border region, where well-drained, sunny conditions with sufficient moisture prevail, and in some places it is the dominant vegetative feature of the landscape. This is one of the most abundant and prevalent shrubs in eastern North America, from

Pine-oak barrens offer the best habitat for American hazel. Note the bushes in the foreground; some of these were so laden they were resting on the ground.

the Great Plains to the coast. American hazel is a frequent understory shrub in dry forests, especially stands of oak, hickory, and pine. It often grows profusely after logging, fire, or storms open up the forest canopy. This shrub also does well in river and stream valleys, on steep slopes or rocky ridges, in abandoned fields, in pine barrens, at forest edges, and along railways, roads, and fencerows.

Due to their abundance, the hazels are among the most important wildlife foods in North America. The nuts are relished by squirrels, mice, flying squirrels, and chipmunks. Bears fatten on them in the late summer, chewing up the nut with both shell and sheath included; in some regions they are even known to make significant migrations to good hazelnut patches. In many areas, hazel twigs are an important winter browse for deer and moose, and the dormant catkins are a major winter food source for ruffed grouse. Hazel brush is cut for food by beavers and is a primary source of both food and cover for cottontail rabbits and snowshoe hares.

Harvest and Preparation

There is a place close to my home that contains a few hundred square miles of sand country that used to be pine barrens. The Forest Service, upon acquiring it, put all of this wasted space to good use by planting jack and red pine for timber. Fifty years later they realized that in doing so they had eliminated the last local strongholds of the sharp-tailed grouse, a barrens-loving species. To compensate for their blunder they started trying to turn some of their clearcuts into grouse habitat once again. The result was several thousand acres of hazel brush with an occasional sharp-tail. It is a hazelnut picker's dream.

People often lament that the squirrels get all of the hazel nuts, but this isn't true. I get some. You can, too, if you get there as soon as they ripen. Wild hazelnuts ripen in late summer, not fall, and most people try to collect them much too late.

Where I live, beaked hazel nuts ripen around August 10 to 25, while American hazels average a week or two later. This is concurrent with the seasons for chokecherries, black cherries, blackberries, and wild rice. At the time that hazelnuts ripen, the involucres are still green. You can tell that they are ripe by prying the husk apart and looking at the nut: the top half of the shell should have turned light brown. If the nuts are unripe, they will be light cream in color. If you try to wait until the *husk* is brown, like many people do, you probably won't get any nuts, because this doesn't happen until weeks after the actual nuts ripen. However, in the occasional years when the hazelnut crop is very heavy, especially in areas where the bushes are predominant, you can get good nuts through the fall and even into winter. But don't count on it.

American hazel bushes loaded with ripe nuts.

I like both kinds of hazelnut, although each has its advantages and disadvantages. American hazel is easier to harvest in quantity. The amounts that can be collected are, in fact, staggering. A single clump of bushes can yield thousands of nuts, and where I pick, there is a sea of hazel brush extending for mile after mile, covering half a township here, two townships there. You can fill a pickup truck in an afternoon. Beaked hazel never reaches this level of dominance, but it is more ubiquitous in much of its range. It bears fewer nuts per bush, but still plenty, and in good years nobody should run out of either kind.

The American hazel's main drawback is that in most years, most of the nuts are empty or wormy, which makes for a lot of wasted labor. On beaked hazel, fewer of the nuts are empty or infested. American hazels will quickly fill a container with their fluffy, voluminous involucres; with beaked hazelnuts you don't have to carry around so much bulk. All things considered, I think American hazels are easier to collect.

The sheaths of American hazelnuts will get your hands sticky with a pleasant, piney aroma; beaked hazelnuts are covered with irritating hairs, like a tamer version of the glochids on a prickly pear, almost requiring gloves for harvest. But then again, I think that beaked hazels taste a little better. I advise picking whichever species is found in your area; they are both excellent. Pick hazelnuts by pulling the entire cluster from the bush, giving it a twist so that you are less likely to pull off the twig.

After harvest, you will have to get the nuts out of their sheaths. The riper they are, the easier they come out. I generally spread the nuts to dry in their sheaths somewhere that the squirrels cannot get them. After a week or so the involucres turn brown and the nuts become easier to remove. *If the involucre sticks tenaciously to the bottom of the nut, this almost always means that the nut is not ripe, or that the kernel inside is bad.* You can use the float test (explained on page 180) on fresh hazelnuts to separate the bad kernels, but it will not work once the nuts have dried for a few weeks.

With American hazel I grab the two halves of the dry involucre and pull apart and dislodge the nut by pushing on it with a finger, after which it usually rolls out. This works for beaked hazels, too, but not as well, and it's hard to grab the involucre with gloves on.

For larger amounts, there is a much more labor-efficient way to deal with hazel nuts. When the involucres of American hazels are dry, I dump a few gallons of them into a wooden barrel and stomp and rub them with my feet until the nuts and husks are separated. Then I just pick out the free nuts. This saves hours over husking by hand. For beaked hazel, the process is similar, but you do not want to dry the involucres. Instead, bury them in wet soil or mud for about

American hazels in the husk. The husks are green, but the nuts are brown and therefore ripe. When they first ripen, the involucres will be very juicy like this. They would need to be dried before the nuts could come out easily.

a month. (Hopefully, they won't be discovered by a squirrel or bear.) During this time the husks and spines will rot and soften, but the shells and kernels will remain undamaged. Then dig up the nuts, put them in a gunnysack, and tread on them vigorously for a while to loosen the hulls. Dump them out of the sack; most of them can be just picked out of the mess by hand. Any that remain in the hulls are easy to get out because the involucres have softened.

Once the nuts are separated from the sheaths they are ready to be cracked and eaten. You can crack them with a conventional nutcracker (although the nuts may actually be too small) or a hammer. I used to crack a handful at a time by pounding them gently in my wooden mortar, but that was before I got spoiled with the super-efficient Davebilt nutcracker, designed for cultivated hazelnuts. In three minutes it can crack what would take me an hour without it. After cracking I just pick out the nutmeats by hand, which is less labor intensive than with many wild nuts.

If you do not want to use your hazelnuts immediately, they store very well in the shell with or without their sheaths attached—although the flavor of the fresh ones is best. However, removing the involucres dramatically reduces the space they take up. (With American hazel, for example, five gallons in the sheath makes about a quart of nuts when removed.) You do not need to refrigerate hazelnuts for storage. As I write this, I am snacking on some American hazelnuts that I picked two and a half years ago, and I can't find any that have gone bad. However, they retain better flavor if kept in the freezer.

Hazelnuts are high in oil and protein. If you were lost in the woods, few foods would sustain you as adequately and pleasantly. I remember Northwoods survival trips as a teenager where I was mighty appreciative of these little nuts, as I

below left Burying beaked hazels in mud to rot off the involucres is the most effective way I have found to hull them. This makes the spines innocuous and the involucres soft but leaves the nuts unaffected. They are laying on the gunnysack in which I stomped them to loosen the husks.

below right With hazelnuts, brown does not mean ripe! The two larger beaked hazels in this photo are insect-infested, as indicated by their inappropriate brown color. The only sound nut here is the small green-husked one.

Beaked (top) and American (bottom) hazelnuts in hand.

sat around the campfire cracking and eating one after another.

Both species of hazelnut were widely used by many Native American tribes. They were often stored for winter use and sometimes served as an important source of calories. They were pounded and mixed with meal or flour to make cakes, served with corn, and mashed and boiled into a milky liquid or soup base. A similar species of hazelnut found in Europe, *C. avellana* was an important food source for Mesolithic hunter-gatherers in many areas of northern Europe (Gregg, 1988; Renfrew, 1973).

You can use your nuts to make hazel milk, a delicious, hearty drink. Put a few cups of hazelnuts into a blender with an equal amount of water and puree thoroughly. Then add an equal amount of water again and bring the mixture to a boil in a sauce pan, stirring occasionally to prevent clumping. Add maple syrup, cinnamon, and a pinch of roasted, powdered dandelion root, and you have a beverage fit for royalty. You can also leave this hazel milk unsweetened and unseasoned and use it as a substitute for milk when baking. Hazelnuts pureed in this way can also be used as a soup base.

If you don't want to invest the effort to make hazelnut-based soup or porridge, you can use them for any of the traditional uses for cultivated hazelnuts (filberts). Most of us have spent spare hours cracking them around the holidays and snacking on them. Wild hazelnuts can be used like filberts in baking, granola, and hot cereal. Hazelnut butter is a popular spread in Europe and also tastes good on this side of the Atlantic. There are many delicious hazelnut or filbert recipes in traditional cookbooks, and wild hazels serve well in any of them.

The hazelnut is another reminder that we do not have to search far and wide for good wild food; we simply need to learn to avail ourselves of the wonderful resources that so generously surround us.

Prickly Pear, Nopal

Opuntia spp.

Cactaceae – Cactus Family

As a child, my life was greatly influenced by a book called _Natural History of Amphibians and Reptiles of Wisconsin_, by Richard Vogt. Not only did this volume give me ideas for weekend and evening activities, it also contained beautiful photographs that helped me envision the snakes and salamanders that I might find on my excursions. But when Vogt said that the endangered ornate box turtle inhabited dry prairies with prickly pear cactus, I had to stop and read that section again. Prickly pear cactus? In Wisconsin? The book even had photos purportedly taken about an hour's drive from my home that showed prickly pears in the background.

My friend Josh had already seen prickly pears, it turned out. We planned a bike trip for that Memorial Day weekend, mostly to look for reptiles—but seeing my first wild cactus would be another highlight. Along a backroad ten miles before our destination, Josh shouted, "Look!" as he came to a sudden halt and pointed toward a grassy slope beside the road. I didn't see them at first—

I was looking for a pile of boards or sheet metal where we might find a bullsnake or a blue racer. "What?" I asked.

"Prickly pears! Can't you see them?"

And there they were, a whole hillside of cactus pads mixed with short, sparse grasses. I threw my precious Trek touring bike onto the gravel and jumped the barbed wire fence before you could say, "Hey dude, who do you think owns this pasture?"

I knew you could eat prickly pear pads because I had seen them in grocery stores, and even once had bought one. I had also read about wild prickly pears in a number of edible plant guides. I had done my book research; it was time to begin the field work.

I gingerly seized a succulent-looking pad and twisted it free. All the spines were on the top, so I took a big, turtle-style bite out of the bottom side and chewed it up as I walked back toward the fence. It tasted just fine, but as I swallowed I noticed a strange uncomfortable feeling . . . no, it definitely qualified as pain . . . in my throat . . . and tongue . . . and cheeks, and the roof of my mouth.

I had never heard of a glochid then. After all, have *you* ever heard of a glochid? Now I know a lot about them—from experience. My mouth was all misery for the next three days, but I didn't let those glochids ruin one of the best weekends of my life. Because we did find a blue racer, and a bullsnake, and a six-lined racerunner, and an ornate box turtle.

Prickly pears used in landscaping provide excellent foraging opportunities, both inside and outside of their natural range. Make sure you ask first.

207

Description

Prickly pears are a variable group of cacti, but for the most part they are easily recognized. They consist of highly flattened oblong or round pads (technically called *cladodes*) fused to one another to form trailing chains on the ground or upright, tree-like structures. Some species are no more than a few inches tall, while others may stand over 8 feet (2.5 m) in height.

Prickly pear pads are defended with two kinds of armor. First, there are the long, clustered, needle-like spines that are easy to see. These are usually more concentrated on the upper rim of the pad. The second line of defense is the infamous inconspicuous glochid. These are tiny, almost invisible, barbed spines, borne in clusters in depressions or pockets called *areoles* distributed across the entire surface of the pad. Glochids detach easily when touched.

The large flowers, consisting of numerous petals, sepals, and stamens, open in midsummer. They are typically yellow but may be orange or reddish, depending on the species. The flowers are borne along the upper rim of healthy terminal pads. The fruit that follows is shaped something like an elongated chicken egg with the wider end sliced off. Prickly pear fruits end abruptly with a symmetrical leathery depression. The fruits, known as prickly pears, or *tunas* in Spanish, also have glochid-bearing areoles on their surface; most species also have spines on the fruit.

Range and Habitat

Prickly pears have a surprisingly wide distribution; they are found through almost all of the lower forty-eight states and into southern Canada. While some species are adapted to warm climates, others thrive in areas with extremely cold winters. Their principal habitat needs are intense sunlight and low levels of soil moisture. These needs are met in deserts, on the Great Plains, and on dry, open slopes at low to middle elevations in the West. In states where you might not expect to find Cacti, they may inhabit dry sandy or gravelly sites exposed to sun, especially on steep slopes.

Prickly pears reach their greatest development in the arid Southwest, where they are a conspicuous and common feature of the landscape. Here there are several species, and some of them grow quite large. Probably the most common is the Engelmann prickly pear *Opuntia engelmannii*, which has elongated pads and juicy, purple fruit. This cactus, found in deserts and on lower mountain slopes, may reach 10 feet (3 m) in height. The pancake prickly pear *O. chlorotica* is tall with large, rounded pads and a thick, central trunk. It prefers rocky sites in mountain foothills. The Santa Rita prickly pear *O. santa-rita* is a striking member of this genus, having large, rounded, purplish or bluish pads and reaching 6 feet (2 m) high. Slightly smaller, the sprawling or brown-spined prickly pear *O. phaeacantha* rarely exceeds 3 feet (1 m) in height. It has oblong pads and produces red to purple fruits.

Leaving the Southwest, prickly pears become less common and smaller, yet they remain excellent food plants and are locally abundant. The bigroot or western prickly pear *O. macrorhiza* is a common species through much of the Great Plains and Mountain West on sandy or gravelly soil. The pads are typically prostrate and the fruits are red and juicy. In the East, small prickly pears such as *O. humifusa* are limited to rocky outcroppings, beaches, barrens, sand

Prickly pears *Opuntia chlorotica* in the Sonoran desert; this one stands about eight feet tall.

dunes, and open areas of very coarse soil, especially those on steep, south-facing slopes. Even where rainfall is heavy, water on these sites drains or percolates fast enough to leave the ground dry, giving the cacti a competitive advantage over other plants.

It is important to realize that most of the common names used here are contrived simply because most people don't like scientific names; they are not in general, standardized use by anybody. All the various species of prickly pear are commonly called "prickly pear." More specific common names are not consistently applied, so you should refer to the scientific names if you wish to cross-reference the individual species. Unfortunately, even the scientific names are often in dispute, and the species frequently hybridize.

Harvest and Preparation

Despite my painful first experience with prickly pear, it has proven itself an excellent food plant bearing four edible products. In many arid areas of the country this cactus is ubiquitous, making it among the most practical wild foods to know. In regions where it is scattered, it is well worth remembering or seeking as a food source.

Flower petal: This is the least known of the prickly pear's edible parts. These are sweet and make an excellent snack when they are in season from late May to mid July. I try to leave the reproductive parts of the flower intact, picking only a few of the petals from each blossom so that they can still fruit successfully.

Pad: The second edible product is the pad. In Mexico, where these are a popular vegetable found in markets, they are called *nopales*. Newly formed

pads, collected at the beginning of the growing season, are best—although older terminal pads can also be used. New pads can be identified by the presence of a small, greenish, fleshy leaf at the base of each areole. These leaves look like spines but are soft and fall off shortly after the pads form. You'll want to collect *nopales* with heavy gloves to avoid being impaled by the spines and glochids. You can grab a small pad and twist it until it detaches. However, Carolyn Niethammer (2004) advises cutting the pad

Prickly pear blossoms are large and attract many pollinators. Most species are yellow, such as this *O. humifusa*, but others may be red or orange.

with a knife about an inch above its base, leaving a stump from which a new pad can re-grow.

Once you have the pad in your possession, you are faced with the task of making it physically safe to eat. It isn't usually too difficult to cut off the larger spines; I often do this by cutting off the rim of the pad (which has most of the spines), then cutting out the few remaining spines. Younger pads may not yet have formed any formidable spines.

The glochids pose a greater problem. You can remove each individual areole with a knife and then rinse the pad, although this can prove quite time consuming. After cutting off the perimeter of the pad, which has the greatest concentration of areoles, I scrub the rest of the surface, going against the direction of the glochids and spines, with a large copper scouring pad, and then rinse thoroughly. Niethammer (2004) recommends scraping with a serrated steak knife. Some authors (Elias and Dykeman, 1982) recommend roasting the pad over a flame, burning off the spines and glochids while simultaneously cooking the flesh.

The skins of the new pads may be tender, but those of older pads should be peeled off before consumption. Cut the pads into strips or chunks and they are ready to be used in a great variety of ways, limited only by your imagination. *Nopales* taste something like green peppers with the tang of purslane. Their texture is mucilaginous, which some people find aversive. Fried with onions, mushrooms, and other vegetables and served over wild rice with Hoisin sauce, they make an excellent dish. They are good served in soups, or just eaten by themselves with a little salt. They can also be eaten raw, and in this state I find them pleasant despite their slimy texture.

Prickly pear pads can be stored by canning, drying, or freezing after parboiling. They will also keep for a month or two in the refrigerator if kept wrapped to prevent them from drying out.

Fruit: The best-known and most commonly eaten part of the prickly

Prickly pear in early summer with young pads. The terminal pads still have the reduced leaves growing beside their areoles, indicating that they are still young and tender.

pear is the fruit or *tuna*. Those of Engelmann prickly pear and several other large southwestern species ripen in July and August, turning to a deep red or purple. They often remain on the pads into October or later, making for a long season of collecting. They are very juicy when ripe and may reach nearly 3 inches (8 cm) in length and weigh up to 2 oz. (60 g). The tunas usually have a few spines along their upper rim, and glochid-filled areoles scattered about their skin. Pick them carefully with gloves or tongs. It is common for prickly pears to fruit so heavily that one can fill buckets in a matter of minutes.

My favorite thing to do with tunas is to clean, peel, and eat them raw, or just cut them in half and scoop out the juicy insides. The taste is surprisingly melon-like, but often with a tang and intensity that melons lack. I have juiced tunas by mashing them raw and then straining through a cloth (something finer than a cheesecloth, since it must catch all the glochids). I don't think I've ever had an easier time juicing anything. The juice can be drunk by itself or mixed with other beverages

A large, juicy fruit of Engelmann prickly pear cut in half. I used the spoon to scoop the pulp from the empty half and eat it.

Even the smaller species of prickly pear, such as this *O. humifusa*, produce good crops of fruit.

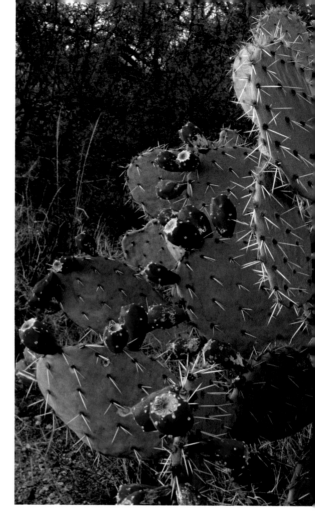

Engelmann prickly pear. The fruit you see here have ripened more than two months ago.

in innumerable ways. It can also be used as a base for prickly pear jelly, wine, or syrup.

If you want to use pulp or fruit pieces, you must first get rid of the spines and glochids. While holding the tunas with tongs or gloves, scrub them with a vegetable brush or copper scouring pad, then rinse them generously. Peeling the tunas does away with any remaining glochids. You can also cut the tunas in half without peeling them and use a spoon to scoop out the seeds and then the pulp.

If you peel the fruit, you still have to separate the seeds. Christopher Nyerges (1999) recommends blending the raw, peeled tunas until they become a watery, seedy pulp, then pouring this pulp through a colander to catch the seeds, leaving a fine puree. Prickly pear puree can be used in drinks, smoothies, jams, ice cream, and in a variety of other ways.

Where I live, the prickly pears *O. humifusa* and *O. macrorhiza* first ripen in late August but the best time for picking is the middle of September. These have much smaller fruit than their southwestern cousins but are produced in abundance. They also have a much more mucilaginous texture and a superb flavor that reminds me of melons, cherries, and apples. The fruit bears glochids but no spines. When fully ripe, the glochids fall out easily. They can be removed by rubbing with a dishcloth, paying special attention to the rim around the end of the fruit, then rinsing. I love to eat these small prickly pears raw and whole.

Prickly pears store well if undamaged. In the Southwest, they commonly remain attached to the pads for months until some animal finally consumes them. I have kept fruit of the eastern prickly pear for more than four months in my refrigerator.

Small prickly pears sliced in half and laid out for drying.

Seeds: The center of the fruit contains a number of edible seeds that are marginally chewable but hard enough to give your jaws a lot of exercise if you choose to do so. These seeds have been ground for flour or gruel and eaten in some cultures (Kindscher, 1987, Moerman, 1998). Their flavor is good, but the modern palate usually takes issue with the great quantity of coarse seedshells.

With four edible products, the prickly pear is one of the most useful wild food plants in North America. After you taste these wonderful foods, the desert doesn't look so barren after all. Amazing, isn't it, what experience does to perception?

Amaranth, Pigweed, Water-Hemp

Amaranthus spp.

Amaranthaceae – Amaranth Family

A friend of mine lives along a muddy Midwestern river, its bed piled deep with the rich topsoil washed out from thousands of acres of upstream farmland. In the summer of 2002 the area was stricken by drought. The river dropped, exposing wide strips of mucky shoreline and creating large mudflats where shallow bends and oxbows had stood only weeks before. I wouldn't have guessed that so many amaranth seeds were there; they must have washed in with the silt during summers past. Soon after the mud was exposed, amaranth shoots covered every inch of it as thick as a well-tended tobacco bed. Blessed with a perfect combination of moisture, full sun, and nutrients, they grew with a lushness and vigor that seemed both reckless and impossible. In a few weeks these plants were chest-high, but still more succulent and tender than many eight-inch shoots in the garden. It was an amaranth lover's heaven, and while visiting I ate them three times a day, for I knew I might never find amaranth growing like this again.

You don't need such particular conditions to avail yourself of this plant, however. All over the world, temperate and tropical, the amaranth has been a friend to humankind, nourishing us for many thousands of years. Few greens have been so widely eaten, and amaranth grain is cultivated and has served as a staple for several cultures. If ubiquitous, delicious, easy, and nutritious are qualities you appreciate, then amaranth should definitely be on your table.

A perfect young *Amaranthus hybridus* shoot.

General Description

The amaranth genus contains just under forty species in North America. All of these are considered edible, but they vary in abundance, size, and palatability. It is impractical in a book of this scope to attempt to identify all of these, so I will just give a generalized description of the group and then discuss some of the more common species individually. (Note: Some taxonomists divide the genus *Amaranthus* into three genera [*Acnida, Amaranthus,* and *Albersia*], but all of them will be classed as *Amaranthus* for our purposes.)

Amaranths are weedy, leafy, annual plants with solid stems growing up to 8 feet (2.5 m) tall. The stems are light green or reddish, slightly grooved, and usually branched when mature. Large amaranth plants have a coarse, bushy appearance and may grow over an inch (2.5 cm) thick at the base. Overall, their form shows a resemblance to the *Chenopodium*s (lamb's quarters and goosefoot), to which they are closely related.

Amaranth leaves are borne alternately, often with branches growing from their axils. Near the end of each branch there are usually several leaves borne quite close together, especially if the inflorescence on that particular branch is small or absent. Petioles range from half as long as the blade to one and a half times as long, and being not particularly stiff they give the leaves a slightly droopy look. Amaranth leaves are simple with entire margins, although the edges may be wavy and somewhat irregular. Leaf shape is usually ovate, spoon-like, lanceolate, or roughly diamond-shaped. The veins form a fairly prominent herringbone pattern. Leaves are typically 2–5 inches (5–13 cm) long.

Several amaranth species have come up in this flooded field after the waters receded, including *A. spinosus, palmeri, hybridus,* and *tuberculatus.*

Amaranth flowers are tiny, unisexual, and greenish; their components are hard to discern. Male flowers have three to five stamens and female flowers have a single pistil. Flowers of both sexes generally have 3–5 sepals. Amaranth flowers are arranged in tiny clusters of three called *dichasia*, and each dichasium has persistent spiny bracts at its base. Many of these dichasia are arranged in spikes or spike-like clusters at the ends of branches or in leaf axils, amounting to hundreds or thousands of flowers per plant. These large, spiny flower clusters, sometimes approaching 12 inches (30 cm) in length, are a prominent feature of mature amaranths, facilitating the recognition of their form.

The fruit of the amaranth is a tiny, inflated, papery capsule known as a *utricle*. The utricle contains a single seed that is rounded or slightly flattened, shiny, and dark.

Although mature amaranths are fairly easy to recognize, the younger plants have no single feature that gives quick and simple identification. Once you become familiar with them they can be easily spotted and identified with certainty, but before this you should closely observe a patch of plants that you

Galeopsis tetrahit: Not an amaranth!

suspect to be amaranth, watching them grow until you see enough features to make your identification certain. While there is no dangerous plant that strikes me as having a particularly strong resemblance to amaranth, many superficially similar plants may grow beside it.

One of its frequent neighbors is the hemp-nettle *Galeopsis tetrahit*. Even though hemp-nettle is a hairy mint (not a hemp, nor a nettle) with square stems, opposite leaves, and pink tubular flowers—and should therefore be easy for even a complete novice to tell from any sort of amaranth with even a bare-bones description—I have been shocked to find that many people mistake it for one. Indeed, I have witnessed wild food educators "teaching" small crowds that *Galeopsis tetrahit* is "amaranth" on two occasions. This is the kind of egregious inattention to detail that gives someone like me night sweats and heart palpitations; it helps me understand how totally ridiculous cases of mistaken identity can take place (such as eating water hemlock believing it to be wild carrot).

Hemp-nettle grows in some of the same habitats as amaranth and has leaves of an arguably similar shape (if you ignore the toothed margins), but that's where the similarity ends. And oh, yeah—it's green. Only the most inexcusable negligence would cause one to eat this herb thinking it was amaranth. *Galeopsis tetrahit* is apparently not dangerous; I know a few people who mistakenly eat it on a regular basis. But having cautiously tasted it, I dislike both the flavor and the hairy texture.

(Young hemp-nettle plants are even more frequently confused with stinging nettle shoots. At least in this case there is a better argument for resemblance. I suspect that *Galeopsis tetrahit* is one of the plants most frequently misidentified by foragers in North America.)

Range and Habitat

Amaranths are found all across North America in weedy situations. They have three requirements: lots of sunlight, exposed soil, and average to high moisture levels. Natural habitats include desert washes, river floodplains, and muddy shorelines, but few plants have benefited from human activity as much as the amaranths. Today they have become among the most abundant, widespread, and aggressive agricultural weeds on earth, the bane of every farmer and gardener. They can also be found at construction sites, dumps, and gravel pits, along roadsides and railroad tracks, or any other place where the soil is disturbed through any human or non-human agent.

Along most large rivers, amaranths will appear in great numbers in summer as the water levels recede, enjoying the moisture and lack of competition on sandbars, banks, and mudflats. Low areas in deserts often produce luxurious amaranth stands once a year, after some spring or summer downpour soaks into the earth. The shoots pop up and grow like mad under the hot sun, until the ground dries out again.

Discussion of Some Individual Species

The most widespread and abundant of the amaranths is *A. retroflexus*, known as redroot pigweed, redroot amaranth, wild beet, rough amaranth, and common amaranth, among other names. Found from East Coast to West, from Florida and Mexico north to Alaska, this weed originally grew in central and eastern North America. To many people this is *the* amaranth, and in some areas it is the only species, particularly where the soil is poor or sandy and the growing season short. It is among our larger species and has robust, erect, spiky flower and fruit clusters that may become enormous. The leaves and stems are both faintly hairy. In general, the leaves are broader and the stem stouter than other tall species of the same height, but the best identifying feature is perhaps the red root.

Almost as common is *A. hybridus*, known as green amaranth, slender pigweed, smooth pigweed, and smooth amaranth. This species has thinner, lighter green, narrower leaves and a more slender, graceful appearance than the former. Its flower clusters are narrower and often curved. *Amaranthus hybridus* is originally a river floodplain species of the eastern United States. It seems to prefer slightly moister and richer soil than *A. retroflexus*, but the two grow together in some areas. Very similar to *A. hybridus* is *A. powellii*, which goes generally by the same common names. This species is native to the Southwest but has spread throughout the United States and southern Canada and is often abundant.

Mature plants of A. *retroflexus* in late summer, showing the spiny seedheads.

A native of the deserts of the southwestern United States is *A. palmeri*, another excellent species for eating. It has spread northward and eastward as a weed over much of the continent. *Amaranthus palmeri* is a tall, robust amaranth with broad leaves and long, narrow flower clusters, the longer of which bend over and droop.

The seedhead of *A. palmeri* is narrow and often droops. The stem is now tough, but the individual leaves can be picked and eaten.

Amaranthus tuberculatus, known as rough-fruited amaranth, rough-fruited water-hemp, or tall water-hemp, is a widespread species of riversides and other moist, disturbed habitats. Growing as much as 8–10 feet (2.5–3 m) tall and having rather narrow, lanceolate leaves, this species produces long, narrow, drooping, terminal flower clusters often interrupted by small leaves. This species, along with *A. hybridus*, formed the amaranth "jungle" that I described at the beginning of this account.

I have never eaten southern amaranth or southern water-hemp *A. australis*, but it deserves mention just for its sheer size. This narrow-leaved amaranth of the southeastern states is the largest North American annual that I have ever heard of—occasionally growing 30 feet (9 m) tall with a "trunk" that may be 12 inches (30 cm) in diameter (Mosyakin, 2003)!

Prostrate pigweed or creeping amaranth *A. blitoides* also has small axillary flower clusters and small spoon-shaped leaves. This species lays on the ground or is slightly elevated, a growth habit distinguishing it from most others. This plant, originally native to central North America, grows on disturbed ground and now ranges through all of the mainland United States and the southern half of Canada. One of its native habitats is prairie dog towns, where it still thrives, but it also grows from less pristine ground, such as sidewalk cracks.

Many other amaranths are found in North America, and all are considered edible.

right The red root of redroot amaranth.

below Creeping amaranth *A. blitoides* growing along a sidewalk and building foundation.

Harvest and Preparation

Both the greens and the grain of amaranth are used as food. Requiring less labor to prepare, the greens are far more popular among foragers today. They can often be collected in enormous quantities and have an excellent mild flavor. Because of amaranth's love for disturbed soil, it is often abundant in areas frequented by people.

Greens: Young amaranth plants can be eaten whole until the stems begin to get tough. The height at which this happens varies greatly according to many conditions, so you'll have to test their tenderness by bending or breaking the stalks. The stems soften a great deal when cooked—you may be surprised to find seemingly tough ones becoming quite tender after steaming or boiling. Experiment with your local species to get a feel for this, and eventually you'll be able to tell just by looking which plants are still tender enough to use. One sign that the stems are getting tough, regardless of size, is the appearance of flower clusters.

Young, tender shoot of *A. palmeri*.

I do not usually like raw amaranth stems or greens, but cooked they are wonderful. Steamed or boiled for a short time, the young stems become softer than asparagus, and the greens are better than spinach. They can be harvested and used just like lamb's quarters, but I actually like the flavor of amaranth much better. I usually eat mine with a little salt after briefly steaming, but they can be used in casseroles, quiches, lasagnas, soups, or any other way you might employ spinach.

After the stalks start getting tough, pick only the tender leafy tops or branch tips, feeling down the stem to find the "bend-easy" point and breaking it there. These tops can be used just like the young plants, and you can collect them until the plants begin flowering.

Once the plants have matured and begun to flower, the stems start to get woody, but the leaves remain good as long as they are green. While older leaves are not as good as the youngest greens, they are still a very satisfactory potherb. Just be sure to pluck only individual leaves and avoid stem sections.

I have tried many species of amaranth and found all of them palatable. Experiment with whatever species is common in your neighborhood.

Amaranth is a hot-weather plant and usually does not begin to grow until late spring or early summer. Once the topsoil is warm, amaranth seedlings will germinate until early fall when the weather cools off. The greatest number, however, will sprout in early to mid summer, often creating a flush of growth that hides the ground from view. As days shorten later in the season, amaranth plants reach maturity at smaller and smaller sizes, and it is harder to find tender growth on these late-season plants.

Amaranth greens are extremely nutritious. A 100 mg portion of *A. palmeri* greens contains 6,100 IU of vitamin A, 80 mg of vitamin C, 411 mg of calcium, and 3.4 mg of iron (Nabhan, 1985).

Grain: Amaranth seeds have been used as a staple food source for thousands of years by many cultures, particularly those in arid and semi-arid regions. There are numerous ethnographic examples of this in the southwestern United States (Moerman, 1998). Not only were amaranths gathered extensively from the wild, they were also a cultivated staple in many places and are still widely grown today. Amaranth flour and grain can be purchased at health food stores and is also used in products such as breads, soups, cereals, chips, and pasta.

The grain is harvested in late summer and fall after the amaranths have gone to seed and the plants have begun to die. To harvest, you can strip the fruit and seed material into a container by hand, let it dry, rub it to loosen the seeds, and then winnow off the chaff. Many species have spiny seedheads and you will not want to remove them by hand. For these, you can cut the whole plant or the large fruiting branches and flail or beat the seeds out onto a clean tarp or sheet. If they are moist, you should dry them before flailing out the seeds.

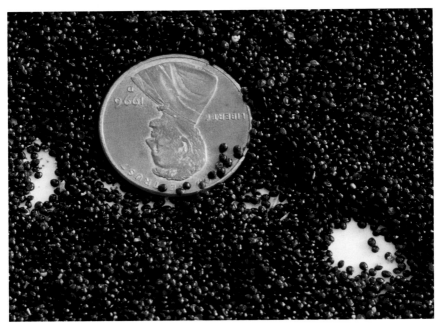

Close-up of amaranth seeds.

Once the seeds are beaten free from their bracts, winnow off the chaff. After winnowing, I rinse the seeds to get them even cleaner. You can then go straight to boiling them, or you can let them dry before grinding. Amaranths growing beside plowed fields often have sand or dirt that has blown and lodged in the bracts. This mixes with the seed and is inseparable from it, so you'll want to avoid such collecting sites.

Wild amaranth seeds are dark brown or black, shiny, and about the size of a large grain of sand. Although they are produced in great abundance, their tiny size makes them difficult to winnow. The bracts of many species are extremely irritating to the throat and mouth, making it imperative to get clean seeds. Were it not for these frustrating drawbacks, I would eat lots of amaranth grain, for the flavor is excellent. Most of my experience is with *A. retroflexus*, and I suspect that some of the other species may have grain that is easier to process. Once harvested the seeds can be stored indefinitely like other grains. Amaranth grain is rich in the amino acid lysine and therefore makes a complete protein when mixed with corn. They are 15% protein (Tull, 1987).

Amaranth grains are usually parched or roasted before being used. This causes the hard, outer shell to split open and reveal the light-colored insides; it also improves the flavor. The seeds are traditionally ground or pounded into a flour or meal. You can do this the old fashioned way with a mano and metate, or you can try a blender, coffee grinder, or flour mill. In my flour mill, many of the tiny seeds squirt out from between the burrs without getting ground. I cook the mixture of ground and unground seeds into a hot cereal, which is delicious. Amaranth flour or meal can also be used in breads, tortillas, pancakes, and as a soup thickener.

Dead amaranth plants along a desert wash, bearing large seedheads. The seeds can be collected from late summer into the winter.

We are a culture obsessed with oversimplification, intent on dichotomizing everything. But if one of our most noxious weeds is also a superb food plant, do we call it *bad* or *good*? Do we love it or hate it? Or do we learn from it that such pre-judgments are unnecessary and blinding?

Dock

***Rumex* spp.**

Polygonaceae – Smartweed Family

As a child, I loved rhubarb and ate it daily during the spring, but we had none growing in our yard. If I wanted some, I had to walk several blocks to my aunt's house or pilfer it from a neighbor. I always kept my eye out for rhubarb. One day I found a plant that looked very much like rhubarb in the tall grass right beside the garage. I knew that raspberries, blackberries, strawberries, asparagus, and carrots could be found growing wild, so I thought perhaps this was the wild form of rhubarb. I pulled up a leaf stalk and tasted . . . it was potently tart—similar to rhubarb but stronger and stringier. From then on I would occasionally eat the stems of this "wild rhubarb" on my forays around town, not learning until a few years later that I was eating a plant known as "dock"—related but certainly not feral rhubarb.

Today, of course, I dread the thought of my own child, or anyone else, jumping to such conclusions based on superficial appearances, but in this case my intuition served me well. In the years since this first taste of dock, I have learned to appreciate it as a versatile, palatable, and abundant food plant.

Patience dock, the standard to which all other docks are compared. No red spots here!

Description

Dock is a group of herbs in the buckwheat family, comprising most of the genus *Rumex* (although some *Rumex*es, like sheep sorrel, are generally not called "dock" and are not covered here). There are numerous species of dock in North America, and all are considered edible, but they do vary considerably in palatability. The best known, and possibly the most abundant, is curly dock *Rumex crispus*.

Curly dock is a perennial that grows from a thick, very deep taproot with yellow interior flesh. This plant is characterized by a basal rosette of elongated lanceolate or nearly linear leaves, rounded or tapered at the base, which can grow up to 20 inches (50 cm) long. The margins are entire but wavy or curly like lasagna noodles—a trait known as "crisped" among botanists. The midrib stands apart from the rest of the leaf's surface as distinctly light green, light purplish-red, or some combination of the two. The petioles of basal leaves are 2–6 inches (5–15 cm) long, up to 0.5 inch (13 mm) thick, solid, somewhat flattened on the top with shallow grooves running their length.

The stem leaves are similar to the basal leaves but are shorter, proportionately broader, and have shorter petioles. At the base of the petiole there is a papery sheath

above Curly dock *Rumex crispus* rosette.

below Mature dock plant.

227

called the *ocrea*. It surrounds the stem and holds a bunch of slime when the plants are young but becomes dry, brown, and brittle later on. Stem leaves are alternate and decrease in size going up the stalk—as does the petiole, which on the uppermost leaves may be shortened to nothing.

Curly dock exists solely as a rosette during its first year or longer, storing energy in its root. Only after this period, the length of which is determined by growing conditions, does it produce a flowering stalk. After flowering, the dock plant does not usually die; it gets a little larger each year and produces more and larger flowering stalks. The leaves are present before and often after flowering, photosynthesizing and storing energy in the root.

The flowering stalks shoot forth in late spring and rapidly reach their full height of 2–5 feet (60–150 cm) by early or mid summer. The stalks are green at first but in maturity may be deep burgundy. Curly dock stems are solid and zigzag gently between their alternate leaves and do not branch beneath their inflorescence. The nodes are prominent, slightly enlarged, and darkened. The stems are glabrous but have fine vertical ridges or grooves giving them texture. An individual curly dock plant may produce one to a few dozen flowering stalks.

In late spring or early summer, curly dock produces numerous flowers in a large, much-branched terminal panicle typically 10–28 inches (25–71 cm) long. Along the various branches of this cluster, the flowers are borne in tiny whorls, each flower hanging on a proportionately long pedicel that has a swollen joint below the middle. Curly dock flowers are tiny—only about 0.13 inch (3 mm) across. They have no petals, three green sepals, and three red sepals. Overall they have a drab reddish or brownish-green look to them.

The flower ripens into a small reddish-brown, three-angled achene.

Curly dock fruit. The triangular papery structures are called *valves* and the white objects that look like seeds are called *tubercles*. The real seeds are hidden under the valves.

The curly or crisped leaves of curly dock.

The inner three sepals enlarge into thin structures called *valves* after fertilization, becoming a three-part papery husk that encloses the fruit. The center of one of these three valves has an enlarged structure called a *tubercle*, which to most people looks like a seed but is not; the other two valves will have a smaller tubercle or none at all. (The size, shape and arrangement of the valves and tubercles are the primary features used in botanical manuals to differentiate the dock species.)

The ripened panicles of curly dock fruit turn dark brown in midsummer; because the rest of the landscape is bright green at this time, they are quite conspicuous. Dock seedheads persist in this state through summer, fall, and often into winter, when the seeds become an important food for deer, pheasants, songbirds, turkeys, and rodents. Dock seedheads are often collected for decorative arrangements.

There are many other species of dock found in North America, some of which strongly resemble the curly dock at a glance and are frequently confused with it. These include western dock *R. occidentalis*, which also has elongated leaves with crisped margins, but these have heart-shaped rather than abrupt or tapered bases. Nancy Turner (pers. comm., 2008) says that this is one of the best docks to use as a vegetable. Yard dock *R. longifolius* (sometimes called

Narrow-leaved or willow dock *R. triangulivalvis*.

R. domesticus) is yet another weedy species with elongate, often crisped leaves, introduced and naturalized in more northern parts of the continent. This species looks much like curly dock, but its valves are larger and lack tubercles. The taste is similar to curly dock, but more bitter. Adding to the confusion we have field dock *R. stenophyllus*, also with narrow, crisped foliage. In truth, few people differentiate these long-leaved dock species; most people simply call all of them "curly dock."

The narrow-leaved or willow dock *R. triangulivalvis* has long, narrow leaves that tend to be flat. Its flower stalks have the habit of branching at the nodes, giving the plant a spreading look. This dock has good flavor, but the leaves are small and the stems are thin and often tough. Another widespread and abundant species is bitter or broad-leaf dock *R. obtusifolius*. This plant can be recognized by its broad, heart-

above Bitter dock *R. obtusifolius* is, not surprisingly, bitter most of the time—although occasionally the flavor of the stalks is mild.

below At maturity, dock seedheads dry out and turn dark brown; the plants are most conspicuous in this stage. This mature patience dock is about eight feet tall. Note the purple stem and broad leaves.

shaped leaves and the coarsely toothed margins of the valves on its fruit. As you might guess from the name, bitter dock is usually too bitter to eat, although mild-flavored individuals are sometimes found.

There are a few native wetland docks: water or pale dock *R. altissimus*, water dock *R. verticillatus*, and great water dock *R. orbiculatus*. All of these species have large, lanceolate leaves; the great water dock is among the largest and most striking of our species.

The matriarch of all docks is *Rumex patientia*, called patience dock or simply patience. This plant was formerly cultivated as a vegetable and is still occasionally grown in gardens today. Found sporadically as an escape across North America, this is *the dock*. It is the largest, reaching 8 feet (2.5 m) in height, with the biggest leaves, which are ovate to lanceolate and about half as wide as they are long. Not only do the massive stalks and petioles dwarf those of our other species, they are also far more tender and have a delicious, mild flavor that sets the standard for docks. If you are driving a country road and spot a clump of dock leaves so robust that you think they might be rhubarb or skunk cabbage, you have probably found patience dock.

In general, the docks are an easy group to recognize. The plant which seems most readily confused with them is the uncommon wild horseradish *Armoracia rusticana*. Since horseradish is edible, the only danger in confusing the two is a dish of greens with a quite unexpected flavor. The prairie dock *Silphium terebinthinaceum* is not a dock at all but a member of the composite family. Burdock is also a composite, not related to dock despite its name.

Indicators of Flavor Quality for Docks

Identifying specific docks with a key is not difficult if you carefully examine the fruit; however, I recognize that most readers will not want to do this. You don't really need to—and due to variable flavor within most species, it may actually be more useful to just look at a few features of the plant and give it a taste test. As long as you know you have a true dock (*Rumex*), look for the following characteristics: long, narrow leaves, smooth surface texture, and no red or purple anywhere on the leaf, midvein, or petiole. (Note that patience dock is an exception to the rule of "long, narrow leaves.") Look for the lightest pea-green petioles. If you find all of these characteristics you almost certainly have a dock with good flavor. Lacking one of these characteristics does not guarantee a bitter plant but does increase the chances. With a little practice you will be able to easily spot good-tasting docks with a high degree of accuracy, even at stages of growth where differentiation of the species with a technical manual would be impossible.

Range and Habitat

Some docks are native and others introduced. Docks are widespread; just about every region in North America has one or more species, although they are localized or absent in desert regions. As a general rule, docks are lovers of sun, moisture, and disturbed ground. However, as perennials they are able to persist for many years after a disturbance. Many are weedy in habit, showing up primarily in open landscapes that have been altered by humans. Highly productive agricultural regions will almost always have an abundance of dock growing in pastures, fallow or untilled fields, along fencerows and field edges, and around barns and other buildings. If you have a yard, you probably have some dock growing in it.

Bitter dock likes moist soil and is quite shade tolerant. It is frequently found along dirt roads or trails through forested areas, but is a common weed generally, inhabiting open areas if there is sufficient moisture. Our native wetland docks are sun-loving but grow in natural habitats.

Harvest and Preparation

Dock is among the most popular wild greens, a folk herb whose use goes way back in European peasant cultures. While some people rave about it, dock also has the reputation of being bitter and unpalatable among others. Indeed, this herb, like many potherbs, ranges from delicious to detestable, and if you pick it without knowledge of the proper indicators of flavor quality (listed above), you are more likely to end up with "survival food" than table fare.

All dock parts contain oxalic acid—a common food constituent that must be consumed in limited quantities. There has been at least one death (Farre et al., 1989) questionably attributed to overconsumption of curly dock greens. In this case, an individual with his health severely compromised (a heavy smoker with diabetes and compromised kidney and liver function) ate an estimated 500 g (1.1 lbs) of dock greens. Reasonably sized portions should not be a concern to individuals in normal health.

Greens: These are the best-known edible part of dock. If you want them tender and palatable, harvest the young leaves in the center of the rosette during

Young curly dock leaves, picked while still rolled up.

Even after unfurling, dock leaves may still be good eating. The fold lines running their length indicate tenderness.

the spring. They do not have to be tiny, just young. The leaves are scrolled up as they emerge, each side unrolling as the leaf lengthens until eventually the blade lies flat. As long as the sides are even slightly rolled up, the leaf will be tender. Often, as you reach into the center of the plant to get the smallest rolled up leaves, you will find them very slimy. Don't worry: the slime is a sign that you are getting leaves at the right stage, and it will rinse off.

Dock leaves will also remain tender for a brief period after they have totally unfurled and flattened out. There are two indicators for this. First, you should see two "fold lines" running lengthwise on the leaf, about halfway between the midvein and the margin on each side. Second, the leaf should pass the "stretch test." Grab it at two points and pull gently and you should actually see the leaf stretch a little bit. If you observe both of these things the leaf should still be tender enough to use for greens. Older leaves are much tougher and usually more bitter.

Although some people eat dock greens raw in salad, I much prefer them cooked. Their flavor is sour but rich and hearty—a taste that many people appreciate. In fact, when I have the participants in my spring foraging classes vote on their favorite wild edible learned over the weekend, about one in four chooses curly dock. The greens can be steamed, boiled, fried, or cooked in the water that clings to the leaves after rinsing. Dock greens are popular creamed and are often served in quiches, omelets, lasagna, or other dishes where spinach is commonly used. They are very high in protein, iron, vitamin C, and vitamin A (USDA, NNDSR 21).

Petiole: These are homologous to rhubarb stems, and the better ones have a similar but milder flavor. I love to eat dock leafstalks raw; they are a refreshing fruity vegetable when no fruits are in season. On larger leaves I also sometimes peel away the blade and eat the midvein. Dock petioles should be uniformly light green for best flavor, and they will be most tender when the leaves are still young.

Flowering stalk: When these are young and tender and less than forty percent of their mature size, they make an excellent shoot vegetable. Dock shoots

Look for petioles that are thick, light green without red streaks, and preferably attached to young leaves. Not all of these qualify. For a very good example, see the patience dock photo at the beginning of the chapter.

above Curly dock shoots at the stage to harvest.   **below** Peeled curly dock shoot.

are not very well known, but are my favorite part of the plant. They are in season from mid spring to early summer. A typical plant produces several stems, and some large ones will have twenty to forty. Cut the shoots at the base or, later, cut the tender top portion that bends easily. (If you want your dock plant to stay vigorous, cut fewer than half of the stalks.) Strip the leaves and peel off the tough and astringent outer layer. You should end up with a light green shoot that has a mild tangy flavor and an agreeable texture that is not fibrous at all. I like these raw but they are especially good cooked and served alone or with other vegetables.

All of the dock parts mentioned can be frozen after parboiling. They can also be pressure canned. I have never experimented with drying the greens.

Root: The yellow root of curly dock (hence another of its common names, yellow dock) is highly regarded as a medicinal; however, it is generally too woody and bitter to be used as a food. I know one individual who sometimes uses curly dock roots as a vegetable, but I have not found any that were palatable to me, and reports of their use as food are rare. I suspect that, like dandelion roots, they may be much better in their first year—but first-year roots comprise a small proportion of the population. Another reported use, which I have not tried, is roasting these roots like those of dandelion or chicory to make a coffee-like drink.

Grain: This is the last and perhaps least edible part of this incredibly versatile food plant. Dock is in the same family as buckwheat, and its seeds resemble those of buckwheat in miniature. From midsummer through autumn—and sometimes well into the winter—the dry, brown fruits of dock can be easily gathered by stripping them into a pail or bag. These can be vigorously rubbed to loosen the papery valves, then winnowed to remove them, leaving behind the small three-angled seeds. These can be ground into a flour or meal or cooked into porridge. But you may not want to.

I have heard about using dock seeds as grain for many years, and occasionally get excited enough to try it. The seeds are easy to gather, the chaff rubs free

Dock seeds after rubbing and winnowing; most of these still have their shell, however.

readily, and it winnows easily from the seeds. But there's no more good news. Each seed has a bulky shell, and if you do not remove it, most of your dock seed flour consists of undigestible roughage. The seeds themselves are unpleasantly bitter. I have tried seeds from *R. crispus*, *R. obtusifolius*, *R. patientia*, *R. triangulivalvis*, and *R. longifolius*, and they ranged from bad to bad. A friend suggested that they could be leached to rid them of their bitter quality, but I have not carried the experiment that far. I have encountered some people who make flour from dock seeds, but they use it in very small proportions where its flavor is masked. Perhaps some species have better flavor than those that I have tried.

With all of the edible products of this mundane weed, you should be able to find at least one that's to your liking. Try it for yourself and see.

Maypop, Passion Flower, Apricot Vine

Passiflora incarnata, P. caerulea

Passifloraceae – Passion Flower Family

We often fail to appreciate the mundane. Thus Floridians ignore the ripe grapefruit in the backyard, New Englanders don't pick their heirloom apples, and pecans in Texas get raked up and hauled to the dump. This occurred to me as I drove past a maypop-laden fence surrounding a lumberyard in southern Missouri. After spotting the vines I took the next exit, backtracked to the parking lot, and proceeded to fill several grocery bags with fruit. In a public place like this, these delicious maypops were available to anybody—and surely they had been seen by thousands. But the first person who felt moved to pick them was a traveler eight hundred miles from home. It makes you wonder what you've been ignoring in your own neighborhood, doesn't it?

Maypop vines growing on a barbed-wire fence.

Description

The maypop is a perennial herbaceous vine with rough, slightly hairy, green stems rarely more than 0.3 inch (8 mm) thick. The vines may grow as much as 30 feet (9 m) long, climbing over fences, walls, bushes, small trees, or buildings. Some-times they trail along the ground or support themselves on weeds and grasses. Maypop vines cling to their supports with long, coiling tendrils.

The alternate leaves are deeply 3-lobed (occasionally 5-lobed), 3–5 inches (8–13 cm) long, and about equally wide. The margins are finely toothed. May-pop leaves are slightly hairy beneath and have a rough texture. They are borne on long petioles, each of which has a conspicuous pair of glands just below the leaf blade.

Maypop is unique among American plants in that its fruit and flower gener-ally go by separate names. Certainly, the striking blossom, 2–3 inches (5–8 cm) wide, is the best-known part of this plant—and it is the state flower of Tennes-see. The form is distinctive: a ring of ten white sepals and petals lays underneath

Passion flower, which turns into a maypop. Arguably the coolest-looking flower in the world. Photo by Steven Price.

a sunburst-like corona of numerous thin, wavy, pink or purple threads. In the center of the flower, five prominent cross-like yellow anthers form a circle beneath three arching styles with enlarged stigmas. Or, in laymen's terms, the flowers look really cool. Just check out the picture.

The fruit, or maypop, is a large berry, usually 1–2.5 inches (2.5–6 cm) long and elliptic, spherical, or egg-shaped at maturity. The maypop's skin is smooth and dark green at first, but slowly gets wrinkly and turns yellowish after ripening. Under the skin, the rind is made of dryish, white, spongy material, and inside of this are many teardrop-shaped, flattened, dark, crunchy seeds with a pitted surface. Each seed is surrounded by a small sac of pale yellowish pulp. Don't ask me why this fruit is called a maypop—I have yet to hear a good explanation. You can step on one to produce a popping sound, but this doesn't explain the "may" part. I have often wondered if the name is somehow derived from an association with the mayapple, which is similar in form and flavor. Unfortunately, nobody seems to know why mayapples are called *may*apples either.

The vine, flower, and fruit of the maypop are all so distinct that it is hard to imagine the plants being confused with anything else. A close relative, the yellow passion flower *Passiflora lutea* grows wild in much of the southern United States. This vine has maple-like leaves and produces a yellow flower and a small, dark purple berry. Another species, *P. caerulea*, has escaped from cultivation in southern California and now grows wild there as a weed. This passion fruit has leaves with five and sometimes seven palmately arranged lobes. The fruits of this species are large and edible, with red pulp around the seeds.

Range and Habitat

Maypop is a plant of the southeastern United States, found as far west as eastern Texas and Oklahoma, and as far north as central Missouri and the southern

edges of Illinois, Indiana, Ohio, and Pennsylvania. This vine grows in brushy, weedy places such as old fields, forest edges, thickets, ditches, roadsides, fencerows, empty lots, and backyards. They regularly

Ripe maypops hanging from the vine.

Picking maypops. As usual, on a fence. The wrinkled yellow ones are also good to eat—very good.

adorn the high fences around power substations. In fact, maypops love fences and are most often seen trailing along barbed wire or chain-link along rural roadsides. They actually seem to be more common along highways than smaller roads. Perhaps this is because the maypop is a sun-loving plant, and larger roadways create sunnier openings. The vines grow best in rich, fertile, sandy soil that is moist but not soaked. They seem to be most common in hilly farm country, but their occurrence can be sporadic and unpredictable.

Passiflora caerulea grows as a weed in disturbed areas near human habitation in southern California, and occasionally in other parts of the southern United States.

Harvest and Preparation

The edible part of this plant is the fruit. The vines are fickle in their production: sometimes laden, other times barren. However, a thick, healthy tangle of vines almost always produces some fruit. The maypop ripens in late summer or autumn, with the peak usually coming in October or early November. They are quite easy to pick, and in good conditions it is possible to fill a large pail in only a few minutes. If you drive around in late fall, keep your eye out for maypops. They are easy to spot: big green eggs dangling from a fence or bush. In many places they are free for the picking, but elsewhere you may need to ask permission. Few people will mind letting you pluck this "weed" from their fence line or ditch.

Maypops are dark green at first, eventually turning yellowish-green or light brownish-yellow. The yellowish ones are ripe, but some of the green ones are too, and discerning which ones to pick can be a little tricky. Wrinkled skin is

above A newly ripe and very ripe maypop broken open to show their insides.

below Starting on the left and going clockwise, these maypops are slightly underripe, just ripe, and very ripe. I ate all three and liked them.

a better indicator of ripeness than color, but perhaps the best way to tell is by weight: ripe maypops usually feel heavier than unripe ones. Of course, you'll have to break some open and check before you get the knack for it. When ripe, the seeds will be dark and the pulp around the seeds will be soft, aromatic, and juicy. Ripe maypops often fall from the vine; if you step on one while picking, it maypop and startle you.

Maypops are close relatives of the cultivated passion fruit *Passiflora edulis*. The taste is quite similar, and I find it absolutely delicious. It starts out rather tangy but gets mellower, richer, and muskier as the fruit yellows. Some people prefer them newly ripened and still green, while others ignore them until they are old, yellow, and wrinkly. John Muir described the maypop as "the most delicious fruit I have ever eaten" (*A Thousand-Mile Walk to the Gulf*, 1916). My favorite way to eat maypops is right off the vine. I just tear them open, suck out the pulp, and discard the skin. The seeds are hard and crunchy; you can swallow them whole, chew them up, or spit them out. I actually like their taste.

I gladly eat about twenty fresh maypops a day, but if you find bucket-loads of them, you can try making lots of fun things. First break them open and scrape out the pulpy insides with a teaspoon. To make pie or jam, add one part of water to four parts of pulp and simmer for ten to fifteen minutes until the little sacs around the seeds break. Then run the pulp through a food strainer or sieve to separate the seeds. The resulting puree can be made into superb jam, pie filling, or fruit leather.

To make juice, add two cups of water for each three cups of pulp and boil gently for twenty to thirty minutes, then strain through a jelly bag. You can use this juice for drinking or for making a light yellow, aromatic jelly. Some people also make maypop wine and use the pulp in smoothies.

I'm sure there are many more great ways to use this delicious and seemingly exotic down-home fruit. Next time you go to the lumberyard, be sure to check around the parking lot.

Toothwort

Dentaria (Cardamine) spp.

Brassicaceae – Mustard Family

When I first learned of toothwort, I read that the plant was so called because of its toothed leaves. That struck me as strange and perhaps unbelievable. Last time I checked, about half the world's dicots had toothed leaves. So why, out of all those thousands of plants, would the genus *Dentaria* be singled out

Cut-leaf toothwort *D. laciniata* in flower.

for recognition of this characteristic? It seems about as likely as an herb being named "green plant" for the color of its leaves.

I had only to dig up the tubers of *D. laciniata* one time to discover a more plausible explanation for the plant's name: the tubers look like canine teeth. In fact, they resemble canine teeth so strongly that, if you find a raccoon skull missing this part of its dentition, you should have no trouble finding a tooth-wort tuber to appropriately fill the vacancy, and few people would notice the substitution without careful inspection.

Description

There are several species of toothwort in both western and eastern North America. Members of the mustard family, all are rather small spring ephemerals with a low, spreading form. The one most common where I live is the cut-leaved toothwort *D. laciniata*. This species typically grows 3–8 inches (8–20 cm) tall. A single, naked stem emanates from the soil and bears one deeply cut, divided leaf. On

Leaves of *D. laciniata.*

flowering individuals the stalk produces a raceme of four-petaled white flowers just above this leaf. On the largest plants this flower cluster might be 6–8 inches (15–20 cm) long and reach a little more than a foot (30 cm) off the ground. The flowers quickly die, after which long, narrow seedpods form in their place.

The tubers of cut-leaved toothwort (which might be more properly called "rhizome segments") are 0.5–1.25 inches (1–4 cm) long and pointed at both ends. They are usually connected in chains, with the sharp end of one attached to the sharp end of the next, but they break apart so easily and the fused area is so small that this can be hard to notice. The color of these tubers is generally a cream or a dull yellow, but where they are growing on the surface and exposed to light they typically become dull green. Two other eastern species with tooth-like rhizome segments are *D. multifida* and *D. heterophylla*.

Another common toothwort of the East is the two-leaved toothwort *D. diphylla*. This species generally grows an opposing pair of leaves upon its stalk, and each leaf consists of three coarsely-toothed leaflets. The large toothwort *D. maxima* has much larger leaves, compound or irregularly divided, with wide leaflets or divisions. Although larger than most species, it still remains generally shorter than knee-high. These two species have irregularly constricted fleshy rhizomes rather than tooth-like structures.

Besides being widespread in the East, many species of toothwort are found west of the Cascades and Sierra Nevada, from southern California north to southern British Columbia. The botanical nomenclature of toothworts in the West is in such a shambles that I will not try to list the species; nobody seems able to agree on what is a species, subspecies, or variety. You will find these plants listed under the scientific names *D. californica, tenella, pulcherrima, gemmata, nuttallii,* and others. Common names include California toothwort, Nuttall's toothwort, yellow-tubered toothwort, milkmaids, and spring beauty.

D. pulcherrima in flower.
Photo by Bill Merilees.

The leaves of *D. diphylla* are quite broad, but the flowers are very similar to those shown for the other species.

The Genus *Cardamine*

Most recent works classify toothworts in the genus *Cardamine*. In this scheme, there is no genus *Dentaria*. People, especially taxonomists, love to dichotomize. Typically, toothworts (*Dentaria*) and bitter cresses (*Cardamine*) are clearly different. Toothworts have enlarged, fleshy rhizomes, while bitter cresses do not. Toothworts have few leaves, while bitter cresses usually have many upon the stalk, and frequently have a basal rosette as well. However, there are a number of plants that do not fit this dichotomy, and are not clearly a toothwort or a bitter cress. This fact has greatly distressed some people and has given other people doctoral theses in taxonomy. The classification that I follow—using the genus *Dentaria*—is generally considered outdated, but it is more useful to foragers. So be aware that if you try to cross reference these plants in other sources, particularly new ones, they will often be found under the genus *Cardamine*.

The bitter cresses are edible, or at least marginally so. Some of them even taste like toothworts. But few of them have any useful underground storage organs, and the information in this account is not fully applicable to them.

Range and Habitat

Toothworts are typical of rich-soiled hardwood forests. In the East they can be found from Minnesota and Arkansas east to Maine and northern Florida, where they are associated with such plants as spring beauty, wild leek, wild garlic, jack-in-the-pulpit, trout lily, and mayapple. In the Pacific states they are found at low to middle elevations in wooded areas, especially along streams and other areas with moist, rich soil.

Toothworts are among the earliest spring ephemerals to emerge and the earliest to die back. Whole patches seem to turn yellow almost overnight, withering away and melting into the leaf litter in a week's time. In some years this plant's growing season is rushed into four weeks, ending as the foliage unfolds on the trees overhead.

Harvest and Preparation

Toothwort is more of a seasoning than a food. And unlike most wild foods, one can make an easy comparison with a familiar cultivated plant to describe its flavor—it tastes very much like horseradish. Perhaps a little less potent than its domestic relative, the horseradish flavor of toothwort is still strong and unmistakable. So if you detest horseradish, feel free to stop reading.

You can get the horseradish flavor from the toothwort's leaves or tubers/ rhizomes. The greens are at their best before the plants flower. They are somewhat milder than the rhizomes and their horseradish flavor is notable but not overpowering. The entire above-ground plant—greens, stems, and even flowers—can be placed on burgers or sandwiches to impart the desired spiciness. They can also be used as a garnish, trailside nibble, or in salads. You can chop the leaves and mix them with cabbage, onion, and wild rice for egg roll filling.

Unlike the greens, which are available for only a few weeks out of the year, the tubers or rhizomes are always in season, so long as you can find them and get to them. Since toothwort often grows in enormous patches

The tooth-shaped tubers of *D. laciniata*.

that carpet many square feet of the forest floor, it is easy to mark an area for harvesting after the visible greenery has disappeared. In fact, the cut-leaved toothwort is so abundant where I live that I can easily find the tubers by "blindly" digging in an area that appears to be good habitat. I like to harvest toothwort tubers with a small, single-handed digging stick such as I use for ground beans.

Many species of toothwort have rhizomes such as this *D. diphylla.*

It is hard to overharvest toothwort because the colony is broken up into so many tiny units. Each tuber or short length of rhizome can generate a separate plant, and there are often dozens of plants per square foot. Unless you dig up an entire area and systematically remove all the tubers, overharvest should not be a problem. However, you should refrain from collecting unless the plants are abundant, and collect judiciously. Luckily

Toothwort fangs. Photo by Russ Lake.

for the toothwort, few people want huge quantities of a horseradish-like seasoning, and impatient people get frustrated with these small tubers.

It is easy to make a horseradish-like sauce from toothwort. Put a half-cup of well cleaned tubers or rhizomes in a blender to pulverize them, then follow a typical recipe for horseradish sauce, using the pulverized toothwort in place of the grated or pulverized horseradish in the recipe.

I have not had the opportunity to eat every toothwort species, but the flavor has been very similar among those species that I have tried. I prefer cut-leaved toothwort only because of its smoother surface texture, which makes the tubers easier to clean.

Garlic Mustard

Alliaria petiolata

Brassicaceae – Mustard family

Once upon a vegetable, there was a flower. And the flower became seed, and the seed spread far, far from the garden where it had originally been planted. Soon the vegetable grew everywhere. But it was no longer a vegetable; it had become the most hated weed in the land. It was the rogue vegetable, the evil plant, the wildflower to end all wildflowers. First posses were formed to fight it, then armies were raised. Propaganda was written and distributed to stir up the public against this evil foreign invader. Yes—garlic mustard—that despicable displacer of our beloved woodland flora. You cannot utter the very name among wildflower watchers without hearing the murmurs and echoes of contempt.

And yet, can we blame a plant for being a plant? Does anyone remember the beginning of the story? Who brought us the garlic mustard in the first place? After all, it is a vegetable.

Leaves of a garlic mustard rosette in autumn. These have a strong flavor and are for seasoning only.

Description

Garlic mustard is a delicate woodland herb that follows the typical biennial pattern. In the first year it exists as a rosette of long-stalked basal leaves, and in the second year it produces a vigorous flowering stalk, then dies after producing seed.

Garlic mustard's basal rosettes contain several simple, kidney-shaped leaves. These are typically 1.5–3 inches (4–8 cm) across. They are as broad as or broader than they are long, and coarsely and irregularly toothed. The petioles are red or reddish green and up to 4 times the length of the leaf blade; they are shallowly channeled and hairy, especially along the upper edge of the channel.

The flowering stalks begin to shoot up in mid spring and reach their full height of 18–36 inches (45–90 cm) within a few weeks. The leaves emanating from the base of the stalk have very long petioles, but these get drastically shorter going up the stalk. Cauline (stem) leaves are borne alternately; they resemble the basal leaves but are proportionately less broad, and those at the top are more prominently toothed. The stalk itself is smooth, rounded, and solid in cross section, and is coated with a light bloom and scattered hairs. It grows rather straight and is generally unbranched except at the top.

Garlic mustard flowers.

251

In typical mustard fashion, the inflorescence atop the stalk consists of several racemes of small, four-petaled white flowers. These mature into 1–1.5 inch (2.5–4 cm) long four-parted ascending pods containing many dark, elongated seeds.

Range and Habitat

Garlic mustard is an invasive exotic weed that is native to Europe and northwestern Asia. It has become well established in many of the hardwood forest areas of eastern North America, west to the Great Plains. It is also found occasionally at lower elevations in the West where the soil is rich and the rainfall adequate. Garlic mustard is known from Utah, eastern Colorado, Idaho, Washington, Oregon, British Colombia, and southern Alaska.

Garlic mustard thrives in rich soil under light to moderately heavy shade. It takes over the understory of oak-hickory and mesic forests alike, crowding out native ground flora. If left unchecked, the forest floor may become a garlic mustard monoculture. In stands that have lost their native flora through overgrazing or other abuse, and in areas where forests have generated in place of prairies and oak savannahs, garlic mustard can invade and take over extremely rapidly. It is also *allelopathic*—chemically inhibiting the growth of competing plants. In stands that still have a healthy population of spring ephemerals and other perennials, the garlic mustard makes inroads much more slowly, but is still invasive.

Garlic mustard has the ability to completely take over the forest floor, crowding out all native vegetation. Pull it out when you see it, and keep the seeds out of your shoes and pockets.

Harvest and Preparation

As its common name suggests, garlic mustard is a mustard with a strong garlic flavor. When used correctly, this herb makes an excellent flavoring. Several times I have had pesto made from the mature leaves. While the pungency was somewhat strong for my taste, this pesto was pleasant when used sparingly. Generally, however, I do not eat the mature leaves of garlic mustard, as the flavor is simply too strong and bitter. Many people have been turned away by this plant's overpowering flavor; if this has been your experience, there is good news ahead.

As with most vegetables, there is a specific stage of growth during which it is ideal to harvest garlic mustard, and there is a specific part that is best to use. And as with many wild edibles, these details seem to be little known.

This is the ideal stage at which to harvest garlic mustard for use as a vegetable.

A nice handful of succulent garlic mustard shoots.

The best part of garlic mustard to harvest is the tender flowering shoot. The time to pick these is just before the flowers open, or when only a few of them have bloomed. The plant is in this stage for only a brief period in mid spring. At this time the flower buds will be clustered near the top, slightly reminiscent of broccoli, and the stalk will have attained about half or less of its final height. The stems will still be succulent and thick in proportion to their height. Bend or break the stalks with your fingers, keeping the tender portion of the top.

For good culinary results with garlic mustard, try to get more stalk and less leaf. Sometimes I use a small portion of the leaves with the shoots in my cooking, but more often I remove and discard all the foliage. Garlic mustard shoots have this plant's characteristic flavor of mustard greens and garlic, but it is mild and the stems are sweet and juicy.

I like to chop up these stalks and use them in salad, or just snack on a few raw. They also make an excellent boiled or steamed shoot vegetable to serve like asparagus, and they are among my favorites while they are in season. I also find much use for tender garlic mustard shoots in soup, where their flavor adds a nice touch.

The flower buds and leafy tops of the shoots are somewhat stronger in flavor but can be used in many of the same ways. A sprig of garlic mustard top goes well on a brat or roast beef sandwich. A creative cook should be able to find many excellent uses for garlic mustard shoots and tops, so long as the potency of the flavor is kept in mind. I usually stay away from the mature leaves and the leaves of first-year rosettes, finding them unpleasantly bitter. However, they can be used as a seasoning.

Garlic mustard stalks can be stored for out-of-season use by pressure canning or blanching and freezing. I have not tried drying the stems or leaves.

I once tried making a mustard-like condiment from garlic mustard seeds, following methods similar to those I had successfully used with wild black mustard seeds. The result was really nasty. There may be a better recipe and better methods than the ones I used, but I tasted nothing in the flavor promising enough to make me want to try again. Looking on the bright side, however, at least I destroyed all those seeds.

I want to emphasize that garlic mustard is an enormous ecological problem. No matter how much you may decide you like it as a vegetable, ***never*** plant it, and ***always*** take care to dispose of any seeds that might have collected in your footwear or clothing before they have the chance to spread. Furthermore, if you have garlic mustard in your woods, take some time in the spring to pull it out before it flowers. If you don't control this weed, you *will* lose your wild leeks, spring beauty, waterleaf, squirrel's corn, Dutchman's breeches, trillium, dwarf ginseng, horse gentian, trout lily, jack-in-the-pulpit, green dragon, pyrola, rattlesnake plantain, shooting star, hog peanut, and a host of other treasures. If you come to enjoy garlic mustard as a food, then your harvesting can become part of your eradication efforts.

Blueberry, Huckleberry, Bilberry

Vaccinium spp.

Ericaceae – Heath Family

It was a calm, hot evening in early August when I parked my car at the intersection of two sand roads in the Moquah Barrens. There were no sounds but the sparse conversation of crickets, cicadas, and a few distant songbirds. I was looking for two things: a place to spend the night, and a place to pick blueberries in the morning. I ran across the open heath, stopping here and there to pick a handful of berries or examine the tracks at the mouth of a hillside burrow. I grabbed my sleeping bag, a half-gallon jug of water, and a tub for collecting, and hauled them to an almost-level grassy spot I had seen at the base of a hill. There were blueberry bushes on all sides.

I lay on my back and watched for shooting stars, listening to a far-off whippoorwill. Coyotes yipped and sang, red bats darted back and forth in the dark sky. I said my prayers, dreamt of tomorrow, and fell asleep with sweetfern heavy in my nostrils.

I awoke in the starry darkness to the sound of soft footfalls and deep sniffing close at hand. My heart started pounding; I knew it was *mukwa*, the no-nonsense

Lowbush blueberry *Vaccinium myrtilloides*.

night shift among berry pickers. He must have gotten a good whiff just then, for his dark form bolted up the hill until all was silent but for crickets. And somehow I fell back asleep.

Before sunrise I woke up for real and, remembering the night's half-sleeping adventure, looked about to make sure I was still in one piece. Then I got to work. By early afternoon I had filled my three and a half gallon tub, all in a little ravine where the moisture collected and the berries grew larger. I still had plenty of time for an invigorating swim at the Cornucopia beach, and a picnic of fresh blueberries, smoked trout, and cold water from the locally famous artesian well.

Now that's a good day if I've ever had one.

Blueberries Versus Huckleberries

Some would argue that only members of the genus *Gaylussacia* are appropriately called "huckleberries," but this doesn't hold up well to linguistic examination. It seems pretty evident how the blueberry got its name, but how about the huckleberry? This name is believed to be a corruption of *whortleberry* or *hurtleberry*—used in England for a species of *Vaccinium*. In the eastern United States, "huckleberry" somehow got attached to the seedy-fruited genus *Gaylussacia*, and "blueberry" was assigned to the soft-seeded, blue-fruited species of *Vaccinium*. When settlers traveled west to areas where *Gaylussacia* was absent, they found quite a variety of *Vaccinium* fruits. Since they needed terminology for this variety and the name *huckleberry* was too catchy to leave alone, it was applied in western North America to those *Vaccinium* fruits which were more sour than the familiar ones from the East. Thus the "huckleberry" group in the East (*Gaylussacia*) is distinctly separate from the "blueberries" (blue-fruited *Vaccinium*). In the West, however, there is not such an obvious or logical distinction: "huckleberries" are those particular members of the *Vaccinium* genus that people have chosen not to call "blueberries." Adding to the confusion is the name "bilberry," given to some of the northern blueberries with more rounded leaves and awned anthers.

If I dared to claim that the beloved mountain huckleberry of the West was really just a sour blueberry, some readers in Montana and BC might throw this book into the fireplace, so I won't go that far. But through this account, I will collectively call the black or blue-fruited species of *Vaccinium* "blueberries" for the sake of convenience, only using "huckleberry" or "bilberry" in reference to the specific kinds that commonly go by those names. This account does not cover any of the red-fruited species of *Vaccinium*, such as cranberries and red huckleberries, for these are generally quite different in flavor and use.

Description, Range, and Habitat

There are about thirty-five species of blueberry in North America. They range throughout most of the continent but occur more sporadically southward, where they are confined to sandy lowlands, rocky ridges, and high elevations. Blueberries are generally absent from rich-soiled hardwood forests, prairies, rich farmland, and deserts. They abound in areas with poor, rocky, or sandy soil, especially those with conifer forests. Blueberries are lovers of acidic ground and are a prominent component of the vegetation of northern and mountainous regions.

All of our various blueberry species are branchy woody shrubs with small alternate leaves and thin twigs; most are deciduous. They range in size from a few inches to 12 feet (4 m) tall. Blueberry leaves are simple and entire or finely toothed, generally ovate or elliptic in shape, and sessile or with very short petioles. Some of the species spread by stolons to form dense colonies.

Blueberries have small bell or urn-shaped flowers composed of five petals that are fused except at the tip. They bloom in spring. The fruits are typically globose and have a "crown" on the distal end composed of five lobes (although on some species this crown is reduced to a short ridge); the berries are flattened or indented under this crown. The berries often have a whitish bloom on their skin. Most people have little difficulty recognizing blueberries. The plants most commonly confused with them are probably "true" huckleberries, salal, and serviceberries, all of which sometimes share its habitat and are also delicious edibles.

We are blessed with so many excellent kinds of blueberries that it would be ridiculous to describe them all here. I'll stick to some of the more widespread, abundant, and popular species.

Starting in the Pacific Northwest, the Alaskan blueberry *V. alaskaense* and oval-leaved blueberry

Flowers of *V. angustifolium*.

V. ovalifolium, a tall species of the Northwest with tangy berries.

V. ovalifolium are abundant in openings in moist coniferous forests, particularly in coastal Alaska and British Columbia. Both of these similar-looking species have broad leaves and reach 6 feet (2 m) in height. Their fruit ripens in July, just after salmonberries, which is earlier than other species of blueberry in this region.

The evergreen or California huckleberry *V. ovatum,* found from British Columbia south through California, is one of the few evergreen species. This shrub reaches 12 feet (4 m) in height and often grows in dense stands in coastal conifer forests. The ovate leaves are shiny, tough, and leathery. The blackish berries ripen in late summer or autumn and often remain on the bushes into the winter.

Leaves and immature fruit of evergreen huckleberry *V. ovatum,* a common species on the west coast.

The popular huckleberry of the mountain west, *V. membranaceum*. This species has large, broad berries.

The dwarf bilberry *V. caespitosum* and the bog bilberry *V. uliginosum* are similar, very short species with highly regarded fruit found across the northern parts of the continent, from West Coast to East. These blueberries are found in bogs, alpine heaths, rocky ridges, and across the far northern tundra where they are a very important wild food. They are collected from late July to September.

The most popular species in the Northwest is *V. membranaceum* (synonym: *V. globulare*), called "black huckleberry" or "mountain huckleberry." Mountain huckleberries are found in coniferous forests that cast moderate to light shade and in forest openings and clearings. They range from Alaska and the Yukon south to Wyoming, Idaho, and northern California, growing from middle to subalpine elevations.

The cultivated blueberry was bred from the highbush blueberry *V. corymbo-*

sum, found in swamp edges and sandy woods from Michigan and Quebec south to northern Florida and eastern Texas. This shrub reaches 12 feet (4 m) in height but 5–9 feet (1.5–3 m) is typical. In some places the highbush blueberry is very common—it dominates huge tracts of the New Jersey Pine Barrens, for example. The fruit is borne in small clusters and is sometimes produced in great abundance.

Several very small northern species, such as this *V. uliginosum*, are known as "bilberries."

The highbush blueberry *V. corymbosum* is the ancestor of our cultivated blueberries. In the wild it commonly grows six to twelve feet tall. Photo by Thomas Vining.

There are several species commonly known as "low-bush blueberry" in the East. The two most common are *V. myrtilloides* and *V. angustifolium*. These are knee-high blueberries of bog edges, sandy pine woods, barrens, burns, roadsides, and other acidic, nitrogen-poor habitats in our northern forests.

If you get some satisfaction in identifying your specific blueberry, go for it—but you don't need to. As long as you have a blue or black fruit from a *Vaccinium* shrub, you know that it is edible and in most cases delicious.

Lowbush blueberry *V. angustifolium*. This species may have dark fruit like this, or they may be coated with a heavy bloom making them appear light blue.

Harvest

Blueberries and huckleberries are among the most sought-after wild fruits in North America. Every summer, all across the northern United States and Canada, these little berries become a focus of activity in rural communities. Weekend berry camps are planned, with families pitching tents along old logging roads. Dusty old pickups are spotted pulled off along backroads at dawn as if it were deer season. Blueberry pies show up at the dinner table, consumed ravenously amidst excited recountings of the day's adventure, as the canning kettle's lid rattles in the background. Blueberry and huckleberry festivals honor the harvest, and seasonal fare goes on sale at local bakeries.

For some, blue-berrying is serious business. In Ontario, Quebec, and Nova Scotia, battalions of pickers spread across the hills and bogs in pursuit of lowbush blueberries. The highbush kind are sought by sly collectors who brave mosquitoes and ply the edges of eastern swamps. Many five-gallon pails are filled with huckleberries from the mountains of British Columbia, Washington, Oregon, and Montana and sold for a handy sum. But the epicenter of blueberry picking is Maine, where thousands of harvesters rake in millions of dollars worth of fruit every year.

The blueberry crop is variable from year to year, depending largely on the weather. Warm, calm, sunny days during flowering ensure good pollination and

Lowbush blueberries begging to be picked.

fruit set, while a wet and sunny summer promotes the development of plump, sweet berries. Other factors, such as browsing, logging, and especially fire, have longer term effects on the blueberry crop. Where I live, the lowbush blueberry season runs from early July to mid or late August. I pick into a shallow, wide dish, setting it on the ground near the bushes and scooting it around as I pick. Picking by hand, a typical rate is 1.5–2 quarts (or liters) per hour, and very good is about 2 gallons (8 liters) per hour.

In some areas it is customary to use a blueberry rake or comb to speed up the picking. This is a tool with long tines mounted on some kind of receptacle with a handle. The thin twigs and leaves slide between the tines, but the wider berries get pulled loose and roll back into the receptacle. When using this tool, don't try to rake too much at one time, and rake only the upper twigs, or your tines will get stuck in the bushes and you'll damage the plants. Under the right conditions, the blueberry rake makes picking *much* faster. However, raked berries will have lots of unwanted leaves, twigs, unripe berries, and other debris that must be removed. In the Northeast and other places where rakes are commonplace, some people have machinery set up to clean out

Blueberry rake.

this trash. If you rake your blueberries and don't have access to such a machine, there are a few ways to get it done. You can remove most of the leaves, twigs, and grass by winnowing, pouring the berries from one container to another in front of a fan. Another technique is to lay a wet cloth over a piece of plywood sloped at about a 45 degree angle. Berries poured onto the top roll down the cloth into a container below, but most of the twigs and leaves stick to the surface. However, neither of these methods gets rid of the unripe fruits.

Some people contend that raking is detrimental to the blueberry resource. While rakes do a small amount of damage to the bushes, so does walking on them. Unless they are egregiously misused, I don't believe that rakes have any significant effect on blueberry patches. If you want to try one, you can make your own, or you can order one from the Hubbard Rake Company of Jonesport, Maine.

Highbush blueberries have somewhat larger fruit than the lowbush species and often lend themselves to easy and fast picking. Because of their height, you can pick them while standing and using a blickey. Since highbush blueberries grow further south than other species, they can often be picked in June and sometimes even May.

Probably the most popular berry in the Northwest is *V. membranaceum.* The state berry of Idaho, this species goes by too many names to keep track of: mountain, black, and thin-leaved huckleberry, mountain or tall bilberry, big whortleberry, thin-leaved blueberry. Those who pick them just call them huckleberries. It is easy to see why these are popular. They often grow in breathtaking abundance. The berries are the largest of our blueberries, occasionally larger than even the most outrageously overgrown cultivated blueberries. Size and abundance combine to make for fast picking, although the berries are borne singly rather than in clusters like most blueberries. Some people improve their harvest rate by using rakes or by beating the bushes over a container. Mountain huckleberries ripen in July, August, and into September at higher elevations.

Raking or combing is very efficient, but you must remove unwanted debris afterward.

Preparation

It feels a little silly to me, telling people how to eat blueberries. Everybody knows they are delicious as a snack, and in pancakes, muffins, or pie. In my opinion, most blueberries are not sour enough to make good jam—I like them just canned by themselves or preserved in a light sugar syrup. Blueberries freeze very well. If you spread them out flat on a cookie sheet before freezing, then put them into bags after they have frozen solid, they will not stick together in one big clump.

In general, those blueberries called huckleberries are more tart than the typical blueberry. Mountain huckleberries have a distinct, tart, musky flavor that some people dislike but many love. They are much better than other blueberries for jams and preserves, but their superiority for pies and eating out-of-hand is in question. For a good read about this awesome berry, along with excellent recipes and an overwhelming dose of huckleberry snobbery, find a copy of *The Huckleberry Book* (1988), by 'Asta Bowen.

My favorite way to preserve blueberries is by drying. In an electric food dehydrator it is easy to dry whole berries, which shrivel into tiny, hard, raisin-like objects. However, I prefer the texture and flavor of blueberries crushed before drying. I generally just snack on dried blueberries by themselves.

If you end up with a good supply of blueberries, you should have no problem using them. Recipes for blueberry pies, pastries, muffins, breads, and dozens of other desserts are easy to find in conventional cookbooks. There are two main differences with wild blueberries: they are less runny because they have a greater skin-to-pulp ratio, and they taste better.

If you've never spent a summer day picking blueberries or huckleberries, it's time you make the pilgrimage. From the interstate, take a two-lane; from there, take a country lane, then a dirt road to a two-track to a foot path. Bring your basket way back into the bushes, hunker down, and get to work.

Cranberry, Lingonberry

Vaccinium oxycoccos, V. macrocarpon, V. vitis-idaea

Ericaceae – Heath Family

I have always been drawn to muskegs. With their cool cushions of sphagnum moss soothing my bare feet, their snowy tufts of cotton grass, and their scattered black spruces rising like crooked spires from the dense low shrubbery, the bog forest is like no place else on Earth. In the summer sun the sedges and Labrador tea give off a rich, spicy scent that will imprint forever upon anyone lucky enough to breathe such perfect air. It was in this enchanting landscape that I long dreamed of finding wild cranberries. And when I finally looked, I found them there, glistening red jewels weighing down their thread-like vines, scattered across everything like hail after a storm. Even better than I had imagined.

Fulfillment is the practice of the right expectations, and this is a life skill that foraging teaches us well.

Small cranberries *Vaccinium oxycoccos* growing on sphagnum moss.

Identification

We have three species of cranberries in North America. Two of these are bog cranberries, and they have been given the straightforward names of small cranberry *V. oxycoccos* and large cranberry *V. macrocarpon*. Our cultivated cranberries are selected varieties of *V. macrocarpon*. The fruit of the wild stock is not as uniform in size and shape as that of the farm-raised cultivars, but otherwise the two are identical. Not surprisingly, the fruit of the small cranberry is somewhat smaller. It also tends to be spherical rather than elliptic in shape, but otherwise it strongly resembles its larger cousin.

The marvelous flowers of large cranberry *V. macrocarpon*. Note the blunter, larger leaves than small cranberry, with less strongly curled margins.

Bog cranberries are small, trailing, woody vines with extremely thin, wiry, much-branched stems. Cranberry vines do not climb by twining or with tendrils; they simply grow over other vegetation and rest upon it. The leaves, like the vines, are tiny, from 0.15 to 1 inch (4–25 mm) long. Borne on extremely short petioles, they are alternate, glabrous, simple, oblong, and evergreen. The edges of the leaves are curled toward the lighter underside.

Cranberry flowers are small but striking, their four pink petals spreading widely or reflexed like those of shooting stars (genus *Dodecatheon*). In the center of each flower, eight long, tightly-clustered stamens protrude, giving it a beak-like appearance. Each blossom is borne singly at the end of a thread-like pedicel many times longer than the flower; the pedicel bears one tiny pair of leaves.

It is not very hard to tell the bog cranberries apart if you wish to do so. Besides having larger fruit, the large cranberry also has much longer vines, which often climb a foot or so up surrounding vegetation, while those of its smaller cousin generally lay on the sphagnum mat. The leaves of the small cranberry are smaller and paler beneath, with more downcurved margins; they also have pointed tips,

This bog forest or muskeg is the classic habitat of wild cranberries. I pick large and small cranberries here; where the two overlap, large cranberries like slightly wetter sites.

while those of large cranberry are more rounded. Small cranberry bears flower and fruit pedicels at the tips of its branches, while large cranberry typically does so around the middle of the branch.

The third wild cranberry, *V. vitis-idaea*, is known as mountain cranberry, highland cranberry, lowbush cranberry, cowberry, foxberry, red whortleberry, redberry, partridgeberry, or, most commonly, lingonberry. This plant has larger, tougher leaves than the bog cranberries. They are blunt-tipped and dotted with black on the underside. The stems of lingonberry are also thicker and stiffer than those of its wetland relatives, and the evergreen leaves are borne more densely. The pink, bell-like flowers have five lobes, but these are not long and recurved as with the other species. Lingonberry produces smaller fruit than even the small cranberry, but they grow in clusters rather than singly.

The only plants that are likely to be confused with cranberry are related members of the heath family such as bearberry (genus *Arctostaphylos*) and creeping snowberry *Gaultheria hispidula*. Bearberry has a red fruit but stiffer stems, and usually grows on dry upland sites. It is sometimes confused with lingonberry, but the fruit is larger and dry and mealy, with five large, hard seeds. Creeping snowberry has a similar vine to the small cranberry, but the miniscule fruit is snow white. Both bearberry and creeping snowberry are edible.

Range and Habitat

Cranberries are found primarily across Canada and the northern third of the United States, extending south to North Carolina and Tennessee in the East and Oregon and Idaho in the West. The large cranberry grows primarily in the eastern United States and southern parts of Ontario, Quebec, and Newfoundland; it is also found less commonly in the Pacific Northwest. The small cranberry grows from the East Coast to the West Coast and ranges north to the Arctic tundra. It grows in Europe and Asia as well. Lingonberries have a similar but more northerly distribution across the northern part of North America, Asia, and Europe, only reaching the lower forty-eight states in New England and the northern Great Lakes.

Where the ranges of the bog cranberries overlap they can sometimes be found growing together. However, the large cranberry is typically found in wetter, shrubbier sites, often at the edge of open water, where it can drape itself over sedges, leatherleaf, laurel, or bog rosemary. The small cranberry is typical of open bogs with sunny, exposed sphagnum moss, which its small vines lay directly upon. Typical habitat for the lingonberry is alpine meadows, rocky outcrops, sparse rocky woods, and tundra. It inhabits places with thin, acidic, and usually rocky soil, in full to partial sun.

Harvest and Preparation

To harvest bog cranberries is to enter a realm into which few people go. The landscape makes me expect to see a majestic moose trodding the wet peat between the well-spaced black spruces. The air is cool and fragrant. Even the ground—if you can call it that—feels different. A sphagnum bog is a place to lose your inhibitions, let Nature touch your skin, and get down into the soft moss to pick cranberries. Set a bowl down beside you and pluck the fruit from the soft cushion as fast as your fingers will go, like cleaning up a bag of candy spilled on a plush carpet.

Some cranberries ripen as early as August, but they reach their prime a month later and can be harvested until they are consumed by birds or covered with snow. If there is no snow, cranberries—even if frozen solid—can be collected all winter. I pick most of mine in October, when few other berries are in season. Ripe cranberries are a mixture of light green, cream, and dark red in color, with red predominating. The small cranberries are often less red than the large species. Cranberries may freeze and soften on the vine without spoiling, meaning you can often collect them in spring after the snow has melted. Such frozen berries will be soft and watery once thawed but retain their good flavor and are much appreciated at a time when no other fruit is available.

Some harvesters use a hand-held cranberry rake, similar to a blueberry rake, where the plants grow in great abundance. However, these are designed for harvesting in the flooded bogs used for cultivated cranberries. Where the cranberries lie on sphagnum, the rake will grab gobs of moss along with the berries. With wild cranberries, the rake works best in dense stands of large cranberry where the vines stand erect, or where they dangle from shrubs well above the sphagnum.

Picking by hand, I can get two to four quarts of small cranberries per hour in a good patch, and roughly twice as many of the larger species. Since the ground is usually wet where cranberries grow, you will probably want to wear rubber boots while harvesting.

Cranberries can be incredibly abundant over large areas, and I know of places where I could pick for days on end without getting halfway across the bog. Cranberries have been an important wild fruit in many areas, and they are still available by the bushel to any forager who seeks a measure of delicious self-sufficiency.

Once gathered, cranberries will easily keep for several weeks or sometimes months in a refrigerator, a root cellar, or even a cool porch if they are kept from freezing. For longer storage you can dry, freeze, or can them in a variety of forms. To separate raked or hand-picked cranberries from their trash, soak about one gallon of berries in 3 gallons of water. Most of the sphagnum will get waterlogged and sink, making it easy to pick out clean berries.

Large cranberry vines with plump fruit, suspended from leatherleaf and bog laurel bushes. These are as large as store-bought cranberries.

Cranberry sauce is probably the most common use of this fruit. Wild cranberries tend to have slightly thicker and tougher skins than their domestic counterparts, so I prefer to make my sauce from pureed rather than whole berries. To get cranberry puree, place the berries in a pot and add a very small amount of water—just enough to wet the bottom and keep the fruit from burning to it. Then cover the pot and turn it on very low heat, stirring occasionally until all the berries have softened and popped. After this, run the cooked cranberries through a fruit strainer. Some screens will separate the skins only, and others will also remove the seeds, but in either case you will lose very little volume of the fruit by straining.

Have you ever seen a recipe for cranberry jam? Probably not by that name. It turns out that cranberry jam is better on turkey than on toast, so we call it cranberry sauce. Use your cranberry puree to make cranberry sauce exactly as if you were making cranberry jam. Use five cups of sugar to six cups of puree. Cranberries have so much pectin that you do not need to add any to get the sauce to jell, although adding pectin may allow you to use less sugar, if that's your preference. Use straight-sided or wide-mouthed jars so that the sauce can be slid out and cut before serving.

If you don't mind the skins or are partial to sauce made from whole cranberries, you can do this, too. Just cook the berries until they pop, as described

Bearberry *Arctostaphylos uva-ursi* sometimes grows in the same habitat as lingonberry and may be confused with it. Bearberries, although edible, are dry and mealy with several large, hard seeds. Photo by Bill Merilees.

above, and mix in sugar to taste. Then water-bath can the sauce. Some people like to embellish the sauce by using orange juice instead of water to cook the cranberries, or by adding grated orange peel to the fruit as it simmers. I prefer mine unadulterated. I like cranberry sauce made from small cranberries slightly more than that made from their larger cousin, but both are fantastic.

To make cranberry juice, put the berries in a pot, cover them with water, and boil until they all pop. At this point I like to take a potato masher and crush the fruit to release more of its juices. Next, simmer it for several minutes longer. Then pour the boiled cranberries into a jelly bag or cloth strainer suspended over a container. Let the liquid drain out slowly over several hours or overnight. If you want clear juice, do not squeeze the bag, but if you don't mind cloudy juice you can make the process go faster by wringing the bag or cloth. Once made, cranberry juice can be easily stored canned or frozen. I like to drink it straight, but most people like to sweeten it or dilute it with apple juice.

Dried cranberries are too sour for most palates, but many people love them with the addition of sugar. Dip whole or halved cranberries in boiling water to break their skins and soften their tissues, soak in a sugar syrup for several hours, and then dry them.

Cranberries have many other popular culinary uses. Often employed in sweet quick breads, especially with walnuts, cranberries add a delicious and distinctive tang. (If you cut the cranberries in half it prevents them from exploding and forming the annoying bubbles that often plague such breads.) Cranberry puree can be used in smoothies. It can also be mixed with applesauce at a ratio of about one part cranberry to five parts applesauce. Not only is cranberry applesauce delicious, it can also be spread thin and dried into a wonderful fruit leather.

Lingonberries are one of the most important of all arctic fruits. Due to their abundance, nutrition, storability, and flavor, they are employed in an incredible variety of traditional dishes from Canada, Scandinavia, Poland, the Baltic states, Russia, and elsewhere. Wild lingonberry preserves imported from Sweden are available at many grocery stores in the United States and Canada.

Being smaller than bog cranberries, lingonberries are more time consuming to pick by hand. However, the Hubbard Rake Company of Jonesport, Maine, modifies one of its rakes specifically for lingonberries, and the berries' growth on dry, rocky ground eliminates the problem of sphagnum moss clogging the tines.

The flavor of lingonberries is similar to that of bog cranberries but is faintly spicy. Like other species of cranberry, lingonberries have a long shelf life in the refrigerator or cellar. Sound, unblemished fruit have been traditionally stored

The lingonberry or mountain cranberry has thicker stems than bog cranberries and usually grows on rocky upland sites.

in unsealed barrels or jars of water, where they last for months without spoiling due to their natural antibacterial properties.

Lingonberry preserves are delicious and very easy to make. They are my favorite cranberry product. Cook six cups of fruit and add three cups of sugar (or adjust to your taste), bring to a vigorous boil, and pour into clean jars like you're making jam. You can make the preserves with or without added pectin. They are delicious on biscuits, pancakes, yogurt, or meats, or just eaten as dessert by themselves. Other lingonberry products include juice, jam, compote, and syrup.

Every year, North Americans eat millions of pounds of cranberries and drink millions of gallons of cranberry juice. Much of our population resides within a short walk or drive of prolific stands of wild cranberry, and these are equal to or better than the store-bought kind, yet few have collected or even seen this delightful little fruit. Venture into a bog some sunny October morning when the tamaracks are glowing with autumn color. When you can pry your eyes away from their smoky gold needles, search the soft moss that muffles your footsteps. Chances are, you will find what you are looking for.

Black Huckleberry

Gaylussacia baccata

Ericaceae – Heath Family

In central Wisconsin there are several thousand square miles of flat, sandy country dominated by pine-oak woodlands and vast wetlands. Although this region was brought national recognition by Aldo Leopold's *A Sand County Almanac*, it attracts few visitors, even from within the state. Tourists need lakes, mountains, coasts, cliffs, or rolling hills. Don't come to the sand counties for these things. There are few panoramic views here; you see Nature "up close and personal."

The sand counties are for people who want to follow wolf tracks along a sand road, or happen upon a Blanding's turtle digging her nest into the shoulder. It is a place for those who revel at the squawking of sandhill cranes coming through the morning fog from a tamarack-studded sedge meadow. But of all the sand counties' treasures, none bring me more daydreams than those hot August afternoons when I wade through the seas of waist-high huckleberry bushes that stretch for miles under the sparse trees. Wearing nothing but a pair of shorts and a blickey, I pick my huckleberries silently, in an all-day meditation on thanksgiving for the things I love.

Eastern black huckleberry in fruit.
This makes my mouth water.

Description

Black huckleberry *Gaylussacia baccata* is a shrub that is typically 2–5 feet (60–150 cm) tall. While it often forms large colonies, its stems do not form thick clumps. In this respect and many others, it resembles its close relatives, the blueberries. The stems do not grow straight and the branches spread widely. The twigs are thin, brown, and finely hairy; the bark becomes dark gray on older growth, with small sections of the outer layer peeling here and there.

The leaves are oval with entire margins that are minutely hairy, typically ranging from 0.75–2 inches (2–5 cm) long. They are borne on extremely short petioles, only 5 to 10 percent as long as the leaf. Huckleberry leaves are somewhat leathery for a deciduous shrub. They are dark, dull green above and lighter beneath with numerous small golden-yellow dots on both surfaces, but these are more obvious beneath. In autumn, black huckleberry is one of the highlights of the country where it grows, as the foliage turns to a striking deep purple.

The flowers appear in late May or June, hanging in small racemes from the twigs. These small, dull, yellow-orange or reddish flowers are only about 0.25 inch (6 mm) long. The corolla is fused into a five-lobed tube, which is bell-shaped and hanging.

The fruit ripens to a purple or blue-black from late July to mid August. Generally less than 0.3 inch (8 mm) in diameter, the round berries resemble blueberries but do not have the five-pointed calyx or "star" on the end. They also contain small, hard seeds that will crunch noticeably when you chew them.

There are some other species of *Gaylussacia* with edible fruit in North America. One of these is the whortleberry or dangleberry *G. frondosa*, found in much of the East. This shrub bears its long-stemmed fruit less heavily than the black huckleberry; it is not as practical to harvest and is therefore eaten less frequently.

Unfortunately, the name "huckleberry" is thrown around quite carelessly. In many areas where huckleberries do not occur, it is common for uninformed blueberry pickers to designate the

Black huckleberry flowers.

darker lowbush blueberries, lacking bloom, as "huckleberries," apparently unaware that huckleberry is in fact a totally different shrub. Other species go by the name "huckleberry" but are not in the genus *Gaylussacia*. These include squaw huckleberry *Vaccinium stamineum* of the eastern United States, and red huckleberry *Vaccinium parvifolium*, a red-fruited, tart species of the Pacific Northwest. The popular huckleberry of the Rocky Mountains is *Vaccinium membranaceum*. This species is part of the blueberry genus and is discussed with that group.

The present account refers to the huckleberries of the genus *Gaylussacia*, focusing on *G. baccata*.

Range and Habitat

The black huckleberry is found in the eastern United States and southeastern Canada, ranging from southeastern Manitoba to southern Ontario and Quebec, south to Georgia, Alabama, and Missouri. Within this region, however, it is not uniformly distributed, being completely absent from large areas while dominating the shrub growth in others. This is due to the black huckleberry's adaptation to very specific situations.

This shrub is most prevalent in acidic, sandy soil 1–3 feet (30–90 cm) above the water table. Where these conditions are met, huckleberries can be extremely abundant. They thrive in the same landscapes as aronia berries, only they don't like their soil quite as moist. The two species often grow intermingled. Black huckleberry grows best where the canopy is thin and sparse, and it can thrive only under those trees that cast light shade. It is also sometimes found in areas of full sun.

Like many plants of acidic lowlands, the black huckleberry can also be found in a seemingly opposite habitat: sandstone outcroppings, ridges, and cliff tops. Colonies on such sites tend to be somewhat smaller and less productive, however.

Harvest and Preparation

When I was too young to drive, my older brother used to bring me to a little swimming hole back in the woods, where forty-foot cliffs rose on both sides of a very deep pool in the stream below. On the top of the cliff from which we jumped into this pool, there was a knee-high patch of huckleberries. Whenever they were available, I'd pick a handful and eat them while I contemplated the next leap. This patch never had more than a few cups of fruit to offer—nor did the other clifftop patches that I knew of—so I never thought much of the huckleberry as a food source. But some years later, when I came across the vast huckleberry thickets of the sand counties, my perception changed dramatically.

Now, at least once a year, I like to set aside a day for picking huckleberries. The peak season is typically from about August 5 to August 20, making them about two weeks later than blueberries in the same area. I pick using a blickey, and the berries, typically borne three to four feet above the ground, are at just the right height for this. In good patches I can collect about three quarts per hour. Using a blueberry rake, one can do much better, but then must clean out the leaves and twigs afterward.

It is common to find large patches where the bushes bear little or no fruit in a particular year. In this case, keep wandering, looking for growing conditions different from the unproductive area. Try to alter the variables of slope, exposure, shade, and moisture, and you are likely to find an area worth picking.

I love huckleberries fresh off the bush, and I gorge on them while picking. The taste is very much like that of blueberries, but better. If I find more than I can eat fresh, I dry, can, or freeze them. Freeze them in a thin layer on a baking tray so they do not stick together, then roll them into a freezer bag for long-term storage. I like to use the frozen fruit on hot cereal or in pancakes, or just to snack on raw. I use canned huckleberries to make pie filling—and in my opinion, black

Open, sandy woods not much higher than the water table: ideal black huckleberry habitat.

huckleberry makes the very best pie. I eat dried huckleberries as a snack whenever I get the urge, and they never last through until the next season.

As with blueberries and serviceberries, I don't find huckleberries sour or tart enough to make very good jam. If you choose to go this route, try to make preserves with as little sugar as possible and add a touch of something sour such as lemon juice. Some people object to the seeds in huckleberries and their products, but I think they are part of the fun of eating this fruit.

Speaking of fun, huckleberries do possess a most peculiar property. When fresh, the juice is clear or nearly so, and the flesh is a very light reddish-purple. But as soon as the flesh or juice dries out, it turns very dark purple. Crush the fresh fruit with your bare hands and you won't notice anything, but look ten minutes later and your fingers and palms will look as if you've been playing in motor oil. After black huckleberries have been dried, eating them will cause an amazingly fast stain on your mouth, tongue, and teeth. I'm not talking about a little grape-tongue; I'm talking about the purplest purple mouth you've ever seen and never imagined. If you do this at the most inopportune times, you will be subject to relentless stares and embarrassing chuckles. But children of all ages get a big kick out of it, and it wears off in an hour or so.

Everybody has heard of the fictional character Huckleberry Finn, but how many people have tried real huckleberries? Don't deprive yourself; in this case, fact is better than fiction.

New Jersey Tea, Oregon Tea, Ceanothus

Ceanothus americanus, herbaceus, sanguineus, and fendleri

Rhamnaceae – Buckthorn Family

There are a myriad of wild teas. But after trying dozens, there are only a few that I keep returning to, craving in the middle of winter when I wish for a taste of summer's greenness. High on my list is this gift of the pine barrens, the New Jersey tea. Every summer, when I visit the sandy pinelands of northern and central Wisconsin, I stock up on a supply for the coming year. And while I get no calories from it, I like to imagine what vitamins might be swarming in the light red infusion. And in any case, it feeds my soul.

New Jersey tea *Ceanothus americanus* in flower. Note the deer damage.

Description

The genus *Ceanothus* contains many species of shrubs found across North America, but particularly in the mountainous parts of the West. Only two eastern species, *C. herbaceus* and *americanus*, are commonly called New Jersey tea. Both shrubs are simply called "New Jersey tea" in botanical manuals, but they are actually quite different. I call *C. americanus* "big New Jersey tea" and *C. herbaceus* "small New Jersey tea." Several western species of *Ceanothus* are also used to make tea. This account refers primarily to the two aforementioned species, but much of the information also applies to other members of the genus.

Big New Jersey tea generally stands 14–36 inches (35–90 cm) high, its growth habit low and shrubby with very thin twigs and branches. The bark is smooth and dark brown, but lighter reddish-brown or green on the new twigs. In winter, the twigs usually die back several inches from the tip.

Leaves are simple, ovate, deciduous, finely toothed on the margins, and borne alternately on very short petioles from 0.25–0.5 inch (6–13 mm) long. Typically ranging from 1.5–3 inches (4–8 cm) in length, the leaves are dark green above and pubescent beneath. Although at first glance New Jersey tea leaves may appear nondescript, one can learn to recognize them readily by their pattern of venation. On each side of the midvein there is one prominent vein which curves out toward the margin of the leaf and then heads back toward the center, forming an arc almost like the parallel veins of lilies. New Jersey tea shares this feature

The dried fruits of *C. americanus*.

Young leaves of *C. herbaceus*, when I like to pick them for tea.

with other members of the buckthorn family, but few other shrubs have veins like this.

Big New Jersey tea is somewhat inconspicuous and tends to be over-looked except when in bloom. The panicle of tiny, five-petaled fragrant white flowers appears in early to mid summer. Later, these mature into small, dry, inedible, three-lobed and three-seeded fruits.

The small New Jersey tea *C. herba-ceus* is similar but shorter, rarely exceed-ing 24 inches (60 cm) in height. The leaves are also much smaller and nar-rower, generally 0.8–2 inches (2–5 cm) long and elliptic or lanceolate. They are somewhat shiny on the upper surface.

The genus *Ceanothus* reaches its greatest diversity in the western United States; Stuart and Sawyer (2001) report forty-three native species for California alone. The shrubs in this genus go by a hodgepodge of names, including ceano-thus, whitethorn, pine mat, glory bush, deerbrush, tobacco brush, mountain balm, Oregon tea, snowbrush, and blue blossom. You wouldn't presume a close relationship by the names. I have not been able to try all of them for tea. Some references lump them all together, but certainly their qualities must vary greatly. For example, I have brewed the leaves of the widespread *C. velutinus* (snowbrush,

sticky-laurel, mountain balm, tobacco brush) and found the tea downright disgusting.

The two western species that I find reported to be used as a tea are Oregon tea *C. sanguineus* and Fendler's buck-brush *C. fendleri*. Oregon tea grows up to 10 feet (3 m) tall, with broad leaves

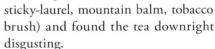

C. fendleri, a small-leaved thorny species of the Southwest that makes a nice tea.

Not all species make good tea. *C. velutinus,* shown here, tastes terrible.

up to 4 inches (10 cm) long. It grows primarily from Montana and Washington south to California. I have not tried this plant, but as the name implies, many others have. Fendler's buckbrush is a small species, seldom exceeding 3 feet (1 m) in height, common in the Southwest. It has large thorns and very small, entire leaves, less than 1 inch (2.5 cm) long. I have made tea from Fendler's buckbrush; it was milder than New Jersey tea but similarly pleasant in flavor. You may have to check regional references or taste your local species to find whether any of the other members of this group make a good tea.

Range and Habitat

In general, the two species of New Jersey tea inhabit well-drained sunny sites that are sandy or rocky. Big New Jersey tea is locally abundant in prairie edge areas, rocky ridges or hilltops, and in dry pine or pine-oak woodlands. It ranges from Quebec to Minnesota, south to Texas and Florida. Small New Jersey tea inhabits similar sites but its distribution is centered on the Great Plains, being absent from most of the eastern United States. The western edge of its range falls in a line roughly from eastern Montana to western Texas.

The various species in the West occupy a great variety of habitats, from deserts to mountain meadows. What they have in common is a proclivity for dry, poor soils and sunlight.

Harvest and Preparation

Pick New Jersey tea leaves at any time in the growing season and dry them out of the sunlight. However, the flavor is best in spring and early summer. To avoid damaging the plants, spread your harvest out rather than stripping all the leaves off a few bushes. I generally leave the terminal leaf or two upon each twig to grow. Never cut whole branches or bushes to make harvest more convenient.

To make tea, boil the leaves for several minutes—the longer the stronger. Be generous with the leaves, as it takes a lot to brew a strong cup. You can use fresh or dried leaves to make the tea, with similar results.

New Jersey tea first turns to an attractive golden color. If you let the leaves steep for longer, the tea will turn a rich reddish-brown. The mild flavor of New Jersey tea suggests both green tea and nettle tea. It is said that this drink was popular during the Revolutionary War, when English tea was under boycott. The cities of Boston, New York, and Philadelphia were supplied with this tea, brought from the pine barrens of New Jersey, hence the name. I don't find this choice a surprise—New Jersey tea is among my favorite wild teas, and to my taste is closest to the true tea in flavor. If it contained caffeine I suspect it would be every bit as popular as Oriental tea.

C. herbaceus in flower, a good time to pick the leaves. Most species in this genus are short shrubs.

C. americanus leaf.

I have read instructions for processing New Jersey tea in an elaborate fashion, by dipping the leaves in boiling water, bruising them, ageing, and then drying the leaves (Gibbons and Tucker, 1978). After having done this with two batches of New Jersey tea, one of each species, I noticed no substantial change in the flavor. I enjoy using the plain leaves, fresh or dried.

It's a good thing that this little bush doesn't grow only in New Jersey.

Wild Strawberry

Fragaria spp.

Rosaceae – Rose Family

Ripe fruit of *Fragaria virginiana*.

My excitement over wild strawberries began the summer after first grade. There was a place on the edge of town that the local kids simply called "Up In the Fields," which was my primary destination for adventure. Shortly after school got out for the year, I took the half-mile trek to get there, shod in the loose-fitting hand-me-down shoes that had once belonged to my older brother. ("Loose fitting" is an understatement; think of a baseball cap on a newborn or a skeleton wearing a backpack.)

While looking for snakes in a rock pile in an abandoned hillside pasture, I came across a patch of wild strawberries full of ripe fruit. I knew strawberries from the garden, and these were obviously the same, only smaller. Not one to pass up free food, I plucked a few and popped them into my mouth. They were ***not*** the same as garden strawberries; they were, as every wild strawberry picker knows, immeasurably better. I cleaned out that patch in minutes, then prowled the fields for more. I soon found myself standing at the edge of a small brook, gazing longingly at a clump of wild strawberry plants on the other side, imagining the luscious fruit hidden under the leaves. As I attempted to scamper across a narrow spot in the stream, I misstepped and sank thigh-deep into the mud. As hard as I tried, I simply could not keep my foot in that shoe as I pulled it from the slurping muck, and once my leg was free, the mud closed up the hole and swallowed the ugly shoe forever.

Many years later I met a beautiful young woman who told me that she loved to pick wild strawberries. Knowing from years of experience that picking with a friend was better than picking solo, I offered to accompany her on such an outing. In several weeks when the proper morning came in early June, we crawled about her chosen pasture, each trying to impress the other with how many berries we collected. Five hours later we had fierce sunburns, two and a half gallons of the best fruit on earth, and something even more precious. We spent the rest of the day making pies, jam, strawberry shortcake, and fruit leather. Four months later we were married, standing outside with that strawberry patch a hundred yards behind us. And while I have a multitude of memories featuring wild strawberries, that one will always be my favorite.

Description

The wild strawberry should be easily recognized by anyone familiar with cultivated strawberry plants, as there are only minor differences. The wild strawberry is a low, herbaceous perennial that spreads by stolons (runners), often forming large colonies. Each leaf is divided into three coarsely, regularly, and sharply toothed leaflets. The leaflets range from 1–3 inches (2.5–8 cm) in length. They are usually covered with fine hairs on the underside which give them a soft, silky feel.

The three leaflets are borne at the top of an erect, hairy petiole that stands 1.5–10 inches (4–25 cm) tall. Plants growing amidst tall grasses and herbs on moist soil grow taller, while the shortest ones are found on dry sites exposed to full sun. Strawberry leaves persist through the winter and are a favorite late fall and early spring food for deer.

The larger fruit to the right, with protruding seeds and pointed tip, is *F. vesca*; those to the left, with depressed seeds, are *F. virginiana*.

Coastal strawberries in flower and fruit.

Flowers are produced in loose clusters of two to twelve atop hairy stalks separate from those bearing leaves, but about as tall. Blooming in early to mid spring, strawberry flowers are about 0.5–0.7 inch (13–18 mm) across, with five white petals and a yellow center. The flowering stems and leaf stems are often red.

There are two widespread species of wild strawberry in North America, the common wild strawberry *Fragaria virginiana*, and the woodland strawberry *F. vesca*. These are generally similar in appearance, but the fruit of the woodland strawberry is more elongated and pointed, and the seeds rest on the surface rather than in small pits like those of the common wild strawberry and the cultivated form. Wild strawberries of both species, however, look essentially like miniature versions of the cultivated fruit. A third species, the coastal strawberry *F. chiloensis*, is confined to the Pacific Coast. The flowers and fruits of this species are larger than those of its inland cousins, and the leaves are more leathery and glossy. Our cultivated strawberry is a hybrid between *F. virginiana* and *F. chiloensis*. Of our three species, the woodland strawberry is the least flavorful—although I certainly don't pass them up.

F. virginiana in flower.

While wild strawberries do not have any dangerous look-alikes, other plants are often mistaken for them. The barren strawberry *Waldsteinia fragarioides* of open northern woodlands is similar in size and growth habit but has yellow flowers and irregularly toothed or lobed leaves; it never produces a strawberry-like fruit. The basal leaves of some cinquefoils, particularly the rough cinquefoil *Potentilla norvegica*, are also frequently mistaken for those of wild strawberry— but again, this species does not produce any strawberry-like fruit. Some of our low, trailing brambles are confused with wild strawberry—especially *Rubus hispidus*, which forms colonies in open bogs and sandy soil. This species flowers at the same time that strawberries ripen; it produces an edible blackberry-like fruit in late summer.

The leaves of rough cinquefoil and other cinquefoils are sometimes mistaken for those of strawberry.

Certainly the most confusing impostor is the Indian or false strawberry *Duchesnea indica*. This plant differs from the true strawberries in that its flowers have yellow petals, but the leaves look nearly identical, only smaller and less hairy. And as if the plant world had conspired to play a big joke on unsuspecting foragers, the false strawberry produces a juicy fruit that looks like a real strawberry but has only slightly more flavor than a water balloon. False strawberries are not toxic—in fact, they seem to be perfectly edible—but they account for many of the comments that wild strawberries are worthless or flavorless.

Everything about the false strawberry *Duchesnea indica* resembles true strawberries. The berry is actually edible but surprisingly flavorless. Photo by Glenn Schmukler.

Range and Habitat

The coastal strawberry *F. chiloensis* is found on sand dunes and bluffs along the entire Pacific Coast of the Americas, and nowhere else. Another species, *F. platypetala*, is found at high elevations in California.

Fragaria virginiana and *F. vesca* are widespread across North America, their composite ranges encompassing nearly all of the United States and Canada, except for the Deep South and desert areas. The common wild strawberry thrives in sunny or partly sunny locations with poor, low-nitrogen soil that is well-drained but receives ample moisture. It tends to be more common northward, in rocky regions, and at higher elevations where such conditions prevail. Wild strawberries are sometimes abundant in meadows, pastures, old fields, lawns, road banks, and along paths and trails. They can also be found scattered in young, open forests. The woodland strawberry tolerates a little more shade and generally occurs in young or open woods with poor soil. It tends not to form large colonies like the common strawberry does, but in some places it is prevalent. Both species are common to abundant over much of their range.

Harvest and Preparation

Wild strawberries ripen in early summer, and in most of their range they are the first, or one of the first, wild berries to become available. Where I live, a few of them will redden in late May, especially on south slopes. The peak of the wild strawberry season in these areas falls in the early or middle part of June, and a few of them remain available into July. The ripening of strawberries coincides with the flowering of blackberries and ox-eye daisies; they are mostly gone by the time that basswoods flower. I have always thought of strawberry picking as the unequivocal beginning of summer.

I cannot deny that wild strawberries are time-consuming to pick—but I can assure you that it is time well spent. In his chapter "Economics of Wild Strawberries" Euell Gibbons (1962) addresses this concern with a beautiful sermon that I need not duplicate and cannot improve upon. Every forager should read this from time to time for inspiration. The message is simple: we do not forage simply for economic gain, but for an experience that we can hardly name or describe. If we can get some delicious, precious, healthy food in the bargain, that is all the better. And certainly wild strawberries fit this description. Perhaps a few fruits are as good, but none are better—and many people simply consider the wild strawberry *the premiere* berry, the pinnacle of fruit flavor experiences. And it is hard to argue with them.

Although I have always loved wild strawberries, my wife is the fanatic in our

A handful of Heaven.

house. She is so devoted to this fruit that she scorns the obese cultivated sort. She has the patience to pick for hours when the going is slow, while I frantically search for a better patch over the next rise. Where we live, strawberry plants are as common as dandelions, but you need to find patches that crop well. These are typically found on roadsides or in neglected fields that have few of the grasses and legumes that hayfields are supposed to have. To get a good crop, you want pleasant, sunny weather while the plants are flowering and ample rainfall while the fruits are forming. Under the right conditions, one person can pick a gallon in about an hour, but typically it takes three to four times that long.

When picking wild strawberries, try to avoid berries that are resting on the soil, or which grow in places where they are likely to collect dust or sand, as it will settle into the pits around the seeds and is nearly impossible to remove. Many people avoid the leafy calyx that comes attached to strawberries, while others remove this annoyance after collection. It makes sense to do this when whole fruits are desired, or when you want to snack on a few, but for larger amounts it is *much* easier to run the berries through a fruit strainer and get a smooth puree. They are soft enough that no cooking is required before straining. After you realize how much time the fruit strainer saves, you will find yourself liking strawberry puree more and more.

There is a plethora of fantastic ways to eat wild strawberries. Most often, they are enjoyed fresh and unprocessed by the handful. But culinary miracles happen when you collect enough to bring home.

My wife's wild strawberry shortcake is the best dessert I've ever tasted. We also make wild strawberry jam and a superb fruit leather from the puree. With their strong, pleasant flavor and mouth-watering aroma, wild strawberries also make great pies. Whole strawberries or strawberry puree, with the optional addition of sugar to taste, make a delicious topping for ice cream and pancakes. Wild strawberry is my fruit of choice to mix into hot cereal made from wapato tubers or lotus nuts.

You can't buy wild strawberries—and if you could they'd cost a hundred dollars a pound. They are the caviar of wild plant foods. Well, maybe that's giving caviar too much credit. But in any case, the only way to experience this bliss on a stem is to go pick it yourself. Just remember the sunscreen.

Black Cherry

Prunus serotina

Rosaceae – Rose Family

At the end of summer when the black cherries ripen, the wild things come to feast. Robins, ravens, catbirds, orioles, and waxwings flit about the tree from dawn to dusk, fickly gleaning cherries here and there. In times past, great flocks of passenger pigeons would descend upon the cherry forests to relieve them of their crop. Mice and chipmunks gather the fruit and pick out the stones, leaving the flesh behind. Raccoons and opossums feed on little else for weeks, leaving piles of their telltale cherry pit scat. Black bears will find small, open-grown black cherry trees and tear off every limb as they pull the fruit within reach, leaving nothing but a seven-foot stub.

It's enough to make you wonder if there's something good about those cherries.

Description

Of all the *Prunus* species in North America, the wild black cherry is by far the largest tree. (Do not confuse wild black cherry, hereafter referred to as simply "black cherry" in this account, with the cultivated black cherry, which is a totally different species with very different fruit.) Black cherry trees commonly exceed 80 feet (25 m) in height, and if left alone rather than cut for their valuable wood, they can easily surpass 2 feet (60 cm) in diameter. They generally have a narrow crown. The entire tree, without its leaves, has a dark appearance. At least when mature, black cherry has very distinct bark, covered with erratic black chips or flakes—often described as a "burnt potato chip" look. The bark of younger trees is very dark, thin, and rather smooth and shiny with numerous small, light, horizontal slits (lenticels).

previous page Ripe black cherries.

left The bark of a black cherry sapling can be told from other cherries by the numerous small, whitish, horizontal lenticels.

right The bark of mature black cherry trees breaks into small, dark plates or scales; this is often called the "burnt potato chip" look.

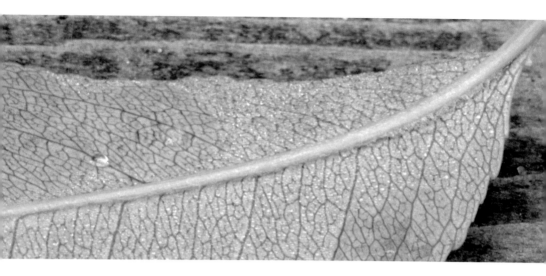

above Rusty fuzz along the bottom of the midvein (although not always present) is sometimes used to distinguish black cherry from chokecherry.

below Black cherry leaves.

Black cherry leaves are alternate, simple, and lanceolate with finely serrated margins. They are narrower, glossier, and darker than the leaves of chokecherry, which is the tree most commonly confused with black cherry. The flowers are produced in late spring or early summer. White with five petals, they hang in racemes of twelve to twenty. The cherries that follow ripen to a dark purple-black in late summer. The individual fruits are about 0.4 inch (1 cm) in diameter, roughly globose or slightly heart-shaped, with a depression where the stem is attached. They hang in 5–9 inch (13–23 cm) clusters of six to twenty cherries. Like other members of the genus *Prunus*, each contains a single stone.

Range and Habitat

Black cherry is one of the most widespread trees in North America, found throughout the eastern and central United States and southeastern Canada, and extending west through Texas, New Mexico, and Arizona.

Black cherry is common in hardwood forests, and in many areas it is a major component. It regenerates well after fires or logging and is a common tree of roadsides, old fields, and fencerows. Black cherry develops best on deep, rich, well-drained sandy loam but is often abundant on dry, poor ground where it tends to be scrubbier in appearance. In the Southwest it grows in moist canyons and river valleys at low to middle elevations.

Harvest and Preparation

Where I live, black cherries usually ripen from late August to mid September, averaging about ten days later than the peak ripening of chokecherries in the same area. The cherries are ripe when they are soft, juicy, and dark purple or black (not red). In years of poor fruiting, the birds will pick off the cherries as they ripen, sometimes sooner, leaving nothing for the human collector. More often, however, these trees fruit copiously.

In many ways, black cherries are an ideal wild fruit. The cherries average larger than choke or pin cherries, and the handful-sized clusters are easily stripped into a container. The crop is often remarkably heavy, and on small open-grown trees the fruit is easily accessible. In fact, the black cherry is so prolific in some areas that it outweighs all other wild fruit combined. All of these factors make black cherry one of the easiest fruits to gather in quantity.

But alas, there is still something left to consider: how does it taste? Black cherry, in my opinion, is the most variable of all wild fruits in flavor. Some trees produce fruit that is so bitter that it is not only unpalatable but, in my estimation,

Racemes of black cherry flowers in early summer.

totally inedible. Other black cherries are absolutely delicious and rival our best cultivated cherries in flavor. Most, of course, are somewhere in between. Some of this variability is due to region or soil. In the area where I live, I rarely find a black cherry tree with fruit worth eating. However, on the rich limestone soils a few hundred miles to the south, the flavor of the typical tree's fruit is passably good, and occasional trees have cherries that are truly excellent. The flavor of black cherries in general seems to be better in some years than others, perhaps due to patterns of rainfall, sunshine, and temperature.

One summer, some friends led me to a fantastic black cherry tree growing in their pasture. The cherries were not only delicious, but enormous—over a half-inch (13 mm) in diameter. We spread clean tarps over the ground beneath the tree, then I climbed up and shook the branches. In this fashion we collected a little over two gallons of fruit in just a few minutes, although it took some time to pick out the twigs and other debris. If the tree had not already been stripped of most of its cherries by birds, the same labor would have yielded several times more fruit. Even if you have to pick black cherries by hand it goes very fast. Under the best conditions I have filled a five gallon pail in less than an hour.

Black cherries are high enough in sugar that they dry to a soft and chewy texture like prunes. It is easiest to dry them with the pits included and simply spit these out as you eat. However, it is much nicer to remove the stones from the pulp with a colander or strainer before drying. Besides being dried, such stone-free pulp can also be used to make jam or other confections.

To make juice, cover the cherries with water and simmer until they become very soft. Crush the fruit gently, then strain it through a cloth or jelly bag. The juice can be used as a drink by itself, although most will prefer it sweetened or mixed with a milder juice. It can also be used to make jelly. In colonial times, black cherries were commonly used for making certain alcoholic beverages, earning them the name *rum cherry*. Of course, you can always just eat them as the animals do, fresh off the tree.

The black cherry kicks off the fall harvest season in an extravagant way. This August, as you pass these often-ignored food trees, take a few moments to taste the fruit that the animals are going wild for. If you find a good tree, treasure it. You might go wild, too.

Sandcherry

Prunus pumila, P. susquehanae

Rosaceae – Rose Family

The Moquah Barrens lies in the center of the Bayfield Peninsula jutting into the south side of Lake Superior. When Europeans first settled the area hardly more than a century ago, they found 150 square miles of sand hills without any flowing water. Scattered pine and oak dotted an otherwise open landscape, a vast sea of knee-high shrubs and bracken fern. The Moquah Barrens has no large rocks, and in those days, neither did it have stumps. It was said that you could drive a Model-T anywhere you wanted over the scrubby heath that held the sand in place.

Today this area remains completely uninhabited, but it is crisscrossed with logging roads and much of the open barrens has been converted to forest. But you can still find solitude. There are breathtaking expanses of heath lands to disappear into, filling bucket after bucket with the same luscious fruit that has long brought *mukwa*, the black bear, to this place every summer. Here the mixture of blueberry, bearberry, sweetfern, and sandcherry covers thousands of acres. When the crop is good, you can pick these cherries to your heart's content. They are hard to overlook but seem practically unknown to the locals who have picked blueberries here all their lives. That's exactly the kind of food I like.

Range and Habitat

Sandcherry is found in the northeastern United States from Pennsylvania and New Jersey north to Maine, and across southern Canada from Saskatchewan to New Brunswick and Quebec. It ranges across the Midwest, south to Arkansas and Tennessee. In the Great Plains, sandcherry is largely absent from the rich soil of the tallgrass prairie region, but becomes common on the drier, poorer soils

previous page Plump, juicy, ripe fruit of beach sandcherries. This is the largest fruit among North America's many wild cherries.

below In the foreground is a dense colony of inland sandcherry in typical pine barrens habitat.

westward, from the Dakotas south to Kansas, west to Colorado, Utah, Wyoming, and Montana. It inhabits sand dunes, beaches along large bodies of water, sandy or rocky prairies and outcroppings, and pine and oak barrens. Due to its specialized habitat, sandcherry is absent from large areas and abundant in others.

Description

This species has the largest fruit of our wild cherries, but it is the smallest plant among them. In fact, the species name *pumila* means "dwarf." Typical height for sand cherry is 14–48 inches (35–120 cm). This shrub spreads by stolons or suckers to form large colonies. There may be single, unbranched whips growing from various points along the stolon, or individual stems may branch out into a small bush. Sandcherry stems often lean over and produce numerous ascending branches on their upper side. Those plants growing on beaches tend to grow significantly larger than those inland, occasionally reaching as much as 5 feet (1.5 m) in height and branching considerably. The bark is dark brown with small lenticels and does not have so strong a cherry scent as choke or black cherry. Some botanists separate sandcherries into multiple species or subspecies, but they all are similar enough in appearance to be discussed together here.

Sand cherry leaves are simple and lanceolate or ovate with finely toothed margins, borne alternately like those of other members of *Prunus*. At 1.5–2.5 inches

Beach sandcherry in flower.

above Sandcherry leaves are similar to black and chokecherry leaves but are much smaller and wider toward the tip.

below Beach sandcherry may reach four feet in height.

Ripe fruit of inland sandcherry.

(4–6 cm) long, they almost look intermediate between choke and black cherry leaves.

Sand cherry flowers are borne in clusters of two to four on long pedicels that hang off the upper few inches of the stalk. About 0.5 inch (13 mm) across, they are white with five petals and open in early May. The cherries turn to a dark purple-black when they ripen in mid to late August. They are usually somewhat oblong and range from 0.4–0.7 inches (10–18 mm) in length. As many as twenty may be borne on a single branch.

Harvest and Preparation

The larger size of the sand cherry makes it easier to collect, but the fact that the fruit grows in small clusters on small bushes makes up for this advantage; all things considered, collecting sand cherries goes a little more slowly than harvesting choke or black cherries. In a good patch, one can gather a few gallons per hour. I usually collect into a wide bowl or basin that sits on the ground, kneeling or squatting as I do so.

Taste the sandcherries to see if they are ripe, for this can be hard to determine visually. They should be soft and juicy with a flavor somewhere between that of black cherry and chokecherry, but closer to the better quality black cherries.

The flavor is far more consistent than that of the black cherry, however, and is generally quite good as long as the fruit is fully ripe.

Because of their larger size and larger stones, sandcherries cannot be run through some fruit strainers. However, they are sometimes large enough to be pitted with a mechanical cherry pitter (Young, 1993). A colander or Foley mill can also be used to separate the pulp, and although it is laborious, the pits can be picked out of the crushed cherries by hand.

Sandcherries, like other wild cherries, can be used to make juice, jelly, and syrup by boiling them in enough water to cover the fruit and then straining the liquid through a jelly bag. Sandcherry pulp can be used for jam or preserves. Sandcherry pie is a local delicacy on parts of the Great Plains (Young, 1993), but I didn't like it enough to make it a second time. This fruit can also be dried, with or without the pits, and its flavor is excellent.

And of course, you can eat them fresh by the mouthful, spitting out the pits as you walk along a quiet sand road some warm August evening. If you're lucky, you'll see Mukwa there, snout low as he sniffs his way through the brush, stopping here and there to deftly slurp off a mouthful of the same sandcherries that brought you into *his* barrens.

Wild Plum

Prunus spp.

Rosaceae – Rose Family

To the forager, those hot days and cool nights at the cusp of summer and fall are the stuff of fantasies the year round. When the first warm breeze of late morning carries not the fragrance of blossoms, but the more subtle aroma of ripening fruit and dried grasses, it's time to store up sweets for the coming cold season. Strolling country backroads or dewy meadows with some free time and a pail, one should not return without some such treasure. Around the next bend or over the next rise one fruit or another is sure to be hanging within reach. And of all the wild fruits native to this land, there is none that outdoes the wild plum in overextending itself for our convenience.

Ripe wild plums _Prunus americana._

Wild plums are short, gnarly trees that tend to form dense thickets.

I have seen wild plum trees so laden with fruit that the tips of their branches were resting upon the ground; as I removed their load the limbs slowly returned to their original position several feet higher. Many times I have gone into a plum thicket with a five-gallon pail and left twenty minutes later because I had no more room in it.

Anybody who is familiar with domestic plum trees will recognize their close wild relatives when they are in fruit, but this season is short and can be easily missed. Thus, most people fail to realize how truly abundant and readily available wild plums are. Almost every town in its range—whether a rural hamlet or an urban metropolis—has thickets of one species of wild plum or another, and it is also a common feature of the countryside. The fruit, fresh off the tree when fully ripe, is a wonderful snack, and many delicious products can be made from it. A plum thicket in bloom is a wonderful sight, and its tangled branches provide food and cover for a host of wild creatures in all seasons.

It is no wonder that many Native Americans once chose to encourage wild plums around their homes and villages. Some still do, and it is a practice that any lover of wild things should consider.

Description

There are several species of wild plum in North America. While there are differences between all of them, they are similar enough to warrant being described and discussed together. Our wild plums are classified in the genus *Prunus* along with cherries, peaches, and apricots. All the wild plums are large shrubs or small trees with a rugged, spreading form reminiscent of an apple tree or cultivated plum. Wild plums often form dense thickets, spreading by root suckers to form clones. Typical height is 6–20 feet (2–6 m); trunks average 1–2 inches (2.5–5 cm) in diameter but may reach 6 inches (15 cm) on larger specimens. The thin bark tends to be relatively light and smooth on young trunks but separates into plates, ridges, or scales on older trunks and turns to a dark gray, brown, or reddish-brown. The branches are stiff, spreading, and somewhat zigzag in form. Many species bear thorns upon some of their smaller twigs, but these are dull—not the needle sharp daggers of hawthorn or honey locust, nor the claws of blackberry or multiflora rose.

Wild plums have simple, serrated, medium-sized leaves ranging from 2–5 inches (5–13 cm) in length. They are borne alternately on proportionately short petioles. The leaves of most species are ovate, oval, or lanceolate with acuminate tips.

These bushes blossom in early spring, often before the leaves have opened up. The flowers are borne in small umbels of two to five on the smaller branches. They are 0.5–1 inch (13–25 mm) across and have five rounded white or occasionally pink petals. Where I live, wild plums are among the earliest bushes to flower, concurrent with serviceberry and just before pin cherry. A patch of plums in full bloom attracts attention to itself, with its snowy white blossoms unobscured

Wild plum flowers. Note the thorn on the nearby trunk.

by any greenery. It is a long time between flowering and ripening of the fruit, so make a note of these thickets and return at the end of summer.

When ripe, wild plums are some combination of reddish, orange, yellow, and blue. They are coated with a bloom, just like cultivated plums. Wild plums range from oblong to globe-shaped. The fruit of larger kinds may reach nearly 2 inches (5 cm) in length, but the smaller species are typically less than 1 inch (2.5 cm) in diameter. Each plum contains a single, oblong, flattened stone like those found in cultivated plums. The skins are thick and tough. When ripe, wild plums are soft, tart, sweet, and juicy.

Range and Habitat

The various species of wild plum are found through most of the United States and adjacent Canada, although they are absent from high elevations, deserts, and the far north.

The Klamath plum *P. subcordata* is found in western Oregon and central California. This is one of the larger species and is popular within its limited range.

The American plum *P. americana* is the most widespread and probably the most commonly eaten species. It grows throughout the Great Plains and most of the Midwestern and Appalachian states, plus it is found scattered at lower elevations in the Rockies. Both the fruit and the tree of this species rank as possibly the largest among the wild plums, and some cultivars have been selected for their fruit.

The Chickasaw plum *P. angustifolia* is a widely distributed species with narrow leaves and small, beautiful, red or yellow fruit. This plum occurs in the southern United

Leaves of *P. americana*. The disease seen in the leaf on the left is quite common.

States from Virginia and Florida west to the easternmost part of Colorado and New Mexico. Chickasaw plums ripen in early to mid summer.

The Canada plum *P. nigra* is another important species, found across southern Manitoba, Ontario, and Quebec as well as the northern tier of states from Minnesota to Maine. Canada plum's fruit is medium-sized but of good quality and is often produced copiously.

The epicenter of wild plum distribution seems to be Missouri, which is home to six species, including the hortulan plum *P. hortulana*, the limited range of which centers on the aforementioned state. The hortulan plum has a rather large fruit. The Mexican plum *P. mexicana*, another fine species, is native to the southern Midwest and south-central states, from Texas to Alabama, north to southern Indiana and southeastern Nebraska. The flatwood plum *P. umbellata* is a small-fruited but popular species native to the Southeast, found primarily in Alabama, Georgia, South Carolina, northern Florida, southeastern Mississippi, and a disjunct area where Texas, Louisiana, and Arkansas meet. The wild goose plum *P. munsoniana* is found scattered through the south-central United States, and the Allegheny plum *P. alleghaniensis* is found in a limited range primarily in the mountains of Pennsylvania and West Virginia, but scattered elsewhere in the East.

All the wild plums are early successional species that grow in disturbed sunny or partly sunny localities. They are found in abandoned farmland and along fencerows, railroads, and roads. They frequently take over vacant lots and abandoned homesteads. Wild plums also occur in such natural habitats as stream valleys and river floodplains, rocky ridges, steep sunny slopes, open woodlands, prairie and field edges, burnt or cut-over lands, pine barrens, young forests, beaches, and riverbanks. Wild plums respond well to human disturbance and are one of the most common wild fruits in many areas.

Harvest and Preparation

While there are many species of wild plum in North America, most of my experience is with the American and Canada plums. The following information reflects this experience, but most of it applies to the other plums as well.

In the upper Midwest the first plums ripen in late August and the last have fallen by the end of September. On any particular bush there is usually less than two weeks between the ripening of the first plum and the dropping of the last, so if you are not paying attention you can easily miss the entire season. You will know the fruit is ripe when it is easily shaken from the limbs or detaches at a light touch. It should be soft and juicy inside, and when fully ripe you should be able to squeeze the pit right out.

Wild plums often produce extravagantly. Color is not a good indicator of ripeness; despite their attractive red, these are still hard and bitter.

If you see a loaded, ripe plum tree, don't plan on coming back in a week; most likely the fruit will be gone by then. Plums tend to ripen and fall almost uniformly, and one windy day can clean off an entire tree. You can pick them up off the ground the next morning, but if you wait much longer insects, animals, and spoilage will get most of the fruit.

The crop of wild plums varies considerably from one year to the next. A plum thicket may be entirely barren one year and produce several gallons the following season. The weather during blossoming is one of the primary factors determining the fruit crop. In late spring one can check a plum thicket to see how well the fruit has set; young plums will appear as hard, green, kidney-bean sized ovals. Unfortunately, there are a large number of insects and diseases that will infect the crop. Plums growing in the shade generally produce poorly or not at all, while those in full sun can be very prolific.

Wild plums can be picked by hand and then dropped into a container— although very ripe ones should be placed gently to avoid bursting them. I like to hold a large bowl directly beneath the branch and loosen the plums with my free hand and just let them roll or fall in; this seems most efficient. With this method I can sometimes get five gallons in as little as fifteen minutes. You can also lay down a cloth or tarp and shake the tree. This is a good option if the plums are out of reach or are scattered widely among thorny limbs. As is always the case when you pick fruit by shaking the tree, you will have to clean out some unwanted debris.

If you pick underripe plums, letting them sit for a few days will soften them up. Very soft plums, however, should be used promptly to avoid spoiling. If you wish to store wild plums for a week or so in the refrigerator, make sure they are treated gingerly, and don't pile them very deep.

The skins of wild plums are very tart and astringent, while the inner pulp is sweet and pleasantly sour, one of the most delicious fruits in nature. For eating fresh, most people prefer to suck out the pulp without chewing up the skin. The key to making the best products from wild plums is to get rid of the skins.

Wild plums make a fantastic jam with a taste similar to that of apricot but stronger. The first step in making jam is to get plum puree. I do this by mashing the ripe fruit and then placing it into a large-holed colander. I press, mix, scrape and turn the crushed plums until I've gotten all the puree I can from the fruit, then discard the skins and stones. The puree is light orange-yellow in color and has the texture of runny applesauce. It oxidizes and turns brown on the surface rather quickly.

Because the plum puree is already rather thick, it jells with less sugar than most other jams: I use a ratio of five cups of sugar to six cups of plum puree for one package of Sure-Jell powdered pectin. I also mix plum puree with applesauce to eat as a dessert. Plum puree is sometimes used to make various savory meat sauces.

Wild plum jelly is also highly esteemed, and when pectin is not used, the runny result is wild plum syrup, sometimes sold commercially as a sweetener for pancakes, biscuits, and the like. Boiling and straining wild plums extracts much of the astringency from the skins and yields an inferior juice that is acceptable for jelly or syrup but not for drinking, unless it is greatly diluted and sweetened.

To get wild plum juice suitable for drinking, take extremely ripe, soft plums and, making a slit in each one, squeeze the contents out by hand, then discard the skins. Put this pulp into a strainer or jelly bag suspended over a container and let it drip slowly for a few hours. Do not squeeze or press, as this will force some of the pulp's tartness into the juice. This process produces a strong, aromatic juice that is just barely mild enough to be enjoyed by itself, and very good mixed with milder juices. It can also be used to make jelly.

Plum puree can also be used to make fruit leather. The uniform texture allows it to dry fast and be spread very thin to make a nice, smooth finished product. The fruit leather is quite sour, even when made from the ripest plums, so you may want to mix the plum puree with applesauce for a more balanced flavor. You can cut wild plums in half, remove the stones, and dry them—but they will not taste like prunes. Despite the super-tart skins, Native Americans formerly dried many plums this way (Kindscher, 1987).

Some people make plum preserves by removing the stones and chopping up the whole fruit, skins included. I prefer the flavor when the skins are not used, however. Again, chopped plums, with stones removed, are sometimes used in pies, but they are just too tart to be used alone. You need to mix them with a milder fruit, like apple or sweet cherry.

In my opinion, the best wild plum products are made with plums that have been scalded and peeled, in the same way that peaches and tomatoes are peeled. Take about thirty plums, put them into a colander, and dip them into boiling water for twenty-five seconds. Then take them out, dip them in cool water, and swish them around for a few seconds. Poke a small slit in the skin and pinch there to peel. It takes a while to peel plums this way, but it is well worth it. Unripe plums peel with great difficulty.

After peeling, the plums can be water-bath canned. Due to their tartness, I prefer them in heavy syrup. They are delicious eaten as dessert like canned peaches, and a delectable hint of almond extract flavor seeps from the pits into

Three gallons of ripe wild plums *P. nigra*. A bowl like this on the kitchen table perfumes the entire house. What really bothers me is that I can see a few spoiled plums in there, but I can't pick them out!

the fruit as they soak in the jar. Peeled and scalded plums can also be pitted and dried, or they can be used in pies, preserves, and other desserts.

Ever since I learned to eat wild plums early in my childhood, I have avidly sought them out as a refreshing late-summer snack. They have become one of my favorite wild fruits to gather, always impressing me with their productivity. When I moved to my current home, I transplanted a plum tree to my yard within the first few days. There were already three at the edge of the backyard, a large thicket down the road, another shortly beyond that, and a half-acre in an empty lot by the schoolyard down the hill. But there are never too many wild plums.

Aronia, ChokeBBBBerry

Aronia spp.

Rosaceae – Rose Family

Chokeberry gets the award for the worst plant name ever given in the English language. Yes—worse than carrion flower, worse than bastard toad flax, and even worse than broomrape. The problem is not so much that *chokeberry* sounds bad—although certainly the name is an insult to a good fruit. More importantly, the name makes the plant almost impossible to communicate about. The vast majority of people, upon hearing or seeing the word *chokeberry*, think that they have just heard or read the word *chokecherry*. (Read carefully; these are two different words.) A typical conversation proceeds like this:

"Another interesting wild fruit is the chokeberry, which is small and black . . ."

"Oh yeah, my mom used to make chokecherry jelly. It was great."

"Actually, I said choke***Berries.***"

Aronia melanocarpa. For juice, seek large, plump berries.

"Yeah, chokecherry jelly. Sometimes we'd eat 'em right off the tree."

"I'm not talking about choke*cherries*; I'm talking about choke***BBBeries***."

"I heard you! What do you think *I'm* talking about?"

On and on it goes. Anybody who has ever tried to teach about this plant knows exactly what I'm talking about. Adding several hundred capital Bs to the middle of the word hardly helps at all. Somehow, certain people find it utterly impossible to grasp the idea that two small dark fruits could have such similar names and still be different entities. This confusing duo might actually rival *prostrate* and *prostate* in the tenacity and humor of their misuse—but at least *prostrate* or *prostate* can be understood by context. In fact, I *guarantee* that somebody has read this far and *still* thinks this chapter is about chokecherries.

So what do you do when a promising fruit is tagged with a name that obscures it into oblivion? Marketers of chokeberry juice were faced with just this problem a few decades ago. The juice sold in much of Europe, where it was lucky enough to have a real name—but how could they sell to American consumers? The answer was simple: give it a new name. How about using the scientific name? Aronia. Ooh, I like the sound of that—elegant and unique, with no excuse for misunderstanding. So it is.

Description

Aronia melanocarpa is a medium-sized shrub reaching maturity at 3–5 feet (1–1.5 m) in height and rarely exceeding 7 feet (2 m). Stems are commonly 0.2–0.8 inch (5–20 mm) in diameter. The thin twigs and branches are gray-brown, sometimes with a purplish hue. Aronia typically forms thickets by rhizomes, and these can be quite dense in full sunlight, but on account of their light, limber stems these thickets are rather easy to pass through.

The leaves of this bush may be small and nondescript, but at the same time their simple symmetry is truly attractive. Indeed, aronia is an increasingly popular landscape plant across much of the continent. Borne alternately on short petioles 0.1–0.3 inches (3–8 mm) long, the leaves are deciduous, 1–3 inches (2.5–8 cm) long and about half as wide. They are ovate, obovate, or elliptic with abruptly pointed tips. Their margins are finely serrated with dull, incurved, gland-tipped teeth. On the upper surface there is a row of dark, hair-like glands on both sides of the midrib—a very good distinguishing feature for this genus, but hard to discern with the naked eye. The leaves are dark green above, lighter green beneath, and glabrous. They are somewhat shiny in appearance, almost giving them a "plastic" look. Aronia foliage turns to a lovely red in autumn. Sandwiched between huckleberry and poison sumac, these three make the most vibrant fall-color trio that we have.

Aronia's attractive, symmetrical leaves are appreciated by landscapers.

In mid to late spring aronia sets out small clusters of four to twenty five-parted white flowers about 0.3 inch (8 mm) across. These are fragrant, insect-pollinated, and quite attractive, as is typical of the rose family. Later they become berry-like pomes with a distinct five-lobed calyx on the end. The fruits reach 0.2–0.4 inch (5–10 mm) in diameter and ripen to a dark purple-black in late summer or early autumn. They hang in red-stemmed panicles. In form, aronia "berries" are essentially identical to the fruits of mountain-ash (genus *Sorbus*) which is indeed very closely related.

Aronia flowers resemble those of blackberry.

The red chokeBBBBerry *A. arbutifolia* is a more southerly species, very similar in appearance but with the twigs and undersurface of the leaves coated by a grayish wool. It also has fruit that ripens to red rather than black. The purple chokeBBBBerry *A. prunifolia* is considered by some botanists to be a distinct species, while others consider it a cross between the red and black species, and some consider it a purple variant of the black chokeBBBBerry.

Range and Habitat

Aronia is an acid-loving shrub of swamps, bogs, lakeshores, and occasionally dry rocky ridges or sandy upland sites. It reaches its greatest abundance in wet, sandy soil in full sunlight, growing at or just above the water table. In such places one can sometimes find enormous patches of aronia. Where there is black huckleberry in lowlands, aronia is almost always found nearby, growing just slightly closer to the water. Although it is far more prolific in sandy regions, aronia can be found growing in bogs on any type of soil.

A. melanocarpa is found from northern Minnesota to Newfoundland, south to Iowa, northern Georgia, and New England. The red aronia berry *A. arbutifolia* is more southerly, found from eastern Texas to Florida and north to New England. This is the chokeBBBBerry commonly found on the wetlands of the Coastal Plain of the Southeast.

Harvest and Preparation

Although it is given minimal attention in the wild food literature, there are thousands of acres of this fruit under cultivation and it is the basis for a substantial industry. Many red-colored Old Orchard brand juices will have "aronia berry juice" on their ingredient list. I have even purchased 100% aronia juice, in a bottle touting this fruit's health benefits, complete with accurate artwork.

So why has so little been written about the wild stock from which the cultivated fruit has been selected and propagated? Good question! Many authors write with disdain about this fruit, calling it inedible and even claiming that the birds neglect to eat it—all of which is totally aronious. I suspect that the most significant reason that this fruit has been neglected is its name.

It is also probable that *making juice* is "too much work" for many people to be interested in, but it is too much fun for me to resist. If it sounds fun to you, then read along.

Fresh aronia fruit is astringent, accounting for the "choke" in chokeBBBBerry. Having tasted a handful, most people stop there, although some good things can be made from astringent fruit. Teresa Marrone's "Pear and Chokeberry Mincemeat Pie" (2004) is an example. However, if you are going to cook with whole aronia berries, you must account for their astringency. Lee Peterson (1977) recommends using them generally like blueberries, but I think that's a recipe for disastrous recipes. Aronia berries are not a very versatile fruit when used whole. They are meant to be juiced.

Aronia berries begin to ripen in mid to late August, and all of them will usually be ready by mid-September. Occasionally, while harvesting wild rice, I take a break on shore where the aronia bushes grow and suck out some refreshing juice before continuing. The berries often remain on the bush until November and sometimes even later, but in other years the bushes get picked clean soon after they ripen. I like to harvest mine as soon as possible after ripening, for I think they taste the best at this stage, and the longer they hang on the twig the drier they become—and a few will spoil. These factors reduce the quality of a batch of juice. Freezing does not improve their flavor—in fact, a very hard freeze is detrimental.

This fruit is highly variable in flavor, and I never pick them without tasting first. The smaller berries often have poorer flavor.

Aronia is becoming increasingly popular as an ornamental planting. The berries are an afterthought and can often be collected in copious amounts around shopping malls, office buildings, parks, schools, libraries, and college campuses. They do not need wet soil to thrive. Landscaping cultivars tend to have large, mild-tasting fruit, making them ideal targets for the urban forager. Much of this fruit hangs on the bushes for months due to the scarcity of wildlife in such urban settings, misleading some to conclude that this fruit is ignored by wild animals. Most of the aronia berries in urban settings dry up and go to waste. Still, make sure to get permission if necessary before you pick.

Aronias often grow in profusion. In some places where I pick, the supply is virtually limitless, with thickets covering acre upon acre. It is not unusual to see the stems arching over from the weight of their fruit, and I have even seen them lying flat on the ground under a ridiculous burden. Since the fruit is borne heavily in clusters at about chest height, a five-gallon pail can often be filled in less than two hours. I grab whole clusters but try to minimize the stems that I pick—although some always get in. The berries are firm enough not to crush when piled deep and are less prone to spoilage than most small fruits; under the right conditions they can keep for a few weeks in the refrigerator. But why wait? Make juice now.

Pour three gallons of aronia berries into a clean five-gallon pail and add about three quarts of water (more if it is late in the fall and the berries are a little dry), then thoroughly mash them with a stomper. Beware of the juice's potent color, so as not to stain clothing or favorite utensils. After the fruit is thoroughly

Close-up of *A. melanocarpa* fruit. The form is virtually identical to that of mountain ash (genus *Sorbus*).

mashed, fill up a nylon jelly bag, wring out the juice until your forearms ache, and discard the dry ball of pulp. Repeat this until the onset of carpal tunnel syndrome or until you have finished, whichever comes first. If you are lucky enough to have a cider press, fill the mesh press bag halfway and squeeze out the juice this way, ensuring a purple cider tray forever. If you like weaker juice, feel free to add more water when mashing the berries. This will give you more volume to show for your efforts, plus it might help you cut yourself some slack so you don't feel like you have to squeeze out those last three drops.

The finished product is a surprisingly mild, dark purple juice that reminds me of a cross between tart cherry, grape, and blueberry. The bitter of aronia berries resides largely in the pulp; the juice is less astringent than blueberry or blackberry juice. And home-made aronia juice is far better than that which is commercially available. I love to drink it plain but many people prefer to mix it with a milder juice such as apple.

Aronia juice is *much* better when cold-pressed from raw fruit as described above; however, some people insist on making a decidedly inferior, indeed almost undrinkable, juice by boiling the berries. Although cooking imparts the pulp's bitterness and astringency to the juice, it does have the advantage of being a bit easier and yielding slightly more juice from the same volume of berries.

This aronia bush, in typical shrub swamp habitat, has small berries—which often have poor flavor.

For cooked juice, add about a half gallon of water to every gallon of berries and mash them, then bring to a boil. Let the fruit boil for about twenty minutes, occasionally using a potato masher to make sure that all the berries are crushed. After boiling, pour the mixture into a jelly bag or cloth strainer and let the liquid drain. Once the pulp has cooled enough to handle you can squeeze out additional liquid if you like, although it will make the juice more cloudy. Some people recommend using a steam juicer.

Aronia juice prepared in either fashion can be used to make jelly (which is better with lemon juice added because it is not very acidic) or syrup, both of which remind me of those products made from wild black cherry. These are both good, but not good enough that I want to give up my aronia juice for them.

What a wonderful, fun, unheralded wild fruit this is. And the most amazing thing is that, after reading all this, impossible as it seems, *somebody* still thinks I'm talking about chokecherries.

Autumnberry, Autumn-olive

Elaeagnus umbellata

Elaeagnaceae – Oleaster Family

I t truly baffles me how the autumn-olive remains one of the biggest wild food
secrets in North America. Over vast regions of this continent it is our most
common wild fruit. I have seen entire pastures overtaken with it, one after
another, sometimes forming autumn-olive thickets covering twenty, forty, or
even a hundred acres. In much of the country this is a regular sight; in fact, it is
considered a noxious invasive weed in many areas and efforts are being made to
eradicate it. Oftentimes, a single bush may be so loaded with fruit that several
gallons may be picked from it, and this can be harvested with surprising efficiency. I have seen bushes so laden that their limbs rested solidly on the ground
under the weight. Recently, I picked eleven quarts from a super-loaded bush—in
less than fifteen minutes! The autumn-olive has received some attention for its

Autumnberry specializes in producing lots and lots of delicious red fruit. This bush is good, but
not exceptional. Note the silvery underside to the leaves.

A typical roadside autumnberry thicket. The bushes are impenetrable and stand about twelve feet high.

content of lycopene, a chemical known to promote prostate health. Tomatoes are generally considered the standard source for this nutrient—but autumn-olives contain about eighteen times as much lycopene as tomatoes (Black and Fordham, 2005). But the most incredible fact about autumn-olives is their flavor: almost everybody loves them.

Growing up, I encountered the autumn-olive quite regularly. I was intrigued by the bush's rugged appearance and by its odd red fruits covered with silvery flakes. Since it is not native, however, this plant was left out of my field guides and ignored by nature writers. Despite the fact that it is an incredible cover and food plant for wildlife, the hunting books and magazines that I read never made mention of it. And although the autumn-olive is a standout among wild fruits, none of my foraging references discussed it. For some years, then, I regularly saw this bush on my excursions but was unable to identify it.

It was Steve Brill's (1994) wild food guide that finally suggested this fruit to me. After verifying the identification with a botanical key, I got my first taste of autumn-olive. I felt ashamed that I had missed out on such a good thing for so long when it had been right there for the picking. But I will miss out no more; I'm making up for lost time and stocking up on lycopene.

I don't mean to make it sound like I'm the only one excited about this fruit. In test plots near Beltsville, Maryland, the USDA has achieved productivity of 3,600–12,600 pounds per acre (4,000 to 14,100 kg per hectare)—without using pesticides or fertilizers (Black and Fordham, 2005). These figures lead me to believe that, during bumper crop years, the largest autumn–olive thickets I've seen, in Kentucky and Tennessee, produce a whopping half million pounds (227,000 kg) of fruit! Not that I need that many, but it's fun to drool over the idea. The authors of the above study believe that this fruit needs a name that connotes a fruity flavor to be widely accepted as food in the United States, suggesting the name "autumnberry."

Description

The autumnberry is somewhere between a hefty shrub and a small, tough, sprawling tree. It usually produces several gnarled and spreading trunks, the largest of which may reach 6 inches (15 cm) in diameter. The topmost limbs of an autumnberry bush rarely reach more than 16 feet (5 m) above the ground. During their first few years, autumnberries are formidably armed with sharp thorns, but older bushes are not nearly so thorny. The autumnberry is typically found in dense, even impenetrable stands. To the trained eye, such thickets can be recognized by this shrub's growth form: trunks strongly arching and producing arched branches, the tips of which droop heavily and often reach the ground.

Autumnberry's leaves are also rather distinct. Elliptic or oval in shape, they are rather tough and leathery for a deciduous shrub. The leaves are dark, dull green on top, and distinctly silvery underneath. Borne alternately, they are

Autumn-olive leaves. Note the silvery undersides.

typically 2–3 inches (3–5 cm) long. The leaf margins are entire and often wavy or slightly curled.

The bark on older autumnberry trunks peels in long, thin, narrow strips, but on smaller trunks and branches it is smooth and grayish green. The twigs and leaves are covered with tiny silvery flakes or scales, a feature that this plant shares with its close relatives the buffaloberries (genus *Shepherdia*).

In mid to late spring the autumnberry produces copious dull yellow flowers in crowded clusters that hang from the leaf axils. Each flower is about 0.3 inch (8 mm) long and consists of four petals joined at the base to form a tube. The blossoms have a very strong fragrance, and a blooming thicket can produce a cloyingly sweet aroma.

Fertilized flowers produce olive-shaped fruits that are typically a little smaller than a currant or pea. Unripe clusters of autumnberries hang all summer long with little change, remaining light, dull green. In fall they plump up and turn to a bright orange-red but remain coated with silvery flakes. Each ripe autumnberry contains one seed, and these are very distinct in appearance. Soft-shelled and constricted to a point on each end, the yellowish-tan seeds have prominent lines running their length.

Autumnberry is fairly easy to recognize, but it is sometimes confused with several related shrubs. Buffaloberries have leaves with shiny scales like autumn-olive, but the scales are more brown in color. Although buffaloberry leaves look similar, they grow in pairs rather than alternately like those of autumnberry. One species of buffaloberry (*Shepherdia canadensis*) is a smaller shrub and lacks

Autumnberry flowers smell "sickeningly sweet."

thorns, while another (*S. argentea*) is similar in size to autumnberry and also thorny. The fruit is reddish but ripens earlier and is less elongated. Autumnberry also has a native relative, the wolfberry or silverberry *Elaeagnus commutata*. This northern shrub inhabits brushy, open areas of the boreal region from Quebec to Alaska. When ripe, the fruit remains green and is covered with silvery scales. The fruit of all three of these related shrubs is edible, so there is no danger in mistaking them for autumnberry.

Another shrub frequently confused with autumnberry is Tartarian honeysuckle (*Lonicera tatarica* and *L. x bella*). Like autumnberry, this is a very common invasive shrub of old fields, disturbed ground, and roadsides. People often mistake the two when they are too lazy or careless to

above The leaves of Canada buffaloberry *Shepherdia canadensis* resemble those of autumnberry but are broader and opposite; the fruit is red and edible but quite bitter.

below Tartarian honeysuckle is a common invasive shrub with inedible red berries that shares most of the habitat and range of autumnberry. Although one must be negligent to confuse these plants, it still happens. Note the paired fruit.

look at identifying details—they can only be mistaken at a superficial glance. I bet you won't do that.

Yaupon holly *Ilex vomitoria*, a shrub whose leaves contain caffeine and are used for tea, also has clusters of small red berries that may be confused with autumnberry. Yaupon is native primarily to the Coastal Plain of the Southeast. While the ranges of these shrubs overlap, they are not often found in the same areas. Yaupon's toxic berries lack the silvery speckles of autumnberry, and each fruit contains four seeds rather than one as in autumnberry. The leaves differ in being evergreen, crenate or toothed, and in that they also lack the silvery flakes of autumnberry.

Russian-olive

The autumn-olive is so named because of its close relationship with another tree, the Russian-olive *Elaeagnus angustifolia*, which is in turn named for its fruit's appearance. Neither of these species is closely related to the true olives (genus *Olea*), and their fruits are not similar to the true olive in flavor, texture, or any other important quality.

Russian-olive *Elaeagnus angustifolia* is a relative of autumn-olive, often confused solely on the basis of its name. It is a medium-sized tree with a notably silver hue.

Russian-olive often fruits heavily.

People have a strong tendency to confuse autumn-olive and Russian-olive—not because they are hard to tell apart, but primarily because of their names. It is hard to speak of one without being asked about the other. Russian-olive is a well-known, non-native tree found in most of the United States and Canada. Like its ecological twin the Siberian elm, this tree can handle extremely hot summers, bitterly cold winters, and severe drought—making it adaptable to places where few other trees can grow. Russian-olive is abundant on the Great Plains and in semi-arid sections of the West. For many miles on the high plains of Wyoming and Colorado, this is the only tree to be seen, and scrubby forests of it have sprung up around many western cities, such as Salt Lake and Denver. It predominates in fencerows and windbreaks over much of the Great Plains.

The Russian olive has much narrower leaves than the autumnberry; they are willow-like with a silvery sheen on both sides. Russian-olive is a spreading tree, growing much larger than the autumn-olive, occasionally over a foot (30 cm) in diameter and 35 feet (11 m) tall.

The fruit of Russian-olive and autumnberry are quite different. The Russian-olive produces a drab, dry drupe about 0.5 inch (13 mm) long, gray-green when ripe and shaped like a miniature olive. The pulp is mealy and sweet, but also astringent. The flavor reminds me a little of dried figs. The seeds are hard and tough but leathery rather than stone-like; they can be chewed with great effort and will eventually give up the tiny but delicious nut-like kernel they contain. Russian-olives often fruit prodigiously, and I would love to find a practical and enjoyable way to use their crop.

Range and Habitat

The autumnberry is native to Asia, where it is one among many *Elaeagnus* species used for food. It was introduced to the United States in 1830. Hu (2005) lists eleven *Elaeagnus* species traditionally used for food in China, and some others are occasionally seen in North America. The autumnberry has been introduced to North America for erosion control, soil improvement, wildlife food and cover, landscaping, and, to a lesser extent, for its edible fruit. Like most exotic invasives, its occurrence is difficult to predict because this depends on both habitat and the happenstance of human introduction. It has not been here long enough for its habitat needs to be thoroughly understood.

The autumn-olive was lauded as a virtual miracle forty years ago; it was intentionally planted by the same government agencies that are now villainizing it and spending millions trying to eradicate it. Latham (1963, p. 19) expressed the prevailing attitude when he said, "These shrubs add beauty to narrow field corners, roadsides, [etc.]—with no evident danger of becoming a pest by spreading onto pastures or well-kept places." Latham then lived in Ann Arbor, Michigan—around which, today, the autumn-olive is the most prevalent shrub, having choked out most native species. I wonder how many of the current ideas espoused by today's natural resource managers will be laughed at in a generation. (I can name a few.)

Autumnberry may be found in southern Canada and all but the driest parts of the United States. In some regions it is rampantly abundant, and I will dare to say that this is *the most common edible wild fruit in the eastern United States.* And it is increasing in the West (Sundberg, 2002)—who knows how common it may be there in a generation or two. It is also a common shrub in parts of Hawaii (Wagner and Sohmer, 1999). Autumnberry is the most prevalent shrub in parts of southern Michigan, Kentucky, Tennessee, Virginia, Illinois, Indiana, Ohio, and several other eastern states. Autumnberry is not hardy in the coldest parts of the United States and is therefore absent from the northern Plains and higher mountain areas.

Autumnberry is one of the few non-leguminous plants able, with the help of certain bacteria called *Frankia*, to fix Nitrogen. This allows it to thrive on impoverished or eroded soils and outcompete other shrubs on such sites. It is precisely for this reason that it was used widely to reclaim and stabilize old mine spoils, eroded hillsides, and newly constructed roadways. Such soil-deprived sites are where it remains most common today, accounting for its abundance in steep, hilly country that has been inappropriately cultivated or overgrazed, and in rocky, sandy, or gravelly areas where the soil is naturally poor.

Autumnberry grows in full sun or light shade. It does not successfully invade mesic hardwood forests but often does well in the sparse shade cast by oaks, hickories, and pines. Autumnberry's competitive edge is further enhanced by its drought tolerance. Like many other exotic shrubs, it loses its foliage later than most native species, giving it an extended growing season but also making it more susceptible to frost damage.

Given the way that birds and mammals relish the fruit and spread its seeds, expect to see autumnberry become more and more abundant over the coming years.

Harvest and Preparation

Autumnberry has an unusually long season of availability. In 2006, I first picked the fruit on August 25; on November 12, even after several hard frosts, I found entire thickets still loaded. The peak season of harvest is roughly September 15 to October 10. The fruit persists later in seasons of a heavy crop.

When autumnberries first turn red they are rather hard, very tart, and astringent due to their tannin content. They can be eaten at this time but are too tart for most palates, although they do make fine jam or jelly. However, the fully ripe fruit are much better. As they sit on the bush they gradually become softer, sweeter, and less astringent. You can judge their ripeness by how easily they pop off their stems when picked; they do not detach easily when under-ripe. And you should taste-test them, for even when fully ripe their flavor varies substantially from one bush to the next.

This is one of the wild fruits that you can really stock up on. It grows in dense hedges along roadways or fence lines and turns abandoned farmlands into wild orchards. Every year you can find a good supply, and in very good years shameful amounts will rot on the bush. The autumnberry clusters often hang along the branches so densely that there is no space between one and the next, creating an elongated "mega-cluster" along the branch. Just one of these mega-clusters can contain several pounds of fruit, and single bushes can produce twenty to eighty pounds of fruit in bumper crop years.

An effective way to pick autumnberries is to hold the laden branch or mega-cluster over a container and loosen the berries with your fingers so they fall in. Try to do this without crushing too many berries and without loosening too many leaves and stems. You can pick autumnberries very fast this way; typical is one to three gallons per hour, depending mostly on the quality of the bush. The low, spreading form means that the bushes bear most of their fruit within easy reach, and often they are so low that I simply place a bowl on the ground beneath the branch as I pick. You can also pick the fruit by laying down a tarp or cloth and beating on the branches. For this the berries must be fully ripe and ready to detach.

As you collect autumnberries you will probably find a disturbing number of Japanese beetles going into your container. They love to hide between the fruit in the clusters, and due to their color are hard to spot there. I know of no good solution to this problem; indeed, these little pests are the biggest trouble with picking autumnberries, and sometimes I spend more time removing and avoiding them than I do picking the fruit.

Upon first turning red, the flavor of autumnberries reminds me of raspberries or pomegranates with the pucker of chokecherries. As they ripen the puckering quality fades, the fruit sweetens, and a hint of tomato flavor develops. I love to eat fully ripe autumnberries straight from the bush. I stuff my face with one handful after another for the first twenty minutes of picking. The seedshells are soft and contain a delicious nutty kernel that seems to disappear in your mouth as you chew. Some people swallow everything, but I spit out the masticated seedshells when I am done absorbing all the flavor possible, then reach for another handful.

I have a number of ways to use those autumnberries that actually do make it into my collecting container. They are good in pie, and they are the berry of choice for making fruit leather. In addition, autumnberries make good jam or jelly and have a most delicious juice.

For all the cooked products that I make, I strain out the seeds first. I do not cook or crush the berries before straining; all I do is try to get rid of the sticks, leaves, and beetles. Autumnberries go through my strainer very easily with little waste, although I may have to run them through an extra time or two to get all the pulp.

Straining will produce a beautiful red puree, but the juice and solids will quickly begin to separate. When this happens you will notice that autumnberry juice has an amazing quality: it is clear. Lycopene, the primary coloring agent, is not water soluble and so remains in the pulp. The solids coagulate into a mass, and this mass slowly shrinks as it releases liquid, almost as if repelling it. You can let a container of puree sit in the refrigerator for a few days and then carefully pour off the clear juice, saving the red pulp for fruit leather, jam, or other fun projects. Or you can keep the two together, mixing well before use. This autumnberry puree stores well frozen.

Once you taste the juice of ripe, sweet autumnberries, you may want to maximize your yield of it. If a better drink has passed my lips, I fail to recollect the experience. A glass of autumnberry juice appears deceivingly like slightly used dishwater—but upon careful inspection one will notice the faintest yellow tone, which hardly hints at the flavor swimming in it. Autumnberry juice is pleasantly acidic like orange juice and at least as sweet. However, juice from under-ripe fruit can be extremely tart.

To get as much juice as possible from your autumnberries, place the puree in a cloth suspended in a bucket and let it drip for a few days, keeping the whole apparatus in a cool place. Almost all the liquid should separate from the pulp without any squeezing involved, and then you can dispose of the solids (or use them, if you really want that lycopene). Sometimes the liquid doesn't separate well—I'm not always sure why—and in these cases I keep the pulp for making other things. Freezing and thawing the puree sometimes seems to facilitate better juice separation.

Besides making a wonderful juice, autumnberry also makes excellent pies, cobblers, and other desserts. If the berries are on the sour side, I mix them with other milder fruits. One problem, however, is that the juice has a tendency to separate from the pulp while cooking and pool in the bottom of your pan. To prevent this, use a little more flour or cornstarch than usual and mix it well into the puree.

The tendency of the juice and pulp to separate affects all autumnberry products. Jam, for example, can get a unique texture and marbled appearance due to

Silver buffaloberry *Shepherdia argentea* in fruit. This relative, native to the Great Plains and intermountain West, looks quite like the autumnberry. Its fruit is also edible but somewhat more tart. Note the blunt leaves and the dark floral remains at the end of the berry.

the pockets of clear liquid that separate while it sets. You can also make a most interesting tart but nearly colorless jelly from the juice.

If I am going to eat autumnberries out of season, my favorite way is in the form of fruit leather. The finest flavor is achieved using ripe, mild berries. For best results, use puree that has had little or none of its juice removed. Mix or beat it thoroughly just before spreading it on trays to dry. The smooth texture of the puree makes for a very fine-looking fruit leather, and the juiciness allows it to be spread very thinly and uniformly on the tray. However, because of the time of year that the fruit ripens, sun-drying is often impossible. I have also done it in the oven, on a rack near my woodstove, and in an electric food dehydrator. The thin layer of pulp dries relatively quickly, especially in the absence of skins. It produces a beautiful red fruit leather, rich in lycopene, that is coveted, bartered, and begged for on account of its flavor.

If our continent is going to be overrun by exotic invasive plants, I pray that there are more of them like autumnberry.

Bunchberry, Dwarf Cornel

Cornus canadensis, Cornus suecica

Cornaceae – Dogwood Family

Like loons and wolves, the bunchberry is a symbol of the Northwoods; but unlike them, it sits still. This characteristic, combined with its unsurpassed beauty, makes the bunchberry perhaps the most popular nature photography subject over half of our continent. Displayed on countless calendars and in every regional photo gallery, this ankle-high plant's remarkable symmetry and color combination, whether in fruit or in flower, captures the eyes and holds their attention like a pretty smile.

To some it is a moral quandary when something so beautiful is also edible. But to me, such beauty is not *destroyed* by being eaten, it is *consummated*. After all, do we not spend hours preparing, decorating, and arranging extravagant meals only to consume them? Neither the bunchberry, nor the platter, if left uneaten, will remain so beautiful forever; indeed, both are beautiful for the very purpose of inviting consumption. So eat without remorse, transforming that physical beauty into something even more wonderful that goes on forever.

A full bunch of ripe bunchberries. Sometimes they rest above the leaves, other times they hang like this.

Description

Bunchberry is a low perennial herb growing from a slender woody rhizome. A member of the dogwood genus and family, it is traditionally treated as a shrub under the argument that its woody portion is underground—although this stretches the definition of "shrub" too much for my comfort. The erect aerial stems are thin and unbranched, typically rising 3–7 inches (8–18 cm) above the ground.

At the top of each of these stems there is a whorl of leaves; usually six on a flowering or fruiting stalk and four on one that is sterile. Occasionally a flowering stalk will bear two whorls of leaves. The stem will have one or more pairs of tiny, reduced, scale-like leaves below the main whorl.

The individual leaves are sessile or with very short stalks. The blades are elliptic to obovate and pointed at both ends, 1–3 inches (2.5–8 cm) long, and smooth with entire margins. The veins are conspicuous and curve toward the tip of the leaf rather than terminating at the margin.

When you look at a blooming bunchberry, it appears as if there are four broad white petals up to 0.8 inches (2 cm) long—but actually these are white bracts that surround a cluster of numerous tiny, yellow-green or pinkish four-parted

What looks like a flower is actually a cluster of them. The four "petals" are actually white leaves, with numerous tiny flowers in the center. Despite these technicalities, it's still beautiful.

flowers, this whole inflorescence giving the illusion of a single large flower. (The same arrangement is found on the flowering dogwood tree *Cornus florida*.) The cluster is borne on a stem 0.5–1.5 inches (13–40 mm) above the top whorl of leaves. Bunchberry's conspicuous blooming occurs in May and June.

The fruit is an elliptic or spherical drupe less than 0.3 inch (8 mm) long borne in a tight umbel-like cluster, each with a single stone. These berries mature from early July to September. Ripe bunchberries are orange-red, as bright as any berry—but the color is only skin-deep. The interior is whitish.

Range and Habitat

Bunchberry is a distinctive plant of cool northern forests, found across the wooded sections of Canada and extending north to Alaska and southern Greenland. One of the most widespread forest plants on our continent, it ranges across the northern tier of United States, being particularly common in the upper Great Lakes states and New England. It extends southward to northern California, Colorado, and Virginia at higher elevations. It is also found in eastern Asia.

The dwarf cornel is a plant of conifer or mixed deciduous-conifer forests, being more abundant where the soil moisture is high and there is partial sunlight. This plant is a lover of organic matter, commonly growing on the mounds of long-rotten logs, old stumps, and mossy places. One site where I pick bunchberries is a rugged cliff top; another is a low forest of hemlock, white pine, and birch; one is a roadside in a tamarack-spruce bog; and yet another is a conifer-studded peninsula in a small lake. Look for bunchberries in association with bluebead lily, blueberry, cinnamon fern, and wintergreen.

There is a second species of bunchberry in North America, even more northerly than the first. The Swedish dwarf cornel or bog bunchberry *Cornus suecica* grows on the tundras from Alaska to Greenland (further south in alpine meadows) and in Europe and Asia as well. This species differs in that the paired leaves below the main whorl on its stem are much larger than those of *C. canadensis*, and in that it has dark purple flowers.

Harvest and Preparation

This is not a very well-known or well-liked wild berry, often being called flavorless by those who disdain it. Certainly the dwarf cornel is no rival to the raspberry. It is true that chewing a single bunchberry delivers little stimulation to the taste buds—but neither does a pea-sized cube of apple flesh, and we love apples. There *is* flavor in bunchberries, but it takes a bunch to get it.

Fruiting bunchberry plants typically have six leaves per whorl.

The bunchberry is not for the impatient; it is for the hungry. Those who mock its mildness have perhaps never been deep in the awesome wilds of the great Northwoods without provisions, seeking breakfast in a misty swamp. Fish cannot be every meal, and greens go only so far. Blueberries, pin cherries, and thimbleberries are all wonderful, but one can't swallow a meal's worth before a bellyache screams in protest and the tongue stings from acid juice. Then you will crave a mild fruit more than soda after french fries. Perhaps the scarlet fooled you, but the bunchberry isn't for dessert—not to be dumped on ice cream as syrup, not to be spread on toast as jam, not to be sprinkled over salad or yogurt—the bunchberry is just food, more aptly compared to tapioca than blueberries.

However, you don't have to be famished to eat them, or even hungry. Curious is quite enough, for if you pick a pinch of bunchberries and don't expect a raspberry, you'll taste what they really are: mild but pleasant and easy to swallow. I can't help but stoop for a handful whenever I see them, whether I'm hungry or not. In some places there are great amounts of them, and it's easy to see that this is a good fruit for any northern woodsperson to know.

Bunchberries ripen in July or early August in the southern part of their range, but further north they may be delayed well into September. They may persist for a couple of weeks or sometimes over a month before being taken by wildlife. I collect bunchberries by crawling or crouching among them, gently grabbing whole clusters at a time and dropping them into a bowl. Their flesh is not dry but neither is it juicy, and a container of bunchberries feels light and airy. You don't have to worry about them smashing, fermenting, or molding in a day like you do with many soft fruits, and they'll easily last a week in the refrigerator.

I enjoy eating raw bunchberries, but the only drawback is the seed. You cannot spit it out because its inseparable from the pulp. There are two choices: you can chew gently in order not to break the seeds and then swallow them with the pulp, or you can crunch up the seeds and swallow them with the pulp. If you're too civilized to swallow seeds you'll have to leave this fruit for the bears.

If you happen upon a bumper crop of bunchberries you can try making bunchberry sauce or pudding. I do this by pounding the berries to a pulp in a mortar, which also crushes the seeds. You can achieve the same with a blender or Vitamix. To the mashed fruit pulp I add a little sweetener and a tart dessert berry like raspberry. This is delicious and refreshing eaten like applesauce. Even if the flavor doesn't impress, the color will.

I have not yet had the opportunity to try the Swedish bunchberry.

Don't fault this nourishing nibble for the mildness of its flavor. Its beauty alone is favor enough to the wilderness wanderer, and everything beyond that is a bonus.

Wood Sorrel

Oxalis **spp.**

Oxalidaceae – Wood Sorrel Family

When I was four years old, my older siblings taught me to eat the wood sorrel growing underneath the front porch of our house. As the first edible wild plant that I learned, it has always occupied a special place in my heart. Every time I nibble on wood sorrel, I am brought back to those carefree summer days of childhood when everything was new and everything new was exciting.

It is a mystery how we learned that wood sorrel was good to eat, but we were not unique in that respect. Across this continent, millions of children graze on wood sorrel as if it were just another kind of candy, and few of them were taught to do this in any formal way or by any adult. Of course, these children don't call the plant "wood sorrel." My family called it "juicies" (always plural), but as far as I know that name was exclusive to the corner of Kickbusch and Prospect in Wausau, Wisconsin. I have met other children who called them "sweets." More widespread names include lemon grass, sour grass, sour clover, and lemon clover. In my neighborhood we called the fruits "nanners" because of their banana-like form, and this is another widely used nickname for the plant.

Yellow wood sorrel, showing banana-shaped seed pods.

O. oregana grows in the rich soil of coastal rain forests in the Pacific Northwest. It has the largest leaves of our wood sorrels.

Description

There are numerous species of wood sorrel found throughout North America. All of them are small, delicate herbs with very thin stems and petioles. Their leaf shape is characteristic and unique. Each leaf consists of three symmetrical leaflets radiating from a central point like clover leaflets. Unlike clovers, however, each wood sorrel leaflet is distinctly heart-shaped or notched. Generally they are strongly creased along the midvein, like a folded paper heart.

Some species of wood sorrel are perennials growing from tubers or rhizomes, while others are annuals. Some, like *Oxalis montana* and *O. oregana*, have no main stalk—only petioles or flower stalks arising directly from underground runners. Other species such as *O. stricta* have short, fragile, branching stems.

The flowers have five petals, five sepals, and ten stamens. Some species are yellow, while others are pink or white. The various species bloom from spring to late summer. After the flowers wither, the plants bear elongated, green, banana-shaped seed pods, 0.3–0.6 inches (8–15 mm) long. In some species these are even borne in banana-like bunches.

Violet wood sorrel, an ephemeral with delicious, tender leaves and petioles.

Range and Habitat

Wood sorrels are found throughout North America. Different species occupy totally different habitats, but all species need shade, moisture, or both. *O. stricta* is a cosmopolitan weedy species found in gardens, along house foundations, and in moist, disturbed soil, usually in partial shade. The violet wood sorrel *O. violacea* is a perennial spring ephemeral, limiting its growing season to the brief period when the soil is moist on its preferred dry, grassy hillsides.

The mountain wood sorrel *O. montana* inhabits moist conifer and conifer-hardwood forests of the eastern United States and Canada. It is strongly associated with hemlock stands and often carpets the duff where few other plants are shade tolerant enough to survive. An ecologically similar species is the Oregon wood sorrel *O. oregana* of the Pacific Northwest. This plant grows in the shady understory of the coastal rain forests. The leaves of Oregon wood sorrel are far larger than those of most other species.

This is just a small sampling of the many wood sorrels in North America; all are considered edible.

Harvest and Preparation

Wood sorrel's main use is as a trailside nibble, and probably no other wild green in North America is so well liked as a snack. All the above-ground parts of the plant can be eaten: stems, leaves, flowers, and fruits. They are edible at any time but are much more pleasant to consume when tender, so the young plants before flowering are best. Texture varies not only over time, but also between the species. *O. montana* tends to be tough, while the leaves of *O. oregana* are quite tender, especially early in the season. The flavor of all species is pleasantly but potently sour, like a rhubarb stalk. It is always interesting to watch people's faces when they taste wood sorrel for the first time, shocked but delighted by the lemony flavor.

The fruits have an interesting appearance and the same pleasant taste. They are so small that it's a major undertaking to acquire even a handful, but with a few excited children, it's quite a fun project.

Besides being used as a snack in the field, wood sorrel greens are excellent in salads, adding a tangy flavor and attractive appearance. Little sprigs make a nice

Violet wood sorrel is one of the few dicots with a bulb. These bulbs, and the tender taproot underneath, are edible.

garnish. You can add wood sorrel greens to soup and other recipes to impart a little acid flavor. However, the stringiness of the older stems really stands out in cooked dishes, and it takes a long time to separate a quantity of leaves from the stems, so it is best to select young, tender plants for cooking. (The exception to this is the Oregon wood sorrel; its large, tender leaves are easy to work with, making it a premiere culinary *Oxalis*.) If I want to add wood sorrel's savory essence to a soup later in the season when the stems are tough, I just grab a bundle by the stalks and dip the whole plants into the boiling pot for about thirty seconds. While holding them in the soup, I comb them with a fork to separate the soft leaves from the stalks and then pull the bundle out.

Wood sorrel can also be used to make a tangy, refreshing, lemonade-like drink. Gather a small heap of the plants, rinse them well, and then chop them fine or process very briefly in a blender. Let the chopped wood sorrel steep in cold water for a while, strain out the vegetation, and serve cold.

The violet wood sorrel, a spring ephemeral of dry prairies, has not only the most tender and delicious greens of any wood sorrel I've tried, but it also has a tiny edible bulb and taproot, both of which are delicious.

A perennial South American species of wood sorrel, *O. tuberosa*, is cultivated for its edible tuber. This vegetable is called *oca* in the Peruvian highlands where it is a common food.

Like many cultivated vegetables such as rhubarb, spinach, and sorrel, wood sorrel is high in oxalic acid. Oxalic acid should be consumed in moderation. There is much ado in the wild food literature about the potential dangers of oxalic acid. It is hard to find an account or recipe for any wild plant known to be high in this chemical that doesn't include a warning to limit one's consumption of it. In line with the preposterous double standard that is applied to wild foods, I have not seen a single oxalic acid warning in a cookbook, produce guide, or gardening manual pertaining to cultivated vegetables. That's because the oxalic acid danger is largely hypothetical, and problems associated with its consumption are unusual and extremely rare. Oxalic acid is a normal part of our diets and is always present in the body because it is produced internally. If wood sorrel was your primary food source for an extended period of time, or you ate an enormous amount at once, the oxalic acid might cause problems. However, that is generally irrelevant to real life.

Yes, twenty million little kids *can* be wrong. (Barney is not cool.) But in the case of wood sorrel, they're onto something.

Honewort, Wild Chervil

Cryptotaenia canadensis

Apiaceae – Carrot Family

As a child I saw honewort nearly every time I ventured into the woods. So mundane a sight was this herb that I never took the time to identify it or even to wonder if it might be edible. Surely, many thousands of these plants have brushed across my bare shins as I stalked the woods in search of mayapples, morels, trout, wild grapes, and such more obvious treasures. In fact, I learned to consider honewort a harbinger of forageable bounty, for it grows best in those rich-soiled woodlands where Nature is most generous with all sorts of gifts.

Some years later I was barefoot, walking through the rich bottomland of a spring-fed stream, shaded by elm, ash, hickory, butternut, maple, oak, and hackberry. Beneath the subcanopy of prickly ash, nannyberry, elderberry, and tangled wild grape vines; under the stinging nettles, gooseberries, ostrich fern, carrion flower, jerusalem artichoke, cow parsnip, cup plant, and hopniss; hidden amongst the wood nettles, clearweed, and ground bean—there was an old familiar weed that I finally took the time to identify. And to my delight, the weed turned out to be a vegetable.

Tender honewort shoot.

Description

Like a host of other useful culinary plants, honewort is a member of the carrot family, the *Apiaceae*. Honewort is attractive but meek; nothing in particular draws one's attention to it. Since it slightly resembles several other plants that may be found beside it, especially when not in flower, your first confident identification of honewort may not be as quick as with some plants.

This perennial herb typically reaches 22–40 inches (55–100 cm) in height at maturity. The stalk is angled at the nodes and typically branches only in the upper half. A large stem is about 0.4 inch (1 cm) in diameter at the base. The leaf

size decreases dramatically going up the stem. The overall form, especially after the foliage has withered, resembles sweet cicely and aniseroot—two edible plants of the same family that commonly share honewort's habitat. However, the honewort's dried fruits are much shorter and stouter; recognizing them, the trained eye can locate honewort patches even in midwinter.

Honewort's leaves are variable and defy easy and concise description. They are divided into three leaflets, each of which is irregularly toothed and sometimes deeply lobed or nearly divided. Basal leaves are larger, more rounded and irregular in appearance, and often deeply ruffled. Upper leaves are smaller and the leaflets more pointed; their patterns of teeth and lobes are less erratic but still irregular. Honewort leaves are glabrous; they are slightly glossy when young but become duller as they age. The petioles of the basal leaves are long and channeled, while the upper leaves are sessile. With practice one can learn to spot honewort's non-descript foliage amidst a collage of lush greenery.

Mature honewort plant, about three feet tall.

Honewort flowers in early summer and doesn't get too extravagant in accomplishing the task. Loose flower clusters grow from the apex of the plant and some of the upper leaf axils. The inflorescence is a compound umbel, but the number of branches at each juncture is few and the pedicels are very unequal in length, making it very easy to overlook this fact. The tiny individual flowers are about 0.15 inches (4 mm) across, consisting of five white petals. The single-seeded fruits are shaped like a stout banana. They are dark brown with a few ridges and stripes running lengthwise. The fruits remain attached to the pedicels well into autumn and sometimes winter.

Many plants can be mistaken for honewort. Buttercups (genus *Ranunculus*) are sometimes confused with it, but they are generally hairy with non-glossy leaves. Buttercups are mildly poisonous and distasteful. Cut-leaved coneflower *Rudbeckia laciniata* (not poisonous) is often found in the same habitat; its flowering stems look very different, and the young leaves can be differentiated by their rough surface and shorter petioles.

The plant most commonly confused with honewort is probably black sanicle *Sanicula marilandica*, and other members of this genus, which are related members of the carrot family. Black sanicle can be distinguished by the larger number of leaflets or divisions (usually four to seven) in each leaf, arranged palmately; its umbellets consist of many short stems packed into a tight, spherical cluster. Differentiating honewort, before flowering, from members of the genus *Sanicula* can be tricky for a beginner—and if you make the mistake, they even smell and taste rather similar. I can find no reliable reports that *Sanicula* is harmful to consume. In fact, Moerman (1998) reports two edible uses for the genus and numerous medicinal ones, while the greens of two species are used as vegetables

Early spring rosettes of *Cryptotaenia* (left) and *Sanicula* (right). The *Sanicula* leaflets are more palmately arranged and not as clearly separated.

Slightly older but still young, honewort leaf on left, sanicle leaf on right.

in China (Hu, 2005). The tubers of *Sanicula tuberosa* are a traditional food for Native Americans in California (Anderson, 2005). However, one should be cautious and avoid accidentally collecting the leaves.

The related edible aniseroot *Osmorhiza longistylis* shares the same habitat; it has much smaller, thinner, and more numerous leaflets, plus a distinct anise aroma. Goutweed *Aegopodium podagraria* is another edible member of the carrot family, found sporadically as a garden escape. It is quite similar to honewort in form, although most cultivated varieties have leaves with white margins. Goutweed can be used as a vegetable like honewort, so there is no danger in confusing them.

The cultivated chervil, a well-known culinary herb used in salads and soups, is *Anthriscus cerefolium*; this species, and two others in the genus, are occasionally found growing wild as escapes in North America, especially the eastern part. For this reason the name "wild chervil" is problematic and necessarily creates confusion. Yet another closely related genus, *Chaerophyllum*, goes by the name of "chervil." I have found varying references to the edibility of this genus but have no experience myself. *Cryptotaenia canadensis*, the subject of the present chapter, is another of the many excellent wild edibles that unfortunately lacks a simple, trouble-free common name.

Range and Habitat

Honewort's habitat is rich, moist soil under hardwood trees in partial to moderate shade. It is particularly common on the higher parts of river floodplains and in fertile valleys, but honewort will show up in nearly any woods in those regions with superb agricultural soils. It likes sandy or loamy soils and generally is absent on heavy clay. Honewort likes moist ground but is not a wetland plant.

346

It does best where bare soil is occasionally available for germination, hence its abundance in floodplains, on steep slopes, in lightly used wooded pastures, and areas otherwise disturbed by human activity.

I encounter this herb frequently when trout fishing. It grows associated with ostrich fern, Virginia waterleaf, wood nettle, carrion flower, aniseroot, wild leek, wild garlic, clearweed, and meadow rue. It seems to thrive under a canopy of oaks a little more than it does under maples, but if you mix a few late-leafing trees such as walnut, hickory, or ash with the maples it does very well there, too. Honewort often does exceptionally well under boxelders; it invades old fields and pastures with them and often grows like a weed under their canopy.

Honewort is found basically throughout the hardwood forests of eastern North America, from southern Manitoba to New Brunswick and south to northern Florida and eastern Texas. It is also found in Hawaii. It is sparsely distributed in parts of this range where the soil is poor. A nearly identical plant, *C. japonica*, is native to Japan and eastern Asia, where it is commonly collected for food and also cultivated. The Japanese call it *mitsuba*.

above Sanicle, flowering top. By this stage, these plants are easy to distinguish.

below Honewort, flowering top.

Harvest and Preparation

In spring, both the tender **young stems** and **leafy tops** of honewort make a delicious cooked vegetable and a wonderful, hearty soup base. The time to gather the stalks is in mid-spring when they are about 8–16 inches (20–40 cm) tall. The season coincides fairly well with the blooming of apples. Go by the bend-easy rule; the stems should easily pinch off at the base. They will feel flimsy when bent but will not snap off like fiddleheads or asparagus—they need to be pinched or cut. I collect these young honewort stalks from plants scattered throughout the colony so as not to overharvest one small patch. I leave the ruffled, rubbery tuft of leaves attached to the top of each stalk. If a recent storm has left a film of silt on the leaves, as is sometimes the case in floodplains, I wash them thoroughly—sometimes in a nearby stream—knowing all too well that some grit will cling in defiance of my best effort. Better yet: if possible, go uphill where the flood did not reach. The smooth stalks are easier to clean than the leaves.

Clean honewort stalks and leafy tops can be steamed or boiled in a small amount of water for five to twenty minutes, depending on your preference. I

right top Mature honewort leaf in summer. The shape is like the spring leaves, but the leaf is not glossy and the margins and texture are rougher.

right bottom The clasping petiole sheath of honewort. Note the smooth surface, without any hairs or bloom. These stalks are prime for eating.

below Note the jagged wings where honewort's leaflets attach. As with the margins, this wing is less jagged on young leaves.

like them just served with a little salt. The stems have a wonderful soft texture and a flavor that is distinct and pleasing but not too strong. Wild chervil stalks are a fantastic vegetable, and they can be eaten raw as well as cooked. They are superb eaten alone or in soups and casseroles.

Young honewort greens have almost the same good flavor as the stems but they never get as tender as I like. I prefer to chop them fine and use them mixed with other vegetables in various dishes rather than serve them alone. You can also eat them raw on sandwiches or in salad.

Whether you boil or steam honewort, be sure to keep the cooking water. Few other herbs produce such a rich, complete-tasting broth all by themselves—only nettles rival honewort in this respect. Add a little salt to this dark green (and probably highly nutritious) liquid to produce a bouillon eminently worth sipping around a campfire in the cool evening air. (It's pretty good in front of a TV, too, I'm told.) To make a hearty honewort broth, be generous with the greens, filling your pot with packed leaves, then filling it to the same level with water. After straining the broth, add a few of your favorite vegetables—perhaps some wood nettles, wild leeks, honewort stalks, a parsnip, a tender peeled thistle stalk, and a few spring beauty roots—and you have a vegetable soup that any cook would be proud of. A fat squirrel or chicken to simmer with your wild chervil greens might launch you to local culinary stardom.

Honewort greens make the best broth in spring at the same time that the stalks are young and tender. However, the leaves can be used at any time during the growing season. Like many woodland herbs, honewort has a second flush of growth in autumn after the canopy leaves have fallen, and the greens can often be collected late into fall.

I have also read that the **roots** of honewort are edible. When I first dug some up, I found them so small that I thought I must be the brunt of someone's joke. I wondered if perhaps they had confused the wild chervil *Anthriscus cerefolium*, which does have a taproot used for a vegetable, with *Cryptotaenia canadensis*. But I cleaned and cooked those tiny little white honewort roots, and they were delicious, so that after three bites I found myself wishing I had collected more than fifteen of them.

Honewort, despite its abundance and superb eating qualities, is not particularly well-known among wild food foragers. This is another case where we Westerners would do well to emulate the Japanese.

Wild Carrot

Daucus carota

Apiaceae – Carrot Family

Iremember visiting my grandparents when I was six years old and seeing some luxuriant wild carrots growing near the base of one of my grandfather's beehives. I had to have one. I slowly approached and carefully attempted to pull out a carrot without disturbing the bees, but I still managed to get stung. I ran into the house crying, but got no sympathy. My grandfather laughed and said, "You got _stung_—that means you _killed_ one of my bees! Do you know how much honey one bee makes?"

Another time, when I was thirteen, my mother brought me to the clinic with a terrible rash, which had persisted for over a week. The doctor asked if I had recently eaten anything "new or unusual." I said no, but my mother commented that I had been eating wild carrots. The doctor's eyes opened wide in terror. (He must have heard horror stories of people confusing wild carrot with poison hemlock.) After his lecture about the danger of eating wild carrot, I plainly told him that wild carrots were not "new or unusual" to me—that I ate them often and had been doing so for a long time. After a sermon about the perils of letting children forage for wild food, he told me to stop eating wild carrots, and my mother halfheartedly seconded the command. Of course, I ignored them both, which is why I grew up to be the wild food guy. We later figured out, with no help from the physician, that my rash was caused by the fabric softener that we were using.

Wild carrot roots are cream-colored, resembling small parsnips, but their scent and flavor is very carroty.

Description

Wild carrot is either the progenitor or the escaped descendent of the cultivated carrot, and the plants look essentially identical. The only part of the wild carrot that differs substantially from the cultivated form is the root. These are thin, white, flexible rather than crisp, and have a thin woody core. They look very much like small parsnips, except they tend not to be so enlarged at the top. Their scent is potently and pleasingly carrot-like.

Wild carrot is typically a biennial. The first-year rosettes contain five to nine lacey, fern-like multi-compound leaves. These leaves are normally 5–10 inches (13–25 cm) long. When the plant grows on bare soil the leaves will lie flat on the ground, but where there is competition they will stand erect. The midrib is thin and grooved. The leaves usually have scattered short hairs that stick out of them at a right angle.

Carrot leaves tend to grow upright with competition, as is typically seen with garden carrots.

A wild carrot rosette in fall. When growing in the open without competition, carrot leaves will rest on the ground or nearly so.

The second-year stalk of wild carrot is light green and rounded in cross section. On its surface there are scattered short hairs sticking straight out. The stalk zigzags gently between its alternate compound leaves, which are similar to the basal leaves. Wild carrot stalks rarely branch except near the top. Normal height at maturity is 3.5–6 feet (1–2 m).

Wild carrot blooms from midsummer to early autumn. The tiny, white, five-petaled flowers are borne in a tightly packed compound umbel 2.5–5 inches (6–13 cm) across. Most of these inflorescences contain a single dark purple flower in the center. This anomalous flower is so small that it can be hard to notice. The smell of wild carrot flowers is spicy and delicious. I used to live near a "hayfield" that grew such a pure stand of wild carrot that a greenhorn might presume the white umbels to be a cash crop. The carrots towered over my head and formed a tangle so dense that I nearly had to burrow to get through it. Walking by this field on a hot August day when the sun was baking the essence out of the blossoms, one could become intoxicated by the sweet carroty scent that drifted across the road.

After flowering, this compound umbel closes up into a tight cluster or "bird's nest," giving the plant another of its common names. The "nest" contains many small, oval seeds covered with tiny, hooked hairs. These seeds may stick to your clothing as you brush against them, although they are far less tenacious and irritating than most kinds of stick-tights.

As a youngster I never had trouble identifying wild carrot, but I eventually learned through the literature that this was considered a difficult and dangerous task. **Indeed, the wild carrot does resemble poison hemlock *Conium maculatum*, and confusing the two could be a deadly mistake.** In fact, **misidentifications have resulted in death**. While all wild plants must be identified with care, the wild carrot deserves special mention due to the danger of its look-similar. The situation is made worse by the fact that the wild carrot's other common name, Queen Anne's lace, is sometimes also used for poison hemlock.

top right The mature leaf of poison hemlock is normally three or four times pinnately compound; the ultimate leaflets are pinnately toothed, incised, or lobed.

below left, center, and right The basal leaf of wild carrot is normally two (but occasionally three) times compound; while stem leaves are often three times compound. The leaflets are deeply and erratically dissected, sometimes to the midrib; the lobes often branch. Note the variability in denseness and pubescence of these carrot leaflets; this is largely an effect of sunlight, soil moisture, and position on the plant (the lacy, nearly hairless leaf is from a mature stalk).

left Wild carrot stems are notably hairy and are not coated with bloom.

below Poison hemlock stems are smooth and hairless with a prominent white bloom. You can see the streak where I rubbed the bloom off with my finger. Also note the stem's erratic purple spots and faint vertical lines. Poison hemlock stems are hollow.

right Wild carrot flowers are borne in a large compound umbel subtended by branching bracts 1–2 inches long.

left Wild carrot's inflorescence is larger and denser than those of poison hemlock, plus they often, like this one, have a dark purple flower in the center, which hemlock lacks.

right Poison hemlock's compound umbel is smaller and sparser than those of wild carrot. The bracts subtending the umbels are about a quarter-inch long.

above Wild carrot root.

below Poison hemlock roots look much like those of wild carrot but are longer and less tapered. Their scent is faint. Note the purple stems. **Deadly poisonous!**

There are other poisonous plants that can be confused with wild carrot. Probably most notable is fool's parsley *Aethusa cynapium*. This annual plant is much smaller than wild carrot, rarely reaching even 3 feet (1 m) in height. It has much smaller compound umbels of white flowers. The leaves are ill-smelling, smooth, hairless, and shiny. Fool's parsley is not native to North America; it is rather rare, being confined largely to the Northeast.

above Poison hemlock often grows in dense colonies like this. It's fern-like leaves are much larger than those of wild carrot.

right Poison hemlock typically grows six to nine feet tall—much taller than wild carrot. It produces numerous compound umbels at various levels.

Wild Carrot vs. Poison Hemlock

Wild carrot, *Daucus carota*	Poison hemlock, *Conium maculatum*
Surfaces with stiff erect hairs	Surfaces lack hair
No bloom (powder) on stalks	Prominent white bloom (powder) on stalks
Petiole channeled, solid	Petiole round, hollow
Stem solid	Stem hollow
Leaflets erratically and deeply lobed, with lobes often branching and sinuous; occasionally divided all the way to midrib. See photos.	Leaflets deeply toothed, incised, or lobed in a distinctly pinnate pattern (pinnatifid). See photos.
Stem light green, sometimes with reddish lines	Purple spots, lines, or zones are prominent on stem
Leaves and stalks with pleasant, carroty scent	Leaves and stems ill-scented
Compound umbels with narrow, branching bracts, up to 2 inches long (almost as wide as umbels).	Compound umbels with short bracts, usually less than .3 inch, not spreading nearly as wide as umbels.
3–16 compound umbels per plant	40–350 compound umbels per plant
Inflorescence 2.5–4 inches wide	Inflorescence 1.25–2.5 inches wide
Basal leaf normally twice compound (although leaflets of the second division may have some lobes divided all the way to the midrib).	Leaf normally three or four times compound
Old, dry umbels curl into "bird's nest"	Old, dry umbels remain in typical form
On typical basal leaf, 1–8 inches of petiole before leaflets appear.	On typical basal leaf, 3–20 inches of petiole before leaflets appear.
Petiole/rachis of basal leaf has leaflets for about 60–90 percent of its length	Petiole/rachis of basal leaf has leaflets for about 50 percent of its length;
Basal petiole/rachis has no abrupt change in angle.	Basal petiole/rachis usually has abrupt angle where division begins.
Shoots up later in spring; two to four weeks after poison hemlock	Shoots up earlier in spring; typically 2–5 feet tall before carrot stems even appear in the same area
Begins blooming 2–4 weeks later	Begins blooming 2–4 weeks earlier
Umbels mostly at or near top of plant	Umbels from middle to top of plant
Roots white with strong carroty smell, generally smaller and more squat	Roots white with faint carroty smell; somewhat larger and proportionately longer
Plants usually 3–6 feet tall when flowering	Plants usually 6–9 feet tall when flowering

This chart lists some distinguishing features of wild carrot and poison hemlock, beginning with those that are easiest to observe and most consistent and reliable. Note that my description of the carrot leaflet is different from that found in most plant manuals: most botanists consider each of the lobes to be leaflets, thus often describing the leaflets as linear. Viewing the leaf, I find this to be a flawed interpretation of its form; the lobes are narrow, but only rarely divided from each other.

This chart may be copied and distributed for educational purposes, but not for sale.

Many other plants also look similar to wild carrot. Among these is yarrow *Achillea millefolium*, which has a distinct, almost piney aroma and much finer leaves than carrot; its flowering heads are arranged in flat-topped clusters, but not umbels. Caraway *Carum carvi*, a locally abundant weed in parts of North America, strongly resembles wild carrot but is shorter and has hairless leaves. The seeds have the same scent as cultivated caraway, as the plants are identical. Caraway's roots are edible like those of wild carrot. Another weed that may be confused with wild carrot is *Anthriscus sylvestris*—one of several species called "wild chervil." This herb tends to be more robust and spreading; its stems and leaves have shorter, stiffer, less erect hairs.

Yarrow is often confused with wild carrot. Compare these flowers to the carrot flower photos.

Range and Habitat

The wild carrot is widely distributed across all of North America except for arid regions, alpine zones, and the arctic. It is most abundant in agricultural regions, sometimes becoming very prolific.

Wild carrot is a sun-loving herb. It frequents such places as old hayfields and pastures, meadows, roadsides, railroad rights-of-way, waste places, even the cracks in urban sidewalks. Since it is a biennial its abundance may fluctuate, often peaking on a site a few years after disturbance occurs. However, it does a fair job of competing with perennial forbs and grasses, holding its own in old fields and meadows. Wild carrot grows in virtually any soil type, from heavy clay to sand or gravel. This plant prefers moderate levels of soil moisture and is absent from very wet or very dry sites.

Harvest and Preparation

The wild carrot provides two excellent vegetables, one of which is underappreciated, and the other of which is practically unknown.

Taproot: As previously described, the taproots are rather small and whitish. The largest wild carrots might be an inch (2.5 cm) thick at the top and eight inches (20 cm) long, although smaller is typical. They average about the size of my little finger. If you don't know what my little finger looks like, look at yours and imagine dirt under the fingernail. If pinkie-sized sounds too small to be

worth your time, you might not be hungry enough for this book. But fortunately for the well-fed majority, it is entirely possible to learn to selectively harvest the larger roots, which grow under the larger and more robust rosettes. I doubt this surprises anybody. The roots also seem to get bigger in loose, fertile, sandy soils than they do in clay. If the soil is rocky, the roots become oddly shaped and are much harder to use and clean.

As with other biennial taproots, wild carrot should be harvested in the fall and early spring from plants that do not have a stalk.

Some people resent that wild carrots are not orange and crisp like their domestic counterparts, but these traits do not make for successful overwintering in the wild. If you can appreciate wild carrots for what they are rather than bemoan what they aren't, you'll find that they are a small but tasty root vegetable with parsnip-like appearance and texture and a wonderful, carrot-like odor and flavor.

left A wild carrot shoot just right for picking.

below Wild carrot shoots, all but one peeled. These have a pleasant carroty flavor and are more tender than they look.

I like to eat wild carrots raw, although their texture is a little stringy. They should be well-scrubbed; peeling removes too much of their volume. Steamed or boiled until tender and then served with a little butter, they make a nice vegetable. Their only drawback is the woody thread that runs through the core, but chopping the roots in short sections makes this hard to notice. You can also split them lengthwise and strip out the woody core. I like to use wild carrots in soups and casseroles, as one would use cultivated carrots or parsnips.

Shoot: The second vegetable produced by the wild carrot (and in my opinion the better of the two) is the tender shoot of the second-year plant in late spring or early summer. These shoots have a carrot-like flavor but are sweeter and much more tender than the roots. They also tend to be larger than the roots, and since they are above ground, they are much easier to collect. And you can tell at a glance exactly how large they are.

Harvest a wild carrot shoot by breaking or cutting off its tender portion, which can be identified by the ease with which it bends. Plants in the right stage for harvest are typically 6–20 inches (15–50 cm) tall. Look for the thickest, most succulent stems you can find.

After maturity, the carrot umbel curls into a "bird's nest" like this. The fruits have spines that catch on clothing.

After cutting the shoots, remove any leaves and peel off the skin. I do the peeling with my fingers, as the skin comes off readily in nice strips. The peeled shoots are a slightly translucent green. I enjoy eating them raw or cooked. They are like tender, green carrot sticks and can be used in any dish where you desire their familiar flavor. And conveniently, they become available just when the roots go out of season.

Other parts of the wild carrot also have culinary use. The seeds have a strong flavor and are sometimes used as a seasoning or tea. The leaves can also been used as a garnish, salad ingredient, or seasoning like parsley.

Fear of misidentification has kept many books from discussing the wild carrot, and most foragers from using it. Some people act as if wild carrot and poison hemlock simply cannot be told apart. That is both ridiculous and unfortunate. These two plants *can* be told apart with absolute certainty by anyone who cares to learn how. And since the wild carrot is a palatable, widespread, and useful wild vegetable, it is worth the effort.

Mature wild carrot in flower. Compared to poison hemlock (p. 359) the carrot plant has fewer and larger flower clusters that are mostly at the top of the plant, longer peduncles, and fewer branches and leaves.

Cow Parsnip

Heracleum lanatum

Apiaceae – Carrot Family

I magine those warm, sunny days in May when spring is easing into summer, when fawns begin to follow their mothers on clumsy legs and the vivid smells of growing plants mix in the humid air. That carefree and hopeful feeling that marks the start of another summer season begins to set in. This is the time for cow parsnip. Growing sometimes several inches a day, its massive hollow shoots sprint toward the sun, carrying a bulging sheath that holds hundreds of flowers waiting to burst forth. These succulent stems have long been sought and relished by Native Americans, particularly in the Rocky Mountains and Pacific Northwest. Sometimes called "Indian celery" or "Indian rhubarb," neither comparison does justice to this unique vegetable.

Cow parsnip in spring with flower bud sheath ready to open. At this time, only the top section of the stalk is tender.

Description

The cow parsnip is in every way unforgettable. Among the most massive herbaceous plants in North America, its sheer size is legendary. Giant stalks tower overhead, topped by saucer-sized flower clusters that inexorably draw the eye their way. The huge leaves, half folded like a grasping hand, the rough lobes like yearning fingers, are somehow almost intimidating. But maybe the most memorable thing about cow parsnip is its overwhelming, odd, spicy-sweet aroma, or the crisp sound of its juicy stalk being broken.

Cow parsnip is an herbaceous perennial that grows from a short, much-branched taproot or what appears to be a cluster of small taproots. Each plant produces a single stem, usually with one or two large leaves growing from the base and a few smaller leaves higher up on the stem. Cow parsnip stems are hollow, faintly grooved and striped lengthwise, and scattered with erect, stiff hairs of varying density. The stalks may be green, purple, or a combination of the two. At maturity, cow parsnip is typically 4–8 feet (1.2–2.5 m) tall with stems 1–2 inches (2.5–5 cm) in diameter.

The alternate leaves grow on enormous hollow petioles that may be 2.5 feet (75 cm) long and 1.6 inches (4 cm) in diameter. The lower leaves are much larger than those growing upon the stem. The base of the petiole on stem leaves

left Mature cow parsnip plants grow up to eight feet tall.

below Cow parsnip's enormous leaf.

Compound umbel of cow parsnip flowers, with green fruits in the background.

expands into a conspicuous papery sheath that clasps the stem. The petioles have a grooved, hairy surface that is essentially identical to that of the stalk.

Cow parsnip leaves are usually divided into three leaflets, each of which may be 8–14 inches (20–35 cm) long and about as wide. The leaflets are hairy, rough, and somewhat ruffled or folded along the veins. Their overall shape is reminiscent of a maple leaf, but they are more erratically lobed and coarsely toothed. The undersides are whitened by a fine, woolly coating.

Numerous flowers appear in early summer, borne in a large, flat-topped compound umbel that may be as much as a foot across. The individual flowers are about 0.25 inch (6 mm) wide with five white, deeply notched petals. Look at them closely and you will see something unusual: they are lopsided, particularly those on the outside of the cluster. The largest of the petals may be three or four times larger than the smallest. The fruit is a flat, elongated disc with two wings and a few lengthwise ribs, each fruit containing one seed. The cow parsnip's fruit is called a *schizocarp*, meaning that it splits into multiple parts when mature. Ripening in mid to late summer, then drying and persisting often until winter, the fruit and seed are very aromatic when crushed and rolled between the fingers.

Cow parsnip's root has white or off-white flesh. If there is a single taproot, it tends to be shallow with numerous side branches, even when growing in loose, rich soil. Older plants often have a cluster of what appears to be many taproots, or a taproot that forks into many parts. The root has a noticeable smell, but it is less aromatic than the aerial portions of the plant.

There really are no plants easily confused with cow parsnip, except perhaps a few rare, closely related, also-edible members of the genus *Heracleum*. Angelica *Angelica atropurpurea* is a related plant of similar size that often shares the habitat of cow parsnip, but its stems are glabrous, purple, and coated with bloom; each angelica leaf has dozens of leaflets as opposed to cow parsnip's three. While there are many poisonous plants among the *Apiaceae* family, and a number of these have white flowers, cow parsnip is so distinct that it is hard to imagine it being confused with any dangerous relative. The leaves and form are so drastically different from those of water hemlock or poison hemlock that even a cursory comparison with the photos should prevent one being mistaken for the other.

Range and Habitat

Cow parsnip is widespread, growing from Alaska to Labrador and south to Arizona, Kansas, and Georgia. However, in the southern part of its range it is confined to cool mountainous areas. This plant is quite common in the northeastern states, the Upper Midwest, the Pacific Northwest, the Rockies, and across the forested regions of Canada and Alaska.

Cow parsnip thrives in rich, moist soil in partial sunlight. It is commonly found in river floodplains and along streams, ditches, lakes, ponds, and marshes. It also inhabits moist woods with sparse canopies, wet meadows, shrub swamps, and any other sites with moist ground and sunlight. Its seeds germinate best on disturbed ground, so look for it especially where floods might occasionally deposit silt or scour away the vegetation.

Harvest and Preparation

Cow parsnip is often described as having a rank, unpleasant smell and an overly strong flavor. In wild food books covering the East it is typically ignored or mentioned only briefly before being dismissed on account of the aforementioned "inferior qualities." In the West, however, where traditional native foodways have persisted much longer and were more thoroughly recorded, we know that cow parsnip was and is used as a vegetable by many tribes; guides to western wild edibles give it far more attention and somewhat more positive reviews. Nancy

Turner (1978) says that this plant was "utilized as a green vegetable by virtually every Indian group in British Columbia. . . . Despite its strong odour, the peeled stems are sweet and succulent." Moerman (1998) lists thirty-eight Native American tribes that were reported to use the plant for food. Cow parsnip does not taste better in the West; it is a good vegetable in any part of its range. The flavor is indeed strong and unique; some people will not like it, while others will relish it—just as with its cultivated relatives such as carrot, caraway, fennel, dill, lovage, cilantro, and celery.

The cow parsnip produces two distinct stalk vegetables which are similar in appearance and are often confused with one another: the **flower stalk** and the leaf stalk or **petiole**. Both are gathered in mid to late spring while they remain succulent and tender, well before flowering occurs. (In my area, these stalks are

This plant has both leaf and flower stalks at the perfect stage to harvest. (A large leaf stalk leans out to the right, while the more upright central one is the flower stalk. The swollen purple area is where the cluster of flower buds is forming.)

Peeling a tender young leaf stalk.   Peeling a tender young flower stalk.

They taste almost as different as they peel.

at their best just after dandelions are in peak bloom.) For either type of stalk, cut them at the base and remove the top leaf and flower bud, then peel the outer layer. Here is where the differences show up. The outer layer of the flower stalk is a thick, solid peel, while the part peeled from the petiole is a thin ribbon of skin with a few string-like fibers. The flavor of the petiole is sweet and fruity, reminding me of celery, dill, and lemon. Some people like them dipped in sugar or chopped in little cross sections and added to fruit or green salad. The flavor of the flower stalk is less sweet—decidedly different but still good. I prefer the flower stalks cooked, especially in soup or pot roast. However, the flower stalks and petioles can be used interchangeably, as long as you expect different results.

The youngest shoots of either type need not be peeled, especially if they are eaten cooked. If harvested too late, cow parsnip stalks will develop a coarse, stringy texture and a strong, soapy flavor.

Also edible are the "**flower buds**" which form singly upon the flower stalk in late spring. Each of these is really an entire cluster of flower buds and stems enveloped by a leafy sheath, which may be up to three inches (8 cm) long. This "bud" and its contents are strong flavored and can be boiled in a few changes of water and used as a vegetable. They can also be chopped fine and used in moderation in soups, casseroles, and other dishes where they serve primarily as a flavoring. Following the suggestion of John Kallas (2003) I have also dried this young flower material after chopping it finely and used it as a seasoning year-round. Upon drying it loses some of its potency but is still a good flavoring.

The youngest leaves of cow parsnip, soon after they emerge, can also be used as a vegetable. Some authors report using them raw in salads, but I don't like them this way. However, they are good in soup or cooked with other vegetables or grains. Any young leaves of cow parsnip can be used, but the basal leaves can be tougher and often have dirt caught in their hairs, so I prefer stem leaves. Young cow parsnip leaves can also be dried and used out of season.

Cow parsnip roots are way too hot and bitter for most palates.

The principal time of year to gather all of these cow parsnip vegetables is from mid spring to early summer—before the plant blooms. In the fall, however, after the flower stalk and large basal leaves have died, cow parsnip often produces a new set of smaller leaves that can be used.

Cow parsnip seeds are powerfully aromatic and can be used as a seasoning in sweet foods. They ripen in midsummer and soon dry out; they can usually be collected until early fall.

With a name like "cow parsnip" one would suspect this plant to have an edible taproot. In fact it does, but this root was not used as food by Native Americans nearly as commonly as the stalks. Some books say that the root tastes like rutabaga, a comment that I believe originated in Huron Smith's *Ethnobotany of the Meskwaki Indians* (1928), in which he states that cow parsnip root, "is cooked like the rutabaga and tastes somewhat like it." I like rutabagas and would not insult them this way. Cow parsnip roots are small and tough and have a very strong flavor, both bitter and spicy. In my opinion, they are not a good vegetable. They can, however, be used in small quantities as a seasoning, much as one would use lovage greens or celery seed. Cow parsnip roots are best collected from fall through early spring, while the plant is dormant.

It is also sometimes written that cow parsnip stalk bases were used as a "salt substitute." Tracing this statement to its apparent original source (Chestnut, 1902), it seems ambiguous whether "salt substitute" simply means a seasoning, or indicates that it actually tastes salty. I suspect the former, and think the repetition of this statement has been misleading.

A very similar cow parsnip, *H. moellendorfii*, is native to northern China and adjacent Korea, where the young plants are used similarly (Hu, 2005). The European cow parsnip *H. sphondylium* is nearly identical to the cow parsnip of North America—indeed, some botanists consider them a single species. It is used as a food in the same ways (Couplan, 1994).

Another close relative, giant hogweed *H. mantegazzianum*, is native to western Asia. It has become an invasive weed in scattered localities in Ontario, the eastern United States, the Pacific Northwest, and elsewhere. This enormous plant has more deeply cut leaf lobes and can grow to 16 feet (5 m) in height. This plant *might* be edible, but its sap is extremely dangerous (see below).

Warning: Cow Parsnip Can Cause Burns

The cow parsnip's juices contain furanocoumarins, which can cause blistering burns if the juice gets on your skin and is exposed to sunlight. (Giant hogweed's sap is apparently much more potent than cow parsnip's; at least the reports seem to indicate this.) Reports of cow parsnip burns are much less common but definitely do happen—my wife and I have both successfully tested this on ourselves. When harvesting and preparing the plant, be careful not to get the juice on your skin. This makes me somewhat uncomfortable, for certainly the juice gets on my lips while I eat the young stalks—yet I have never had any sort of rash from these, nor have I ever found reference to this being a problem. Perhaps we all lick our lips well enough. Perhaps the offending chemicals are concentrated in the skin, being removed when we peel them. Perhaps the furanocoumarins are not yet developed in the tender young stalks. The Thompson tribe of British Columbia claim that, if eaten in large quantities, raw cow parsnip would "burn like pepper" (Turner et. al 1990). To be safe, I try to eat them in the shade and rinse my lips afterward, but I have no evidence that this is actually beneficial.

The only way to know if you like cow parsnip is to try it. These sweet, aromatic stalks are one of the many intense food experiences that only foragers get to enjoy. And whether you enjoy it or not, I guarantee you'll never taste anything else quite like it.

Black Nightshade

Solanum nigrum, S. americanum, S. ptychanthum, S. douglasii, **and other closely allied species**

Solanaceae – Nightshade Family

The very word "nightshade" causes many foragers to shudder with apprehension. It seems that everybody has heard of "deadly nightshade" and written off the entire group as too scary to contend with. How lucky we are that our ancestors were more confident in their botanical skills—for the amazing nightshade family has given us many cultivated fruits and vegetables, including potatoes, tomatoes, eggplants, bell peppers, hot peppers, ground cherries, and tomatillos.

Black nightshade is a common weed found on all the inhabited continents. It has a long and well-established history as a food source for numerous cultures

A cluster of black nightshade *Solanum ptychanthum* berries, some ripe and some green. Note the wings or ridges that run lengthwise on the stems.

around the globe. In fact, it is among the most widely used and well-documented wild foods in the world, rivaled in this respect only by a few other ubiquitous weeds such as lamb's quarters, amaranth, and stinging nettle. There are probably over two billion people for whom the black nightshade is a regular or occasional item of diet. Yet in the predominantly "white" parts of the world—Europe and North America—the *Solanum nigrum* complex is widely believed to be extremely poisonous. The contradiction is stark, confusing, and quite amazing.

> "The leaves and tender shoots are boiled in the same way as spinach and are eaten in many parts of India . . . The berries, when ripe, are often eaten by children and are sometimes used for preparing pies and preserves."
>
> —Chopra, Badhwar, and Ghosh, 1965, p. 670.

> "Every intelligent child shuns the fruit of this weed . . . the poisonous properties of which are undoubted. Children who have eaten the fruit have died soon after from its effects."
>
> —"W.W.," in *The Gardener's Chronicle of London*, March 21, 1909.

> "Ripe berries . . . are frequently eaten raw as fruits, particularly in parts of Africa. They are also widely used in pies and preserves, and sometimes as a substitute for raisins in plum puddings, particularly in North America. They can also make a delightful jam."
>
> —Edmonds and Chweya, 1997, pp. 56–57.

> "The berries are poisonous, and will produce torpor, insensibility, and death."
>
> —Brown, 1867, p. 110

> "I have eaten pounds of pies, preserves, and fruit sauces made of the ripe berries."
>
> —Gibbons and Tucker, 1979, p. 251

One can't help but wonder how such discrepancies can coexist. But before we look at this question in detail, let's introduce the plant.

Description

Authorities today recognize a number of similar species that used to be lumped together under one name, *Solanum nigrum*. All of these are called "black night-shade" and exhibit only minor differences. In North America, *S. ptychanthum* dominates in the East, and *S. americanum* dominates in the South. The Great Plains is home to *S. interius*, and *S. douglasii* is found in the Southwest. *S. nigrum* is native to the Old World, particularly Europe and the Mediterranean; it is rather rare in North America, where it has been introduced. In most older works, all of these species are called *S. nigrum*. Today, many authors speak of "the *Solanum nigrum* complex," which refers to all of the dozens of black nightshade species around the world formerly called *S. nigrum*. It is usually impossible to tell from older sources if the plant under discussion would now be classified as *S. nigrum* or some other species. This account pertains to those members of the *S. nigrum* complex found in North America. I use the name *S. nigrum* when referring generally to the black nightshades of this complex. I also use the names originally given in the sources I cite, but readers should be aware of the unique ambiguity of this group.

The black nightshade that abounds in my area, *S. ptychanthum*, is an annual herb with relatively weak, unarmed, smooth, usually hairless stems that branch widely and freely. Large specimens stand 3 feet (90 cm) high and span 4 feet (120 cm) or more in width, usually with the lower branches resting directly on the

Small but mature black nightshade plant, showing flowers and berries, both green and ripe.

ground. However, like most weedy annuals, this plant can be sexually mature at almost any size, sometimes fruiting when no more than 3 inches (8 cm) tall.

The leaves are alternate, dark green, soft, rather thin, and often riddled with bug holes like those of amaranth, which they somewhat resemble. The young leaves may have a coppery or purplish sheen on the underside. The size of the leaves is quite variable, while the shape is moderately so, ranging from ovate to lanceolate to diamond-shaped. The margins may be entire or have sparse, rounded teeth. The leaf surfaces are glabrous or sparsely hairy. Petioles are 1.2–2.5 inches (3–6 cm) long, usually with a faint wing on each side. These wings extend to the branches and main stalk, which often has several short wings or ridges running lengthwise.

The flowers appear as early as June and continue being produced into autumn; they are most prevalent in late summer. Hanging in small clusters from the leaf axils, the blossoms grow on pedicels that are often unequal in length. The inconspicuous five-petaled flowers are whitish and about a half inch across. In form they resemble tomato flowers.

The fruit is almost perfectly spherical, about the size of a pea or a blueberry, green at first but turning purplish black when ripe. They are subtended by a persistent five-parted calyx that is slightly smaller in diameter than the fruit. The skins are somewhat tough, like tomato skins, and encapsulate a soft, juicy interior with numerous seeds.

Our other species of black nightshade are quite similar, although some may be hairier or taller, with fruit that is more or less glossy, or exhibit other minor differences. Readers who wish to separate the individual species will need to refer to more technical botanical manuals, as that is beyond the scope of this book.

There are a number of toxic nightshades that must be avoided. Among these is belladona *Atropa belladona*, which has been frequently confused with black nightshade (and also shares that common name). Differentiating this plant from black nightshade will be discussed at length later. Bittersweet nightshade *Solanum dulcamara*, while a member of the same genus as black nightshade, is very easy to tell apart. This species is a semi-woody vine with large, deeply lobed leaves. The striking purple flowers are borne

Bittersweet nightshade *S. dulcamara* (not edible) is very easy to tell from black nightshade, but the catch-all name "deadly nightshade" is sometimes used for either.

in panicles of about a dozen, ripening later into oblong red berries. Bittersweet nightshade is a common weedy vine of semi-shaded localities and often grows on hedges, fences, and porches. The bright red fruits seem to attract children, but they are somewhat poisonous. **Read the above description of black nightshade carefully, as there are a number of other nightshades with toxic fruit.**

Range and Habitat

Black nightshade is found just about anywhere in the world where there are weeds. It occupies gardens, yards, agricultural fields, construction sites, and other areas where humans disturb the soil. Natural habitats include river floodplains, steep banks, flooded areas, and storm-damaged woods. It typically persists at a site for only one to three years before being crowded out by perennials, unless the ground is disturbed repeatedly. The seeds can persist viably in the soil for years, waiting for the proper germinating conditions to present themselves. Unlike most weedy species, black nightshade seems to prefer light to moderate shade.

The Mystery of a Myth

Are ripe black nightshade berries toxic?

Let's take a scientific approach to this question. Two hypotheses have been presented: (1) The ripe berries of black nightshade are edible. (2) The ripe berries of black nightshade are deadly poisonous. (Note that, throughout this discussion, I am referring to the ripe fruit unless otherwise specified.)

Hypothesis 1 is supported by the actions of hundreds of millions of people who have consumed the plant, plus the actions of untold ancestors who have handed the tradition down to them. The literature contains a wealth of information pertaining to the consumption of black nightshade berries. Schilling et al. (1992) report that the berries are eagerly sought and eaten by children in India. They are also eaten in China (Hu, 2005), the Philippines (Siemonsma et al. 1993), Nepal (Manandhar, 2002), Java (Duke, 1987), southern Europe (Couplan, 1998), South Africa (Quin, 1959), New Zealand (Crowe, 2004), and Ethiopia (Guinand and Lemessa, 2001). They were eaten by the Mendocino Indians of California (Chestnut, 1902) as well as the Tubatulabal (Voegelin, 1938). In Turkey, the berries are traditionally used in sweets (Dogan, et al., 2004). Edmonds and Chweya (1997) report the fruit being eaten in Bolivia, Peru, Hawaii, Sierra Leone, Ethiopia, Tanzania, Namibia, South Africa, and Uganda. Some relatively recent wild food authors report their own consumption of these berries (Gibbons and Tucker, 1979; Nyerges, 1999).

Furthermore, black nightshade has been cultivated for over a hundred years in European and American gardens for its edible fruit, sold under the name of "garden huckleberry," "sunberry," or "wonderberry." The wonderberry, now known to be an African species of black nightshade *S. retroflexum* (Defelice, 2003; Heiser, 1969), and not the special new hybrid that plant breeder Luther Burbank once claimed, was described in a 1909 seed catalog as "like an enormous rich blueberry. Unsurpassed for eating . . . The greatest garden fruit ever introduced" (from Heiser, 1969, p. 64). Relatively recent authors in the United States and England have recommended this fruit for pies and jam (Fisher, 1977; Simms, 1997). A quick Internet search shows that these black nightshades are still available from some seed companies.

I can add my own experience to this list. I began eating wild black nightshade berries at the age of twelve and have avidly sought them since. I have eaten the berries on many hundreds of occasions—sometimes more than a cup at a time. I eat them because I find them delicious. After introducing my wife to them, she decided that we would encourage the volunteers in our garden. In my wild food workshops and in everyday life, I have fed the plant to a few hundred people, most of whom liked the fruit, and none of whom were harmed by it. I have met a few dozen people who, like me, make the berries regular fare when available. Most of them learned this from books or fellow foraging hobbyists, but a few reported that eating black nightshade berries was a family tradition. The same friend who taught me to eat this fruit started feeding them to his son at two years of age.

The conclusion that black nightshade berries are not toxic is supported by additional evidence. In one German study, no alkaloids could be detected in twenty-two samples of ripe fruit of *S. nigrum* (solanine, atropine, and other nightshade toxins are alkaloids) (Frohne and Pfander, 2005). Cippolini and Levy (1997) state that *S. americanum* fruit has "negligible levels" of alkaloids. Voss et al. (1993) studied the toxicity of black nightshade berries (*S. ptychanthum*) in feeding experiments with rats. Even when fed a mixture of ripe and unripe berries as 25 percent of the diet for several weeks, no mortality was observed.

Since untold millions of people eat black nightshade berries, we should see cases of poisoning in the medical literature quite frequently if hypothesis 2 (that the ripe berries are extremely poisonous) is correct. It seems that there would be legal action against the seed companies that sell the plant, or the authors and publishers of the many books that extol its edibility. Contrarily, I can find no record of such a lawsuit, nor of any documented case of poisoning by ripe black nightshade berries in the last fifty years. The evidence is conclusive that black nightshade berries are edible.

However, we are still left with explaining the origin of such a pervasive myth. Literature from the 1800s contains a few accounts of poisoning by ripe *S. nigrum* berries. These cases seem to be confined to Europe. Chopra et al. (1965) presume that, because the ripe berries are known to be edible, all such accounts refer to unripe berries. This conclusion at first appears sound, but closer examination renders it untenable, since some of the cases specify that ripe berries were the agent of poisoning. Many modern authors cite the fact that the unripe fruits are toxic as justification for the berries' reputation as deadly, and suggest that this means that the fruit should be avoided entirely. This is nonsense. Unripe may-apples are very toxic (Turner and Szczawinski, 1991) yet this plant's ripe fruit is not shrouded in horror. In fact, many common fruits are poisonous when unripe, and this doesn't seem to worry us at all. While the unripe fruits should probably be avoided (although this, too, is disputed by some), and credible poisonings have been attributed to them (Chopra et al. 1965), this in no way justifies or explains the fear with which the plant is typically treated.

A significant observation is that, in the late 1800's, cases of reported poisoning from ripe black nightshade berries almost completely cease; to the best of my knowledge, the last documented case in the English language occurred in Ireland in 1952 (Towers, 1953). What happened? Certainly, the plant didn't transform from deadly to delicious over a few generations. And Europeans continue to be affected by *other* poisonous plants.

The discrepancy in the literature is commonly explained away by the proposition that individual plants vary widely in the toxicity of their berries. This makes no sense; it cannot account for the cessation of reported poisonings, nor can it explain why the poisonings are reported in a limited geographical area. If chemical variability of individual plants accounted for the differing reports of edibility, then we would see poisonings occurring most often where the berries are eaten most often. Instead, the converse is true; the reported poisonings are concentrated in Europe, one of the few places on Earth where the berries are not regularly consumed.

It has also been argued that the toxicity varies on a larger scale, with some populations, species, or subspecies being deadly, while others are edible. Although highly unlikely (there is no known case of plants this closely related having fruit that varies by such extremes), this explanation is conceivable. But again, if this is true, why would the poisonings in Europe have ceased? Why would analysis of European berries show them nontoxic (Bruneton, 1999)? Why would Gerarde and Dioscorides, both Europeans, call them harmless (Defelice, 2003)? Why would Couplan (1998) claim that the ripe berries are eaten raw or cooked in parts of southern Europe? Where are the documented cases of poisoning?

Even in Europe, the toxicity of *S. nigrum* berries has always been disputed. The famous botanist Michel-Felix Dunal (1813) of Montpellier, France, ate the berries on several occasions and claimed them harmless. This made quite an impression on his contemporaries, and he was much quoted by incredulous Nineteenth-century authors. Balfour (1873, p. 462) stated of *S. nigrum*, "It contains a small amount of solanine in the juice of the stem and berries, but it may be eaten as food, as in France." François Couplan, Europe's leading authority on edible wild plants, tells me that he eats these berries often and loves their addictive taste. He adds that, while people in Europe generally believe them poisonous, there is "no toxicity whatsoever" in the ripe fruit (pers. comm., 2009).

Fortunately, there is a perfectly good explanation for all of this. In Europe there is another plant sometimes known as black nightshade: *Atropa belladonna*, a well-known poisonous plant that has been used for centuries in medicine and murder. The primary toxic (and medicinal) constituent of *Atropa belladonna* is atropine, which causes a whole suite of neurological and physiological effects. Common names for this plant include "belladonna" and "deadly nightshade"; unfortunately, due to its black berries, it is also occasionally called "black nightshade." The shared common name makes confusion likely, and the physical similarities of the plants only exacerbate the problem. Elizabeth Daly's 1963 novel *Deadly Nightshade*, the plot of which revolves around a case of poisoning by nightshade berries, demonstrates how false conclusions are an easy task for the lazy or uninformed. At one point, Daly's detective says, "*Solanum nigrum Linnaeus*. Also 'Black, Deadly, or Garden Nightshade. Also *Atropa belladonna*.' That's the poison."

Daly's mistake has been made again and again; it inundates the older literature, and is still made with frightful regularity today. I am convinced that this confusion accounts for the reputation of ripe *S. nigrum* berries as toxic. I am not the first to conclude this; Dunal (1813) made exactly the same argument 200 years ago in France. Displaying the fear-mongering suspension of logic that often accompanies the discussion of black nightshade berries (and wild foods in general), one of Dunal's critics made a strident but worthless effort to discredit him by pointing out that the *raw leaves* have caused poisonings, stating that this "places beyond doubt the often contested toxic properties" of *S. nigrum* (Tardieu and Roussin, 1875, p. 925, translation mine). Of course, this has nothing to do with the berries. Interestingly, in French, *S. nigrum* and *Atropa belladonna* also share common names, and the idea that *S. nigrum* berries are extremely toxic is still deeply entrenched in France today. As in the English sources, older accounts of black nightshade poisonings in France are highly suspect, such as a case reported by Dufeillay (1838), in which the poisoned children described the berries as *red*.

The confusion between *Atropa belladonna* and *Solanum nigrum* is a problem that has long been recognized in the English-speaking countries as well. In a medical treatise on treating cases of poisoning, Murrell (1884, p. 111) says that *S. nigrum* is often mistaken for belladonna, adding, "Medical witnesses and coroners often wrong on this point." In *A Manual of Toxicology*, John James Reese (1874, p. 450) states that

> "There is great discrepancy among authorities about the poisonous properties of the above two species of Solanum [*dulcamara* and *nigrum*]. . . . Some have supposed that the cases of poisoning that have been ascribed to the two species were, in reality, to be accredited to the *Deadly Nightshade* (belladonna), which had been mistaken for the others."

The following anecdote shows that the confusion has gone both ways:

> "Solanum Nigrum has often been mistaken for Belladonna. A physician in Ohio confidently said to me, that Belladonna grew plentifully in every part of his county, and upon my questioning the accuracy of his statement, he produced a very fine specimen of Solanum Nigrum, saying, 'If that is not Belladonna, what is it?'"

> —Hoyt, 1874, p. 374

Indeed, the poisoning symptoms described in the old accounts usually suggest atropine poisoning rather than that of solanine. The fact that this myth originated in Europe, the primary natural range of belladonna, and has persisted most tenaciously there, lends further support to this conclusion. In contradistinction to the case with *S. nigrum*, the medical literature contains hundreds of cases of poisoning by *Atropa belladonna* berries. These cases are easily found and consistent in their described symptoms, and many of them occur quite recently. When you consider that *S. nigrum* is a far more common and widespread plant, eaten regularly around the world, there should be millions of such cases if it were equally poisonous. This is perhaps an appropriate place to point out another obvious fact: myths of toxicity are commonplace (in fact, I'd argue that they are a universal feature of human culture) while myths of edibility are exceedingly rare, since they are soon discredited.

People have an amazing ability to make our observations coincide with a preconceived belief (see *Don't Make it Fit*, p. 33). In 1978, a red panda escaped from a zoo in Holland. Local newspapers informed the public, in hopes that the animal could be recaptured, but by this time, the panda had already been found dead near the zoo. Yet over a hundred sightings of the panda were reported, all of which occurred after the animal was dead (Feder, 1996). These people weren't reporting the panda because they had seen it; they were seeing the panda because it had been reported. Similarly, it seems that reports of poisoning from

Belladonna vs. Black Nightshade

Atropa belladonna (belladonna)	*Solanum nigrum* complex (black nightshade)
Fruit borne singly in leaf axils	Fruit borne in axillary clusters
Conspicuous, shiny, cherry-sized fruit	Pea-sized fruit, dull, inconspicuous
Five-pointed calyx more than twice as wide as berry	Five-pointed calyx, about as wide as berry, or less
Flowers bell-like, 1 inch (2.5 cm) long, purple or purple-brown	Flowers white or off-white, five petal-like spreading lobes, 0.4 inch (1 cm) wide
Leaves rarely bug-eaten; margins entire	Leaves usually bug-eaten; margins may be entire, sinuate, or dentate
Upright form, usually taller than wide	Spreading form, usually wider than tall
Rare in North America, confined largely to the coasts	Common weed throughout North America

black nightshade berries occurred because the plant was believed to be toxic, rather than the converse.

The black nightshade is not the only European plant to be subject to a toxicity myth of such stark contrast to reality. As surprising as it sounds, the parsnip *Pastinaca sativa*, the very same plant that is available in markets and grocery stores all across the northern hemisphere, which has been grown for thousands of years for its esculent roots, is widely reported in wildflower books to be *deadly poisonous*. This myth, like the black nightshade myth, probably arose as a way of keeping people from collecting the plant in the wild and confusing it with toxic relatives.

By the late 1800s, at least in the United States, some authorities began to cautiously challenge the myth. Behr (1889, p. 201) says, "It is not poisonous in California, at least under ordinary circumstances. The same species is common in Europe, where it is considered poisonous." In 1905, Botany professor Charles Bessey wrote a letter to *American Botanist* regarding this inversion of thought:

> "[This] reminds me of an incident which occurred in my class in Botany nearly thirty five years ago. I was lecturing on the properties of the plants constituting the Solanaceae, and, as a matter of course, said that the berries of the black nightshade (*Solanum nigrum*) were poisonous. A young fellow from Fort Dodge, Iowa, spoke up and said that the people

below left Black nightshade in flower. Note the bug-eaten leaves and the flowers and fruit borne in umbels.

below right Belladonna *Atropa belladonna*, the true deadly nightshade, in flower and fruit. Note the long bracts, large, shiny berry borne singly, entire leaf margins, and purplish flower. Photo by Bill Merilees.

in his neighborhood made them into pies, preserves, etc. and ate freely of them. I answered him, as became a professor of botany, by saying that as it was well known that black nightshade berries are poisonous, the student must have been mistaken. . . . After a while, however, I learned that the people in central and western Iowa *actually did* eat black nightshade berries, and they were not poisoned either. Later, I learned the same thing in Nebraska for this species."

Since then, the obvious fact that black nightshade berries are not deadly poisonous has been slowly and reluctantly accepted. This is often expressed with guarded language and reservation, but at other times it is stated plainly that the berries are edible and delicious. Most scholarly works since about 1960 agree that the ripe berries of the *S. nigrum* group are edible or at least nontoxic.

Interestingly, despite the fact that enormous numbers of ethnographic sources describe the berries being used as food, and despite the fact that legions of people willingly, gladly, and *repeatedly* eat them, the wild food literature has become one of the loudest voices contributing to the fear that surrounds this plant. Peterson's field guide (1977) lists it as "poisonous," accompanied by a skull and crossbones. Elias and Dykeman (1982) lump it with other nightshades as poisonous. Henderson (2000, p. 189) nebulously suggests an unspecified danger: "Although some nightshades actually bear edible fruit, none of them are worth the risk." Tull (1987, p. 186) says, " I consider the whole plant potentially deadly and leave it alone." (Here she misleadingly cites Heiser [1969], but in that source Heiser's discussion of black nightshade's toxicity is poorly constructed, conjectural, and flippant—*and* he tells us that he made and ate a black nightshade pie!) Many other wild food books take the very reasonable position of not discussing the matter. However, I am proud to align myself with the significant minority of authors (Gibbons and Tucker, 1979; Nyerges, 1999; Couplan, 1998; Van Wyk, 2005) who unabashedly proclaim the ripe fruit edible.

Still, I wondered if, very rarely, ripe black nightshade berries contain an abnormally and dangerously high concentration of solanine. It seems possible. Put into perspective, this fact shouldn't even be particularly alarming; virtually all edible plants contain toxic compounds. There are numerous documented poisonings from potatoes *Solanum tuberosum*, several of which have resulted in death (McMillan and Thompson, 1979; Bruneton, 1999; Hansen, 1925). Curly dock *Rumex crispus* remains a popular wild edible, despite the fact that, rather recently, a fatal poisoning was attributed to it (Farre et al., 1989). Does this happen with black nightshade? With this question in mind, I sought the last reported case of poisoning (nonlethal, incidentally) by ripe black nightshade berries, which occurred in Ireland and was recorded in an article entitled, "A Case of Poisoning by Solanum nigrum" (Towers, 1953).

Here, again, is a case of name misapplication. Throughout the article, there is conclusive evidence that the plant that was actually responsible for this poisoning was *Atropa belladonna*. The victim's description of the plant and its berries strongly suggests belladonna, and is scarcely compatible with the characteristics of *S. nigrum*. The symptoms described clearly fit those associated with atropine (the primary toxin in belladonna) rather than solanine (the toxin found in *unripe* black nightshade berries). I was prepared to carefully advance this argument, but fortunately our good Dr. Towers does this himself—unwittingly testifying convincingly against his own conclusions. He attests (p. 79), "Having thus reviewed the pharmacology of atropine, it is possible to see that this case under discussion shows most of the classical features associated with the drug." However, atropine is not found in *S. nigrum*; it is commercially extracted from *Atropa belladonna*, from which its name is derived. Towers apparently was unaware of this. He clearly writes under the assumption that what is true of one of these nightshade is also applicable to the other. The prevalence of this irresponsible attitude makes careless investigation of this plant no surprise. Indeed, the two-page commentary following the clinical notes mentions *S. nigrum* only once, in the first sentence. Amazingly, thereafter, the text refers only to belladonna and atropine. Towers concludes (p. 80) by stating that the victim's symptoms "fit in with the classical features of poisoning by atropine caused by eating berries of the deadly nightshade type." The name "deadly nightshade" is properly applied to belladonna, not *S. nigrum* (although it is often mistakenly applied), and of the two species, only belladonna contains atropine. By this point, his article has quietly transformed into "a case of poisoning by *Atropa belladonna*"—which should have been its title.

Through an extensive search of literary sources and correspondence with experts (including Jennifer Edmonds, probably the world's leading authority on black nightshades), I have been unable to locate a single credible, documented case of poisoning from the ripe berries of any member of the *S. nigrum* complex. There is simply no basis for the contention that they are toxic.

The Second Myth: Black Nightshade Greens

As well documented as black nightshade berries are as a food source, the greens are even better documented. In fact, they are perhaps the most commonly eaten wild greens in the world. Black nightshade greens are regularly consumed in virtually every tropical and subtropical country on Earth, as well as occasionally in the temperate zones. Again, European and North American literature often calls these greens poisonous or deadly, but authors from the tropics hold a completely different attitude. Consider this:

"The tender shoots, young leaves and unripe green fruits are eaten as a vegetable, raw, cooked or steamed (for 5–10 minutes), alone or in combination with other vegetables. . . . *S. americanum* is used as a green vegetable throughout South-East Asia and the green fruits can be bought in the local markets. It is common in the vegetable assortment of large supermarkets. . . . Being a common crop of home gardens and a common weed of cultivation, its importance is considerable."

—Siemonsma and Pilvek, 1993, p. 253

These authors conclude their account by suggesting that black nightshade should receive more research attention as a food crop. Nowhere in their rather lengthy treatment of this plant do they even mention any concern over toxicity. And note their repeated mentioning of the *green fruits* as food. (Be aware, however, that analyses have clearly shown the green fruit of at least some species to contain high levels of solanine. I advise against eating them.)

Chopra et al. (1965, p. 670) tell us, "The leaves and tender shoots are boiled in the same way as spinach and are eaten in many parts of India." The young greens are eaten in Vietnam (Tanaka and Ke, 2007), Nepal (Manandhar, 2002), and China (Hu, 2005). Couplan (1998) says that black nightshade greens are the most popular vegetable in Madagascar; he says (pers. comm., 2009) that they are eaten at "almost every meal." In three villages in Tanzania, Fleuret (1979) found black nightshade to be the second most commonly eaten wild green—only amaranth was eaten more. The greens were also sold in local markets. Purseglove (1968, p. 65) says that *S. nigrum* "is extensively used as a pot-herb in Africa and Asia, in spite of the fact that it is reputed to be poisonous in Europe." Heiser (1969) found the greens regularly for sale in vegetable markets in Guatemala. Edmonds and Chweya (1997, p. 56) summarize, "Leaves and tender shoots are widely used as vegetables throughout the world . . . All the species [of black nightshade] are used as pot-herbs or leaf/stem vegetables more or less throughout their respective ranges in Africa, Asia, Malesia and the Americas." They record the greens being consumed in Guatemala, Mauritius, Hawaii, Papua New Guinea, the Seychelles, Australia, Greece, and fourteen African countries. Black nightshade greens are eaten so frequently and widely that documenting it in this way is as superfluous as documenting the edibility of onions.

Looking to uphold the Western notion that this plant is deadly poisonous, some suggest that the edibility of tropical forms differs from ours. There is nothing to support this idea. The most widespread black nightshade of the Old and New World tropics is *S. americanum* (Edmonds and Chweya, 1997), but this species is also widespread in the United States. Black nightshade was said to be "the most relished potherb" of the Cherokee (Witthoft, 1947). Couplan (1998) reports it being eaten in southern Europe. In Wisconsin, Minnesota, and surely elsewhere in the United States, black nightshade greens are actively sought and regularly eaten by Hmong immigrants.

But some Americans desperately want us to disbelieve this plant's edibility. Based on her interpretation of one anecdotal account, Fackelmann (1993) conjectures that people who eat black nightshade greens must first undergo a lengthy process of building up a tolerance to solanine—otherwise they will be poisoned. Although she provides no scientific evidence to support this specious and ridiculous claim, it has been widely accepted as fact. Fackelmann makes it sound as if only a few obscure, impoverished cultures eat this vegetable, when in fact it is a common food for hundreds of millions of people in dozens of countries, sold in grocery stores and produce markets. The tone of her article is condescending and ethnocentric. I know several Americans, including myself, who have eaten these greens safely without building up a tolerance. This doesn't mean that black nightshade greens can be used without caution; they sometimes contain the toxin solanine (Frohne and Pfander, 2005). For guidelines on their safe use, see the preparation section on pages 390–392.

Harvest and Preparation

Berries: Black nightshade berries are delicious, abundant, widespread, and easy to harvest. Only eat the ripe berries, which turn juicy and dark purple-black. (A few species, such as *S. villosum*, have berries that ripen to yellow or orange, but these are not commonly found in North America.) Do not eat partially ripe berries that still contain green lines, and do not eat ripe berries if they taste bitter or unpleasant to you. As always, eat small portions your first few times.

Don't imagine that black nightshade berries are a substitute for blueberries or any other familiar fruit. Their flavor is most like that of ground-cherries (genus *Physalis*)—like fruity tomatoes. Generally, I eat the berries raw. Whenever I happen upon a plant bearing ripe fruit, I eat as many as time or the supply allows. They are excellent in salad—although being perfectly round they tend to roll off your fork, and they're usually too small to spear with a tine. Alas, the conundrums of a forager. I also like them in tacos or burritos, where they aren't so mobile. They are good in certain soups or pasta dishes.

Black nightshade berries are also used to make uniquely delicious fruit sauces and jams. They remind me of ground-cherries, blueberries, and tomatoes, but their tiny seeds are slightly hot, especially when cooked. (To get in the right mood for this chapter, I savored some nightshade jam from our refrigerator.)

The flavor and texture can be altered by straining out the skins and seeds. They make good pies, and a few can be added to applesauce to enhance the color.

Black nightshade berries begin ripening in midsummer and continue late into the fall, often past light frosts. It is not uncommon to find flowers, unripe fruit, and ripe fruit on the plant at the same time. I have no special tricks for picking them, which I typically do while sitting comfortably beside a prolific plant. The branches droop and the fruit is often borne near the ground; in this case, wash the berries carefully. From the best plants you might get over a quart of fruit, but it will go as slowly as picking blueberries.

I was once exploring an acquaintance's garden with him. When I found a black nightshade plant loaded with fruit and began eating them, he said, "Nightshade? My grandmother used to make nightshade sauce when I was little, but I never knew what nightshade she used." He tasted a handful, smiled at the flavor, then confirmed, "Oh yeah, this was definitely it." We talked a little of the sweet nightshade sauce that his grandmother in South Dakota made, which the family relished on pancakes and ice cream. He remembered this sauce fondly, saying that as a child he "wanted all he could get."

Greens: The young, tender leafy shoots of black nightshade, before the plants have flowered, make an excellent potherb—in my opinion equal in

Black nightshade, mature plant.

Black nightshade, young shoots.

quality to amaranth and lamb's quarters. Gather thick, juicy shoots that stand upright, snap easily when bent, and do not need to be cut. You will find these mostly in early or mid summer. They should be boiled before being eaten. Their rich, mild flavor and soft texture leave no question as to why they are a popular vegetable in much of the world. The older growth, however, is bitter and should be avoided.

Although the greens are the most commonly eaten part of black nightshade worldwide, they contain varying amounts of the bitter toxin solanine. (Solanine is also found in tomatoes, potatoes, eggplants, bell peppers, and even cherries.) As with the ripe berries, I have been unable to find any documented cases of poisoning from eating the properly cooked young greens. Although Edmonds and Chweya (1997) report that toxic alkaloids are not present in the vegetative parts of the plant, others have reported solanine in some leaf samples (Frohne and Pfander, 2005).

The youngest, tenderest shoots are generally not bitter. As the plants age, the bitterness (and presumably, the solanine content) increases—sometimes substantially. I reiterate here that the older growth, or any greens that are distastefully bitter, should not be eaten. Marshall (2001) interviewed villagers in Kenya and found that, while black nightshade was the most favored and most commonly eaten green, they recognized and avoided those with certain subtle characteristics that denoted bitterness (older, tougher, drier stems with full-grown leaves, especially stems that spread horizontally). Marshall reported that her informants preferred it because, unlike amaranth, it could be eaten every day without making one feel sick.

The bitter quality of black nightshade greens has been overemphasized by Western authors whose attitude about the plant is irrationally negative. After all, many of our more popular greens are bitter (dandelion, chicory, escarole), toxic when raw (marsh marigold), or toxic when too old (pokeweed). When collected at the correct stage and prepared properly, black nightshade greens are not only safe to eat, but are a palatable, nutritious, and wholesome food.

When collecting black nightshade greens, follow these guidelines to avoid ingesting excessive solanine: (1) harvest only the young, tender growth, generally before the plants flower. (2) Boil them in a full pot of water for ten to fifteen minutes, drain the water, and repeat this process if any bitterness remains. (3) Do not eat oversized portions. (4) Do not eat them if you find the bitterness strong or distasteful. (5) Stick to those species which have a well-established traditional use as food. (Among North American species, this means *S. americanum* and *S. ptychanthum*.)

Some Western authors, attempting to explain away the obvious edibility of a plant that their culture erroneously believes to be poisonous, suggest that black nightshade greens are eaten regularly by hundreds of millions of people only because of their medicinal properties. It is true that this plant is traditionally considered a health tonic by many cultures, as well as a remedy for numerous ailments, including malaria, dysentery, and schistosomiasis (Gbile and Adesina, 1988). Studies have also demonstrated that these greens have antiviral, anticancer, and antiparasitic properties (Gbile and Adesina, 1988; Bose and Ghosh, 1980). However, these are secondary benefits; most people who eat these greens clearly do so because they like them and are hungry. Black nightshade greens are also extremely nutritious, providing a much appreciated rich source of proteins, amino acids, minerals, and vitamins (Edmonds and Chweya, 1997).

Some who remain afraid to try black nightshade act as if those of us who eat it are foolish and irresponsible. Meanwhile, hundreds of millions of people eat it anyway. I counter that it is irresponsible, and a bit ethnocentric, to insist on perpetuating this myth in the absence of any supporting evidence. After all, both the tomato and potato were once considered poisonous in Europe.

Bugleweed

Lycopus spp.

Lamiaceae – Mint Family

Few people have ever seen a four-toed salamander. Tiny and silent, crypti-cally colored like a faded stick of cinnamon, these delicate predators lurk under logs and leaves in cool, shaded forests. As a child I read that "only the most patient and ardent naturalists find them," and since that's what I wanted to be, I looked for them. Many years later, I still make it a springtime ritual to search for the elusive four-toed salamander, and I still get a rush of adrenaline with every one that I uncover.

Finding the half-rotten trunk of some maple that fell into a pond several years ago, I carefully lift the layer of moss that grows on top of it. With luck I may spot a tiny amphibian pressed into a crevice or curled into a ball. I admire its etched and sculpted form and its beautiful color, and observe the rapidly vibrating fold of skin beneath its tiny lower jaw. Amazed that such a delicate-looking thing with

Finding a four-toed salamander *Hemidactylium scutatum* is one of foraging's priceless perks.

such tiny bones can live for decades, keeping its lungless body moist enough all the while to respire through its skin, I gently lay the moss back over it.

It may take some time to find this creature—but as I search I can't help but notice a most peculiar snow-white object embedded in the moss here and there. Scarcely an inch long, looking like a bunch of miniature dough balls stuck together, these are the tubers of the northern bugleweed. I pluck a few and pocket them to bring home and savor, along with the memories of a lifetime of spring salamander hunts.

Description

Bugleweeds, also called water-horehounds, are members of the genus *Lycopus* in the mint family. Although none are toxic, only some of them produce edible tubers, and these vary in size and palatability. Like other mints, bugleweeds have square stems and opposite pairs of leaves. However, *Lycopus* can be told from other members of the mint family by the presence of *all* of the following characteristics: They are not distinctly aromatic, the leaves are toothed, the flowers are sessile and less than 0.25 inch (6 mm) long, the corolla and calyx appear regular or nearly so, and there are two fertile stamens.

Bugleweeds are small to medium sized herbs, ranging from 4–32 inches (10–80 cm) tall. The stems are thin and fragile, rarely exceeding 0.2 inch (5 mm) in width. They are erect or leaning with few to no branches.

The leaves are coarsely toothed, more so on the terminal half. They are light green, roughly ovate or lanceolate, tapered at both ends, fairly consistent in size upon the plant, sessile or nearly so, and 0.5–2 inches (1–5 cm) long. Bugleweed's tiny, tubular, four- or five-lobed white or pink flowers grow in small, whorl-like clusters from the leaf axils.

Warning: Bugleweeds often grow near water hemlock, a deadly poisonous plant whose tuberous roots may be similar in size and shape when the plants are very young. Study the photos and descriptions carefully to avoid any such mistake.

Range and Habitat

There are several species of *Lycopus* in North America. The widespread *L. americanus* and *L. virginicus*, and the introduced *L. europeas*, do not produce tubers. Northern bugleweed *L. uniflorus*, sessile bugleweed *L. amplectens*, stalked bugleweed *L. rubellus*, narrow-leaved bugleweed *L. angustifolius*, western bugleweed *L. asper*, and possibly others, all produce edible tubers. Collectively, this group is found across the United States and southern Canada wherever there is moist soil. Bugleweeds grow in or near all kinds of wetlands, in heavy shade to partial sunlight.

Northern bugleweed is our smallest species and has very small white tubers, up to 0.8 inch (2 cm) long and is common along shady or semi-open ponds, marshes, bogs, brooks, swamps, and other wet areas. It is found across the northern forests of the United States and southern Canada. Sessile bugleweed is considered the best of this group by Fernald and Kinsey (1943); this plant is found on wet, sandy ground on the Coastal Plain from Massachusetts to

right Close-up of the stem of a fruiting *L. rubellus*.

below Flowers of rough or western bugleweed *L. asper.*

Florida and occasionally inland. It produces elongated white tubers, tapered at both ends and usually slightly curved, with multiple constrictions giving them a segmented look. The narrow-leaved and stalked bugleweeds are both similar to the sessile bugleweed and have relatively large tubers. The western bugleweed, found from the central United States west to British Columbia and California, has slightly narrower tubers.

Harvest and Preparation

The various species of bugleweed are all used in the same way. These perennial mints produce small tubers just below the surface, embedded usually in moss, mud, loose sand, or gravel. These tubers can be collected during the root season, from fall through spring. You can get them by digging carefully around the base of the plant while tugging gently on the stem. If the stems are withered or gone,

Water hemlock root (far right) among northern bugleweed tubers. They grow in the same habitat and I often find them inches apart. Water hemlock typically has a branching cluster of enlarged roots, but very small plants may have a single, enlarged tuberous root, like the one here. Note the different color, rougher surface, and the lack of regular constrictions. Water hemlock roots will normally have a rosette attached, while bugleweed will produce only a single stem. Water hemlock roots are creamy or light yellow inside, with faint yellow veins (or developing such veins after short exposure to air) while bugleweed tubers are uniformly whitish inside. Water hemlock roots have a scent reminiscent of carrots and paint, while bugleweed tubers have minimal scent. **Study carefully! Water hemlock is deadly poisonous and eating one root could kill you.**

just dig where the plants were growing. The excavation of bugleweeds usually requires no implements because the root system is so close to the surface. A bare hand can usually pull up the clumps of sphagnum moss or sift through the loose sands where the tubers are hidden. In some areas I have had the luck of pulling up plants with many tubers attached with only minimal digging.

It is important not to overharvest bugleweed. Leave a generous number of tubers behind as you collect. Always leave much of the colony undisturbed, and don't collect them except where they are common and seem to be thriving.

I pluck the larger tubers from their rhizomes and replant the smaller ones. The tubers turn green where exposed to light, but these green ones taste good too. If you are collecting a little late in the spring you will find young shoots growing from the ends of the tubers. These are safe to eat but may become slightly bitter. When collecting northern bugleweed I often rinse them nearby and nibble them raw. Otherwise I bring them home to cook. I rinse them, pull off any attached roots, scrub them to loosen any sand, then rinse them again. They can be boiled, steamed, fried, or cooked in almost any fashion.

Bugleweed tubers are mild and slightly sweet. They are crispy when raw but tender and somewhat starchy when cooked. They are quite similar in every way to the Chinese artichoke or "crôsne" *Stachys sieboldii*, a rather uncommon cultivated vegetable from the mint family, popular with some European and Asian chefs and occasionally sold in stores in North America. Bugleweed

above Tubers of *L rubellus*, a larger species of bugleweed.

below Northern bugleweed *L uniflorus* tubers. The dead stem from last year tells you where to look for tubers in spring.

tubers have a flavor that most people find pleasant. They are good eaten alone as a cooked vegetable, seasoned as you wish. They can also be used in any dish where you might appreciate a small chunk of tasty carbohydrate.

Because bugleweed tubers in my area are not easy to collect in volume, I have not tried storing them in any way. They certainly could be kept in damp sand in a root cellar or preserved by pressure canning. And I suspect that pickled bugleweed tubers would be a conversation-generating finger food.

Bugleweed is a fine plant to know if you reside near a supply—which may be more likely than you think, for this herb does a good job of remaining inconspicuous. Just be careful not to step on a salamander.

Northern
bugleweed
L. uniflorus
plants.

Elderberry

Sambucus spp.

Caprifoliaceae – Honeysuckle Family

For part of my childhood my parents owned an old farmhouse near a marshy lake, and at the edge of the yard there was a large thicket of American elderberries. One time when my friend Paul was visiting, the bushes were especially loaded with berries, and we decided to pick some. My dad noted our enthusiasm and said that if we picked enough, he would make some elderberry wine. Excited to be part of such a project, we brought back eight gallons of elderberries less than an hour later. My father took one full pail and said that would be enough for his purposes, leaving us with three gallons of leftover fruit. We promptly did what any two level-headed thirteen-year-olds would do and began an "elderberry war"—throwing them at each other and mashing them into each other's faces and bodies while wrestling and giggling. This gave us the brilliant idea of stripping down to our shorts, stomping the berries to a pulp in the pail, and rubbing the juice into all of our exposed skin to color ourselves purple. We then walked the three miles to town, hoping to attract attention to ourselves, and responding in unison, "We are the Purps," on the few occasions when we got some. I think it was Smurf envy. Finally, an old woman working in her flower garden stood up and shouted in the same disapproving tone of voice that seemed to follow me through my childhood, "You foolish boys! Very funny to cover yourselves in elderberry juice. It'll never wash off! You're gonna have to go to school like that. You'll be purple for *weeks*!"

We looked at each other in horror. Ashamed by our lack of foresight, we walked sheepishly to the nearby lake, wondering how she *knew* it was elderberry juice. (Perhaps she once had boys of her own.) We jumped into the muddy water

previous page Heavy, ripe clusters of American elder fruit.

below An American elder clump loaded with fruit.

and found that the purple color rinsed off with little trouble. Exiting the lake and celebrating our victory over ornery, fear-mongering elderly people, it dawned on us that she had *tricked us into de-purpling ourselves.* Our relief transmuted to anger: all that effort for *nothing*! We had walked three miles only to be duped! We cursed her all the way home and swore never to listen to our elders again.

Lucky for those of you satisfied with your skin tone, there are even better uses for elderberries.

Identification

All of our native elderberries are medium to large shrubs or small trees with pinnately compound leaves. The best-known species is the American elder *Sambucus canadensis* (often considered the same species as the common black or sweet elder of Europe, in which case it is known as *S. nigra*). This is a medium-sized shrub, typically fruiting when 5–12 feet (1.5–4 m) tall, although it may grow much larger in the South. It spreads by rhizomes to form clones, some of which are very dense and cover large areas. Individual elderberry stems are proportionately stout but weak and have few branches. The twigs are thick and the buds are small and conical, either brown or green. The bark of mature stems is light brownish-gray and rather smooth but for a sparse spackling of warty lenticels. Inside these stems there is a large, white pith.

American elder has large, opposite, pinnately compound leaves sometimes as much as 20 inches (50 cm) in length. The leaf typically consists of seven leaflets, which are sharply serrated, 2–5 inches (5–13 cm) long, elliptic with sharply pointed tips, and sessile or growing on very short petioles. The leaves and stems of elderberry give off a strong, unpleasant odor when cut or bruised.

The small, white, five-petaled flowers, about 0.25 inch (6 mm) across, are produced in rounded, somewhat flat-topped clusters called *cymes* at the ends of the branches. These cymes are typically 4–9 inches (10–23 cm) across, and each can contain hundreds of flowers. The fragrant blossoms open in late June and July.

The elderberry fruit is a tiny drupe, generally about 0.13 inch (3 mm) in diameter. Dark purple and juicy when ripe, they make up for their lack of size with copious production. American elderberries ripen in July, August, and September, the plump clusters often drooping under their own weight.

The western counterpart is the blue elder *S. cerulea.* This plant is similar to the American elder but larger in all respects, occasionally becoming a tree as much as 40 feet (12 m) tall. The individual berries are larger, as are the cymes they are borne in; clusters have weighed in at more than 2 pounds (1 kg). The fruit is dark blue but coated with a prominent white bloom.

The Mexican or desert elder *S. mexicana* is another blue-fruited species; it is similar to the blue elder and is often considered to be a form of that species. Some botanists recognize other species, such as velvet elder *S. velutina*, which is very similar in appearance to desert elder but has more velvety leaves. Other botanists lump most of the black- and blue-fruited types, such as desert, velvet, blue, American, and European black, into one mega-species encompassing an enormous range of variability on three continents, in which case they would all be *S. nigra*. This debate is not of great concern to the average forager, but anyone personally familiar with the blue elder thinks of it as quite distinct from the eastern species.

Red elder is easily distinguished from our other species by the shape of its fruit clusters: rounded or cone-shaped, much like grape clusters, rather than flat-topped like the other elders. The ripe fruit is usually bright red, but occasionally it may be yellow-orange, and in some parts of the Rockies it is black. It ripens much earlier than other elders; where red and American or blue elders grow beside one another, the red elder's fruit ripens about the time the first flowers appear on the darker species.

There is a small, herbaceous species of elderberry, *Sambucus ebulus*, native to Europe. This plant is rare as an escape in North America, being known only from a few sites in Quebec, New York, and New Jersey. The berries, which are bitter, disagreeable, and toxic (Couplan, 1999), are dark purple-black like those of the American elder, but the ripe clusters are oriented skyward rather than drooping. The leaflets are more linear and are reported to have a strong disagreeable scent. The flowers have pinkish centers.

Some botanists recognize three different species of red elder (two American and one Eurasian): *S. pubens*, *S. racemosa*, and *S. callicarpa*. Other authorities lump them all together as one. In any case, all of the three aforementioned scientific names refer to "red elder." **Red elderberries are not similar in flavor or use to the black and blue kinds. Their harvest and preparation require special consideration and are discussed in a separate section.**

When the large pith of an elderberry stem is pushed out, it forms a hollow wooden tube that people have found many uses for over the ages. These hollowed stems have been used as maple sap spiles, blowguns, and more commonly, the fashioning of flutes and whistles. In fact, the scientific name *Sambucus* comes from *sambuke*, a Greek word for a musical instrument traditionally made from elder wood. The tradition of making instruments from elderberry stems was surprisingly widespread. Some recent authors have warned against all such uses because of the plant's toxic qualities, but I doubt that there is any legitimate danger unless you eat the flute right after making it, and I challenge anyone to present an actual case of elder whistle or elder spile poisoning.

Range and Habitat

These well-known fruiting shrubs are found nearly everywhere in North America, from the deserts of the Southwest to the Pacific Coast, through the Rocky Mountains and Great Plains to the wooded East Coast and the boreal forests of the North.

The American elder is found from Minnesota south to eastern Texas and east to Florida. The northern edge of its range extends through southern Ontario and Quebec to Maine and New Brunswick. It is found in rich, moist soil with ample sunlight, being especially common in open areas along waterways, ditches, and fencerows. American elder is commonly found in association with stinging nettle, American elm, jerusalem artichoke, hopniss, Joe-Pye weed, and dogwood.

The blue elder is found in southern British Columbia and scattered about the western third of the United States, where it grows on rich soil in open and semi-open sites at low to middle elevations. It is commonly found in valleys, along cliff bases, roadsides, fencerows, and streams, at forest edges, and under power lines. This species is most prevalent in California, Oregon, Washington, Idaho, and Utah.

The Mexican elder is found in California, Arizona, southern New Mexico, and southern Nevada. This species inhabits places where there is moisture in the desert regions, such as ditches, streamsides, river valleys, and drainages.

Red elderberry is found across the southern boreal forests of Canada and roughly the northern half of the lower forty-eight states, extending even further south in mountainous areas and north to Alaska along the Pacific Coast. This species tolerates more shade and poorer, more acidic soil than our other elders but still thrives upon moist ground and disturbance. It is often abundant in old fields and farmsteads, and along field edges, roads, and trails. Occasionally red elder becomes a predominant shrub under a canopy of pine, aspen, or other trees that cast a light shade. It does surprisingly well in some very polluted or human-altered sites, springing readily from collapsed homes and the sites of razed buildings.

Blue elder may be a shrub or a small tree such as this one.

Harvest and Preparation – Blue and Black Elderberries

The elderberry is one of North America's most popular wild foods. Not only is it abundant and conspicuous over much of its range, it is also remarkably easy to gather due to its copious production of large fruit clusters. Any enterprising forager in elderberry country can find thickets bearing far more of this opulent fruit than he could use. The largest clusters will weigh well over a pound, and generally every one of them hangs within easy reach. It is quite commonplace to fill a five-gallon bucket with elderberries in a matter of fifteen to twenty minutes. They will be loosely packed due to the stems, but this is still a considerable haul.

The fruit ripens from midsummer to autumn, generally later further north or at higher elevations. I have seen American elders ripen in July in the southern United States, but where I live they are not ready until the later part of August or early September. Elderberries in the southwestern deserts will ripen in July, but blue elderberries in many mountainous parts of the West ripen in late September and October. If the berry crop is light, birds may pluck them all before they fully ripen, but more often the clusters hang for several more weeks, thinning gradually as the berries get carried away a few at a time until finally the cymes are left naked. In the occasional bumper crop years the elders may remain loaded for two months, extending the harvest season well into fall.

Blue elderberries. Note the heavy bloom coating the fruit.

However, if you find a loaded elderberry bush late in the season, be skeptical. All elderberries are not equal. Birds know this, and they have a serious sweet tooth, often gleaning the last berry from a tasty tree before moving on to the insipid ones. Before filling your pail, test the elderberries from your chosen bush to see if they are fair representatives of their kind.

Once you find your elderberry patch, picking is simple. Most are within easy reach, although a berry hook may be necessary on some larger trees, especially with blue elder. I pinch, bend, and twist the stem of the whole cluster—simply yanking often pulls off the ends of the branches. Some people use pruning shears to make a clean snip; so do I, on the rare occasions when I have them on hand. The hard part about elderberries isn't collecting them; it's knowing when to stop.

Warning: Some people experience nausea after eating elderberries, raw or cooked. This is more commonly reported with raw fruit. Consume elderberries sparingly and cautiously until you are comfortable that they will not adversely affect you. There is widespread suspicion that the seeds are the culprit.

Although I have lumped the black and blue elderberries together here for discussion, they are quite different in flavor. The blue elderberries of the West are, in my opinion, vastly superior to the American or black elder of the East. Blue elderberries have a pleasant, fruity, grape-like sourness that makes them ideal for pies, jellies, and drinks. American elderberries, in comparison, are bland and somewhat bitter, with that "rank eldery taste" that Euell Gibbons kept mentioning, and I keep tasting. I am convinced that if the two grew together, almost everybody would ignore the American elder. But considering the price of airfare, I suspect that we easterners will keep on using what we have and calling it good enough.

American elderberries can be eaten raw straight from the bush, although few people seem to enjoy them this way. However, I often snack on them while afield. Blue elderberries are much better, and I greatly enjoy eating them raw. I sometimes swallow the berries, while other times I spit them out after sucking out the juice. In general, elderberries have a poor reputation as a fresh fruit, but wonderful things can be made from them.

The first step in preparation is to remove the tiny fruits from their stems. Many people do this with a fork, combing the berries off the clusters. This works alright but leaves many of the smaller stems attached to the berries and is extremely time consuming. Using your fingers goes slower, but does a better job of getting clean berries. Another method is to put a piece of hardware cloth with half-inch holes over a wash basin and drag the elderberry clusters across it. This yanks the berries off their stems, after which they fall into the basin below.

The best method for removing elderberries from their stems is to put whole clusters in the freezer, loosely arranged on a tray of some sort. After they have frozen solid, rub the clusters between your hands and the berries will snap off the stems easily, rolling out like spilled BB's. This works amazingly fast—it takes only a few minutes to separate a gallon of berries—and it produces a cleaner finished product than any other method I've seen. You can immediately re-bag and freeze the berries for storage, and they will not stick together. Or you can proceed to making any of the many famous elderberry products.

It is not absolutely necessary to de-stem the elderberries if you are going to juice them, especially when the clusters are very plump and have a high fruit-to-stem ratio. My friend Rose Barlow simply puts whole fruit clusters into a steam juicer and is happy with the product she gets. I remove the larger stems and mash the fruit, then squeeze the juice from this pulp in a jelly bag. I do not notice a flavor from the stems this way, perhaps because the mash is not boiled before the juice is extracted. Pressing raw elderberries like this produces a thicker, stronger juice than one gets from steaming or boiling, but it yields less volume.

To make juice by boiling, de-stem your elderberries, place them in a large pot, add about a quart of water for each gallon of fruit, and bring to a boil. When the fruit has softened, mash it gently, boiling for a total of fifteen to twenty minutes. Then strain the juice through a jelly bag or cloth—and don't squeeze if you want the juice to have the nicest color. Elderberries contain a sticky, greenish, latex-like substance that will stick to cooking utensils, especially when the fruit is boiled.

Elderberry juice is often drunk as a tonic. It has been shown to be effective at reducing the duration and severity of flu symptoms (Brown, 2004) and may be effective against other viral infections. Elderberries are also high in vitamin C, potassium, and phosphorus (USDA, NNDSR 21). Small bottles of elderberry extract are sold for its immune-boosting and other health benefits.

I like to store elderberry juice by water-bath canning. Most people prefer it diluted and sweetened or mixed with milder juices such as apple. Even though I sometimes make an ugly grimace after gulping a small glass of pure, thick American elderberry juice, I always feel good about it afterward, and usually I crave it beforehand. I have also had many wonderful punches and other nonalcoholic drinks that included a portion of elderberry juice.

Long before Elton John sang about it, elderberry was famous as a wine ingredient, and it remains one of the most popular fruits for home winemakers. Euell Gibbons gives an oft-cited recipe in *Stalking the Wild Asparagus*. The beauty of wine is that it is a way to store all those phytonutrients from elderberries—without cooking or refrigeration.

Elderberry jelly is also highly regarded by many—although by itself the fruit of the American elder is not acid enough to make a good jelly, so traditionally lemon juice is added. Any very sour fruit juice will work, however. Good candidates include wild grape, common barberry, crabapple, apple, buffaloberry,

Oregon grape, and red raspberry. I have not tried all of these, and each would impart its own distinct flavor, but mixing in any sour fruit juice will make a better jelly than using American elderberry alone. Blue elder, being sour, makes a very good jelly by itself. You can also make elderberry jam, but most people prefer the seeds to be strained out.

It is generally agreed that fresh American elderberries are not good for pies and other typical wild berry fare, but blue elders are highly esteemed for such goodies. Drying is sometimes said to improve the flavor of American elderberries, and is a good way to store the fruit. Separate the berries from their stems and dry them in the sun, on a tray in the oven, or in a food dehydrator. Gibbons was a big fan of these dehydrated elderberries and even claims that, "All the rank elder taste is dissipated in drying." But I still don't like them very much, and the annoying seeds remain. At your convenience you can reconstitute the dried fruit by pouring a little boiled sugar water over them and letting them sit. These can be used in muffins, pies, pancakes, and the like.

Warning: Every part of the elder besides the flowers and ripe fruit is considered toxic. Do not eat the stems, bark, leaves, roots, or unripe fruits, for they all contain cyanide-producing glycosides and possibly other toxins. This warning goes for all elderberry species.

Flowers

The elder's culinary value is not solely invested in its fruit; the flowers also have many traditional uses. The clusters of small white flowers bloom in early to mid summer and are often borne profusely, making roadside thickets look like anachronistic snowbanks from a distance. The flowers are often called "elder blow" in the culinary tradition.

My favorite elder product is the tea made from the flowers. I make this tea by bringing about two cups of water to a boil in a medium saucepan, removing it from the heat, and placing three or four elder flower cymes upside down in the pan. The stems will stick out of the water, leaving just the flowers submerged. I let them steep for five to fifteen minutes and drink the tea with no sweetener added. It has a hearty but gentle flavor, faintly sweet, that reminds me just a little bit of pancakes. The tea looks like urine but tastes much better and is reputed to cure headaches. I do not strain it because I enjoy chewing the occasional flower parts that swim around in it. Elder blow tea is sometimes used to make wine.

Of course, if you pick the flowers you are preventing fruit from forming. If this bothers you, you can gently shake or rub the clusters over a container, letting the loose elder blow fall in. These loose flowers will already be spent, and taking them will leave any fertilized fruit intact. Elder flowers can be added to

above Water hemlock's leaf differs from elderberry's in being twice compound with smaller, more numerous leaflets.

below left Flowers and leaves of American elder.

below right Water hemlock sometimes grows beside elderberry and is about the same height; don't accidentally grab a cluster of its flowers. Note that the water hemlock flowers are borne in compound umbels (elderberry's are not) with the umbellets well-spaced, while the entire inflorescence of elderberry is crowded.

Elder vs. Water Hemlock

Sambucus spp. (elder)	*Cicuta* spp. (water hemlock)
Leaves once compound	Leaves two or three times compound
Typically 5–9 leaflets	Typically 18–40 leaflets
Petioles lack papery sheath at base	Petioles with papery sheath at base
Surface of stalk with corky lenticels	Surface lacks lenticels
Flowers in cymes	Flowers in compound umbels
Woody shrub	Perennial herb
Stems pithy	Stems hollow

pancakes, muffins, or other baked goods to impart their pleasant flavor. You can also dry the flowers for use out of season.

Warning: Small flowering elderberry plants might be confused with water hemlock, which looks remotely similar and flowers at about the same time and often grows in the same habitat. Of course, elderberry is a bush and water hemlock is herbaceous, but it can grow quite tall. See page 409 for characteristics used to differentiate the two.

Red Elderberry

It is commonly written that red elderberries (*Sambucus racemosa, S. pubens, S. callicarpa*, depending on the classification followed) are inedible or even poisonous, even though it is well documented that they were a widely used and important food source for First Nations in the Pacific Northwest (Turner, 1975), and they are still eaten there and elsewhere today. However, **they should always be cooked, as the raw berries are reported to be toxic and cause nausea.**

Red elderberry is among the first woody plants to leaf out in spring, and it flowers soon after the leaves emerge. The bright red fruit ripens in early summer, about the same time as wild strawberries—usually before the other elders even begin flowering. Red elders often produce copious amounts of fruit, and the clusters have a very high fruit-to-stem ratio.

Red elderberries. Too bad they don't taste as good as they look.

Red elderberry flowers.

Red elderberry does not have a fruity flavor; there is very little sweetness or sourness to it. Most who try it find it disgusting, and part of this disgust stems from its failure to meet the expectations evoked by its bright color. The taste is like bland, slightly bitter tomatoes. One traditional use was to steam and dry the berries. They were later rehydrated and eaten with eulachon grease, sometimes mixed with other berries (Turner, 1975). The juice has been used to soak salmon before baking.

I have encountered a few recommendations for making red elderberry jelly. After having tried the raw fruit many times, I embarked skeptically but hopefully on this project (since red elder is among the most abundant berries where I live). After boiling the berries for about twenty minutes, their terrible smell disappeared and the flavor became almost tolerable. I then juiced the fruit and made jelly, which was a beautiful bright red. In flavor it was perhaps the most boring, worthless jelly that I have ever made, although it wasn't totally disgusting.

Last summer I gathered five gallons of red elderberries for more experimentation. After de-stemming, I cooked the fruit and let the juice drain out by gravity through a cloth. Since the initial taste of the light red juice reminded me of tomatoes, I used it as the base for a soup. The juice tasted so bad, however, that I couldn't consume anything I made from it. I took the cooked, drained berries and ran them through my fruit strainer. Curiously, I got a thick, dull yellow puree that tasted like slightly bitter cooked squash. I followed a squash soup recipe and thought the result was pretty good, but not exceptional.

Few modern foragers use the red elderberry. This plant has great genetic variability across its enormous range, and the flavor probably varies from one place to another. Perhaps it is more palatable in the Pacific Northwest. However, my communications with others in that region do not confirm or even suggest this. It is also possible that it was eaten more in some areas, such as coastal British Columbia, where plant foods comprised a small percentage of the diet, simply because of its comparative availability, or perhaps because it satisfied a common nutritional craving by providing essential nutrients in a consumable form. Nancy Turner (pers. comm., 2008) tells me that it is an acquired taste. It's one that I haven't acquired yet, but also have not given up on. With the right preparation methods or recipes, red elder might be an excellent food.

Red elder flowers can be used for tea like other elder flowers, although I do not like them as much.

Don't let any of this talk about poisonous leaves and stems scare you away from the elderberry. After all, a bush so valuable has every right to protect itself. There are truly few plants that offer such diverse ways to be appreciated as the amazing elderberry.

Jerusalem-artichoke

Helianthus tuberosus

Asteraceae – Sunflower Family

As I was growing up, most of the adults in my life were unsupportive of my wild food habit. One of the few who encouraged me in my pastime was my sixth grade teacher. After I told him about some of my foraging experiences, he asked me if I had ever eaten jerusalem-artichoke. I had never heard of such a plant, and I couldn't imagine that something with this exotic-sounding name was actually native or wild in the Midwest. I wasn't sure what to make of the question—whether he had changed the subject to discuss some interesting culti-vated vegetable, or perhaps was just pulling my leg—but I told him no. Sensing

Jerusalem-artichoke flower. Many other common sunflowers have dark centers.

my uncertainty, he described the plant as resembling a sunflower and having edible tubers, promising to bring some in for me to try.

A little later in autumn, he dangled a clear plastic bag full of small pieces of an unfamiliar vegetable in front of the class. After a brief lecture about the plant, he passed the bag around and invited us to try them. I was one of the few who did, and that taste sparked a quest to find wild jerusalem-artichoke that was not consummated for a decade.

I read about the plant, but none of my books had good descriptions or depictions of it. So I dug up every species of wild sunflower that I found, sifting the soil in search of tubers. Those poor wild sunflowers—I must have pulled out hundreds over the years: giant sunflower, woodland sunflower, Maximilian sunflower, but never that elusive *Helianthus tuberosus*. One of my high school teachers said they grew in huge colonies along the roadsides near her house. My books said they were abundant and widespread, growing like weeds. Yet no amount of digging under the wrong sunflower would procure me a tuber.

Thank God for Mark and Jon. Were it not for these guys, who collaborated to teach me what real jerusalem-artichokes looked like, the woodland sunflower might be extinct by now.

First, Mark ordered some cultivated "sunchoke" tubers from a seed catalog as starters. He planted them in his garden, which happened to be in the field near my cabin, since it was sunny there and he was living in the woods in a birchbark wigwam nearby. Like most people who live in wigwams these days, he moved out after a short time, leaving me a little clump of sunchokes. The deer never let these plants get more than knee-high, so I transplanted some tubers to a site *right* next to my cabin—a place that wise deer avoid. The next summer the jerusalem-artichokes grew to be eight feet tall, blocking the beautiful sunset view from my favorite window. I began to understand how they could be considered a nuisance. Yet even though, by staring at them every day, I learned exactly what they looked like, I still could not find a single specimen growing wild.

Jon told me of a place nearby where hopniss grew and mentioned that he might have seen some jerusalem-artichoke there as well. I went there to search for the hopniss, having concluded that sunchokes grow only in my blind spot. When I found the hopniss and dug some up, I happened upon an odd-looking, finger-like tuber in the sand beside them. It was utterly different from the cultivated jerusalem-artichokes that I had grown accustomed to, so at first I didn't recognize it. But I looked around to see what plant might have produced such a tuber, and the most likely candidate was some sort of wild sunflower that looked like a smaller, thinner version of the jerusalem-artichokes trying to engulf my house.

I found it! Releasing eleven years of failure, I let out a triumphant shout. And since then, I have had no trouble finding jerusalem-artichokes.

Description

The jerusalem-artichoke's Latin name, *Helianthus tuberosus*, means "tuberous sunflower"—an excellent name for this plant. Unfortunately, however, this species has no good common name. Not only is "jerusalem-artichoke" long and cumbersome, it is misleading because this plant is not an artichoke and does not come from Jerusalem.

You will notice that I leave the "jerusalem" part of this sunflower's name uncapitalized. This is not an accident. We do not capitalize words such as "afghan" which may be derived from proper nouns, but which have evolved through usage into common names with no ethnic or geographic meaning. But the "jerusalem" part of jerusalem-artichoke does not even appear to be geographic in origin; it is believed to be a corruption of the Spanish or Italian word for sunflower (*girasol* or *girasole*). Thus it is doubly appropriate not to capitalize it.

Because "jerusalem-artichoke" is such a misfitting name, new ones have been proposed over the years to replace it. There has been an attempt to market the cultivated tubers as "sunchokes." I question the wisdom of promoting the word "choke" in the name of any food, preferring the less common "sunroot." However absurd, "jerusalem artichoke" remains the best known and most widely used name for this distinctly American vegetable.

Jerusalem-artichoke is closely related to the cultivated sunflower, and the resemblance is quite apparent. Typical height at maturity is 5–9 feet (1.5–3 m). The stalks are usually 0.4–0.8 inch (1–2 cm) thick at the base. They are straight and unbranched except near the top, with very little taper. Their surface is covered with short, stiff, raspy hairs that give the stems a sandpapery feel. This is an important feature, since it can help to identify the dead stalks in late fall, winter, and early spring, when the tubers are at their best.

The only other wild sunflower whose stalk has a similar surface texture is

This is a clump of the cultivated "sunchoke," slightly more robust than typical wild plants but otherwise identical. Note that most leaves are paired, but the upper leaves on the taller plant to the right become alternate.

the wild sunflower *H. annuus*, the ancestor of the cultivated sunflower. However, the wild sunflower has a proportionately thicker stem than jerusalem-artichoke and produces spreading branches. Also, the leaves of wild sunflower are broader and mostly alternate, the flowers are larger, and the plant tends to grow in disturbed soil and usually does not form dense colonies.

Jerusalem-artichoke leaves are simple, entire, usually serrate, and lanceolate or narrowly ovate. They are coarse and raspy like the stems, especially when growing in full sun, and are larger and broader than those of most other species of *Helianthus*, growing 4–10 inches (10–25 cm) in length. The leaves on the lower part of the plant are opposite, but near the top they are sometimes alternate, especially on large, robust specimens. They are borne on winged petioles about

left Note the short, stiff hairs that cover the jerusalem-artichoke's stem.

below Leaves of jerusalem-artichoke growing wild in a river floodplain.

A clump of wild jerusalem-artichokes in early autumn. This is the best time to look for colonies of this plant.

one third of their length. Another distinct feature of the jerusalem-artichoke leaf is the presence of two prominent secondary veins, one on each side of the midvein. These originate near the base of the leaf but stop near the midpoint of the margin.

The composite flowerheads of jerusalem-artichoke open in late summer and fall. They emblaze many roadsides and meadows with their striking beauty. Usually 2–3 inches (5–8 cm) across, they look like miniature sunflowers except the disks in the center are yellow and proportionately much smaller. Each stalk bears four to eight of these blossoms in a loose terminal panicle.

The vegetable for which this plant is famous grows 1–4 inches (2.5–10 cm) under the surface of the soil. Small rhizomes radiate from the base of the stalk, growing horizontally. Toward the end, these rhizomes gradually widen into a tuber. Typically 2–5 inches (5–13 cm) long, these tubers come to an abrupt point at the end. At the widest point, just behind the tip, the larger tubers may reach 1.25 inches (3 cm) in diameter. The skin is smooth except for a few rings or constrictions, which bear occasional buds. The tuber is usually gray, cream, or light brown in color, sometimes with a reddish hue. Inside, the tubers are solid and semi-opaque without noticeable fibers.

Jerusalem-artichokes were once an important food in Europe; they were widely adopted there long before the potato. As the potato was incorporated into the European diet, jerusalem-artichoke became gradually less important, and today it is of minor significance. However, it still produces phenomenal yields: of all known crops, only corn produces more edible calories per acre under cultivation (Kays and Nottingham, 2008).

Various cultivated varieties of sunchoke have been selected and bred. The tubers of these plants are larger and thicker than typical wild stock and some have shapes that deviate dramatically from the wild plants. People who have become familiar with the cultivated jerusalem-artichoke may have trouble recognizing the tubers of the wild form.

Most of the information on jerusalem-artichoke pertains to the cultivated forms—this is true even of the wild food literature. Many authors are only familiar with the cultivated plant and have assumed that the wildlings are identical or very similar. This has resulted in much confusion where the culinary qualities of the two differ. The situation is complicated by the fact that the wild stock varies; somewhere in the vast range of this plant there are probably some original wild specimens with the odd tuber characteristics of the cultivated forms, from which the cultivars were long ago selected. Additionally, cultivated plants have often escaped and have no trouble surviving in the wild. In this chapter I am referring to typical wild forms unless otherwise specified, but I will try to discuss the entire range of variation of all forms that readers might encounter.

Range and Habitat

The jerusalem-artichoke is native from the Great Plains eastward. It ranges from Texas to Georgia, north to Saskatchewan and Quebec. It is most abundant in the center of that range. It is also found as an introduced or escaped plant at scattered sites around the western United States.

Like most weeds, the primary natural habitat of this species is in river floodplains. It is also found along small streams, lakeshores, and sunny wet areas where the soil is sand, loamy sand, or sandy loam. In its natural habitat, jerusalem artichoke often grows along with hopniss. It is also frequently associated with American elder and stinging nettle.

The jerusalem-artichoke has benefited greatly from human disturbance of the landscape. In areas of good agricultural soil these plants are often abundant along roadsides and ditches, in abandoned fields, and in other open areas—as long as there is ample moisture in the soil.

The wild type is to be expected in river floodplains and other natural habitats. In farm country you may encounter escapees from cultivation.

Harvest and Preparation

The best time to harvest sunroots is late fall, winter, and early spring. You can get them in the early or middle part of fall, but they will be unripe and usually less than full size. Timing is very important with sunroot due to their high content of the non-digestible starch inulin. With the onset of cold weather, the tubers convert their inulin to simple sugars, making them sweeter to the taste and more readily digestible. The difference in flavor is dramatic.

If jerusalem-artichokes are eaten when they are full of inulin, they will cause *horrendous* gas and sometimes diarrhea in many individuals—unless they are *very* well cooked. You might not have read "horrendous" loud enough; few people will ever experience worse flatulence. The Dakota in Minnesota relegated jerusalem-artichoke to the status of starvation food "from dread of its flatulent qualities" (Prescott, 1849, p. 452), and many modern foragers avoid it for the same reason. Indeed, in certain circles this tuber has earned the uncouth but accurate name of *fartichoke*.

The gassy quality is presumably due to the high levels of inulin. Being indigestible, it passes into the lower alimentary canal where it is broken down by bacteria in our gut. There are two ways to avoid this: either you can eat them only when they are fully ripe, or you can cook them for a very long time, since prolonged heating breaks down the inulin into simpler sugars. The wild tubers generally cause gas worse than the cultivars, which makes me suspect that there may be more than inulin at play.

I prefer to harvest my sunroots with a shovel, but a digging stick or trowel can also work. The tubers of cultivated forms may be right near the base of the stalk, but wild types tend to bear the tubers further away—sometimes more than a foot (30 cm). They are typically found 1–4 inches (2.5–10 cm) deep. These tubers are often easy to harvest in quantity where the plants grow in dense colonies. Other times they will be found spread around and mixed with other vegetation, in which case the tubers are more sparsely distributed and harder to collect. For wild forms, it works best to just dig in the middle of a dense patch; trying to follow rhizomes, or to dig up individual plants, is often futile.

Many people who plant jerusalem-artichoke comment that they cannot get rid of it no matter how hard they try to dig up every tuber produced. As long as you leave some tubers behind, digging actually benefits the colony; the loosening of the soil is comparable to cultivation, causing the remaining plants to grow more vigorously the following season. In fact, under unfavorable soil conditions, the plants are *only* able to survive if they are dug up regularly; they will slowly die out if left alone. I am convinced that the plant evolved symbiotically with herbivores who cultivated it by rooting for the tubers.

If not used immediately after harvest, sunroots should be stored in a way

above Spring is an excellent time to harvest jerusalem-artichokes once you learn to identify the old, dead stalks. These wild tubers came from very rich soil and are rather robust. The ideal time to collect them would have been two weeks earlier than this, before growth had commenced.

below Wild jerusalem-artichokes are more apt to look like this, although they are quite variable. These were collected in October and came from rather poor sandy soil.

Tubers of the most common variety of cultivated jerusalem-artichoke or sunchoke.

that prevents the loss of moisture. I keep mine in a plastic bag in the refrigerator, or in a pail of moist sand in the root cellar. Like most wild root vegetables, jerusalem-artichokes can be subjected to freezing temperatures without harm, but a very hard freeze will kill them. If stored properly, sunroots will keep all winter, but the surest bet is to leave them in the ground until needed.

Jerusalem-artichokes are generally very easy to clean because their skin is smooth. Scrub or brush them, rinse, and cut out any dirt pockets or bug holes. After cleaning, I sometimes peel the skin with a sharp knife or vegetable peeler. This isn't necessary, and I assume that the skins contain some good nutrients, so refrain unless you feel that there are culinary benefits to peeling.

I use jerusalem-artichokes as a baked or boiled vegetable. Because of their flatulent property, I cook them for one to six hours, depending on the time of year (longer cooking earlier in fall, shortest cooking in winter and spring.) They have a rich, pleasant, almost buttery flavor that is good alone or with other vegetables. Sunroots are one of my favorite soup ingredients. With cooking, they soften dramatically.

I don't eat wild jerusalem-artichokes raw, because of the gas factor. How-ever, some of the thicker and sweeter cultivated varieties, when totally ripe, are excellent in salad. I peel them and slice them into thin chips. These add a nice crunchy texture to a salad and are a refreshing snack all by themselves.

Jerusalem-artichokes are often described as potato-like, but I advise you to ignore this analogy. There have already been enough unsatisfactory attempts to use this vegetable as a potato substitute. You can boil and mash them, and they are good, but they are not like mashed potatoes in texture or flavor. You can slice them thin and eat them scalloped or fried, but they will not have the potato's starchy texture, nor will they become equally crispy. It is best to enjoy sunroots for what they *are* rather than for what they aren't.

Jerusalem-artichoke seeds look like miniature sunflower seeds, and their taste is similar. However, they are too small to be of any practical value to humans.

Jerusalem-artichoke is among the best-known wild vegetables in North America. It has long been cultivated and can be purchased today in many health food stores. It was used widely by Native Americans and was an important article of food for some groups. If you take the time to learn to identify this not-so-descript wild sunflower, you will have access to a delicious, abundant, versatile, and easily collected vegetable. You will understand why the plant remains among the most popular wild foods today. Just don't collect it in September and eat it raw. Especially not if you're expecting company.

Ox-Eye Daisy

Chrysanthemum leucanthemum (Leucanthemum vulgare)

Asteraceae – Sunflower Family

There is something redeeming about an abandoned, worn-out hayfield. Like the one just uphill from my cabin, where I like to stand at sunset and peer down upon my modest handiwork—the most prominent feature in yet another abandoned hayfield.

Every old field tells a story. This one, of settlers who came only four generations ago, seeking what we always seek: wealth—this time in the form of cheap land and white pine. When the great trees were sawn through, wedged over, bucked up, and hauled away, all by the hard labor of men and harnessed beasts, the land was bought up by some hopeful Scandinavian immigrant who cut and burned the remaining timber as fast as he put up a home, barn, and fence posts. As he did so, the cougars and wolves were poisoned, trapped, or shot, and the moose and caribou evicted. Year by year he grubbed out and burned up stump

The ubiquitous ox-eye daisy flower.

after stump after stump and filled in the wounds to make this smooth, tillable twenty acres—a toil that nearly every person to gaze upon this field since then has taken for granted. Spring after spring, wheat was planted on the steep slope, and with every tilling a portion of its scant topsoil washed down to Lake Superior until finally the land was "wheated to death," left with nothing for soil but sticky red clay, worthless for growing grain. In a great exodus the locals never mention, like some almost-forgotten family scandal, this farmer and his wife packed up and left the house to rot. The collapsed remains of a cedar shake roof now supporting sheets of moss, old pine boards with empty holes where nails have rusted away, all heaped into a crumbling fieldstone foundation with red fingers of dogwood creeping out of the cracks, home now to a porcupine and a weasel; this scene may not immediately evoke images of late-night arguments, screaming matches and worse, broken dreams and crying children, unpaid bills stacked on the dresser, cursing the cow, and neglected apple trees. But it takes all of this, and usually more, before a man abandons the house that he has built with his own hands and lets it decay.

Most of the neighbors left, too, but a few stayed and switched from wheat to dairy or sheep, and one of them planted this field to hay. But even the hay wouldn't take on this hostile clay slope, devoid of organic matter. All that it could support were daisies, orange hawkweed, and wild strawberries. So to these it was left.

That's the story these daisies tell in June, their blossoming beauty mocking the toil of the men who despise them, the fragrant snowy hillside proclaiming their victory. Their roots hold down the scant soil that they are slowly rebuilding. But the daisies are not the whole story of this land—only the current sentence. Where is it headed? Nobody can say for certain, but if I can see back to the white pines, towering over oaks and birches, then I can see forward to them, too, standing tall again. The old tragedy ends with daisies, but so begins the new story—one that we and our children will write.

Description

The ox-eye daisy is a perennial herb with a tough root that spends most of its life as a dense basal rosette, sometimes with dozens of leaves. These leaves are very dark green and rarely more than 5 inches (13 cm) long and 2 inches (5 cm) wide. They are widest near the tip, tapering gradually to a narrow base and flattened petiole. The margins are coarsely and irregularly toothed, sometimes lobed. The leaf surfaces are glabrous.

In late spring or early summer the ox-eye daisy sends up one to several flowering stalks. These are typically about 0.25 inch (6 mm) thick, 14–30 inches

A large, lush rosette of ox-eye daisy in late summer. This plant provides a salad green or garnish most of the year.

(35–75 cm) tall, and unbranched. The alternate stalk leaves are much smaller than the basal ones. Both petioles and leaves decrease in size going up the stem, and the upper cauline leaves are sessile or clasping.

The solitary, flat flowering heads are 1.2–2.5 inches (3–6 cm) across, composed of yellow disk flowers surrounded by a ring of fifteen to thirty-five beautiful white rays about 0.4–0.8 inch (1–2 cm) long.

There are several other nonnative species of *Chrysanthemum* found in North America; most occur uncommonly and sporadically. The corn chrysanthemum, corn marigold, or corn daisy *C. segetum* is a daisy with yellow rays; it is occasionally grown for its edible greens, which resemble the leaves of ox-eye daisy. Costmary *C. balsamita* is a strongly aromatic relative with much smaller flower heads, used as a seasoning.

Range and Habitat

The ox-eye daisy is not a North American native, but it has spread as a weed across nearly all of the continent. This daisy is dependent on disturbance, thriving upon the activities of humans. It is generally found near buildings, in yards, along roadsides, and as a weed in fields and pastures. Daisies do best in soil that is well watered but well drained. They compete most vigorously where the soil is exposed or impoverished and has little organic matter.

Harvest and Preparation

Ox-eye daisy is a strong-flavored herb that is somewhere between a salad green and a seasoning. The tender young stems, flower buds, and leaves can all be eaten, but the leaves are by far the most popular. Most commonly, ox-eye daisy greens are eaten raw as a trail nibble. They are also excellent in salads, sandwiches, and tacos. Tilford (1997) claims that they are sometimes served in salads at gourmet restaurants. I find them refreshing and delectable raw, but am not fond of them cooked. Ox-eye daisy greens are aromatic and have a distinct sweet flavor that is hard to describe. Some people are reminded of carrot, mint, or tarragon, others of sage or arugula, and some even mention pepper. You'll have to try it and see for yourself. Daisy greens are used sparingly for their unique flavor; they are generally not the centerpiece of a dish.

The largest and most succulent leaves grow in the basal rosettes. These are always available from early spring to late fall, and I have collected them at any time of winter when the ground was without snow cover. The leaves on the flowering stalks are much smaller than the basal leaves; however, unlike many greens, they retain their pleasant flavor and texture even as the plant matures and blooms.

The tender young stems and unopened flower buds can be used in the same ways as the greens and have a similar but not identical flavor; both have their

own unique texture. It is also reported that the flower heads have been used to make wine (Couplan, 1998).

The various edible parts of ox-eye daisy do not have great subsistence value. However, they are pleasant flavorings and salad greens that are widely available throughout the growing season. Once you start nibbling, you might keep nibbling for the rest of your life.

The entire stem and all the leaves of this daisy shoot are tender and delectable.

The Lettuce-Dandelion Group

(Tribe *Lactucaceae* of the Aster Family)

There are numerous wild edibles within the enormous family *Asteraceae*. A subgroup of this family, known to botanists as the *Lactucaceae* (lettuce) tribe, contains several well known edible plants which are often confused with each other. Members of the lettuce tribe are distinguished from other composites by two characteristics: their sap is milky, and their heads contain only petal-like ray flowers. There are seven genera which comprise the most common, widespread, and useful food plants within the lettuce tribe: *Cichorium* (chicory), *Hypochaeris* (cat's ear), *Lactuca* (lettuce), *Prenanthes*, *Sonchus* (sow thistle), *Taraxacum* (dandelion), and *Tragopogon* (salsify). I call these seven the **lettuce-dandelion group**. Many wild food authors lump several of these species and genera together for discussion, but in fact the specific details of their collection, preparation, and culinary attributes are often quite different.

Many of these plants, such as dandelion and chicory, are famously hard to tell apart—yet the existing wild food literature does little to address this confusion. Botany manuals focus on identifying these plants when they are in flower or fruit, but this is of limited use to the forager, who generally eats them while they are still young. Fortunately, all of these plants can be readily distinguished at any time in their growth cycle by characteristics of their stems and leaves. The following key, designed with the forager in mind, should clear up this confusion, especially when used in conjunction with the photos and descriptions found in the specific plant accounts that follow.

This is not a key to the entire lettuce tribe, which includes dozens of genera and hundreds of species, many of them edible. If your plant is not a member of the six genera listed above, the key will be useless in identifying it. In other words, the key cannot *identify* wild lettuce, but it can differentiate wild lettuce from sow thistle, if you already know that you have one or the other. Mixing up the species in the lettuce-dandelion group is not dangerous, but it might mess up dinner.

Also note that, while hairy cat's ear *Hypochaeris radicata* is edible and is part of the key, it is not covered in an account in this book.

above Flower of hairy cat's ear *Hypochaeris radicata*.

right Leaves of hairy cat's ear *Hypochaeris radicata*.

Key to the Lettuce-Dandelion Group
(Focusing on leaf and stem features)

If you are not yet comfortable or familiar with dichotomous keys, here is a great one to start with. After finding a member of this group, start at the beginning of the key. Choose carefully which of the couplets describes your plant, proceeding until you have arrived at the correct genus.

1. All leaves long and narrow, grass-like, v-shaped in profile, margins smooth and entire; latex light brown: *Tragopogon* (salsify).
1. Leaves toothed, lobed, or with wavy or irregular margins: all others, go to 2.

2. Basal leaves borne on long petioles roughly equal to or longer than the blade; blade widens abruptly from petiole. Blade and petiole form a 90–130 degree angle: *Prenanthes*.
2. Leaves clasping, sessile, or with proportionately short petiole; blade widens gradually: all others, go to 3.

3. Midrib cross-section forms a low, rounded hump on leaf underside: *Taraxacum* (Dandelion), *Cichorium* (Chicory), or *Hypochaeris* (Cat's ear), go to 4.
3. Midrib cross-section triangular, forming a sharp or nearly sharp keel: *Lactuca* (lettuce) or *Sonchus* (sow thistle), go to 6.

4. Leaf generally without erect hairs (may have very fine wool laying down, especially on midvein): *Taraxacum* (Dandelion).
4. Leaf with notable erect hairs: *Cichorium* (Chicory) or *Hypochaeris* (Cat's ear), go to 5.

5. Erect hairs on all leaf surfaces, almost evenly distributed: *Hypochaeris* (Cat's ear).
5. Erect hairs most prominent on midvein, especially below: *Cichorium* (Chicory).

6. Erect hairs or spines found along the keeled bottom of midvein, latex white or light brown: *Lactuca* (lettuce), except *L. muralis*.
6. Erect hairs or spines absent from bottom of midvein; leaves with curved auricles at base where attached to stalk; latex white: *Sonchus* (sow thistle).

Wild Lettuce

Lactuca spp.

Asteraceae – Sunflower Family

Whoever first said "The Devil is in the details," must not have liked details. And I doubt that he was an economic botanist. Because when it comes to edible wild plants, the *miracle* is in the details. It is the details that give one the power not only to identify plants, but also to select the best specimens among them. The nuances of texture, color, size, and timing are the key to gustatory delight in all cooking—but especially with wild foods.

So do not shy away from details; and don't resent Nature for being so replete with complexity. That is its glory, not its downfall. We owe our very intelligence to this miraculous complexity. It is not the burden of the naturalist to learn this complexity; it is the awesome reality. More than anything else, which of these

A cluster of upright *L. canadensis* leaves in mid-spring, about to bolt. This species collected at this stage is a remarkably good salad green.

attitudes you choose will determine your success as a naturalist. So learn your details with joy, remember them with pride, and experience them with gratitude. Let the details excite you—for there are enough of them to excite you for the rest of your life.

Many people consider wild lettuce a second-rate salad plant with an unpleasant bitterness, and a mediocre potherb that requires water changes to tone down its flavor. So did I—before I learned the wonderful details.

Description

North America is home to twelve species of *Lactuca*. The basic wild lettuce that I will first describe is *Lactuca canadensis*. I will then give the differences of several other species as compared to this template.

Lactuca canadensis, commonly called "yellow lettuce" or simply "wild lettuce," is the best species to use for food. In my workshops, as well as in everyday life, I refer to this plant as "good lettuce." Good lettuce is a biennial or perennial, accumulating energy for one or more years as a rosette before flowering.

The rosette leaves are typically 5–10 inches (13–25 cm) long and very deeply lobed. The leaves resemble those of dandelion but tend to be lighter green in color with proportionately longer lobes. The lobes also tend to be proportionately longer than those of dandelion. The leaves of good lettuce are usually glabrous except for a row of long, thin hairs that is usually found on the midrib.

left The leaves of good lettuce *L. canadensis* are extremely variable. Notice how the lower ones here have long lobes, but some of the upper ones are entire, almost grass-like. All of the leaves on a particular plant may fit one extreme or the other.

below The base of a *L. canadensis* rosette, showing light brown latex where the leaves and stalk were picked. This specimen is unusually hairy because its locale is a sunny south slope—plants in moist soil in shade may be nearly hairless.

L. canadensis leaf with row of erect hairs along the midvein. All wild lettuces except *L. muralis* have such a row of hairs or spines along the midvein's bottom, although it is often sparser than in this example.

All parts of the plant exude a latex when broken; this latex quickly turns light orange-brown upon exposure to the air.

When flowering, *L. canadensis* sends up a vigorous, straight, unbranching, hollow stalk that typically reaches 5–9 feet (1.5–3 m) in height. The stalk leaves generally have fewer and longer lobes than the basal leaves, but they are remarkably variable—sometimes being deeply lobed, other times being long and almost grass-like. Atop this stalk is a cluster of numerous composite yellow flowers that resemble miniature dandelions. Each of these blossoms is about 0.3 inch (8 mm) across. At first the flower cluster is tightly packed, but later it spreads into a fairly loose panicle.

Bitter lettuce *Lactuca biennis* (also called tall or blue lettuce) is at first glance similar to the preceding species. However, the leaves of bitter lettuce tend to have

Wild lettuce is unusual in that it begins blooming when the heads are still tightly clustered and the stems remain meristematic. This is bitter lettuce *L. biennis.*

A few weeks later, this bitter lettuce stalk has opened up into a spreading panicle, with each head well separated.

much larger lobes and terminate with an arrowhead shape, unlike *L. canadensis*. Also, the leaves of *L. biennis* have scattered hairs across their underside, and the latex is white. *Lactuca biennis* in the flowering stage gets tall indeed. While typical height is 6–11 feet (2–3.5 m), I have seen plants as much as 16 feet (5 m) tall! The blossoms of this plant are a light, dull bluish white and are smaller than those of *L. canadensis*.

Another common species of wild lettuce, and the one commonly believed to be the ancestor of our cultivated lettuce, is the prickly lettuce *L. serriola*. Unlike the first two species described, *L. serriola* is an exotic plant that came to North America as an agricultural weed.

Prickly lettuce can be readily told from good and bitter lettuce by its solid stems and its leaves, which have stiff bristles along the margins and on the bottom of the midvein. These are not nearly as formidable as thistle thorns, and really they are harmless, but they are just stiff enough to get your attention. The leaf margins are often reddish. Prickly lettuce also tends to be a shorter and stouter plant, rarely exceeding 5 feet (1.5 m) in height. The flowers of prickly lettuce are yellow, resembling those of good lettuce.

A peculiar feature of prickly lettuce is that its leaves will turn to optimize their exposure to sunlight. It is common to find all the leaves in plane with one another, giving the impression that the entire plant has been pressed between

left Flowering panicle of *L. serriola*. In flower, lettuces are easy to distinguish from sow thistles by the much smaller and more numerous flowerheads in a spreading panicle.

right Prickly lettuce *L. serriola* is the ancestor of cultivated lettuce, although it is generally quite bitter. Note the leaves twisting in the sunlight.

below Prickly lettuce *L. serriola*. The leaves and petioles have twisted to optimize exposure to sunlight.

two pieces of plywood. When this occurs, prickly lettuce can easily be distinguished at a glance. This trait has earned it the alternate name of compass plant—but this epithet causes confusion, because it is normally associated with the genus *Silphium*.

Lactuca serriola is more often confused with sow thistles than with the other lettuces, but it can easily be told from them by the solid stem and the spines on the bottom of the light midvein.

The three species mentioned above are the most common and widespread wild lettuces in North America. Wild food books generally lump them together for discussion, which is unfortunate because their eating qualities are remarkably different. Most of this account will focus on good, bitter, and prickly lettuce, but there are several other wild lettuce species in North America, some native and some exotic. All are edible, but I have not tried every one of them.

Lactuca floridana, known as Florida or woodland lettuce, is a tall, blue-flowered species of woodland openings, roadsides, stream banks, and brushy areas in the eastern United States and Canada, being most common in the Southeast. The leaves often have long petioles, or they may resemble those of *L. biennis*; the latex is white.

Lactuca ludoviciana, called western, prairie, or biannual lettuce, is found in fields and prairies. It is most common in the Plains but is found throughout the western two-thirds of the United States. The flowerheads, larger than our other lettuces, are light blue or pale yellow. The leaves, like those of prickly lettuce, are spiny on the margins as well as the bottom of the midvein. They are somewhat bitter but good when young and tender.

Lactuca pulchella, usually called blue lettuce, is a weedy perennial primarily found in western North America. It rarely exceeds 4 feet (1.2 m) in height and bears leaves with a small number of deep sinuses and large lobes.

Wall lettuce *L. muralis* is an abundant weed about human habitations in the Pacific Northwest. This lettuce has tiny yellow flowerheads with only five ray florets each. The leaves have a small number of large triangular lobes, with a very

Leaves of *L. muralis* are characterized by having most of their leaf surface in the terminal lobe.

Western lettuce *L. ludoviciana* is a native species that has prickly midveins and leaf margins. It can be hard to tell from prickly lettuce when young, but the leaves do not twist in the sunlight. The young leaves make a slightly bitter salad green and a nice potherb when boiled and drained.

large terminal lobe. This lettuce lacks the hairs on the bottom of the midvein and is sometimes classified in its own genus as *Mycelis muralis*. The leaves and shoots are somewhat bitter but acceptable in salads when young.

Launea intybacea, another related species called "wild lettuce," is a weed found in parts of Florida and Texas. This species is also edible (Whetstone and Brodeur, 2006), but I have never eaten it and it is not a subject of this chapter.

Range and Habitat

The two common native wild lettuces, *L. canadensis* and *L. biennis*, are found throughout most of North America in wooded areas. Both are occasional members of the forest understory that reproduce prolifically after disturbances such as construction, logging, or windstorms. They tend to be common in river-bottom forests, along roads and trails, in old fields that are becoming overgrown with

left Good lettuce on the left, bitter lettuce on the right, showing typical height differential. While it is hard to explain the difference between these two verbally, it can easily be seen—and tasted.

right This flower stalk shoot of *L. canadensis* is tender and delicious, especially when cooked, with a flavor very different from that of the young leaves. You can eat it down as far as it is tender. Note that no flowers have opened yet—an indication of good quality.

brush, and in the woods along field edges. They occasionally grow as weeds in the shadier parts of people's yards. Typically, good and bitter lettuce are found in the same kind of habitat, but at any particular site one or the other predominates for reasons that I am unable to discern.

Prickly lettuce is a plant of open country. It is locally abundant in pastures, old fields, roadsides, vacant lots, and agricultural fields. Like most exotic weeds, *L. serriola* is distributed widely across the more agricultural and heavily populated parts of the continent. It is known from across the lower tier of Canadian provinces and every state but Alaska.

One or more species of wild lettuce is present in every part of the continent, save for the Arctic. In arid regions they are confined to irrigated croplands.

Harvest and Preparation

Lactuca canadensis, harvested at just the right time, is a superb salad material. You want to get the leaves of plants in their *flowering* year, but just as the flower stalk is first beginning to push above the root crown. Ideally, the stalk will be 6 inches (15 cm) high or less, and it will be hard to notice because at this stage it is obscured by the leaves around it. The leaves of a basal rosette in a non-flowering year will be few and lie flat on the ground or nearly so; however, a rosette that is just about to send up a flower stalk will have a dense cluster of leaves that stand more or less erect—and this is what you're looking for. These leaves will also tend to be lighter green than those on non-flowering plants, and they are generally more folded along the midrib.

Look for these densely packed clusters of light green upright leaves in late spring or early summer. At this stage not only the greens, but also the shoot hidden among them, make a good base for a salad. There is no wild green that more closely approaches the flavor and texture of cultivated romaine lettuce. The leaves get progressively less palatable as they age, but are never totally inedible.

In early to mid summer, the rapidly growing lettuce flower stalk and the cluster of young flower buds at its apex make an excellent vegetable. These stalks and buds will be tender and break easily like the finest spears of asparagus, and can be cooked similarly. Their flavor is hard to describe, having a faint peppery quality that mingles with a rich green sweetness.

I consider *L. biennis* only marginally edible, on account of its overpowering bitterness. The name "bitter lettuce" seems to spontaneously generate when people taste this plant, and it is easy to remember. The flavor is unfortunate, because it is such an abundant plant. Every year I find succulent, tender specimens and just have to try them, for they look so good. And each time I have to spit them out after a few seconds. If you are going to eat this species, the greens are at their

Rosette of bitter lettuce. Compare to the photo of good lettuce at the beginning of the chapter.

least bad in the same stage of growth described for harvesting the last species. You can boil the leaves in a couple water changes to reduce their bitterness, and they actually turn out reasonably good. The shoots of bitter lettuce are massive and succulent. Deer love them. But not only do they have the potent bitterness of the leaves, they are also imbued with a terrible metallic flavor that stimulates contorted grimaces on most human beings. However, on several occasions I have cooked these huge, tender shoots in multiple water changes and rendered them mild enough to eat.

Occasionally, I have found bitter lettuce rosettes with leaves that were less bitter than usual—fine to mix with a few other greens, but nothing to write home about.

One would think that *L. serriola*, as the ancestor of the garden varieties, would be a fantastic salad plant. In fact, it's not too bad when extremely young—well before the flowering stalk begins to grow. At this time, the prickles will be so underdeveloped as to be totally innocuous. This species can also be a good potherb at this stage. As prickly lettuce gets older, it soon becomes extremely bitter.

In general, the other wild lettuces are primarily salad plants. They can also be used on sandwiches or as a raw nibble, much as one would use their cultivated counterparts. You can also eat lettuce greens as a potherb, but they will shrink drastically. The greens must be gathered when very young to be their most palatable, and even then many of our species are mediocre in flavor. Feel free to experiment with any of the other wild lettuces; there may be wonderful details waiting for you.

Sow-thistle

Sonchus spp.

Asteraceae – Sunflower Family

When I was eighteen I started building a little log cabin in northern Wisconsin near Lake Superior—the fulfillment of a childhood dream. It was a steep learning curve with many setbacks, so I didn't get to move in until I was twenty-one. With all those years of anticipation, it was one of the most exciting events of my life, and I still vividly remember many things from that first year in my cabin. I didn't have to go find Nature anymore; it came to me, and surrounded me. Like the snowshoe hare that lived beside the cabin, the weasel that raised her family in the wall, the great horned owl who hooted from the peak of the roof, the phoebe who nested under the eaves, and the six-foot wall of sow-thistles that sprang from the crumbling clods of red clay along the foundation, their brilliant golden blossoms swaying gently in the hot breezes of July. In this new place, an old familiar plant suddenly caught my attention and made my acquaintance.

A large, robust prickly sow-thistle *Sonchus asper*, just beginning to flower.

The distinct auricles of prickly sow-thistle.

Description

North America is home to three widespread and common species of sow-thistle, all of them introduced from the Old World. Sow-thistles are closely related to the dandelions and wild lettuces, a fact which will come as no surprise to anybody who has looked at them. In fact, some people lump the sow-thistles and lettuces together for discussion (Henderson, 2000), which I think is misleading. Many people have trouble telling these two groups apart, but the sow-thistles have no hairs or spines on the bottom of their midvein, as lettuces do.

The better edible part of the sow-thistle, in my opinion, is the young stalk. Find this when it is still very short but about to bolt. Break it off just above the base, strip off the leaves, and steam or boil it to produce an excellent vegetable; they are also good raw. To make these sow-thistle stalks truly excellent, peel off the outer skin before eating, as this layer contains most of the bitterness.

François Couplan (1994, 1998) is apparently quite fond of sow-thistle greens and praises them highly, calling them "one of the very best of all wild salads"—but few New World authors agree with him. Henderson (2000, pg. 155) says the flavor "ranges from bland to bad." I find this a little strange considering the popularity of chicory, dandelion, and marsh marigold among North American authors, for all of these plants seem to me at least as bitter as sow-thistle. I believe that, just as with the wild lettuces, the variety of opinions about sow-thistle stems partly from the variety of species, and the failure of many people to distinguish the particular kinds they are eating and writing about. Their culinary qualities differ substantially.

Perennial sow-thistle is primarily a source of leafy greens. These range from mild to bitter, and I cannot tell which are which by looking, so I just taste them and see. The younger leaves, harvested in spring and early summer, are more tender but not necessarily less bitter. The stems are generally too thin to use as a vegetable. This is my least favored species to gather.

Common sow-thistle's young leaves are a popular wild potherb and salad green; they are probably the best of our three species. The stems are often quite robust, and if peeled when still young and tender they make a succulent vegetable, raw or cooked. Their mild sweetness is much appreciated in salads or as a snack. The stalks are excellent stir-fried or steamed with other vegetables.

Prickly sow-thistle also produces excellent young stalks. After peeling, these stalks are light green, hollow, tender, sweet, and mild in flavor. They are delicious raw or cooked. The leaves are fairly good when very young, but the spines soon become a serious drawback.

Next time you're weeding your garden, keep your eye out for this invader. I'm not saying you should let it grow where you don't want it. But if you must get rid of it, do it at just the right time and get some food out of the deal.

Prenanthes, White Lettuce

***Prenanthes* spp.**

Asteraceae – Sunflower Family

Prenanthes is a simple and unassuming plant for much of its life: a root with a leaf. Later, if it enjoys some economic success, it might even grow a second leaf. Prenanthes persists like this year after year, storing energy in its root, until one spring it decides that it is finally ready for *the big event*. In this long-awaited growing season, the culmination of the plant's life, it transforms into something totally new: a tall stalk decorated with showy, drooping flowers. This terminal phase is apparently so bold and memorable that nobody seems to have noticed that anything came before it; I have never found a single written description of

Prenanthes alba leaves; this is what the plant looks like for most of its life.

what prenanthes *usually* looks like, nor of its life cycle. This seems like forgetting that salmon come from the ocean.

If you want to eat prenanthes, it is more important to know what it looks like during its first six years than during its last six weeks. And I'm assuming that you *do* want to eat prenanthes. Or at least, you're assuming that I do.

Description

The genus *Prenanthes* contains a number of species in North America. These plants go by a variety of common names, including white lettuce, rattlesnake root, and lion's foot. Since these names are inconsistently used and all are ambiguous in one way or another, I like to "commonize" the scientific name of the genus as "prenanthes," which means "drooping flower." The description I give pertains to *P. alba*, the species I am most familiar with.

The leaf shape of *Prenanthes alba* is remarkably variable. The youngest basal leaves, under an inch long, are arrowhead-shaped and flat with smooth margins. As they grow, the leaves become coarsely but sparsely toothed, and the reflexed lobes at the base grow wider. The largest leaves become deeply and erratically lobed and coarsely toothed. These larger leaves may reach 12 inches (30 cm) in length. The basal leaves of prenanthes grow on a petiole that is 0.6–1.2 times the length of the leaf blade and may be up to about 8 inches (20 cm) long. The petiole is light red or reddish green and has a groove running its length. It rises at about a 60 degree angle to the ground, but the leaf blade is roughly horizontal. The surface of the leaf is sometimes glossy and glabrous, but at other times it is quite hairy on the underside, especially when growing in the open. The leaves, and all other parts of the plant, exude a white latex when injured.

In this photo there is a striking array of shapes and sizes of *P. alba* leaves.

Prenanthes leaves may become deeply and erratically lobed such as these.

Study the leaf photos carefully, for if you want to enjoy prenanthes at its best, you'll need to recognize it in the absence of a flowering stalk. If you have any uncertainty, observe the plants until you find prenanthes in flower for positive identification, then thoroughly familiarize yourself with it so that you can recognize the lone basal leaves with ease.

As mentioned previously, prenanthes spends most of its life with just one or two leaves photosynthesizing and storing energy in its root. In the spring of its final year, the plant starts out with three to five large basal leaves—this is how you can tell in May which plants will be flowering in August. The flowering stalks are leafy, hollow, and unbranched except in the inflorescence, attaining 1.5–6.5 feet (0.5–2 m) in height. The leaves get progressively smaller and less lobed as one ascends the stem, and the petioles get shorter; the uppermost leaves are sessile.

The inflorescence occupies the upper third of the stem. It is much branched, with each branch terminating in a small cluster of nodding composite flowerheads. These are composed of an elongated cluster of usually nine white or pink ray florets with protruding, forked styles. These florets are surrounded by elongated, strap-like, light purple to greenish bracts. The entire flowerhead is usually a little over a half inch (8 mm) long. A prenanthes stalk in bloom is a dazzling sight. Flowering occurs in August or early September.

All our species of prenanthes are variations on this theme. Some are taller or smaller, hairier or smoother; some have smaller flower clusters, and some have leaves that tend to be more or less lobed. However, once you become familiar with one species of prenanthes, you should be able to recognize any members of this genus. Note, however, that several are rare or protected in different areas.

left When it finally blooms, prenanthes sends up a magnificent, towering stalk.

below Prenanthes flowers are very attractive.

Range and Habitat

The various species of prenanthes are found throughout most of the moist forests of the United States and southern Canada, with greater diversity east of the Great Plains. The western rattlesnake root *P. alata* inhabits stream banks and moist forest edges at low to middle elevations in the western United States.

Prenanthes alba is widespread in the eastern United States. This herb never grows in pure stands and doesn't have a particular habitat where it dominates, but it is one of the most ubiquitous woodland plants, being found in virtually every forest type in at least small numbers. Occasionally, where the soil is disturbed in semi-sunny situations such as young forests, stream valleys, rocky slopes, and recently logged tracts, this plant is abundant.

Other species of prenanthes are found in similar wooded or semi-open habitats.

Harvest and Preparation

Prenanthes is a green, leafy vegetable that is used like wild lettuce. The young, tender basal leaves, characterized by a rubbery feel and more glossy appearance than the older foliage, make a good salad green. These are not very well known,

You could eat any of the leaves shown, but the small, glossy, meristematic leaf to the right is ideal. It almost looks as if the larger leaf is trying to protect it from me.

but in my opinion they exceed the quality of several more popular related greens, such as sow thistle, dandelion, chicory, and most of the wild lettuces. The flavor is reminiscent of dandelion greens but milder, although still stronger than the best *Lactuca canadensis* leaves. Prenanthes leaves excel in texture, however, being extremely tender when young. Older leaves do get more bitter, and the variability from one plant to the next can be significant and hard to predict or account for. If the leaves are boiled and the water drained, most of their bitterness can be eliminated, leaving behind a pleasant flavor like that of cooked dandelion greens.

You can eat the tender leaves and tops of the plants as they send up flowering stalks in midsummer. However, the greens upon the stalks are more bitter than the basal spring leaves. I usually don't collect the stalks of flowering plants because I like to let them go to seed. When picking the basal leaves, I never take all of them from a plant, and I collect only in areas where they are common. Harvesting leaves will not kill the plant, but it will steal some of its energy and set back its flowering. I never gather large amounts of prenanthes—just a trailside nibble or enough for a serving of salad or pot greens.

Next time you're hiking in the spring woodlands, keep your eye out for this unobtrusive leaf. Once you learn to spot it, you'll see it more and more, giving you access to another excellent green for your wild salads.

Dandelion

Taraxacum officinale

Asteraceae – Sunflower Family

In the beginning of my wild food workshops, one of the most frequent questions that I am asked is: "You're not going to make us eat dandelions, are you?" This isn't posed by people who are afraid to try new things, for such people wouldn't come on a foraging trip to begin with. It is asked by people who have already tried dandelion greens on their own and found them bitter and unpalatable. At the same time, dandelions have a legion of enthusiastic defenders and evangelizers. Why the paradox?

Part of the problem resides in the wild food literature, which in my opinion downplays the bitterness of this herb and over-sings its culinary praise, misleading beginning foragers into thinking that they should immediately fall in love with a dandelion salad or plate of cooked dandelion greens. This just isn't so.

People climb mountains to see flowers less striking.

Even when carefully collected and properly prepared, *many people will dislike dandelion greens*—especially at first, and sometimes always. I know that swarms of dandelion lovers will be angry when I say this, but I think the conclusion is inescapable.

Dandelion greens are no more bitter than many of the salad greens commonly sold in supermarkets—in fact, they *are* sold in many supermarkets. But how much do you eat bitter greens? The answer to that question gives you a good idea how much use you have for dandelion greens. Denouncing the people who dislike bitter greens as having an "unsophisticated palate" will do nothing to improve the dandelion's reputation; it will only alienate the skeptics and make them more certain that we foragers are just delusional health nuts. Many people aren't compelled to culinarily imitate the French or Italians. For some open-minded people, the best reason to eat something is still because they like it, and dandelions may have failed to qualify.

However, the common disappointment with dandelions is just as much the fault of neophyte foragers.

In late May, shortly after my tenth birthday, my mother told me that dandelion greens were edible. She was cautiously trying to nourish the interest she was beginning to notice in me, and I think she figured that dandelion was the easiest and safest thing to identify. I asked her how I should prepare them, and she told me she thought they were just boiled. Within minutes I was excitedly pacing the lawn with an empty salad bowl. I found some nice-looking, large leaves at the edge of the yard in a place that was too steep to mow, picked a bunch, and came back into the kitchen. I boiled the leaves in a saucepan, forked them out, sprinkled on some salt, and started eating. I made it through several forkfuls, but only due to the momentum of my excitement. The greens were a little tough and very bitter. Not nearly as good as Lucky Charms or Froot Loops.

Many people have had a first dandelion experience like mine. But it wasn't the dandelion's fault that I collected leaves of the wrong size at the wrong time of year and had unrealistic expectations of them. It is a natural human tendency to want to experience a food all by itself, just to "feel it out" and decide what we think of it before accepting it into our diet. When we do this with dandelion greens, we are likely to reject them.

We don't, as a general practice, eat potatoes, dandelions, or any other vegetables "all by themselves." We eat them prepared in very particular fashions mixed with other ingredients and seasonings in very specific proportions, a fine art known as *cooking*. Dandelion greens are a popular food around the world and have long been cultivated as a vegetable. There are hundreds of delicious traditional dishes based upon them. For a plant to have entered so deeply into the food traditions of so many cultures, there must be something good about it. Although the greens are inherently bitter, it is a pleasant, clean bitter that one can become accustomed to and eventually even crave—and the other flavors of the plant are superb. Don't let that initial flavor scare you off; let it guide you in how to use this plant.

If at first you aren't crazy about the greens, the dandelion's incredible health benefits should give you ample reason to eat this herb in innocuous, diluted quantities. If your palate just won't become "educated" to them, that's alright. The greens may be the best-known dandelion product, but to me they are the least interesting. This much-despised weed offers something for everybody. In fact, all of its parts are edible. So if you have written off the dandelion, prepare to give it another try.

Description

The dandelion is probably the most recognized plant in North America, but we'll describe it here just for the exercise. It is an herbaceous perennial that never has a true stem. All of its leaves are basal, forming a rosette. The leaves are 4–16 inches (10–40 cm) long and get wider toward the tip. They are broken by erratic deep lobes which usually point back toward the base of the leaf. The leaf margin is extremely variable; it may have many deep lobes or few to none. Generally, leaves growing in the shade have fewer and shallower lobes. The midrib is usually lighter in color than the leaf blade. I'm proud of you for reading this far; almost everybody skips dandelion descriptions, including me. All parts of the plant, except the flowers, contain a white latex.

Flower stalks (peduncles) emanate directly from the root crown at the center of the rosette. These are hollow, leafless, and unbranched, reaching 4–18 inches (10–45 cm) in height and occasionally taller, especially in the shade. The stalk may be red-tinged, but in shade they are pure light green. Their surface may be glabrous or covered with extremely fine wool. Each stalk terminates in a single composite flowerhead—the familiar yellow dandelion—composed of many ray florets. The dandelion is, in my opinion, one of our most beautiful flowers. Soon after blooming, the white, fluffy head of parachuted seeds appears.

Can you imagine spring without 'em?

above Where there is more moisture and shade or competition, dandelion greens are less lobed and stand erect, like these. These look better for eating.

below Especially when growing in sunlight, dandelion leaves may be deeply incised, with tooth-like lobes pointing toward the center of the rosette.

A few plants are frequently confused with dandelion. Chicory and wild lettuce rosettes look remarkably similar, although in flowering stages there is no chance of confusing these plants. Hairy cat's ear *Hypochaeris radicata* and its close relatives are also sometimes confused with dandelion at a glance, but they can be readily told apart. For more details, see the key on page 428. Luckily, all of these plants are edible. The red-seeded dandelion *Taraxacum laevigatum* is a very similar, closely related, and widespread weed; it is also edible.

Range and Habitat

The common dandelion is a Eurasian native that has naturalized throughout the United States and Canada, becoming perhaps the most ubiquitous plant on the continent. Dandelion is most common in hayfields, pastures, meadows, lawns, parks, gardens, empty lots, and other disturbed areas. It is also plentiful along forested roads and trails, and can be found scattered deep into the woods, especially on hillsides. Dandelions appear in at least small numbers in every upland, non-arid habitat, from full sun to heavy shade, but they thrive in full sun. They can handle virtually any soil but do best in productive agricultural soils with good moisture levels. Dandelions are most abundant in agricultural and residential landscapes.

Harvest and Preparation

Greens: Dandelion greens are usually picked in early spring before the plants have flowered. The best leaves grow in rich, moist soil in locations where the plants do not get mowed. If there is a little shade or competition, the leaves usually stand erect rather than lie on the ground, which means they are more likely to be clean. Don't pick leaves from dandelions that grow all alone on bare ground exposed to full sun, as these usually have a stronger flavor, tougher texture, and dirt clinging to them.

The best dandelion greens, collected in early spring, are milder in flavor and more tender than the older leaves, but they are still somewhat bitter. Many dandelion aficionados claim that the spring greens are not bitter. I think this may be because, to most people, "bitter" means "I don't like it," and "I like it" means "not bitter." I suspect that even the staunchest dandelion defenders can taste something bitter in them, but many feel like admitting to the bitterness would be conceding defeat (like the guy who slathers Tabasco sauce on saltines at a party and eats them jovially while claiming, "It's not *hot*.") It is easy to get around the observation that dandelions are bitter by defining *bitter* as "too bitter."

Even Peter Gail, a dandelion lover if ever there was one, agrees:

> "Dandelions are inherently bitter. You need to know that from the start. But, because they are so nutritious and have so many potential health-giving properties, it is worth finding a way to mask or reduce the bitterness." (Gail, 1994, pg. 14)

Dandelion greens are generally eaten as a spring tonic. In former times, before the advent of technology that facilitated the availability of year-round produce of all sorts, dandelion greens were far more popular. After a long winter without fresh vegetables, these nutrient-packed greens were strongly craved—and with good reason. Dandelion greens are extremely high in vitamins A, K, and beta carotene. They are also high in vitamins E, C, thiamine, riboflavin, B6, folate, and the minerals calcium, iron, potassium, and manganese (USDA NNDSR 21). The traditional process of boiling and draining reduces some of the nutrients, but still leaves an incredibly nutritious food.

It can be hard to differentiate between liking something's taste and simply craving it; both play a part in the dandelion's popularity. People who really enjoy dandelion greens will eat them all summer. Indeed, I feel that the difference between the flavor of spring and summer dandelion greens is often exaggerated.

Dandelion leaves are eaten raw or cooked. In a salad I like them mixed with milder greens. If you use them alone a heavy application of dressing helps mask the bitterness. More often, dandelion greens are used as a potherb. After washing thoroughly, the leaves can be steamed or cooked in a covered pot with only the rinse water clinging to them. If you find the flavor too strong, you can boil them in voluminous water for five to ten minutes and then drain, which will eliminate much of the bitterness. This is how I usually cook my dandelion greens, often serving them with butter and a dash of salt.

There is probably more written about dandelion greens than any other wild vegetable, and I won't repeat most of that here. If you want to explore this fascinating green further, an excellent and interesting source of information in Peter Gail's *The Dandelion Celebration*, a small volume devoted fully to this herb's history, lore, nutrition, and culinary use. Within it you will find a variety of recipes, both traditional and innovative.

Some people store dandelion greens in quantity by freezing (parboiling first) or canning. A fresher storage method for the winter months is to dig up fall roots and store them in sand or soil in a bucket or box, leaving them outside in the cold. Later in the winter, bring them into a basement or cellar and the crowns will send up several crops of new leaves.

Crowns and Buds

A dandelion's taproot usually begins an inch (2.5 cm) or so below the surface of the soil. From the top of the root a funnel-shaped "crown" of leaves grows up to the surface and beyond. In early spring when the leaves are just beginning to grow, this crown consists of several young, tender, yellowish-white leaves and embryonic flower buds in the middle. If you cut the dandelion root just below its top you can pry out this crown. Cut the root carefully so there is just enough of it left to hold the crown together, then peel away the outermost leaves, which will be dirty. Now your dandelion crown is ready to eat in a salad or ready to cook.

I find these crowns preferable to the greens. They still have a little of the plant's characteristic bitterness, but when cooked it is lost in a sea of rich flavors. I usually boil or steam them. They are excellent in soups or just served with the seasonings of your choice.

However, the crowns are dirty—and hard to clean. It is a lot of work to get this small vegetable, and by the time one adds trimming, peeling, and rinsing, it is terribly frustrating to still find sand crunching between your teeth. This frustration caused me to nearly give up on dandelion crowns until one day I came up with a novel way to harvest them, which I have come to call *gouging*. Now I eagerly anticipate dandelion gouging every spring and eat more of the crowns than I do of the greens.

I harvest the crowns with a modified teaspoon, which I appropriately call my *gouger*. I found a teaspoon (silverware, not a measuring spoon) with a very stiff handle and neck and a rather narrow tip (it's hard to find such a teaspoon, but vital to making a good gouger) and filed the outer edges until they were sharp. That's it; the tool works perfectly.

left This cluster of dandelion buds is what you use the gouger on.

right A gouged dandelion crown, my favorite part of the plant.

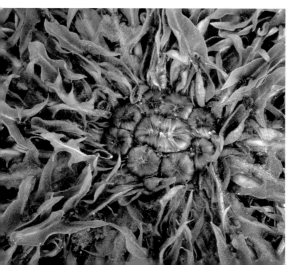

Find a large dandelion plant (the small ones are not worth your time) in early spring, before those in your area flower, and look into its crown. Just at or below ground level you will probably see a cluster of flower buds. Push the top of your spoon down along the edge of this cluster of buds about 0.5–0.8 inch (1–2 cm), depending on the size of the plant, then start to pry up as you continue pushing the spoon in. Soon the buds and some of the leafy material at the center of the crown will pop out of the ground. With a little practice you'll be able to guess how deep to gouge so that you can get as much of the crown as possible without going too far and getting dirt.

Gouging is very easy compared to digging the roots, cutting off the crowns, and then cleaning them. It is also more likely to result in a dirt-free final product. Another advantage to gouging is that it damages the plants far less than removing the whole crown and root top; you will be able to scoop out the centers of the same plants year after year. The season for gouging lasts right up until the flower stalks begin to grow, pushing the buds above the surface of the ground.

Flowers and Stalks

The dandelion's flower and flower stalk are the parts that I eat most often. I love to pluck a long, juicy stalk at its base and eat my way to the flower. They are quite bitter, but for some reason I really like them. I crave them, eating them pretty much every day from spring to fall, and those who know me have learned that I can hardly refrain from picking one that catches my eye. For an interesting dish, you can cook the flower stalks into "dandelion noodles." Find long stalks growing in shade or mixed with tall herbs and grasses, picking only those with young blossoms and light green stems. Remove the flowers, boil the stalks for ten minutes in a full pot of water, drain, salt, and serve.

The blossoms are picked and separated from the green bracts so that all one has is the yellow flower material. This has a variety of uses, including being the base for the famous dandelion wine. The blossoms can also be used fresh in salads, or they can be cooked with other vegetables. Fresh or dried they can be steeped to make a tea. Another popular use is dipping them in batter to make fritters.

Roots

The dandelion is a perennial that grows from a long, fleshy taproot. During the first year of growth this taproot resembles a slender parsnip. It is generally light on the surface with flesh almost uniform in cross section. During later years the surface becomes rougher and darkens, the center often develops a dark core, the

above Roasted dandelion roots, which need to be ground before brewing.

below Old dandelion plants with large roots, good for making "coffee."

bottom The root of a one-year-old dandelion plant makes a tender vegetable when cooked.

root often splits open lengthwise, grows large branches, and the top of the root becomes "multi-headed," growing additional necks each with its own crown.

Young dandelion roots make a decent vegetable; old roots are distinctly inferior. Small roots are not worth your time. So what you want are big, young dandelion plants, and you get these only under the best growing conditions. Crop fields and gardens tend to be good places to find dandelion roots for eating. The best time to get them is fall, but you can dig them year-round.

Thoroughly washed and scrubbed, dandelion roots can be simply boiled and served with a little salt and butter. As you'd expect, they have a hint of bitterness, but otherwise they are very tender and exhibit a fine and delicate flavor that reminds me a little of salsify. Dandelion roots can be used as you would use other root vegetables.

Unfortunately, since dandelion is a perennial and most plants live for several years, only a small percentage of the available roots are young enough to be nice and tender—and it's hard to tell the plant's age by looking at the rosette. However, roots of any age can be used to make another famed beverage: dandelion coffee. Dandelion root coffee has been drunk in Europe since ancient times and is still a commercially available commodity. This caffeine-free drink is considered a super healthy habit, but I drink it only because I like it. In fact, I prefer it over coffee, and I suspect that if dandelion were endowed with caffeine and coffee was deprived of this stimulant, the world would drink billions of dollars' worth of dandelion and the coffee tree would be an unknown component of African highland flora.

To make dandelion coffee, dig and wash a mess of roots and then proceed according to the instructions given in the next chapter for chicory. The flavor is said to be best in autumn or very early spring, but the roots can be used any time. I actually prefer dandelion root coffee to chicory, and, at least for me, it acts as less of a diuretic.

Isn't it remarkable how something so mundane can be so amazing? Hopefully this account can get you excited enough to try something new with dandelions, regardless of your past experiences with them.

Chicory

Cichorium intybus

Asteraceae – Sunflower Family

I know that this is a book about food, but to me, chicory has always been, above all, about beauty. Many photos display the startling deep blue of the individual blossoms, but this fails to convey the awesome spectacle of a country road at dawn on the fourth of July, winding along a pastured stream valley nestled between rugged wooded hills, with the chicory flowers lining each shoulder, held up by erratic stems so thin and green that they aren't visible from afar, making each distant blossom appear as a blue star, shining as it basks in the morning sun. Growing up, we used to take a road called the Blue Star Highway on the way to my grandparents' house, and I like to imagine that it was named for just such a sight.

If you want to share this beauty, you'd better hurry, for this most beautiful flower will close up before noon on a sunny day. But if you miss it, remember this forager's lesson: good things may not last, but to the faithful they come again.

previous page Chicory flowers.

below Chicory rosettes look remarkably like dandelion at a glance, although the midribs are often tinted red.

The two bottom leaves, with hairy midveins, are chicory; the upper leaf, glabrous, is dandelion. They're easy to tell apart if you look closely.

Description

Chicory is a perennial herb that grows from a large, deep taproot. It produces a basal rosette of leaves which looks remarkably like that of dandelion, to which it is related. These two plants are frequently confused in the rosette stage, and many people collect the greens indiscriminately. Chicory leaves tend to be slightly less deeply lobed than those of dandelion, but this characteristic is highly variable in both species. The primary distinction of chicory leaves is that they have long, erect hairs on their midrib, which dandelion leaves lack. The leaves are typically 3–10 inches (8–25 cm) long. Like dandelion, all parts of the plant except the flowers contain a white latex.

Chicory produces a thin, tough stalk with a small number of prominent, wide-spreading branches that zigzag between their multiple flowering heads. In this stage it has no resemblance to the dandelion. The stalk itself is a curious thing, looking almost as if somebody built a plant and forgot the leaves—or shrunk them on purpose so the flowers wouldn't be obscured. The stalk is typically 1.5–4 feet (45–120 cm) in height, but occasionally it exceeds 6 feet (2 m).

The stalk has alternate leaves, but except near the base, these leaves are so small that they generally remain unnoticed. The tiny upper leaves are sessile; they are entire or toothed rather than lobed.

The composite flower heads are well-spaced along the stalk and its branches, growing from the axils of the reduced leaves. Borne singly or in sets of two or three, the flowering heads are sessile or nearly so. When open, each flower head is 1.2–1.7 inches (3–4 cm) across, consisting of ray florets only. The tips of the outer rays are notably jagged, showing five teeth. The flowers are usually blue, but occasionally they are pink or white. Chicory flower heads open at dawn and remain open until late morning, sometimes longer if it is cloudy. They also will occasionally be open when it is cloudy during the afternoon. Each flower is open for one day only, and only a few will be open on the same day on a particular

A clump of chicory in typical roadside habitat.

plant. After the tiny dry fruits mature and blow away, the stiff floral bracts remain, often persisting through the winter. This facilitates easy recognition of the chicory stalk even long after it has died and dried up.

Range and Habitat

Introduced from Europe, chicory has naturalized and can now be found through most of the United States and Canada. In some regions it is an abundant weed, while in others it is inexplicably absent. But overall it is one of our more common herbs on disturbed ground.

Chicory has essentially three habitat requirements: full sun, well-drained soil, and disturbed ground. These conditions consistently occur on the shoulders of roads and highways, which is where chicory is usually seen. In fact, it is surprisingly difficult to find chicory growing very far from a roadside. Other habitats include railroad tracks, yards, hayfields, pastures, abandoned farm fields, fencerows, vacant urban lots, sidewalk cracks, along building foundations, and steep open hillsides.

Harvest and Preparation

Chicory has a long history of cultivation for both its leaves and roots and is still grown commercially and in gardens today. Among the cultivated forms are witloof chicory, which produces blanched leaves through *forcing*—growing indoors in reduced light during the winter. These forced chicory greens are called "Belgian endive." Some varieties are self-blanching—they don't need to be starved of light to produce light-colored leaves. Other varieties are grown for their thick leaf stalks (these are sometimes called "asparagus chicory") or for their dandelion-like leaves and roots (these are often called by the confusing name of "Italian dandelion").

In the wild, however, chicory leaves do not turn into "Belgian endives." Wild chicory greens are collected in early spring before the plant produces a stalk. They are used raw in salads or cooked as a potherb.

I have only one problem with chicory greens, and it's a big one: they are very bitter. Fernald and Kinsey (1958, pg. 369) write, "In spring the leaves are gathered somewhat indiscriminately with dandelion greens, having the same excessively bitter quality which some people find palatable in a potherb." I'm not one of those people, and I find that chicory greens are substantially more bitter than those of dandelion. I like them only when they are collected very early in the spring, at a time when they are so small as to be hardly worth the

In very early spring, chicory leaves may lack lobes. However, these are the mildest-tasting leaves, and this is the best time to get the crowns.

above Chicory crowns are best when the leaves have barely emerged, but they are smaller and harder to find.

below You can cut or gouge the crowns from slightly older chicory plants and trim the bitter leaves (or eat them, if you wish).

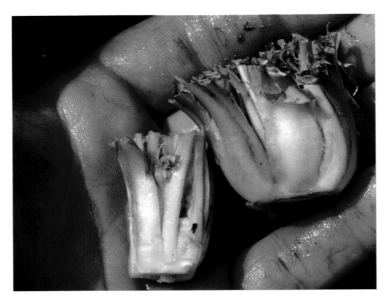

468

effort of collecting. Later in spring, I can tolerate them used quite sparingly in a salad. For a potherb I cook them in two waters to leach out some of the bitterness, but I generally don't do that anymore, because there are so many wonderful greens available at this time of year. Chicory seems to be a very well-known wild green, but I wonder how much this is due to the plant's familiarity because of its cultivation.

In early spring, chicory has a "crown" of young, developing leaves clustered at the top of its taproot. These are less bitter than the green leaves after they have begun to grow. Chicory crowns are harvested and used like those of dandelion. In my opinion they taste almost, but not quite, as good.

Chicory Roots

First-year chicory roots can be used as a cooked vegetable similar to dandelion and salsify, but this use is fraught with problems. The first-year roots are small; they comprise only a small fraction of the population, and it is hard to tell which ones are young by their rosettes. Another annoyance is the plant's tendency to grow in hard, gravelly soil that is difficult to dig and encourages poor shape in the roots. For this reason the use of chicory root as a vegetable is mostly con-fined to cultivated plants.

However, chicory roots of any age can be used to make the famous chicory coffee, by far the most popular use of this plant in the wild. This is an ancient

Chicory roots collected for roasting.

tradition in Europe, perhaps older there than the use of coffee itself. Chicory is grown commercially for this purpose and the prepared root can be purchased from some coffee suppliers and health food stores.

(Note: The following process is used to make a drink from chicory or dandelion root.) To make this beverage, dig and wash a mess of roots in autumn or early spring, when the plants do not have flowering stalks. Then dry the roots, either whole or cut into smaller pieces beforehand. A week or two on a rack or tray at room temperature should be sufficient, and once dried they will last for years. Roast the dried roots for twenty to sixty minutes in an oven at 325 degrees F (163° C) until they are brown and brittle. Watch them carefully to achieve the darkness of roast that you prefer.

In different sources you will see widely varying instructions for both roasting time and temperature. I have made good root coffee following different guidelines; what is most important is to recognize the proper color and texture of the final product you want. Many accounts do not specify if the roots are dried first or are being roasted fresh. I have done both successfully, but fresh roots require much longer roasting, and this is usually done at a lower temperature. It is also difficult to uniformly roast fresh roots. Roasted chicory roots can be ground in a flourmill, coffee grinder, blender, or mortar. Ground or whole, they can be stored in an airtight jar.

I brew chicory or dandelion coffee by adding one or two teaspoons of the ground, roasted root per cup of water and boiling for about three minutes, then pouring it into a coffee strainer and letting it percolate. You can also brew it in a percolator exactly like coffee, but the brief boiling extracts more flavor. While chicory does not taste exactly like coffee, it is close, and I actually prefer it. I like mine with a little milk and maple syrup. However, it acts as a strong diuretic.

Salsify, Oyster Plant, Goat's Beard

Tragopogon spp.

Asteraceae – Sunflower Family

I am always intrigued by the comparison of wild and cultivated food plants. Some of the best wild foods have never been cultivated. Some of our best cultivated foods were derived from wild ancestors that were mediocre, unpalatable, or even poisonous. Some of our domesticated plants are so utterly different from their wild ancestors as to be scarcely recognizable. Other cultivated vegetables are virtually identical to their wild brethren and can successfully go feral at the drop of a hat. A few, like asparagus, are sought when growing feral, while others are almost totally ignored. Salsify is in the latter category: the wild plants

If the salsify rosette didn't look so grass-like, this plant would be a much more popular wild edible. The leaves at the center of this rosette are at a good stage for eating. Young spiderwort (genus *Tradescantia*) plants look similar, but their leaves do not have latex.

are essentially identical to cultivated forms in appearance and quality, but they are only rarely collected.

Surely this versatile vegetable would be more commonly collected if it did not hide so well amongst the grasses. A trained eye is required to spot its long, grass-like leaves in a meadow. But eyes can be trained, and in this case the reward is well worth it, for salsify is both abundant and delicious, and it offers several different vegetables available over much of the year. So let me introduce you to this excellent and underappreciated food plant.

Description

There are three similar species of salsify found in North America, all of them introduced from Europe. For the forager it is not important to distinguish them, since all three are harvested and eaten in the same ways and are comparable in flavor. Salsify is a biennial herb with a stout, fleshy taproot. The first-year rosette consists of numerous linear, grass-like leaves up to 14 inches (35 cm) long. When growing on bare ground the leaves often spread out wide, lying flat upon the soil, but under competition from neighboring plants the leaves stand erect.

Although at a glance the salsify rosette looks grass-like, there are many distinctions which allow one to spot this composite. First is the existence of the rosette itself: few grasses have numerous leaves radiating symmetrically from a single point as in a salsify rosette. Another characteristic is the deeply folded, V-profile leaves of salsify. Grass leaves may be creased in this way, but rarely so deeply. Salsify also has a distinctly light-colored midvein, which grasses lack. If in doubt, break a leaf in the middle; on salsify you will note that the midvein is enlarged and hollow or airy, while in grasses this is never the case. And most reliably, a torn salsify leaf will exude a latex, white at first but soon turning brown—no grasses produce latex.

In its second year the salsify produces an erect flowering stalk typically 1–5 feet (30–150 cm) tall. It is a lover of warm weather and so does not begin growing until mid to late spring, but once the stalk begins to shoot up it reaches its full height in a few short weeks. The stem typically forks into two to thirty branches. Each branch terminates in a composite flowerhead, and after these bloom, new branches will sprout from some of the leaf axils below. I once counted 229 flowerheads on a large purple salsify plant in Victoria, British Columbia. Salsify stems are smooth, glabrous, solid, and round in cross section, generally ranging from 0.2–0.8 inches (5–20 mm) in diameter.

The stem leaves are alternate, linear, and clasping. They resemble the basal leaves but are shorter, proportionately broader, and somewhat wider at the base. All portions of the plant contain latex.

above left Flower of *Tragopogon dubius*. The bracts extend well beyond the yellow rays.

above right Flower of *T. pratensis*. The bracts are shorter than the rays.

below right Flower of *T. porrifolius*. This is the least common wild species but it abounds in some regions.

Salsify blooms from late spring through early summer, with a few stragglers continuing into August. The terminal flowering heads are 1.2–2 inches (3–5 cm) wide, borne singly, consisting only of ray florets, the outer ones much longer. Our more common species, *Tragopogon dubius* and *T. pratensis*, have yellow rays, while on the less common *T. porrifolius* they are dark purple. These plants are also known to hybridize, producing flowers with orange and reddish hues. Behind the flowers are ten to fourteen narrow, pointed, green bracts; on *T. pratensis* they are shorter than the rays, while on the other two species they are longer.

Salsify flowers open at dawn, unless it is cloudy—and in any case they close by midday. This has led to the plant being called "jack-go-to-bed-at-noon" in England. The name salsify is also derived from this behavior: *solsequium* (sunflower) in Latin corrupted to *salsifis* in French and finally *salsify* in English, although earlier competing spellings and pronunciations in England included *salsisix, salsafy,* and *sassafy*.

After flowering the heads close, then reopen a few days later as round, fuzzy seedheads consisting of dozens of elongated, beak-like achenes (what a layperson would call a seed) attached to a receptacle, each achene with a plume or *pappus* to catch the wind for dispersal. These fluffy heads can reach 3 inches (8 cm) in diameter. Because of them, many people call this plant "giant dandelion." Salsify heads are the most commonly noticed part of the plant; nearly everybody recognizes them, though perhaps not by name. Their most amazing feature, however, is invisible from afar. At a distance, the seedheads and the individual "parachutes" look dull white. But carefully pluck one and hold it up close to your eye. Each pappus is shaped like an inverted umbrella; hold it so that the sun shines into its bowl of interlocking fibers. The pappus of purple salsify will be golden brown, but those of the yellow species will shine like dazzling golden threads.

Once the salsify has flowered and released its seeds by mid to late summer, the plant dies and withers away.

Mature salsify plant with unopened flower buds, recently closed flowerheads, and the familiar seedheads.

Range and Habitat

All three of our species are nonnative, weedy, and widespread, inhabiting disturbed, sunny ground. Taken collectively they range across all of our continent, absent only from the northernmost and southernmost areas. Habitats include roadsides, railways, abandoned fields, meadows, crop field edges, backyards, vacant lots, urban waste areas, gravel pits, construction sites, riverbanks, and beaches. Their love for full sunlight can hardly be overemphasized. *T. dubius* prefers dry sandy or gravelly sites, while the other two species thrive with a little more soil moisture. However, they are all opportunists and their habitat needs overlap, and occasionally two or three species are found growing together.

On good soil salsify is especially dependent on soil disturbance, without which it soon gets outcompeted by tough perennials like timothy grass, goldenrod, and milkweed. Salsify is a lover of snowplows, which move around gravel and debris and gouge sod, creating good germination sites. This is why you will often see good stands of it along road shoulders and parking lots.

T. dubius is especially common in semi-arid sections of the West. The largest salsify plants I've seen were on the shoulders of interstate highways in Montana, Oregon, Idaho, Utah, and Colorado—where I wouldn't pick them, but conditions are perfect for their growth. The ground-hugging rosettes are too low to get mown, receiving full sunlight with little competition. Any rain that falls runs to the edge of the pavement before percolating, effectively irrigating the plants. The roots grow enormous under these conditions, and the second-year plants grow so fast that they can attain full height, flower, and go to seed between mowings by the highway department. Under these conditions I've seen salsify plants 6 feet (2 m) tall with stems over an inch (2.5 cm) thick, bearing over a hundred flowerheads.

Harvest and Preparation

Salsify is cultivated for its edible **taproot**, although it is not nearly as popular now as it was formerly. Taproots of wild plants can be used just like those of the cultivated form. Although they tend to be smaller, their flavor and texture are in no way inferior. Salsify roots are stout, cream-colored or light brown, rarely branched, and strongly tapering. They may be over an inch (2.5 cm) thick at the crown but rarely exceed 8 inches (20 cm) in length.

The time to harvest salsify roots is fall, winter (if you can get to them), and early spring. As with other biennials, do not harvest roots from plants with a stalk—seek rosettes only. These vegetables are easily dug with a regular shovel. Leave half or more of the plants to go to seed. After you scrub and wash the

Typical wild salsify roots. They are so tender that it can be hard to get them out of rocky soils without breaking, as happened here.

roots, they can be cut into sections and cooked in any way you please. Use them promptly, for cut ends will quickly discolor to a dark reddish brown. Salsify roots become very tender when cooked and have a mild flavor that has earned them such names as *oysterplant* and *vegetable oyster*. The flavor is rich, hearty, slightly sweet, and filling—perhaps even meaty—and these qualities are widely appreciated. I love salsify roots boiled until tender, drained, and then served with a sauce of butter, salt, and dill weed. They are excellent scalloped, mashed with potatoes, mixed with sweet corn, or served with other cooked vegetables like broccoli and carrots. Salsify roots also make a superb addition to a stew or pot roast.

Salsify roots can be stored all winter in a root cellar. Like parsnips, they can even tolerate light freezing without damage. They will last quite a while in the refrigerator if kept in a plastic bag to prevent drying out. They can also be stored by pressure canning. I have not tried drying or freezing them.

Salsify shoots—a fantastic and little-known vegetable. It only took a few minutes to gather these.

Actually, every part of the salsify plant is edible when it is tender. In the second year, just before the flower stalk shoots up, the rosette will produce a cluster of upright, light green **leaves** in its center. These leaves are very tender and have a mild, lettuce-like flavor. They make an excellent salad, the only drawbacks being their grass-like form and rapidly discoloring latex.

When the **shoot** is still very tender, up to a height of about 4–16 inches (10–40 cm), it can be cut at the base and eaten with its attached young leaves. These shoots are good when eaten raw and exceptional when cooked and served like asparagus. They are my favorite part of the plant.

Salsify shoot in late spring, about eighteen inches tall. A superb specimen to harvest.

left Flower bud and "fistulous peduncle" of *T. dubius*.

right *T. pratensis* has smaller flower buds, and the peduncle (stem) is not enlarged, nor as sweet.

Salsify produces a fourth vegetable—in early to midsummer when such things can be hard to find: the **flower bud**. These have a mild, sweet flavor and cook up nice and tender; they are excellent steamed and served with a little butter. Be certain to get the flower *buds* (pre-flowering) rather than the closed up heads *post-flowering*; the latter will be about twice as big and will usually show a little tuft of pappus near the end, plus the bracts will not be closed as tightly or

A handful of flower buds and peduncles.

as neatly as those on a bud that has not yet opened. The smaller buds are better than the larger buds that are nearly ready to open.

Even better than the flower bud is the fast growing, 3–7-inch (8–18 cm) stem (**peduncle**) that bears it. Remember that fast means tender—and few things grow as fast as salsify peduncles. One day there is but a tiny bud peeking from a leaf axil, and two days later there is a 6-inch (15 cm) stem in the same place, terminating with a flower bud nearly ready to open. I make my way through a salsify patch picking one or two of these from each plant until I get a small handful. I usually eat both the stem and bud at the same time, but the stems taste better. These peduncles are the sweetest part of the plant and I like them best raw, sometimes eating them in the field and saving the flower buds to be cooked later. On *T. pratensis* the flower stems are rather slender, but on the other two species they become enlarged and hollow, with *T. dubius* having the best flavor. Since new flowers appear erratically upon the plant for two to three weeks after the first heads have bloomed, the season for the flower buds and peduncles lasts fairly long.

Posing as a tuft of grass, the rosettes of salsify grow unobtrusively but abundantly in meadows and on roadsides across North America. Learn to spot this disguised composite and you will have one more gourmet vegetable, bearing five edible parts, conveniently at your disposal. One more weed come to life and given meaning, one more secret brought to light: how beautiful it is to forage!

Bibliography

Adovasio, J.M., J.D. Gunn, J. Donahue, and R. Stuckenrath. 1978. "Meadow-croft Rock Shelter, 1977: An Overview." *American Antiquity* Vol. 13 No. 4, pp. 632–651.

Allen, Geraldine A. and Kenneth R. Robertson. 2002. *"Erythronium." Flora of North America* Vol. 26, pp. 153–164. Oxford: Oxford University Press.

Anderson, M. Kat. 2005. *Tending the Wild: Native American Knowledge and the Management of California's Natural Resources.* Berkeley: University of California Press.

Anderson, M. Kat and Michael G. Barbour. 2003. "Simulated Indigenous Management: A New Model for Ecological Restoration in National Parks." *Ecological Restoration* Vol. 21 No. 4, pp. 269–277.

Angier, Bradford. 1969. *Feasting Free on Wild Edibles.* Harrisburg: Stackpole.

Angier, Bradford. 1974. *Field Guide to Edible Wild Plants.* Harrisburg: Stackpole.

Bailey, L.H. 1916. *The Standard Cyclopedia of Horticulture.* New York: MacMillan. Vol. IV.

Balfour, Edward. 1873. *Cyclopaedia of India and of eastern and Southern Asia, Commercial, Industrial, and Scientific* (Ed. 2). Scottish and Adelphi Press.

Barley, T. M. and Ronald L. McGregor. 1986. *Flora of the Great Plains.* Lawrence: University of Kansas Press.

Barnes, Burton V. and Warren H. Wagner, Jr. 1981. *Michigan Trees.* Ann Arbor: University of Michigan Press.

Basgall, Mark E. 1987. "Resource Intensification Among Hunter-Gatherers: Acorn Economics in Prehistoric California." *Research in Economic Anthropology* 9, pp. 21–52.

Bean, Lowell John. 1972. *Mukat's People: The Cahuilla Indians of Southern California.* Berkeley: University of California Press.

Behr, Hans Herman. 1889. "On the Poisonous Plants Indigenous to California." *American Druggist* Vol. XVIII No. II.

Benoliel, Doug. 1974. *Northwest Foraging.* Lynnwood, WA: Signpost.

Black, Brent and Ingrid Fordham. 2005. "Autumn olive: weed or new cash crop?" *Proceedings of the Mid-Atlantic Fruit and Vegetable Convention* 2: 15–16.

Boas, Franz. 1921. *Ethnology of the Kwakiutl.* Bureau of American Ethnology, 35th Annual Report, 1913–14, pp. 43–1473.

Bowen, 'Asta. 1988. *The Huckleberry Book.* Helena: American Geographic.

Bowers, Janice Emily. 1993. *Shrubs and Trees of the Southwest Deserts.* Tucson: Western National Parks Association.

Brill, Steve. 1994. *Identifying and Harvesting Edible and Medicinal Plants in Wild (and Not So Wild) Places*. New York: Morrow.

Brothwell, Don R. and Patricia Brothwell. 1969. *Food In Antiquity*. London: Thames & Hudson.

Brown, Donald J. 2004. "Standardized Elderberry Syrup Shortens the Severity and Duration of Influenza in Adults." *Journal of the American Botanical Council* No. 63, 16–17.

Brown, O. Phelps. 1867. *The Complete Herbalist; or, The People Their Own Physicians by the Use of Nature's Remedies*. O. Phelps Brown.

Brown, Tom Jr. 1985. *Tom Brown's Field Guide to Wild Edible and Medicinal Plants*. New York: Berkley.

Bruneton, Jean. 1999. *Toxic Plants Dangerous to Humans and Animals* (Translated from French by Caroline K. Hatton). Paris: Lavoisier.

Buchholtz, K. P., B.H. Grigsby, O.C. Lee, F.W. Slife, C.J. Willard, and N.J. Volk. 1960. *Weeds of the North Central States*. Urbana: University of Illinois Agricultural Experiment Station.

Chadde, Steve W. 2002. *A Great Lakes Wetland Flora* (Ed. 2). Laurium, MI: Pocketflora Press.

Chestnut, V.K. 1902. "Plants Used by the Indians of Mendocino County, California." *Contributions From the U.S. National Herbarium* 7, pp. 295–408.

Chopra, R.N., R.L. Badhwar, and S. Ghosh. 1965. *Poisonous Plants of India* Vol. II. New Delhi: Indian Council of Agricultural Research.

Cippolini, Martin L. and Douglas J. Levy. 1997. "Why Are Some Fruits Toxic? Glycoalkaloids in *Solanum* and Fruit Choice by Vertebrates." *Ecology* Vol. 78, No. 3, pp. 782–798.

Clarke, Charlotte Bringle. 1977. *Edible and Useful plants of California*. Berkeley: University of California Press.

Coon, Nelson. 1957. *Using Wayside Plants*. New York: Hearthside.

Couplan, François. 1994. *Guide des plantes sauvages comestibles et toxiques*. Paris: Delachaux et Niestlé.

Couplan, François. 1998. *The Encyclopedia of Edible Plants of North America*. New Canaan, CT: Keats Publishing.

Crowe, Andrew. 2004. A Field Guide to the Native Edible Plants of New Zealand. Auckland: Penguin.

Cowan, C. Wesley and Patty Jo Watson (Eds.). 1992. *The Origins of Agriculture: An International Perspective*. Washington, DC: Smithsonian.

Defelice, Michael S. 2003. "The Black Nightshades, *Solanum nigrum* L. et al: Poison, Poultice, and Pie." *Weed Technology* Vol. 17 No. 2, pp. 421–427.

Densmore, Frances. 1928. "Uses of Plants by the Chippewa Indians." *Forty-Fourth Annual Report of the Bureau of American Ethnology*.

Derby, Blanche Cybele. 1997. *My Wild Friends: Free Food From Field and Forest.* Northampton, MA: White Star Press.

Derby, Blanche Cybele. 2001. More *My Wild Friends.* Northampton, MA: Wild Weed Woman Press.

Derig, Betty G. and Margaret C. Fuller. 2001. *Wild Berries of the West.* Missoula: Mountain Press.

Deshpande, Usha S. and S.S. Deshpande. 1991. "Legumes." *Foods of Plant Origin: Production, Technology, and Human Nutrition.* (Eds. D.K. Salunkhe and S.S. Deshpande) pp. 137–300. New York: Van Nostrand Reinhold.

Detling, LeRoy E. 1936. "The Genus *Dentaria* in the Pacific States." *American Journal of Botany*, Vol. 23 No. 8, pp. 570–576.

Diamond, Jared. 1997. *Guns, Germs, and Steel: The Fates of Human Societies.* New York: Norton.

Dogan, Yunus, Suleyman Baslar, Gungor Ay, and Hasan Huseyin Mert. 2004. "The Use of Wild Edible Plants in Western and Central Anatolia (Turkey)." *Economic Botany* Vol. 58 No. 4, pp. 684–690.

Dufeillay, M. Pihan. 1838. "Observations d'empoisonnement par les Baies de Morelle noir, *Solanum nigrum*" *Journal De La Section de Medecine de la Societe Academique du Departement de la Loire-Inferieure.* Vol. 14. Nantes: Mellinot.

Duke, James. 1987. *CRC Handbook of Medicinal Herbs.* Boca Raton: CRC Press.

Dunal, Michel-Felix. 1813. *Histoire naturelle medicale et economique des Solanum et des genres qui ont ete confondus avec eux.* Paris: Montpellier, Koenig & Renaud.

Edmonds, Jennifer M. and James A. Chweya. 1997. *Black Nightshades.* Solanum Nigrum *L. and related species. Promoting the conservation and use of underutilized and neglected crops. 15.* Institute of Plant genetics and Crop Plant research, Gatersleben /International Plant Genetic Resources Institute, Rome, Italy.

Elias, Thomas S. 1980. *Trees of North America.* New York: Times Mirror.

Elias, Thomas S. and Peter A. Dykeman. 1982. *Field Guide to North American Edible Wild Plants.* New York: Outdoor Life Books.

Elmore, Frances. 1976. *Shrubs and Trees of the Southwest Uplands.* Tucson: Southwest Parks and Monuments Association.

Elpel, Thomas J. 2000. *Botany in a Day* (Ed. 4). Pony, MT: HOPS Press.

Elpel, Thomas J. 2002. *Participating in Nature* (Ed. 5). Pony, MT: HOPS Press.

Emery, Carla. 1994. *The Encyclopedia of Country Living (An Old Fashioned Recipe Book)* (Ed. 9). Seattle: Sasquatch Books.

Fackelmann, Kathy. 1993. "Food, Drug, or Poison?" *Science News* Vol. 143 No. 20, pp. 312–314.

Fagan, Brian. 2003. *Before California.* Lanham, MD: Rowman and Littlefield.

Farrar, John Laird. 2006. *Trees of the Northern United States and Canada.* Ames: Blackwell.

Farre, M. et al. 1989. "Fatal Oxalic Acid Poisoning From Sorrel Soup." *Lancet* 2 pp. 8678–8679.

Feder, Kenneth L. 1996. *Frauds, Myths, and Mysteries: Science and Pseudoscience in Archaeology* (Ed. 2). Mountain View, CA: Mayfield.

Fergus, Charles. 2005. *Trees of New England*. Guilford, CT: Globe Pequot.

Fernald, Merritt Lyndon and Alfred Charles Kinsey. 1958. *Edible Wild Plants of Eastern North America*. New York: Harper & Row.

Fischer, Pierre C. 1989. *70 Common Cacti of the Southwest*. Tucson: Western National Parks Association.

Fish, Paul R., Suzanne K. Fish, Austin Long, and Charles Miksicek. 1986. "Early Corn Remains from Tumamoc Hill, Southern Arizona." *American Antiquity* Vol. 51 No. 3, pp. 563–572.

Fisher, B. 1977. " 'Instant' Fruit – It's hard to Ask More." *Organic Gardening and Farming* 24, pp. 74–75.

Fleuret, Anne. 1979. "The Role of Wild Foliage Plants in the Diet: A Case Study from Leshoto, Tanzania." *Ecology of Food and Nutrition* Vol. 18, pp. 87–93.

Fordham, I.M., B.A. Clevidence, E. R. Wiley, and R. H. Zimmermann. 2001. "Fruit of the autumn-olive: a rich source of lycopene." *HortScience* Vol. 36 No. 6, pp. 1136–1137.

Frohne, Deitrich and Hans Jurgen Pfander. 2005. *Poisonous Plants*, Ed. 2. (Translated from German by Inge Alford.) Portland, OR: Timber Press.

Gail, Peter. 1994. *The Dandelion Celebration*. Cleveland: Goosefoot Acres.

Gbile, Z.O. and S.K. Adesina. 1988. "Nigerian *Solanum* Species of Economic Importance." *Annals of the Missouri Botanical Garden*, Vol. 75 No. 3, pp. 862–865.

Gebauer, Anne Birgitte and T. Douglas Price (Eds.) 1992. *Transitions to Agriculture in Prehistory*. Madison: Prehistory Press.

Gibbons, Euell. 1962. *Stalking the Wild Asparagus*. New York: McKay.

Gibbons, Euell. 1964. *Stalking the Blue-Eyed Scallop*. New York: McKay.

Gibbons, Euell. 1966. *Stalking the Healthful Herbs*. New York: McKay.

Gibbons, Euell. 1971. *Stalking the Good Life*. New York: McKay.

Gibbons, Euell. 1973. *Stalking the Faraway Places*. New York: McKay.

Gibbons, Euell and Gordon Tucker. 1979. *Euell Gibbons' Handbook of Edible Wild Plants*. Virginia Beach: Donning.

Gifford, E. W. 1971. "Californian Balanophagy." *The California Indians, A Source Book* (Eds. R. F. Heizer and M. A. Whipple). Berkeley: University of California Press.

Gilbert, Elizabeth. 2002. *The Last American Man*. New York: Penguin.

Gilmore, Melvin R. 1977. *Uses of Plants by the Indians of the Missouri River Region*. University of Nebraska Press (reprint: original publication 1919).

Gleason, Henry A. and Arthur Cronquist. 1991. *Manual of Vascular Plants of Northeastern United States and Adjacent Canada* (Ed. 2). Bronx: NY Botanical Garden.

Glover, Ian C. 1977. "The Late Stone Age in eastern Indonesia." *World Archaeology* Vol. 9 No. 1, pp. 42–61.

Gregg, Susan Alling. 1988. *Foragers and Farmers: Population Interaction and Agricultural Expansion in Prehistoric Europe.* Chicago: University of Chicago Press.

Grimm, William Carey. 1957. *The Book of Shrubs.* New York: Bonanza.

Grodner, Michele, Sara Long Anderson, and Sandra DeYoung. 1996. *Foundations and Clinical Applications of Nutrition.* St Louis: Mosby.

Guinand, Yves and Dechassa Lemessa. 2001. *Ethiopia: Famine Food Field Guide.* Addis Ababa: UN-EUE.

Haaland, Randi. 1995. "Sedentism, Cultivation, and Plant Domesticaiton in the Holocene Middle Nile Region." *Journal of Field Archaeology* Vol. 22 No. 2, pp. 157–174.

Hall, Alan. 1973. *The Wild Food Trailguide.* New York: Holt, Rhinehart, and Winston.

Hall, Thomas F. and Willam T. Penfound. 1944. "The Biology of the American Lotus, Nelumbo lutea (Willd.) Pers." *American Midland Naturalist* Vol. 31 No. 3, pp. 744–758.

Halpin, Anne Moyer, ed. 1978. *Unusual Vegetables.* Emmaus, PA: Rodale.

Hammami, H. and A. Ayadi. 2008. "Molluscicidal and antiparasitic activity of *Solanum nigrum villosum* against *Galba truncatula* infected or uninfected with *Fasciola hepatica*." *Journal of Helminthology* Vol. 82 No. 3, pp. 235–239.

Hamel, Paul B. and Mary U. Chiltoskey. 1975. *Cherokee Plants and Their Uses—A 400 Year History.* Sylva, NC: Herald Publishing.

Hamerstrom, Frances. 1989. *The Wild Food Cookbook, From the Fields and Forests of the Great Lakes States.* Amherst, WI: Amherst Press.

Hansen, Albert A. 1925. "Two Fatal Cases of Potato Poisoning." *Science* 61, p. 340.

Harlow, William M. and Ellwood S. Harrar. 1941. *Textbook of Dendrology*, (Ed. 2). New York: McGraw-Hill.

Harries, W.N., F.P. Baker, and A. Johnston. 1972. "An outbreak of locoweed poisoning in horses in Southwestern Alberta." *Canadian Veterinary Journal* Vol. 13 No. 6, pp. 141–145.

Harrington, H.D. 1967. *Edible Native plants of the Rocky Mountains.* Albuquerque: University of New Mexico Press.

Harris, Ben Charles. 1961. *Eat The Weeds.* Barre, MA: Barre.

Harshberger, John W. 1916. *The Vegetation of the New Jersey Pine Barrens.* Philadelphia: Christopher Sower.

Hedrick, U. P. 1919. *Sturtevant's Notes on Edible plants.* Albany: J. B. Lyon.

Heiser, Charles B. Jr. 1969. *Nightshades: The Paradoxical Plants.* San Francisco: W.H. Freeman.

Heizer, R.F. and A.B. Elsasser. 1980. *The Natural World of the California Indians*. California Natural History Guides 46. Berkeley: University of California Press.

Helbaek, Hans. 1964. "First impressions of the Catal Huyuk plant husbandry." *Anatolian Studies* 14, pp. 121–123.

Henderson, Robert K. 2000. *The Neighborhood Forager: A Guide for the Wild Food Gourmet*. White River Junction: Chelsea Green.

Henry, C.J.K. 1990. "Body mass index and the limits of human survival." *European Journal of Clinical Nutrition* 44, pp. 329–335.

Herrick, James William. 1977. *Iroquois Medical Botany*. Ph.D. thesis, State University of New York, Albany.

Hesiod. *The Works and Days* (translated by Richard Lattimore, 1991). Ann Arbor: University of Michigan Press.

Hibler, Janie. 2004. *The Berry Bible*. New York: Harper Collins.

Hitchcock, Susan Tyler. 1980. *Gather Ye Wild Things*. New York: Harper & Row.

Horn, Dennis and Tavia Cathcart (Eds.). 2005. *Wildflowers of Tennessee, the Ohio Valley, and the Southern Appalachians*. Auburn, WA: Lone Pine.

Hoyt, P. B. 1874. "*Solanum nigrum* (Deadly Nightshade)." *American Observer Medical Monthly* Vol. II, 1874, pp. 372–384.

Hu, Shiu-Ying. 2005. *Food Plants of China*. Hong Kong: Chinese University Press.

Hyatt, Philip E. 2006. "*Sonchus*." *Flora of North America* Vol. 19, pp. 273–276. Oxford: Oxford University Press.

Kallas, John. 2003. "Cow Parsnips." *The Wild Food Adventurer*, Vol. 8 No. 1.

Kari, Priscilla Russel. 1995. *Tanaina Plantlore: Den'ina K'et'una* (Ed. 4). Anchorage: Alaska Natural History Association.

Kavasch, E. Barrie. 2005. *Native Harvests: American Indian Wild Foods and Recipes*. Mineola, NY: Dover.

Kays, Stanley J. and Stephen F. Nottingham. 2008. *Biology and Chemistry of Jerusalem Artichoke* Helianthus tuberosus *L.* Boca Raton: CRC Press.

Kershaw, Linda. 2000. *Edible and Medicinal Plants of the Rockies*. Auburn, WA: Lone Pine.

Keys, Ancel, Josef Brozek, Austin Henschel, Olaf Mickelsen, and Henry Longstreet Taylor. 1950. *The Biology of Human Starvation* (2 Vols.). Minneapolis: University of Minnesota Press.

Kindscher, Kelly. 1987. *Edible Wild Plants of the Prairie*. Lawrence: University of Kansas Press.

Kingsbury, John M. 1965. *Deadly Harvest: A Guide to Common Poisonous Plants*. New York: Holt, Rinehart, and Winston.

Koenig, Walter D. and Lauryn S. Benedict. 2002. "Size, Insect Parasitism, and Energetic Value of Acorns Stored by Acorn Woodpeckers." *The Condor* Vol. 104 No. 3, pp. 539–547.

Koenig, Walter D. and M. Katy Heck. 1988. "Ability of Two Species of Woodland Birds to Subsist on Acorns." *The Condor* Vol. 90 No. 3 pp. 705–708.

Korstian, C.F. 1927. *Factors Controlling Germination and Early Survival in Oaks.* Yale University School of Forestry Bulletin 19.

Krakauer, Jon. 1993. "Death of an Innocent: How Christopher McCandless lost his way in the wilds." *Outside*, Jan. 1993.

Krakauer, Jon. 1996. *Into The Wild*. New York: Villard. (Also, 2007 printing with certain alterations.)

Krumm, Bob. 1997. *The New England Berry Book*. Helena, MT: Falcon Press.

Ladd, Doug. 2001. *North Woods Wildflowers*. Helena, MT: Falcon.

Ladd, Doug and Frank Oberle. 2005. *Tallgrass Prairie Wildflowers* (Ed. 2). Guilford, CN: Globe Pequot.

LaFrankie, James V. 2002. "*Maianthemum*." *Flora of North America* Vol. 26, pp. 206–210. Oxford: Oxford University Press.

Lamothe, Ron. 2007. *The Call of The Wild* (Documentary film). Terra Incognita Films.

Lamothe, Ron. 2009. "*Into The Wild" Debunked*. http://www. Terraincognitafilms .com/wild/call_debunked.htm.

Larson, Gary E. and James R. Johnson. 2007. *Plants of the Black Hills and Bear Lodge Mountains* (Ed. 2). Brookings, SD: South Dakota State University.

Latham, J. Edward. 1963. "The Autumn-olive." *The American Biology Teacher*. Vol. 25 No. 1, pp. 18–20.

Lentz, David L. 1991. "Maya Diets of the Rich and Poor: Paleoethnobotanical Evidence From Copan." *Latin American Antiquity* Vol. 2 No. 3, pp. 269–287.

Leopold, Aldo. 1949. *A Sand County Almanac*. Oxford: Oxford University Press.

Lindley, John and Thomas Moore. 1876. *The Treasury of Botany*. London: Longmans, Green, and Co.

Loewen, Dawn C., Geraldine A. Allen, and Joseph A. Antos. 2001. "Autecology of *Erythronium grandiflorum* in Western Canada." *Canadian Journal of Botany*: Vol. 79 No. 4, pp. 500–509.

Logan, William Bryant. 2005. *Oak: The Frame of Civilization*. New York: W. W. Norton.

Lyle, Katie Letcher. 1994. *The Wild Berry Book*. Minocqua, WI: Northword.

Manandhar, Sanjay. 2002. *Plants and People of Nepal*. Portland, OR: Timber Press.

Marrone, Teresa. 2004. *Abundantly Wild: Collecting and Cooking Wild Edibles in the Upper Midwest*. Cambridge, MN: Adventure Publications.

Marshall, Fiona. 2001. "Agriculture and Use of Wild and Weedy Greens by the Piik Ap Oom Okiek of Kenya." *Economic Botany* Vol. 55 No. 1, pp. 32–46.

Mason, Sarah L. R. 1992. *Acorns in Human Subsistence*. Ph.D. Dissertation, University College of London.

Mason, Sarah L. R.. 1995. "Acornutopia? Determining the Role of Acorns in Past Human Subsistence." *Food in Antiquity*, pp. 12–24. Exeter, UK: University of Exeter Press.

Matsuyama, T. 1981. "Nut Gathering and Processing Methods in Traditional Japanese Villages." *Affluent Foragers: Pacific Coasts East and West*.

S. Koyama and D.H. Thomas (Eds.), pp. 117–139. Senri Ethnological Studies 9. Osaka: National Museum of Ethnology.

Mazuelos Vela, F., F. Ramos Ayerbe, and J.A.F. Ros de Ursino. "Le Fruit du Chene (*Quercus ilex*). *Oleagineux* Vol. 22 No. 3, pp. 169–171.

McMillan M. and J. C. Thompson. 1979. "An Outbreak of Suspected Solanine Poisoning in Schoolboys: Examination of Criteria of Solanine Poisoning." *Quarterly Journal of Medicine* 48, pp. 227–243.

McPherson, Alan and Sue A. Clark. 1977. *Wild Food Plants of Indiana and Adjacent States*. Bloomington: University of Indiana Press.

Medsger, Oliver Perry. 1939. *Edible Wild Plants*. New York: Macmillan.

Meyers, Katherine J., Tedmund J. Swiecki, and Alyson E. Mitchell. 2006. "Understanding the Native Californian Diet: Identification of Condensed and Hydrolyzable Tannins in Tanoak Acorns (*Lithocarpus densifolius*)." *Journal of Agricultural and Food Chemistry*, No. 54, pp. 7686–7691.

Moerman, Daniel E. 1998. *Native American Ethnobotany*. Portland, OR: Timber Press.

Mohney, Russ. 1975. *Why Wild Edibles? The Joys of Finding, Fixing, and Tasting*. Seattle: Pacific Search.

Mosyakin, Sergei L. and Kenneth R. Robertson. 2003. "*Amaranthus*." *Flora of North America North of Mexico*, Vol. 4. Oxford: Oxford University Press.

Muenscher, Walter Conrad. 1951. *Poisonous Plants of the United States* (Rev. Ed.). New York: Macmillan.

Muir, John. 1916. *A Thousand-Mile Walk to the Gulf*. Boston: Houghton Mifflin.

Murrell, William. 1884. *What to do in cases of poisoning* (Ed. 4). London: H.K. Lewis.

Nabhan, Gary Paul. 1985. *Gathering the Desert*. Tucson: University of Arizona Press

Newcomb, Lawrence. 1977. *Newcomb's Wildflower Guide*. Boston: Little, Brown.

Niehaus, Theodore F. and Charles L. Ripper. 1976. *A Field Guide to Pacific States Wildflowers*. Boston: Houghton Mifflin.

Niethammer, Carolyn, 1974. *American Indian Food and Lore*. New York: Collier.

Niethammer, Carolyn. 2004. *The Prickly Pear Cookbook*. Tucson: Rio Nuevo. North Dakota Department of Health and U.S. Centers for Disease Control, News Release, Nov. 5, 2008.

Nyerges, Christopher. 1999. *Guide to Wild Foods and Useful Plants*. Chicago: Chicago Review Press.

Ortiz, Beverly R (As told by Julia F. Parker). 1991. *It Will Live Forever: Traditional Yosemite Indian Acorn Preparation*. Berkeley: Heyday Books.

Oslund, Clayton and Michele. 2002. *What's Doin' the Bloomin'?* Duluth, MN: Plant Pics.

Pavlik, Bruce M., Pamela C. Muick, Sharon G. Johnson, and Marjorie Popper. 1991. *Oaks of California*. Los Olivos, CA: Cachuma Press.

Peattie, Donald Culross. 1953. *A Natural History of Western Trees*. Boston: Houghton Mifflin.

Peattie, Donald Culross. 1964. *A Natural History of Trees of Eastern and Central North America*. Boston: Houghton Mifflin.

Peterson, Lee. 1977. *A Field Guide to Edible Wild Plants of Eastern and Central North America*. Boston: Houghton Mifflin.

Phillips, Jan. 1979. *Wild Edibles of Missouri*. Missouri Dept. of Conservation.

Phillips, Steven J. and Patricia Wentworth Comus (Eds.). 2000. *A Natural History of the Sonoran Desert*. Tucson: Arizona-Sonora Desert Museum Press.

Pinkava, Donald J. 2003. "*Opuntia*." *Flora of North America North of Mexico*, Vol. 4. New York: Oxford University Press.

Plug, I. 1981. "Some Research Results of the Late Pleistocene and Early Holocene Deposits of Bushman Rock Shelter, Eastern Transvaal." *The South African Archaeological Bulletin* Vol. 36 No. 133, pp. 14–21.

Pojar, Jim and Andy Mackinnon (Eds.). 1994. *Plants of the Pacific Northwest Coast*. Vancouver, BC: Lone Pine.

Prescott, Philander. 1849. "Farming Among the Sioux Indians." *U. S. Patent Office Report on Agriculture*, pp. 451–455.

Purseglove, J. W. 1968. *Tropical Crops: Dicotyledons 2*. New York: Wiley.

Quin, P. J. 1959. *Food and Feeding Habits of the Pedi*. Witwaterssrand University Press.

Renfrew, Jane. 1973. *Palaeoethnobotany*. London: Metheun.

Rhoads, Ann Fowler and Timothy A. Block. 2005. *Trees of Pennsylvania*. Philadelphia: University of Pennsylvania Press.

Rhoads, Ann Fowler and Timothy A. Block. 2007. *The Plants of Pennsylvania* (Ed. 2). Philadelphia: University of Pennsylvania Press.

Rossen, Jack, Tom Dillehay, and Donald Ugent. 1996. "Ancient Cultigens or Modern Intrusions? Evaluating Plant Remains in an Andean Case Study." *Journal of Archaeological Science*, Vol. 23 No. 3, pp. 391–407.

Royer, France and Richard Dickinson. 1999. *Weeds of the Northern US and Canada*. Renton, WA: Lone Pine.

Sahlins, Marshall. 1972. *Stone Age Economics*. Piscataway, NJ: Aldine.

Saunders, Charles Francis. 1976. *Edible and Useful Wild Plants of the United States and Canada*. New York: Dover (reprint: original publication 1920).

Schilling, E.E., Q.S. Ma, and R.N. Anderson. 1992. "Common Names and Species Identification in Black Nightshades, *Solanum* sect. *Solanum* (Solanaceae)." *Economic Botany* No. 46 Vol. 2, pp. 223–225.

Schofield, Janice J. 1989. *Discovering Wild Plants: Alaska, Western Canada, The Northwest.* Anchorage: Alaska Northwest Books.

Servello, F.A. and R.L. Kirkpatrick. 1989. "Nutritional value of acorns for ruffed grouse." *Journal of Wildlife Management* Vol. 53 No. 1, pp. 26–29.

Seymour, Tom. 2002. *Foraging New England.* Guilford, CN: Globe Pequot.

Shen-Miller, J., Mary Beth Mudgett, J. William Schopf, Steven Clarke, and Rainer Berger. 1995. "Exceptional Seed Longevity And Robust Growth: Ancient Sacred Lotus From China." *American Journal of Botany* Vol. 82 No. 11, pp. 1367–1380.

Shils, Mauriuce E., James A. Olson, and Moshe Shike. 1994. *Modern Nutrition in Health and Disease*, (Ed. 8), Vol. I. Philadelphia: Lea and Febiger.

Siemonsma, J. S. and Kasem Pilvek (Eds). 1993. *Plant Resources of South-East Asia No. 8: Vegetables.* Wageningen: Pudoc Scientific.

Simms, C. 1997. "Garden Huckleberries." *The Garden*, Jan 1997, p. 19.

Smith, Huron H. 1928. "Ethnobotany of the Meskwaki Indians." *Bulletin of the Public Museum of the City of Milwaukee* 4, pp. 175–326.

Smith, Huron H. 1932. "Ethnobotany of the Ojibwe Indians." *Bulletin of the Public Museum of the City of Milwaukee*, Vol. 4, pp. 327–525.

Smith, Huron H. 1933. Ethnobotany of the Forest Potawatomi Indians." *Bulletin of the Public Museum of the City of Milwaukee* Vol. 7, pp. 1–230.

Smith, J. Russell. 1929. *Tree Crops: A Permanent Agriculture.* New York: Harcourt, Brace.

Soper, James H. and Margaret Heimburger. 1982. *Shrubs of Ontario.* Toronto: The Royal Ontario Museum.

Stern, Kingsley R. 2006. *Introductory Plant Biology* (Ed. 10). New York: McGraw-Hill.

Strother, John L. 2006. "*Lactuca.*" *Flora of North America* Vol. 19, pp. 259–263. Oxford: Oxford University Press.

Stuart, John D. and John O. Sawyer. 2001. *Trees and Shrubs of California.* Berkeley: University of California Press.

Sundberg, Scott. 2002. "New Records for Oregon." *Oregon Flora Newsletter* Vol 8 No. 2. Corvallis: Oregon State University.

Suttles, Wayne. 2005. "Resource Management: Incipient Agriculture?" *Keeping It Living.* D. Duer and N. Turner (Eds.). Seattle: University of Washington Press.

Tanaka, Yoshitaka and Nguyen Van Ke. 2007. *Edible Wild Plants of Vietnam.* Bangkok: Orchid Press.

Tardieu, Ambrose and Zacharie Roussin. 1875. *Etude medico-legale et clinique sur l'empoisonnement* (Ed. 2.) Paris: Bailliere et Fils.

Tatum, Billy Jo. 1976. *Billy Jo Tatum's Wild Foods Field Guide and Cookbook*. New York: Workman.

Taylor, Walter W. 1972. "The Hunter-Gatherer Nomads in Northern Mexico: A Comparison of the Archival and Archaeological Records." *World Archaeology* Vol. 4 No. 2, pp. 167–178.

Teit, James A. 1928. "The Salishan Tribes of the Western Plateaus." *Bureau of American Ethnology Annual Report*, Number 45.

Thompson, Steven and Mary. 1972. *Wild Food Plants of the Sierra*. Berkeley: Dragtooth Press.

Tilford, Gregory L. 1997. *Edible and Medicinal Plants of the West*. Missoula: Mountain Press.

Towers, Robert P. 1953. "A Case of Poisoning by Solanum nigrum." *Irish Journal of Medical Science*, 1953; No. 6, pp. 77–80.

Treadwell, Edward and Thomas P. Clausen. 2008. "Is *Hedysarum mackenziei* (Wild Sweet Pea) Actually Toxic?" *Ethnobotany Research and Applications* Vol. 6 : 319–321.

Trimble, H. 1896. "The Tannins of Some Acorns." *American Journal of Pharmacology* 68, pp. 601–604.

Tull, Delena. 1987. *Edible and Useful Plants of Texas and the Southwest*. Austin: University of Texas Press.

Turner, Nancy J. 1975. *Food Plants of British Columbia Indians, Part 1/Coastal Peoples*. Victoria, BC: British Columbia Provincial Museum.

Turner, Nancy J. 1978. *Food Plants of British Columbia Indians, Part 2/Interior Peoples*. Victoria, BC: British Columbia Provincial Museum.

Turner, Nancy J. and Sandra Peacock. 2005. "Solving the Perennial Paradox: Ethnobotanical Evidence for Plant Resource Management on the Northwest Coast." *Keeping It Living*. D. Duer and N. Turner (Eds.). Seattle: University of Washington Press.

Turner, Nancy J. and Adam F. Szczawinski. 1979. *Edible Wild Fruits and Nuts of Canada*. Ottawa: National Museum of Canada.

Turner, Nancy J. and Adam F. Szczawinski. 1991. *Common Poisonous Plants and Mushrooms of North America*. Portland, OR: Timber Press.

Turner, Nancy J., Laurence C. Thompson, M. Terry Thompson, and Annie Z. York. 1990. *Thompson Ethnobotany: Knowledge And Usage Of Plants By The Thompson Indians of British Columbia*. Victoria: Royal British Columbia Museum.

USDA, National Nutrient Database for Standard Reference, Release 21 (2008)

Vance, F.R., J.R. Jowsey, J.S. McLean, and F.A. Switzer. 1999. *Wildflowers of the Northern Great Plains* (Ed. 3). Minneapolis: University of Minnesota Press.

Van Wyk, Ben-Erik. 2005. *Food Plants of the World*. Portland, OR: Timber Press.

Voegelin, Ermine W. 1938. "Tubatulabal Ethnography." *Anthropological Records* Vol. 2 No. 1, pp. 1–84.

Voss, Edward. 1972. *Michigan Flora*, Vol. 1. Ann Arbor: University of Michigan Press.

Voss, Edward. 1985. *Michigan Flora*, Vol. 2. Ann Arbor: University of Michigan Press.

Voss, Edward. 1996. *Michigan Flora*, Vol. 3. Ann Arbor: University of Michigan Press.

Voss, Kenneth A., William J. Chamberlain, and Lucas H. Brennecke. 1993. "Subchronic Toxicity Study of Eastern Black Nightshade (*Solanum ptychanthum*) Berries in Sprague-Dawley Rats." *Journal of Food Safety* Vol. 13 No. 2, pp. 91–97.

Wagner, W.L., D.R. Herbst, and S.H. Sohmer, 1999. *Manual of Flowering Plants of Hawaii* (Rev. Ed.). Honolulu: University of Hawaii Press.

Wagnon, K.A. 1946. "Acorns As Feed For Range Cattle." *Western Livestock Journal* Vol. 25 No. 6 pp. 92–94.

Waino, W.W. and E.B. Forbes. 1941. "The chemical composition of forest fruits and nuts from Pennsylvania." *Journal of Agricultural Research* 62, pp. 627–635.

Weatherbee, Ellen Elliot and James Garnett Bruce. 1979. *Edible Wild Plants: A Guide to Collecting and Cooking*. Ann Arbor: Weatherbee and Bruce.

Weber, William A. 1976. *Rocky Mountain Flora*. Boulder: Colorado Associated University Press.

Whetstone, R. David and Kristin Brodeur. 2006. "*Launea.*" *Flora of North America* Vol. 19, p. 272. Oxford: Oxford University Press.

Whitaker, John O. Jr. 1996. *National Audubon Society Field Guide to North American Mammals*. New York: Knopf.

Wiersema, John H. 1997. "*Nelumbonaceae.*" *Flora of North America North of Mexico* Vol. 13. New York: Oxford University Press.

Witthoft, John. 1947. "An Early Cherokee Ethnobotanical Note." *Journal of the Washington Academy of Sciences* Vol. 37 No. 3, pp. 73–75.

Young, Kay. 1993. *Wild Seasons: Gathering and Cooking Wild Plants of the Great Plains*. University of Nebraska Press.

Glossary

Abscission: The natural separation of two bonded parts (such as a deciduous leaf from its twig before falling), usually occurring at a predetermined point, the *abscission zone*.

Achene: A dry, single-seeded fruit that does not naturally split open.

Acuminate: Tapering to a long, narrow, needle-like point.

Aerial: Growing in open air (as opposed to under the ground or water).

Alternate: Growing from opposite sides of a stalk at *different* points along its length (rather than at the same point as in opposite leaves). Not paired.

Anther: The pollen-bearing part of the stamen.

Antinutrient: A chemical that interferes with the body's absorption or utilization of nutrients.

Astringent: Causing the constriction of tissues.

Axil: The upper angle where a leaf or petiole joins a stem.

Basal: Growing from the base of the plant, attached near ground level.

Berry hook: A pole or stick with a hook on the end, used to pull down and hold out-of-reach branches for fruit picking.

Biennial: A plant that normally has a two-year life cycle, spending the first year as a stalkless rosette storing energy, and using that energy to produce a flowering stalk the second year, after which the plant dies. Biennials may spend multiple years as a rosette before flowering, however, if the growing conditions are poor.

Blanch: To briefly boil a vegetable in order to destroy enzymes and kill individual cells; generally done before freezing. Also, to cover growing plants so as to keep light from them, making them grow lighter in color, more tender, and less strong in flavor.

Blickey: A berry-picking container that straps onto the waist, leaving both hands free.

Bloom: A thin waxy or powdery coating that can be rubbed off. Often found on fruit and smooth herb stems, bloom gives the surface a lighter hue.

Boreal forest: The plant community that dominates most of Canada's forested regions, characterized by fir, spruce, aspen, white birch, and other northern plants.

Bract: A small, modified leaf found directly beneath a flower or flower cluster.

Bulb: A modified bud, such as an onion, in which the leaves are enlarged and thickened to store energy.

Calorie-day: The number of calories per day needed by an individual.

Parts of a Regular Flower

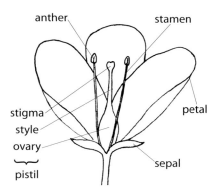

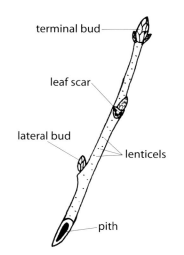

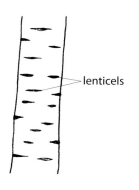

Calyx: The sepals of a flower, collectively. These sometimes remain attached to fruit after the flower has been fertilized.

Cambium: The layer of dividing cells that lies between the wood (xylem) and bark (phloem), and which produces both. Cambium is often erroneously called "inner bark." It would be more proper to call it "outer wood" because it generally remains attached to the trunk when bark is peeled off. In truth, however, it is neither bark nor wood.

Catkin: A soft, spike-like inflorescence of numerous small, petal-less flowers, often drooping.

Cauline: On or pertaining to the stem; often used in contrast to *basal*.

Chaff: The unwanted, inedible dried flower and fruit parts that are separated from a grain by rubbing and then removed by winnowing.

Chambered: Divided into compartments, often with hollow spaces, by transverse partitions; said of pith.

Channeled: Having a groove or depression running its length; usually said of petioles.

Climax community: A plant community that persists indefinitely in the absence of significant environmental changes; the last stage in plant succession on a particular site.

Clone: A colony of genetically identical plants or stems that have propagated themselves through some form of vegetative reproduction; a clone is essentially one large plant with many stems.

Cold storage: Storing food in a cool but not frozen environment.

Colony: A group of many individuals or stems of the same species of plant found growing together.

Composite: A flower cluster that appears as one flower (such as dandelion) in which many tiny florets are clustered on a receptacle. Also, any plant of the Composite family, all of which share this characteristic.

Compound: A leaf that consists of multiple leaflets (see *divided*).

Contradictory confidence: Such absolute certainty in a plant's identity that you would be willing to contradict anybody who told you otherwise; the same level of confidence with which you recognize familiar plant foods like bananas or pineapples.

Corm: The base of an upright stem, enlarged to store energy.

Corolla: The petals of a flower (collectively).

Corrugated: Having a rough surface texture formed by valleys, ridges, wrinkles, or folds.

Cotelydon: A seed-leaf; the portion of the seed that becomes a leaf upon germination, or this leaf. Dicots have two, monocots have one. Cotyledons are the first leaves to appear when a seed germinates; on dicots they are always paired and often look quite different than typical leaves.

Crenate: With rounded teeth on the margin; wavy or scalloped.

Cyme: A broad, flat-topped or convex cluster of flowers, the center flowers opening first.

Deciduous: Dying and falling away from the plant at the end of the growing season.

Dermatitis: Rash or irritation of the skin.

Dichotomous key: A tool used for identifying plants by repeatedly deciding which of two technical descriptions applies to it, narrowing down the number of possibilities

Flower/Fruit Clusters

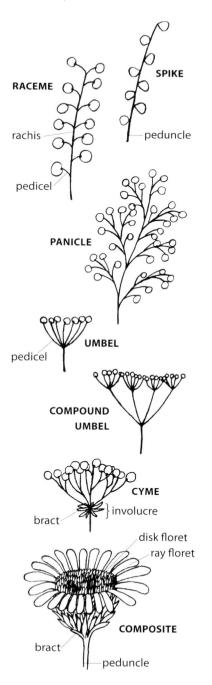

RACEME
SPIKE
rachis
peduncle
pedicel
PANICLE
UMBEL
pedicel
COMPOUND
UMBEL
CYME
bract } involucre
disk floret
ray floret
COMPOSITE
bract
peduncle

Simple Leaf Shapes

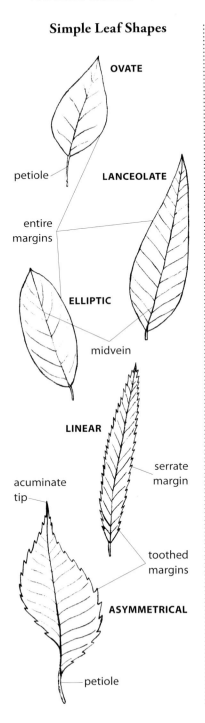

OVATE

petiole

LANCEOLATE

entire
margins

ELLIPTIC

midvein

LINEAR

serrate
margin

acuminate
tip

toothed
margins

ASYMMETRICAL

petiole

with each set of descriptions until the species is identified.

Dicot: (Short for dicotyledon) One of the two major divisions within the Angiosperms (typical flowering plants). Dicots generally have net-patterned veins, a main central root, and two seed-leaves (cotyledons) when germinating. Examples include maple, strawberry, dandelion, and clover.

Divided: A leaf that is indented nearly or fully to the midrib or base, forming separate and distinct contiguous sections of leaf surface. The term *compound* is usually reserved for those leaves that are divided all the way to the midrib or base, and whose leaflets are somewhat consistent in form and arranged in a describable pattern.

Drupe: A fruit with pulp surrounding a seed with a tough outer layer.

Dry-mesic: Referring to forests or prairies with slightly less soil moisture than those classified as *mesic*. One of the five divisions of the soil moisture gradient (wet, wet-mesic, mesic, dry-mesic, dry) used by ecologists to classify or describe ecosystems.

Ecoculture: The management of natural ecosystems to increase their production of economically useful plants. In distinction to *agriculture* and *horticulture*, which both entail removal of natural ecosystems and their replacement with plant communities that would be impossible without vigorous human maintenance.

Economic botany: The study of the material uses of plants (food, fiber, lubricant, soap, perfume, recreational drug, medicine, etc.).

Edible plant: A plant, one or more parts of which can normally be consumed at a certain stage of growth, prepared in a particular fashion, and eaten in a certain manner, with no significant ill effects. *Edible plants can also be poisonous!*

Emergent: Extending above the water.

Entire: A leaf or leaflet with no divisions, lobes, or teeth.

Ephemeral: A plant with a very brief growing season. Spring ephemerals begin growth very early in spring and usually die back by late spring or early summer.

Ethnobotany: The study of how people or cultures relate to plants, materially and perceptually.

Ethnography: The description of human cultures; a branch of anthropology.

Fiddlehead: The shoot of a fern, upon which the end parts are coiled or drooping rather than pointed.

Float test: Placing nuts in water to see if they float; typically, good nuts will sink and many bad ones will float.

Floret: One of the many tiny flowers in a composite cluster; also, a grass flower.

Flower bud: A flower that is not ready to open; the bud that will later become a flower.

Flower stalk: A stalk that bears a flower or flowers; sometimes used in distinction to the leaf-stalk or petiole.

Fruit leather: Thin sheets of dried fruit pulp.

Genus: A taxonomic group above the species but below the family; a group of closely related species.

Glabrous: Smooth; lacking hairs or bristles.

Gland: A structure that secretes a liquid, such as oil or resin. These usually protrude and are often shiny and darker than surrounding tissue. Some similar-looking structures that have no secretory function are also called glands.

Leaf Shapes

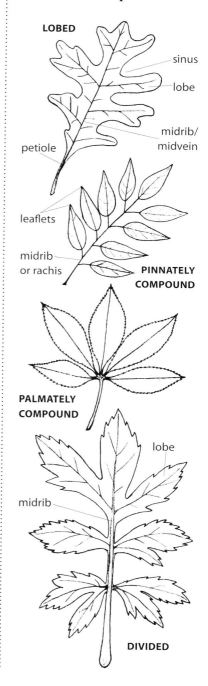

Leaf Patterns

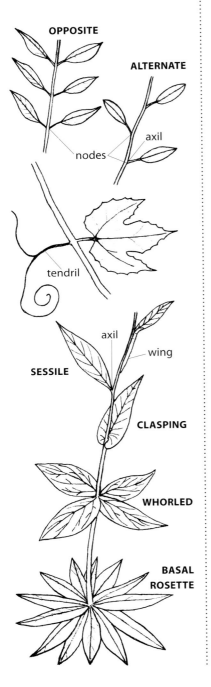

Globose: Spherical or roughly spherical.

Glochid: The minute, barbed, hair-like spines of some cacti.

Greens: The edible leaves or leafy portion of a plant.

Herbaceous: Having no perennial woody tissue above ground.

Inflorescence: A flower or cluster of flowers and all that comes with it, such as stems and bracts; the whole flowering portion of the plant.

Inulin: A non-digestible starch that can be broken down by prolonged cooking, inulin is found in many underground vegetables, which convert it to simpler, digestible sugars before using it to fuel growth.

Involucre: Collectively, the bracts immediately beneath an inflorescence.

Kernel: An edible seed, or the edible portion of a seed.

Lanceolate: Shaped like a lance head: much longer than wide, broadest near the base, tapering to a pointed tip.

Latex: A white, milky sap that dries as a rubbery substance, used to heal wounds.

Leaflet: One of the smaller leaves or blades within a compound leaf.

Leaf scar: The mark left on a stem or twig where a leaf or petiole was formerly attached.

Lenticel: A small corky spot on the bark of small trees and shrubs.

Lobe: An extension of a leaf blade; a division of a leaf that is broadly attached rather than constricted or stalked at the base, as on the leaves of white and red oak.

Margin: The outer edge of a leaf.

Mast: Collectively, the nuts produced and dropped by a tree or stand of trees. Often used in the ambiguous construction *mast* *year*, which is usually intended to mean a year when the mast is heavy or abundant.

Meristem: The zone of a plant where cell division and growth occurs. There is an *apical meristem* at the tips of the branches; this is where the plant increases in length. *Lateral meristems* (cambia) occur under or within the bark of plants, and account for increases in diameter.

Mesic: A forest or prairie with a medium level of soil moisture (also, mesophytic); in the East, a *mesic forest* is a rich hardwood forest dominated by long-lived species such as sugar maple, beech, basswood, yellow birch, hemlock, and white ash.

Midrib: The main vein of a leaf, especially one that is enlarged and provides support, as on most divided leaves; sometimes also used to refer to the rachis (main stalk) of a compound leaf.

Midvein: The main vein of a leaf. Same as *midrib*, except in connotation; the main vein is more commonly called a midvein if it is relatively small, as one finds on most simple leaves.

Monocot: (Short for monocotyledon) One of the two main divisions within the Angiosperms (typical flowering plants). Monocots generally have parallel veins, no main taproot, and a single seed-leaf (cotyledon) when germinating. Examples include grasses, sedges, arums, onions, Solomon's seals, and lilies.

Mucilage: A sticky or slimy substance, usually indicating the presence of dissolved starches. *Mucilaginous* refers to plants or plant parts containing mucilage, or which produce mucilage when chewed.

Nodding: Hanging downward; usually said of flowers.

Underground Parts

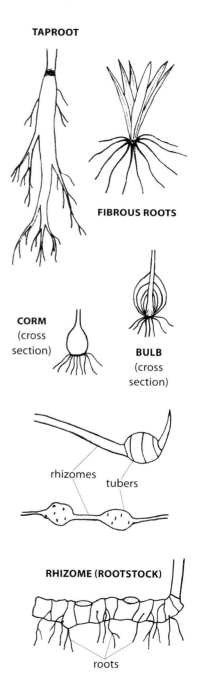

TAPROOT

FIBROUS ROOTS

CORM (cross section)

BULB (cross section)

rhizomes   tubers

RHIZOME (ROOTSTOCK)

roots

Node: The point on a stem where one or more leaves are borne.

Nutmeat: The edible portion of a nut.

Obovate: Egg-shaped in outline but broader near the tip rather than near the base.

Opposite: Growing from the same point along a stalk but on opposite sides of it; paired. (Alternate leaves grow on opposite sides at *different* points.)

Ovary: The lower portion of a pistil, usually enlarged, in which the seed or seeds are produced. The ovary ripens into a fruit.

Ovate: Roughly egg-shaped; somewhat longer than broad, with the widest part near the base.

Palmate: Hand-shaped, having several finer-like lobes.

Palmately compound: Having several leaflets radiate from the same point.

Panicle: A flower cluster with a compound branching pattern, the branches growing from an elongated central stalk. Grapes are a well-known example.

Pappus: Bristles or hairs on the achene of a composite, often used to catch the wind for dispersal. (An example is the "parachute" attached to a dandelion seed.)

Parch: To heat and cook (a grain) to harden the kernel and make the chaff brittle.

Pedicel: The stalk of an individual flower or flowerhead in an inflorescence with multiple flowers or flowerheads.

Peduncle: The stalk of an entire inflorescence or a solitary flower.

Perennial: Any plant that typically lives for more than two years.

Petal: One of the innermost set of modified leaves of a flower, usually brightly colored.

Petiole: The stem or stalk of a leaf.

Phenology: The timing and sequence of seasonal biological events, and the study of this timing and sequence.

Pinnate: Feather-like; with leaflets, branches, or veins arranged in two rows along opposite sides of a midvein or midrib; the most common form for ferns, also seen in most legume leaves and compound tree leaves such as walnut, hickory, and ash.

Pistil: The central female part of the flower, which receives the pollen. It is usually much larger than the stamens (if both present).

Pith: The soft, spongy material found in the center of many stems.

Pome: A fleshy fruit with a cartilage-like core, such as an apple or pear.

Potherb: A green eaten after boiling or steaming.

Prostrate: Lying flat on the ground; not erect.

Pubescent: Covered with hairs.

Puree: The pulp of fruit after the seeds, skins, and stems have been removed by straining.

Raceme: A flower cluster in which each flower is borne on a stem emanating from an elongated central stem.

Rachis: The central axis or stem of a compound leaf or inflorescence.

Receptacle: A surface, often spongy in texture, into which flowers or fruits are inserted or attached.

Rhizome: A horizontal stem of a perennial plant, found under or on the ground, usually thick and rooting at the nodes.

Rib: A pronounced vein (also called a nerve) in a leaf.

Root: The part of a plant which serves to anchor it and absorb water and dissolved nutrients. The root does not have leaves or buds.

Root crown: The transition area from root to stem.

Root season: The time of year when most underground vegetables should be harvested: from late summer to mid spring (being best from late fall to very early spring).

Rootstock: A rhizome that is enlarged to store energy.

Rosette: A circular cluster of leaves radiating from the same point, usually a root crown or the base of a stem.

Samara: A winged fruit, such as maple, ash, and elm seeds.

Sepal: A member of the outer ring of modified leaves in a flower. Sepals may be green or they may be colored like typical petals.

Scape: A leafless stem of an inflorescence (peduncle) arising directly from the base of the plant. Examples include dandelion and wild leek.

Serrated: With sharp teeth of somewhat uniform size.

Sessile: Attached directly, without a stalk or petiole.

Shoot: Rapidly growing stem or stalk of a plant, like asparagus. Leaves may be present, but are not fully formed and comprise a small portion of the shoot's volume.

Simple: Not compound; a single-leaf unit.

Sinus: The space between two lobes of a leaf.

Spike: An elongated, unbranched flower cluster in which the flowers are attached directly to a main stem without individual stems.

Stamen: The male, pollen-bearing part of a flower. Usually multiple.

Stigma: The part of the pistil that receives the pollen.

Stone: A seed with a hard shell that is enclosed in a fruit; a pit.

Straining: The process of removing seeds, skins, stems, and other unwanted coarse material from fruit or berry pulp.

Style: The portion of the pistil that connects the ovary and stigma.

Succulent: Thick, fleshy, and juicy.

Tannin: A complex organic acid that precipitates protein. Tannins are common in many plants and cause astringency.

Taproot: A primary, central root that grows downward rather than laterally or horizontally.

Tendril: A modified leaf or branch that grasps or coils around other objects to support a vine.

Terminal: At the tip or end.

Tuber: An enlargement of a stem in which energy is stored, primarily in the form of starch.

Umbel: A flower cluster in which all of the flower stalks radiate from the same point.

Vegetative reproduction: Any form of reproduction or propagation that does not involve seeds, such as spreading by tubers, suckers, or rhizomes.

Venation: The pattern and characteristics of the veins in a leaf.

Wing: A thin, flat, usually leafy extension from a stalk, petiole, fruit, or other plant part.

Winnow: To separate kernels or seeds from chaff using wind, air, or the different rates that different materials fall or travel through the air.

Wool: Long, matted hair, lying on the surface of a plant rather than erect.

Xylem: The tissues of a plant that transport water and minerals from the roots to the other organs; xylem usually has structural functions as well.

Index

About the Author

Since childhood, foraging has been Samuel Thayer's passion. He has spent his life studying wild food, putting his knowledge into practice, and sharing it with others. Sam began teaching in 1995 and since then has led plant walks and taught foraging workshops around the country. His first book on edible wild plants, *The Forager's Harvest*, has won three awards and has been a perennial Amazon.com category best-seller.

Sam earns his living as an author, speaker, wild rice harvester, and maple syrup producer. He lives in the woods of northern Wisconsin with his wife, Melissa, and their daughter, Myrica. Wild food is a daily part of their diet.

Sam with a boatload of wild rice. Photo by Joe Eucolono.